TROUBLE MAKER

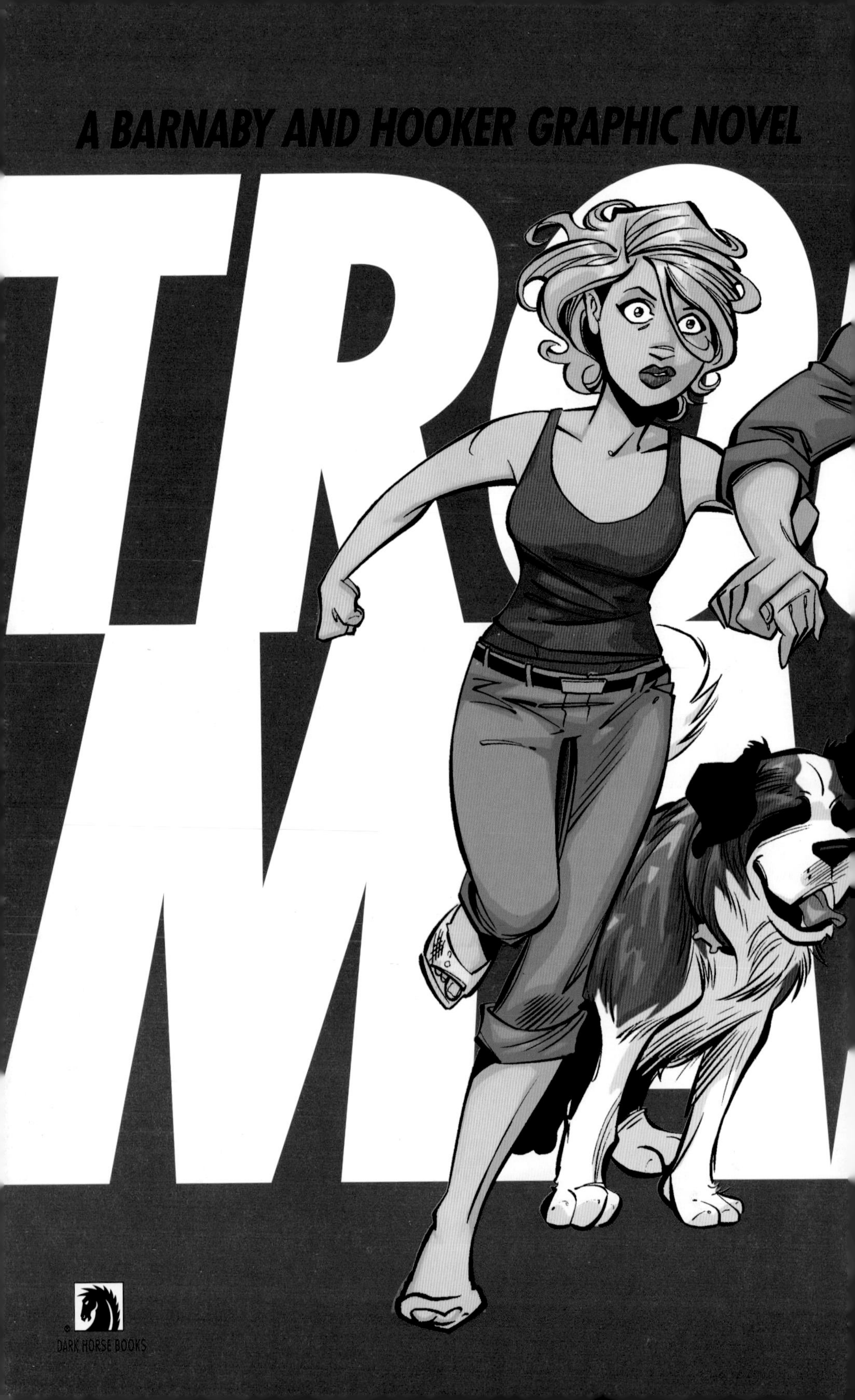
A BARNABY AND HOOKER GRAPHIC NOVEL
DARK HORSE BOOKS

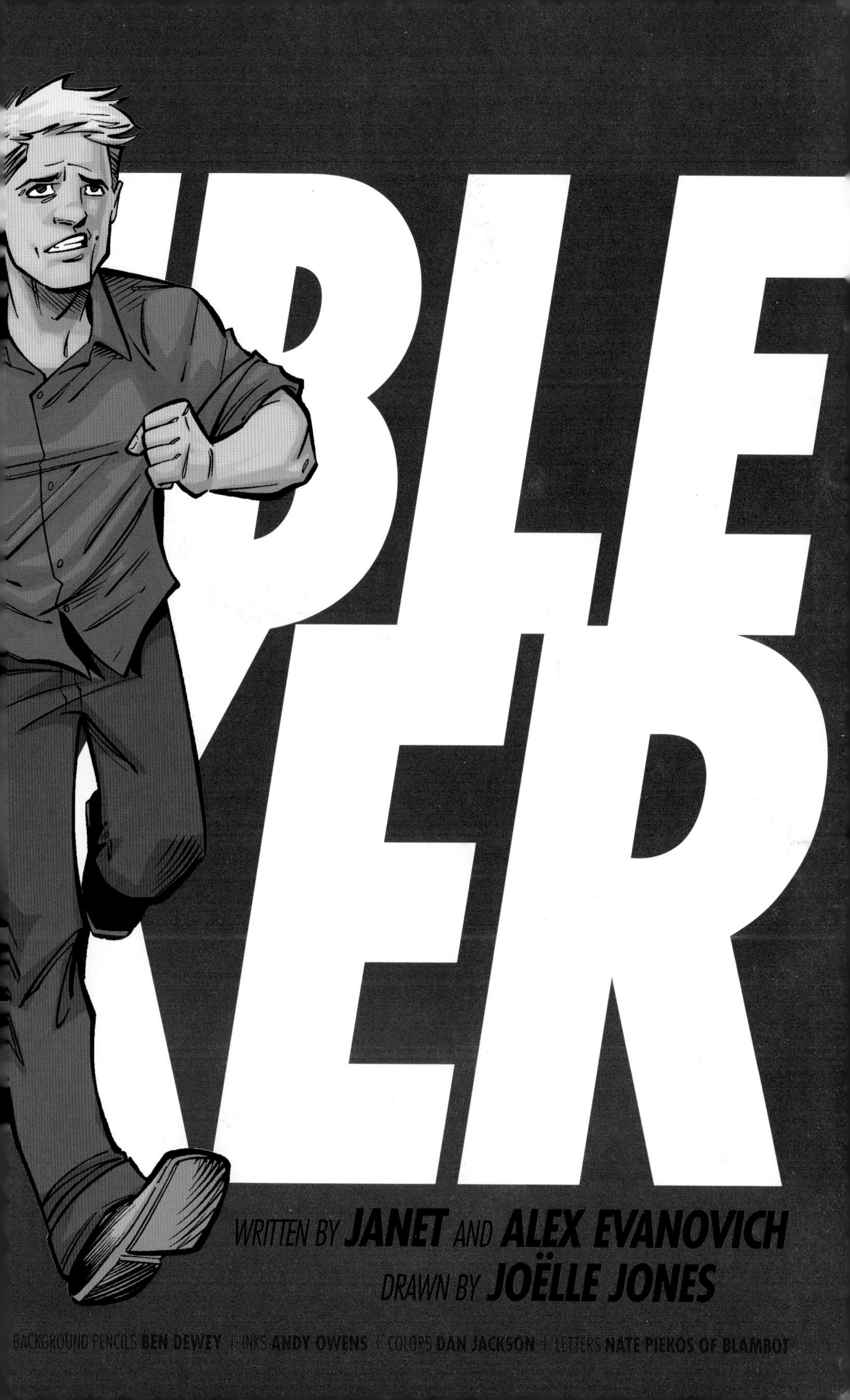

BLE
ER

WRITTEN BY **JANET** AND **ALEX EVANOVICH**

DRAWN BY **JOËLLE JONES**

BACKGROUND PENCILS **BEN DEWEY** | INKS **ANDY OWENS** | COLORS **DAN JACKSON** | LETTERS **NATE PIEKOS OF BLAMBOT®**

For Barnaby,
the greatest St. Bernard
a girl could have.

President & Publisher
MIKE RICHARDSON

Editor
SIERRA HAHN

Assistant Editor
FREDDYE LINS

Collection Designer
DAVE NESTELLE

Special thanks to Anita Nelson and Dark Horse Comics for giving
us the opportunity to make a lifelong dream come true.

Thanks also to Matt Dryer and Lia Ribacchi.

executive vice president Neil Hankerson • chief financial officer Tom Weddle • vice president of pub-
lishing Randy Stradley • vice president of business development Michael Martens • vice president of
business affairs Anita Nelson • vice president of marketing Micha Hershman • vice president of product
development David Scroggy • vice president of information technology Dale LaFountain • director
of purchasing Darlene Vogel • general counsel Ken Lizzi • editorial director Davey Estrada • senior
managing editor Scott Allie • senior books editor Chris Warner • executive editor Diana Schutz • director
of design and production Cary Grazzini • art director Lia Ribacchi • director of scheduling Cara Niece

Published by Dark Horse Books
A division of Dark Horse Comics, Inc.
10956 SE Main Street
Milwaukie, OR 97222

www.DarkHorse.com
www.Evanovich.com
www.JoelleJones.com

To find a comics shop in your area, call the Comic Shop Locator Service toll-free at (888) 266-4226.

First edition: July 2011
ISBN 978-1-59582-722-7

10 9 8 7 6 5 4 3 2 1
Printed at 1010 Printing International, Ltd., Guangdong Province, China

HOW TO READ A GRAPHIC NOVEL

Just because *Troublemaker* is Janet's first foray into graphic novels, that doesn't mean her prose fans can't get the same amount of enjoyment when they pick up a copy of this best-selling book!

AT 3 A.M. THIS MORNING FELICIA CALLED TO TELL ME SHE'D HAD A "VISION" AND ROSA WAS IN TERRIBLE DANGER.
HERE.
THE LAST TIME FELICIA HAD A NIGHT-TIME "VISION" ABOUT ROSA BEING IN TROUBLE, IT WAS BECAUSE THE TWO OF THEM HAD EATEN DINNER AT FAT MONDAY'S. THE CRISIS WAS SOLVED WITH AN ANTACID.
CHICKEN SALAD?
TURNS OUT FELICIA'S "VISION" MIGHT BE LEGIT THIS TIME. ROSA NEVER RETURNED FROM A WEEKEND TRIP TO THE FLORIDA KEYS.
DON'T BE SO PICKY, BARNEY. IT CHICKEN AND IT DEAD.
WAVE IT.
PLUS WE FOUND THIS VOODOO DOLL AT ROSA'S CIGAR-ROLLING STATION WHERE SHE WORKS. THERE WAS A NOTE ATTACHED...

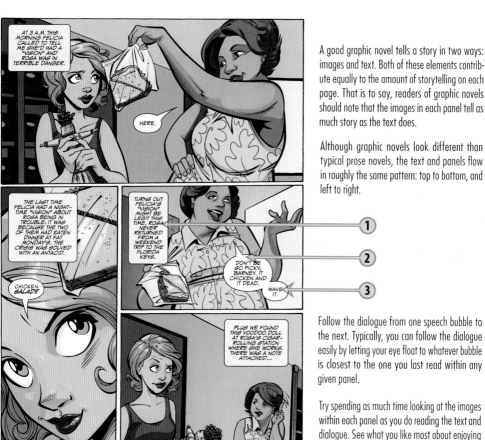

A good graphic novel tells a story in two ways: images and text. Both of these elements contribute equally to the amount of storytelling on each page. That is to say, readers of graphic novels should note that the images in each panel tell as much story as the text does.

Although graphic novels look different than typical prose novels, the text and panels flow in roughly the same pattern: top to bottom, and left to right.

Follow the dialogue from one speech bubble to the next. Typically, you can follow the dialogue easily by letting your eye float to whatever bubble is closest to the one you last read within any given panel.

Try spending as much time looking at the images within each panel as you do reading the text and dialogue. See what you like most about enjoying sequential art, and focus on what draws you into the story the most.

Don't be surprised if a character isn't describing an action or an emotion. That's what the images are for! Let the character's body language and panel environments tell you what else is going on.

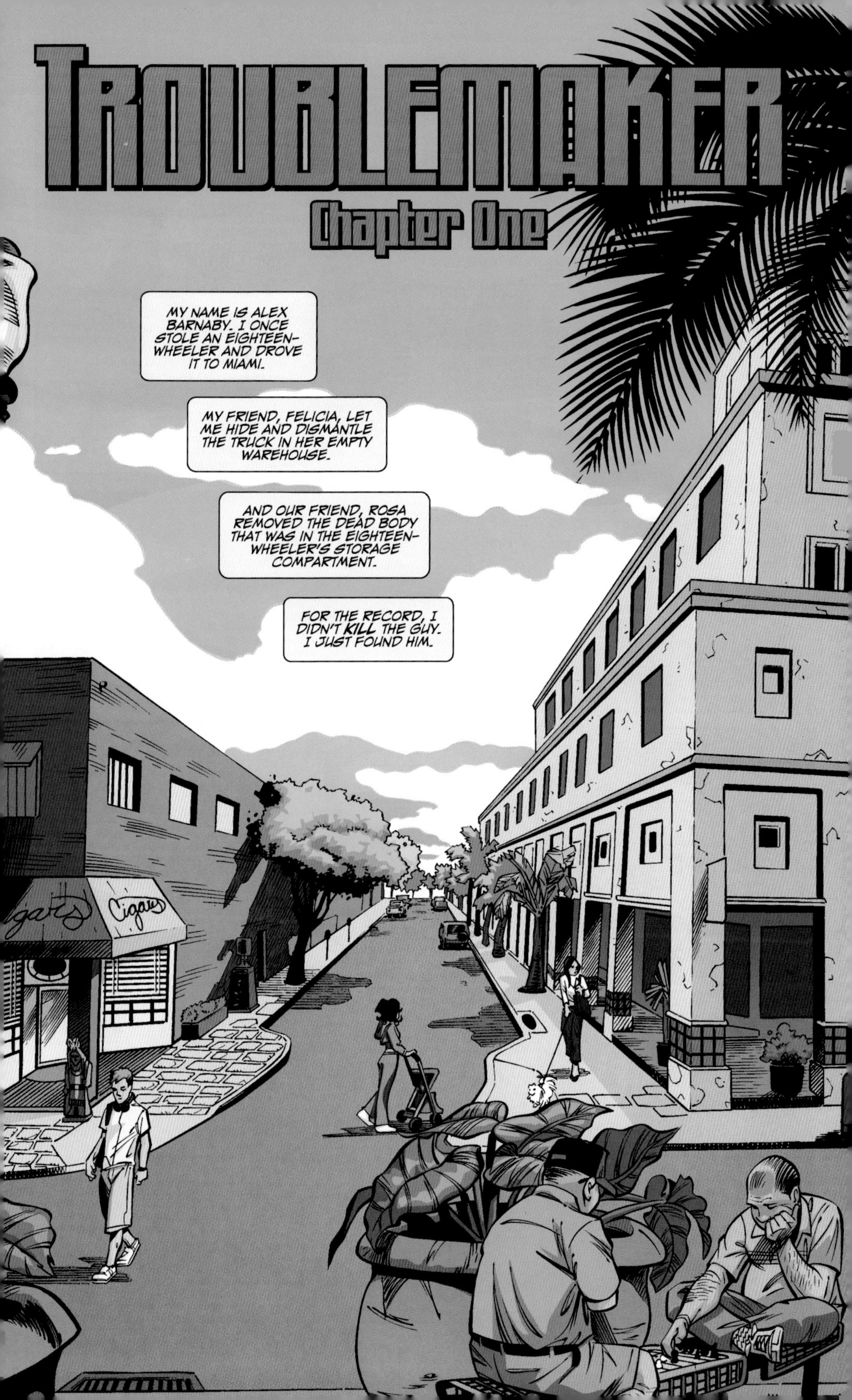
TROUBLEMAKER
Chapter One
MY NAME IS ALEX BARNABY. I ONCE STOLE AN EIGHTEEN-WHEELER AND DROVE IT TO MIAMI.
MY FRIEND, FELICIA, LET ME HIDE AND DISMANTLE THE TRUCK IN HER EMPTY WAREHOUSE.
AND OUR FRIEND, ROSA REMOVED THE DEAD BODY THAT WAS IN THE EIGHTEEN-WHEELER'S STORAGE COMPARTMENT.
FOR THE RECORD, I DIDN'T **KILL** THE GUY. I JUST FOUND HIM.
Cigars

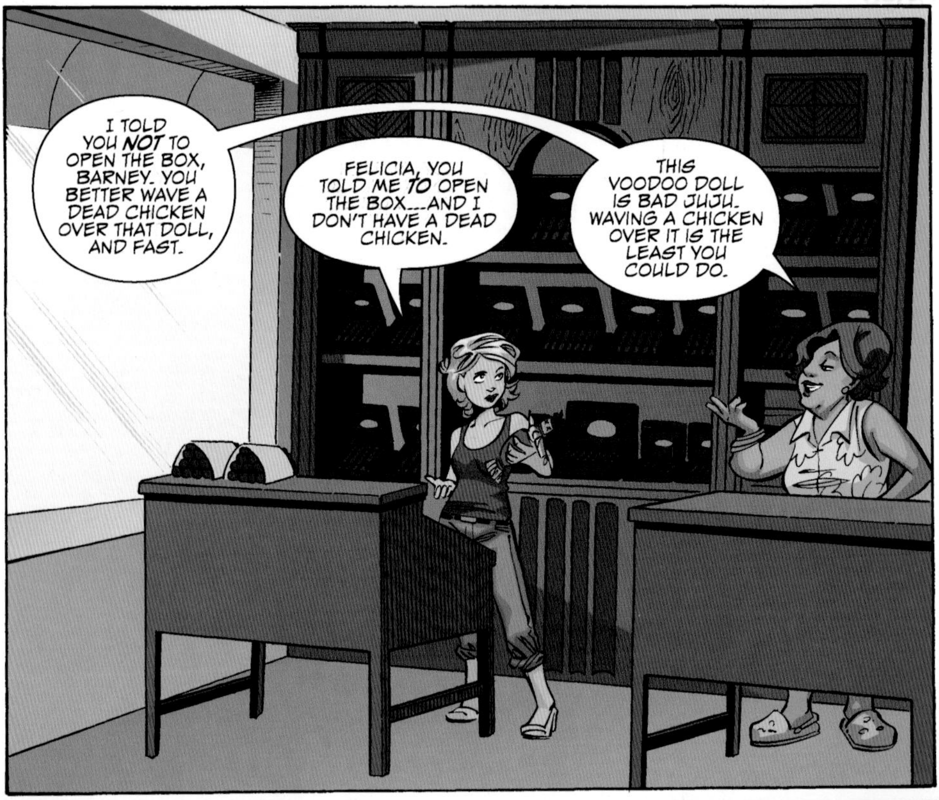
I TOLD YOU NOT TO OPEN THE BOX, BARNEY. YOU BETTER WAVE A DEAD CHICKEN OVER THAT DOLL, AND FAST.
FELICIA, YOU TOLD ME TO OPEN THE BOX...AND I DON'T HAVE A DEAD CHICKEN.
THIS VOODOO DOLL IS BAD JUJU. WAVING A CHICKEN OVER IT IS THE LEAST YOU COULD DO.

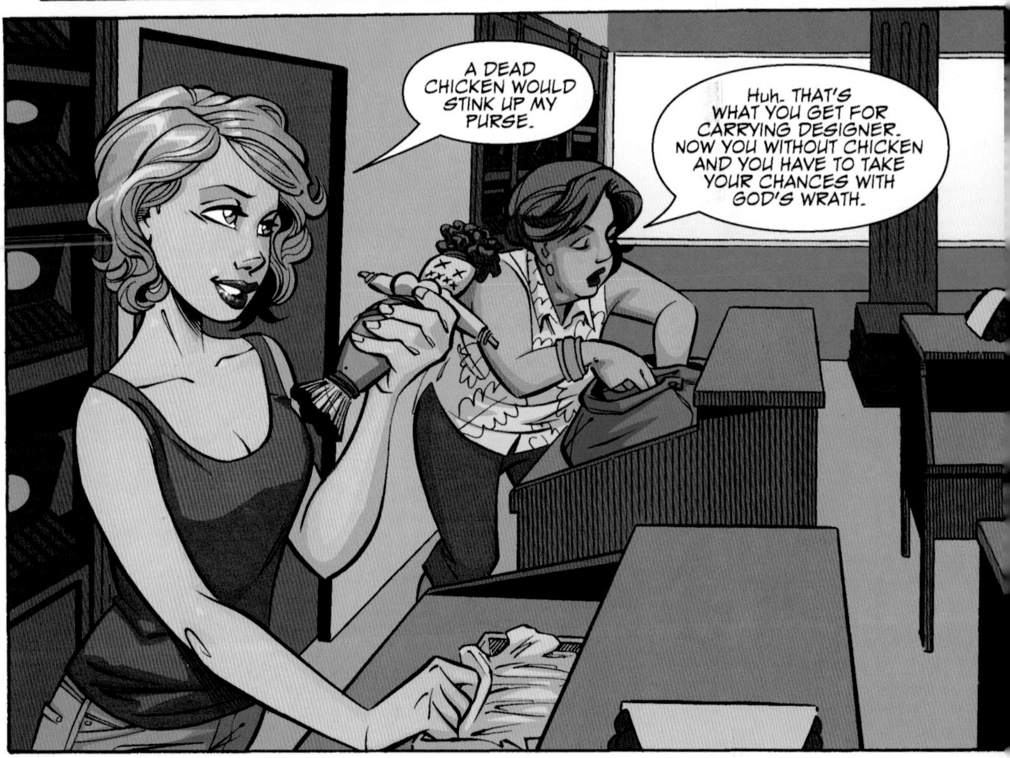
A DEAD CHICKEN WOULD STINK UP MY PURSE.
Huh. THAT'S WHAT YOU GET FOR CARRYING DESIGNER. NOW YOU WITHOUT CHICKEN AND YOU HAVE TO TAKE YOUR CHANCES WITH GOD'S WRATH.

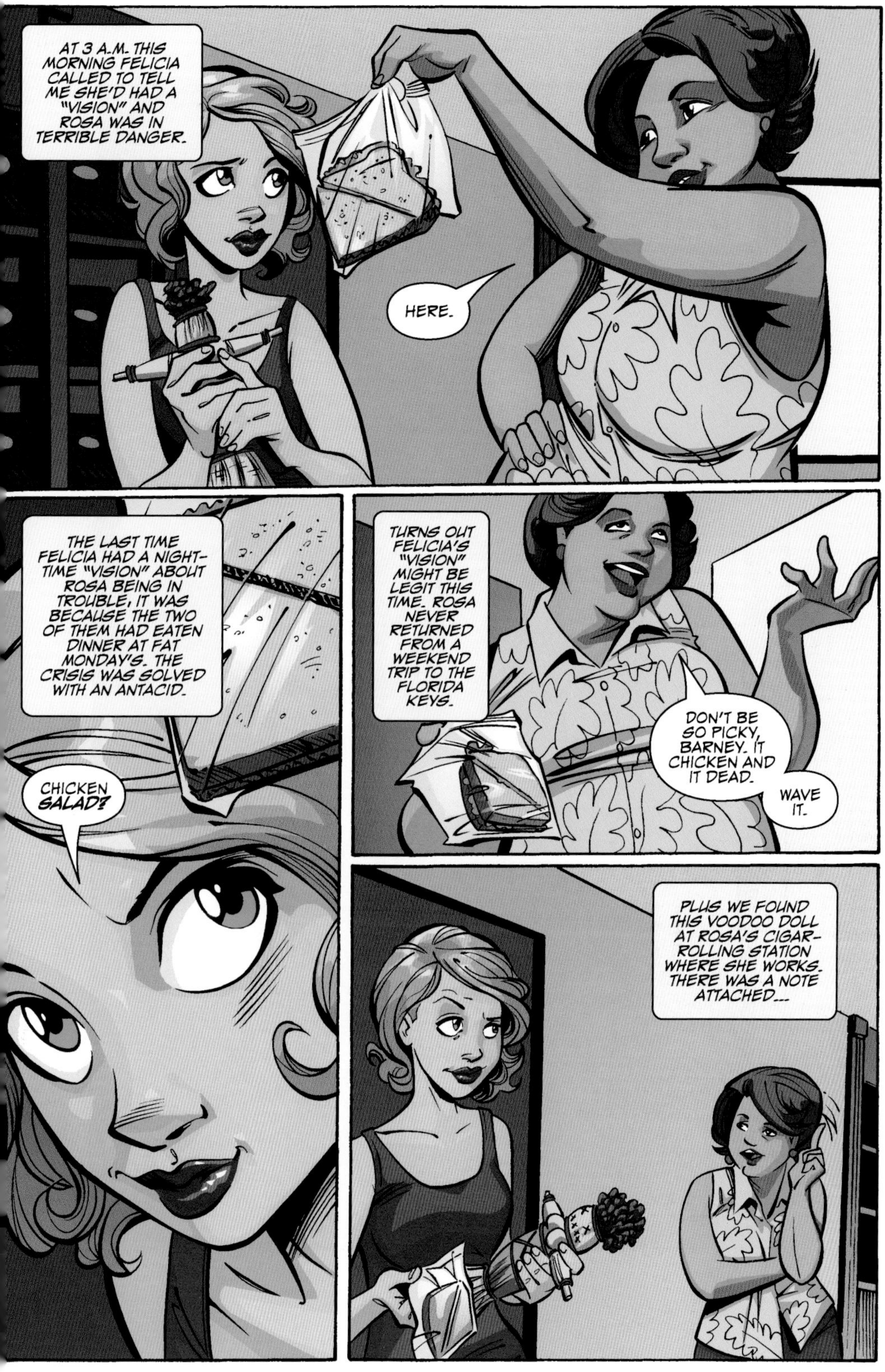
AT 3 A.M. THIS MORNING FELICIA CALLED TO TELL ME SHE'D HAD A "VISION" AND ROSA WAS IN TERRIBLE DANGER.
HERE.
THE LAST TIME FELICIA HAD A NIGHT-TIME "VISION" ABOUT ROSA BEING IN TROUBLE, IT WAS BECAUSE THE TWO OF THEM HAD EATEN DINNER AT FAT MONDAY'S. THE CRISIS WAS SOLVED WITH AN ANTACID.
CHICKEN SALAD?
TURNS OUT FELICIA'S "VISION" MIGHT BE LEGIT THIS TIME. ROSA NEVER RETURNED FROM A WEEKEND TRIP TO THE FLORIDA KEYS.
DON'T BE SO PICKY, BARNEY. IT CHICKEN AND IT DEAD.
WAVE IT.
PLUS WE FOUND THIS VOODOO DOLL AT ROSA'S CIGAR-ROLLING STATION WHERE SHE WORKS. THERE WAS A NOTE ATTACHED...

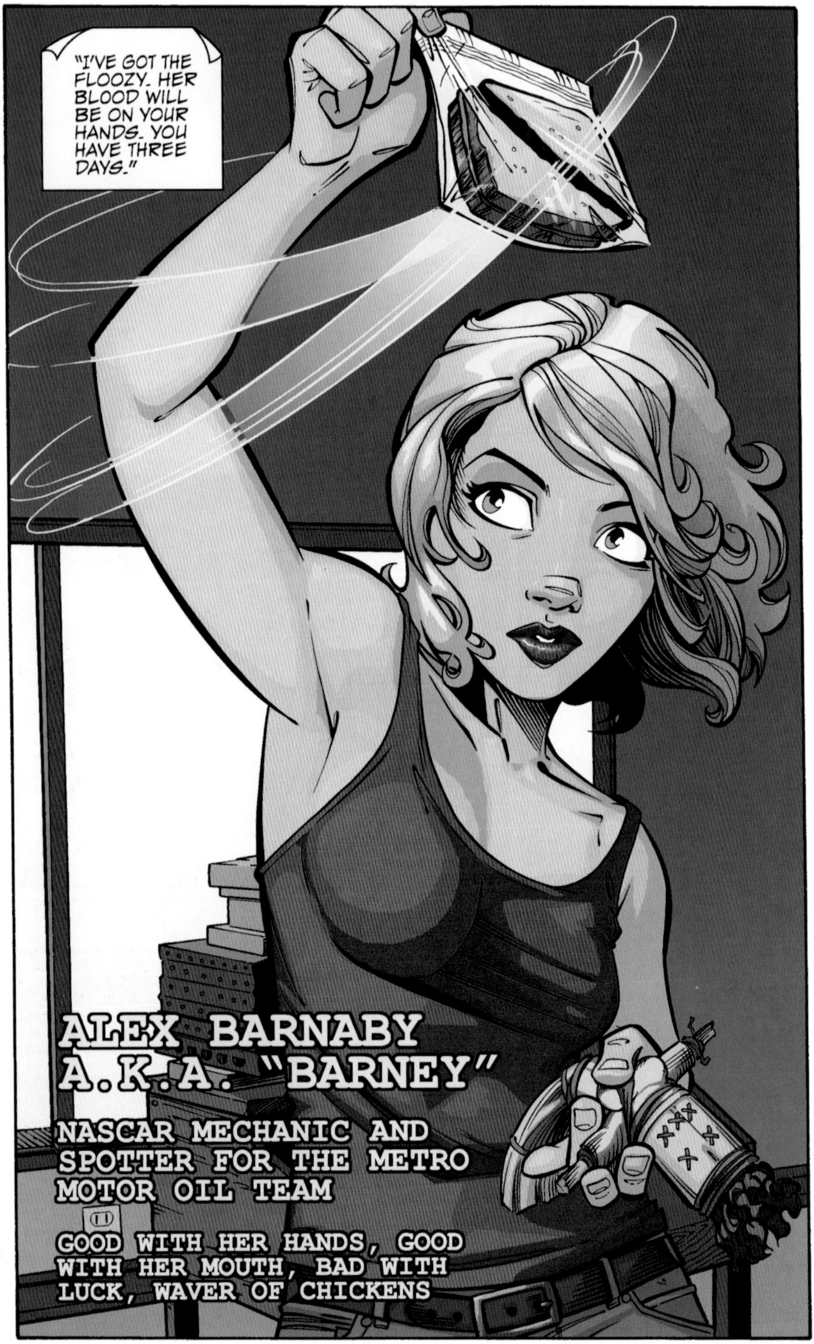
"I'VE GOT THE FLOOZY. HER BLOOD WILL BE ON YOUR HANDS. YOU HAVE THREE DAYS."
ALEX BARNABY
A.K.A. "BARNEY"
NASCAR MECHANIC AND SPOTTER FOR THE METRO MOTOR OIL TEAM
GOOD WITH HER HANDS, GOOD WITH HER MOUTH, BAD WITH LUCK, WAVER OF CHICKENS

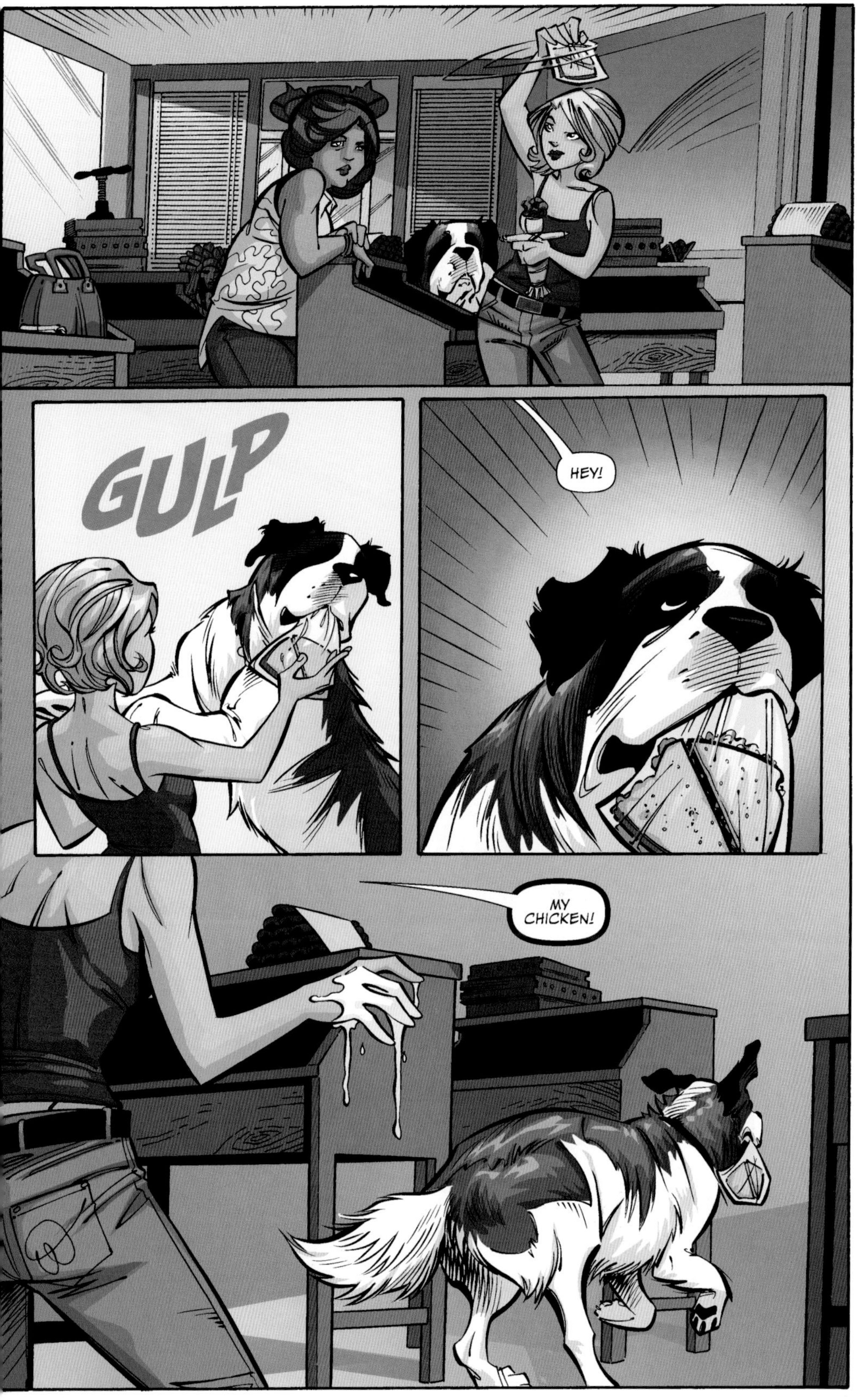
GULP
HEY!
MY CHICKEN!

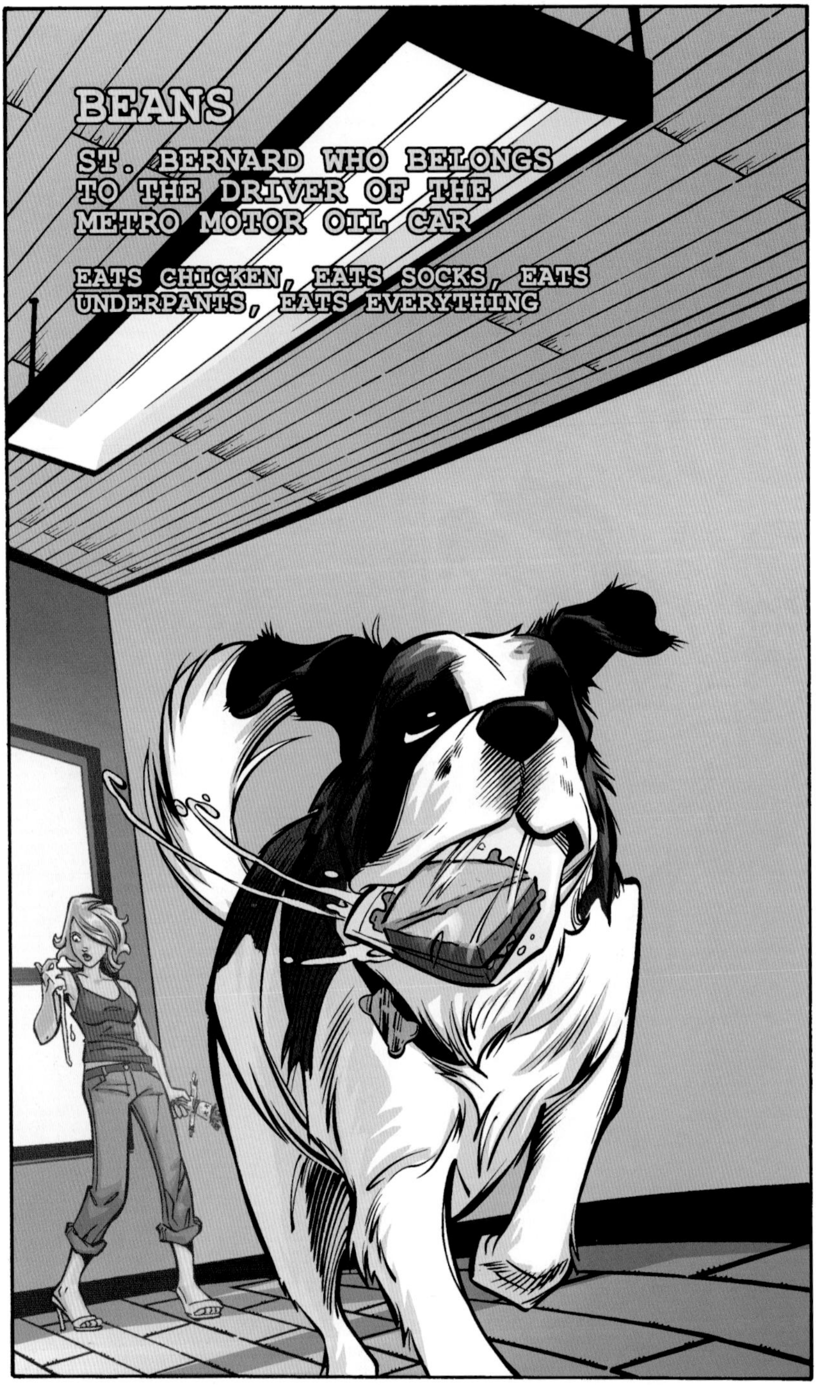
BEANS
ST. BERNARD WHO BELONGS TO THE DRIVER OF THE METRO MOTOR OIL CAR
EATS CHICKEN, EATS SOCKS, EATS UNDERPANTS, EATS EVERYTHING

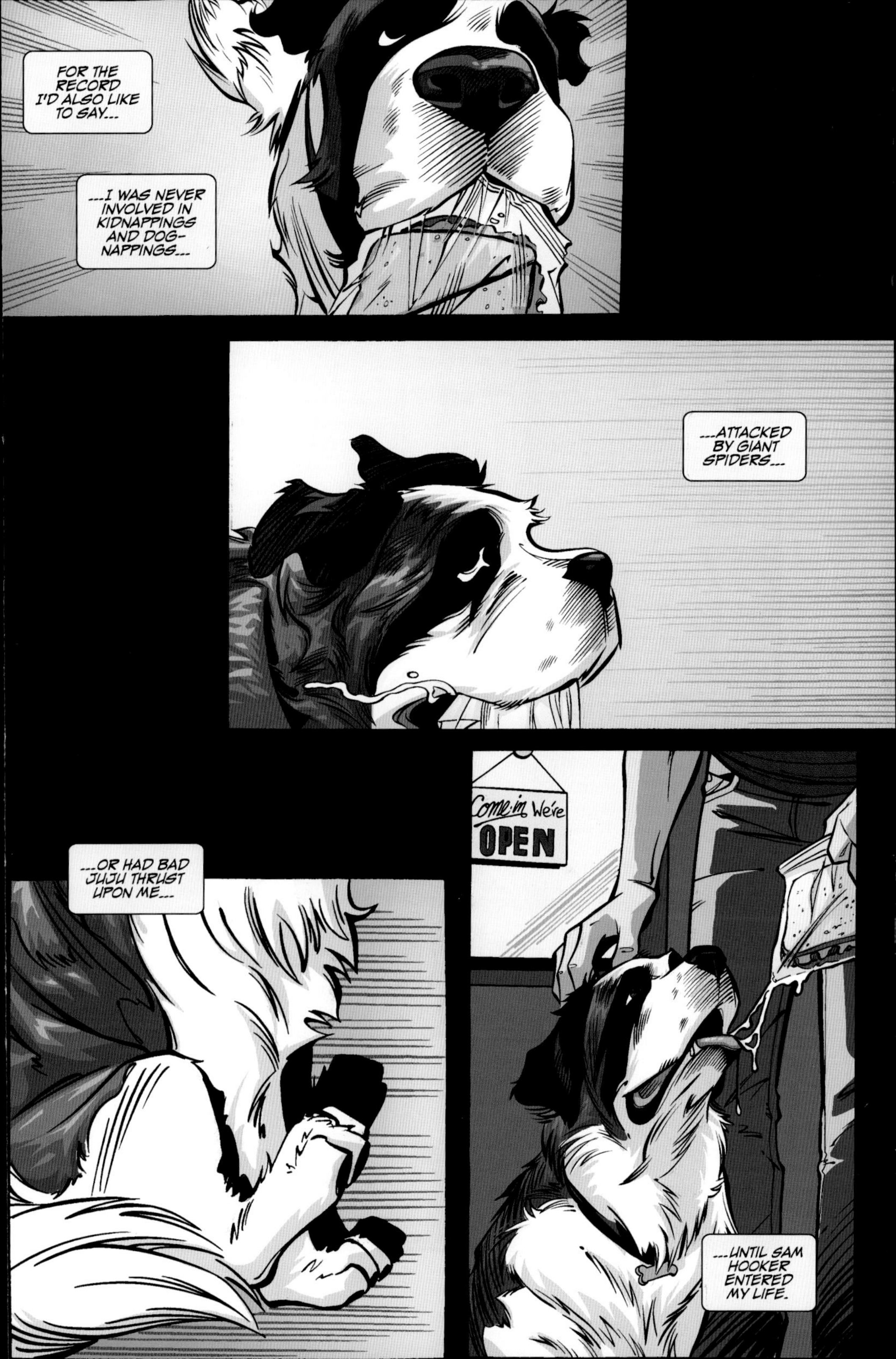
FOR THE RECORD I'D ALSO LIKE TO SAY...
...I WAS NEVER INVOLVED IN KIDNAPPINGS AND DOG-NAPPINGS...
...ATTACKED BY GIANT SPIDERS...
Come in We're OPEN
...OR HAD BAD JUJU THRUST UPON ME...
...UNTIL SAM HOOKER ENTERED MY LIFE.

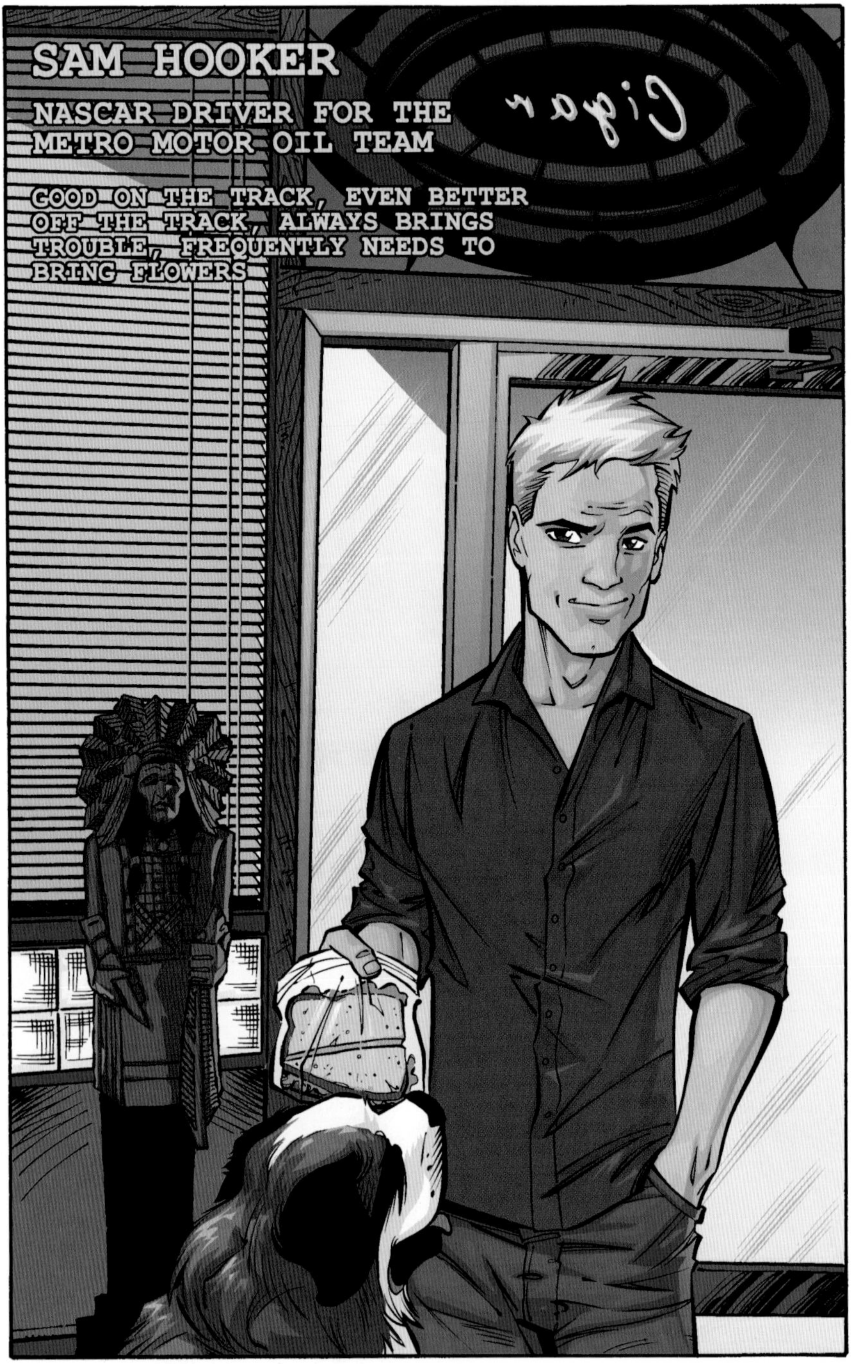
SAM HOOKER
NASCAR DRIVER FOR THE METRO MOTOR OIL TEAM
GOOD ON THE TRACK, EVEN BETTER OFF THE TRACK, ALWAYS BRINGS TROUBLE, FREQUENTLY NEEDS TO BRING FLOWERS

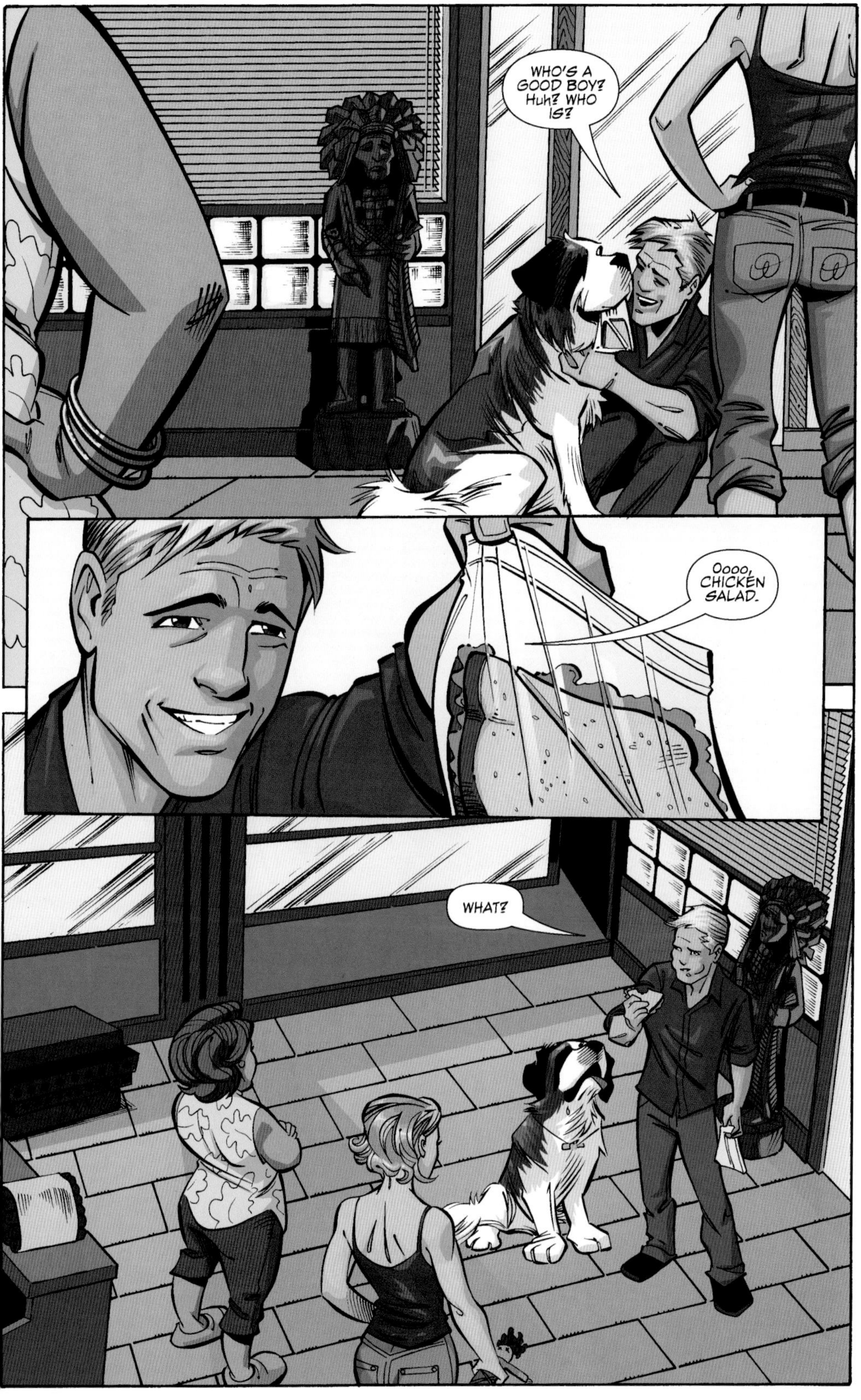
WHO'S A GOOD BOY? Huh? WHO IS?
Oooo, CHICKEN SALAD.
WHAT?

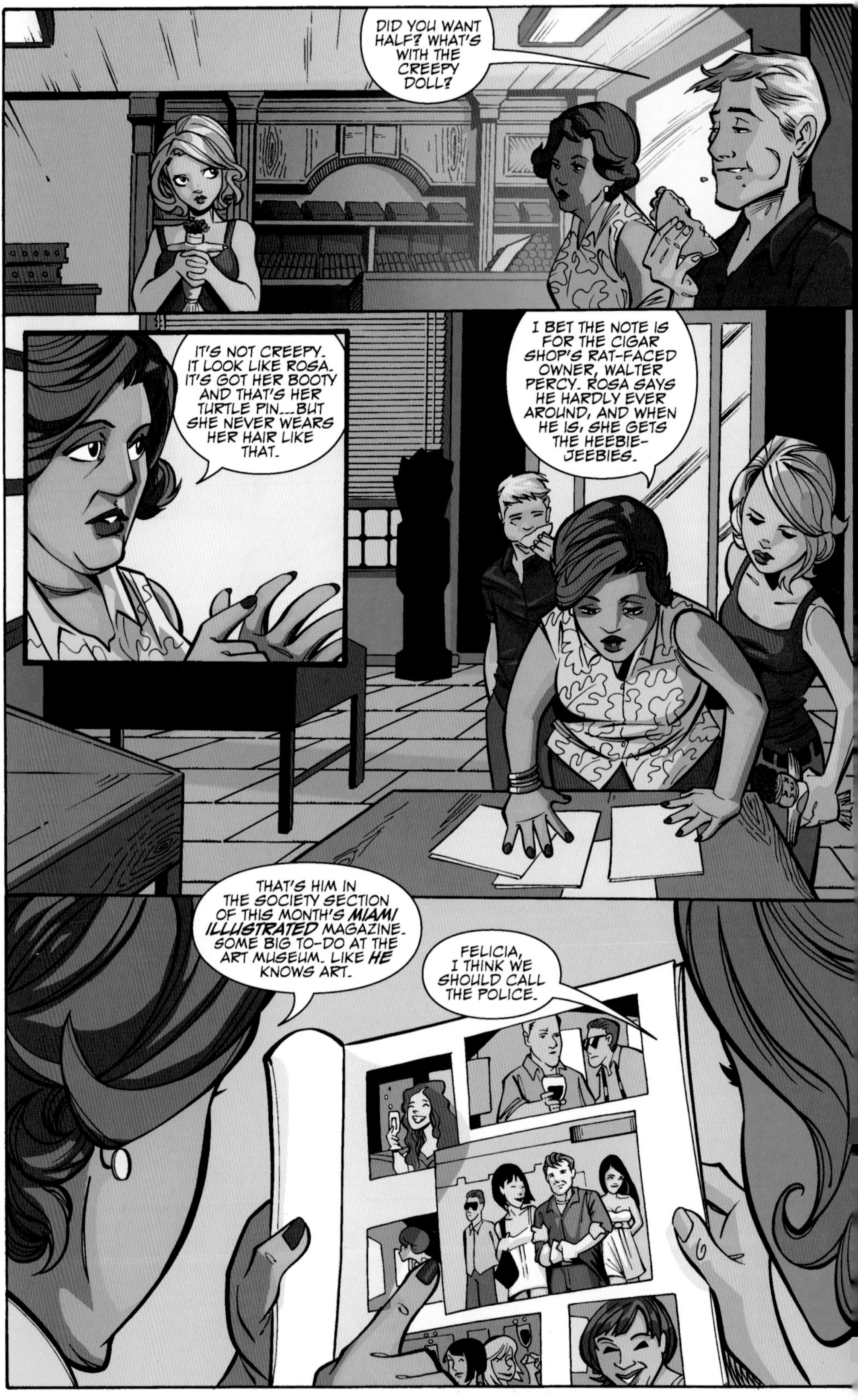
DID YOU WANT HALF? WHAT'S WITH THE CREEPY DOLL?
IT'S NOT CREEPY. IT LOOK LIKE ROSA. IT'S GOT HER BOOTY AND THAT'S HER TURTLE PIN...BUT SHE NEVER WEARS HER HAIR LIKE THAT.
I BET THE NOTE IS FOR THE CIGAR SHOP'S RAT-FACED OWNER, WALTER PERCY. ROSA SAYS HE HARDLY EVER AROUND, AND WHEN HE IS, SHE GETS THE HEEBIE-JEEBIES.
THAT'S HIM IN THE SOCIETY SECTION OF THIS MONTH'S ***MIAMI ILLUSTRATED*** MAGAZINE. SOME BIG TO-DO AT THE ART MUSEUM. LIKE ***HE*** KNOWS ART.
FELICIA, I THINK WE SHOULD CALL THE POLICE.

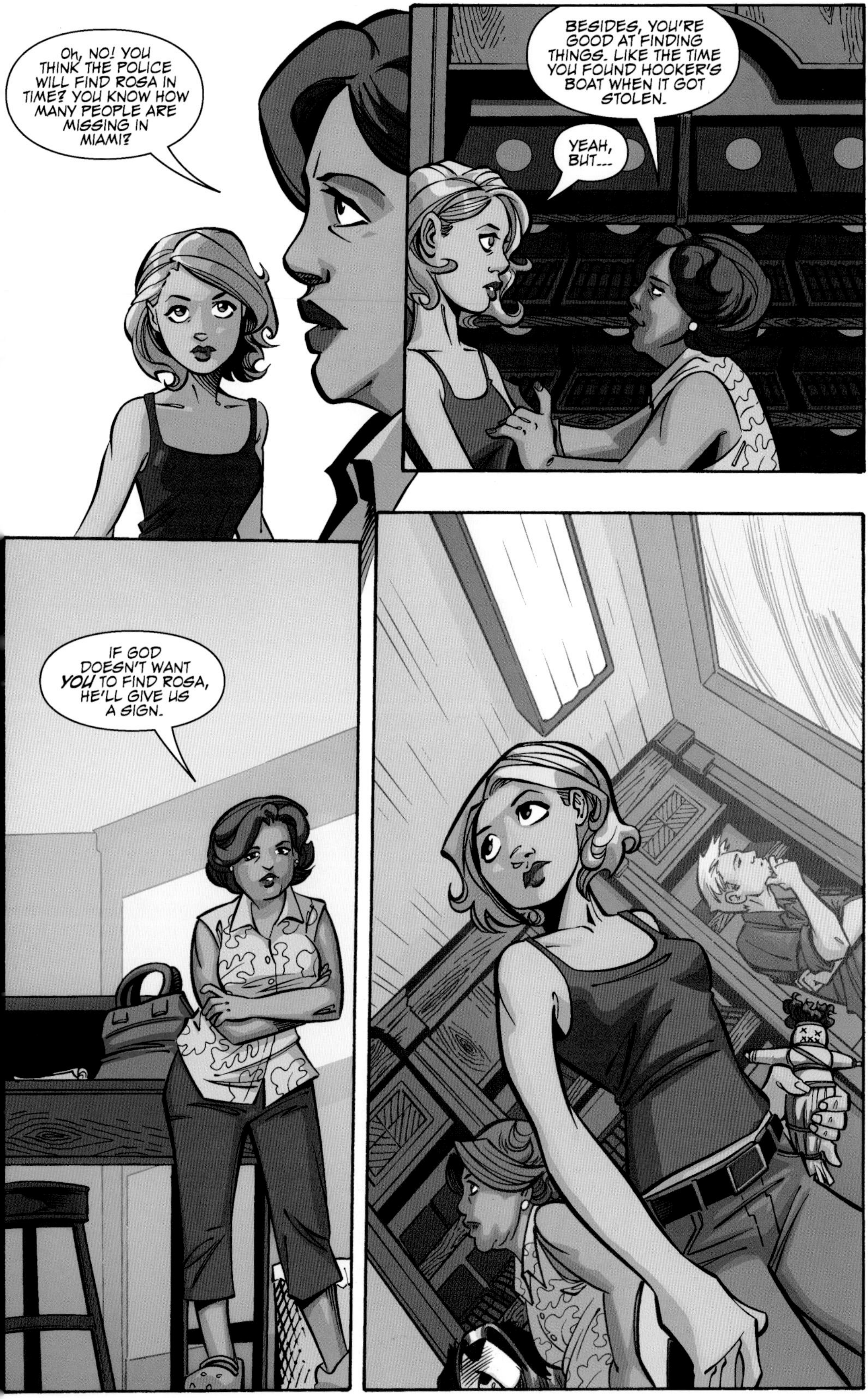
Oh, NO! YOU THINK THE POLICE WILL FIND ROSA IN TIME? YOU KNOW HOW MANY PEOPLE ARE MISSING IN MIAMI?
BESIDES, YOU'RE GOOD AT FINDING THINGS. LIKE THE TIME YOU FOUND HOOKER'S BOAT WHEN IT GOT STOLEN.
YEAH, BUT...
IF GOD DOESN'T WANT YOU TO FIND ROSA, HE'LL GIVE US A SIGN.

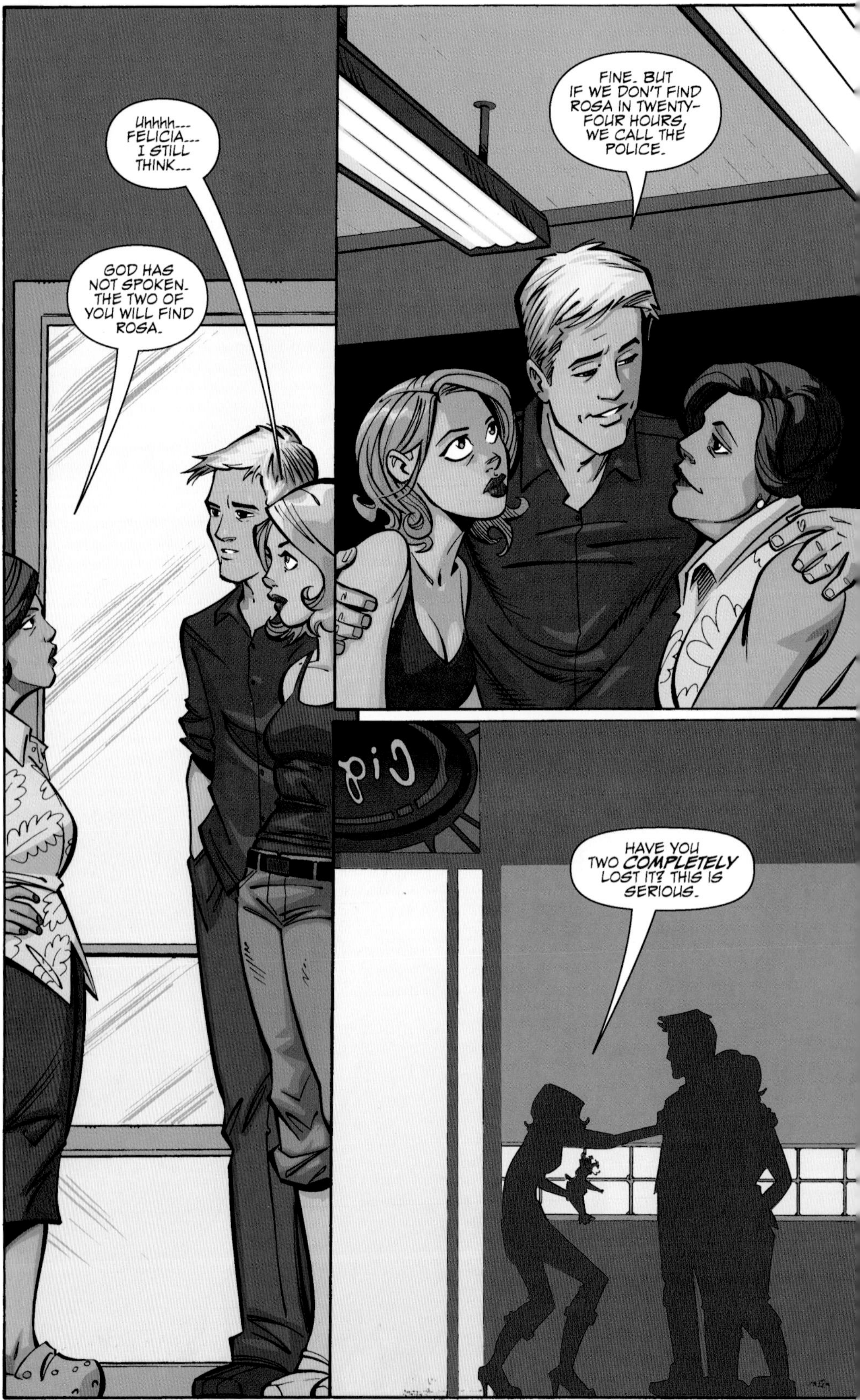
UHHHH...
FELICIA...
I STILL
THINK...
GOD HAS
NOT SPOKEN.
THE TWO OF
YOU WILL FIND
ROSA.
FINE. BUT
IF WE DON'T FIND
ROSA IN TWENTY-
FOUR HOURS,
WE CALL THE
POLICE.
HAVE YOU
TWO *COMPLETELY*
LOST IT? THIS IS
SERIOUS.

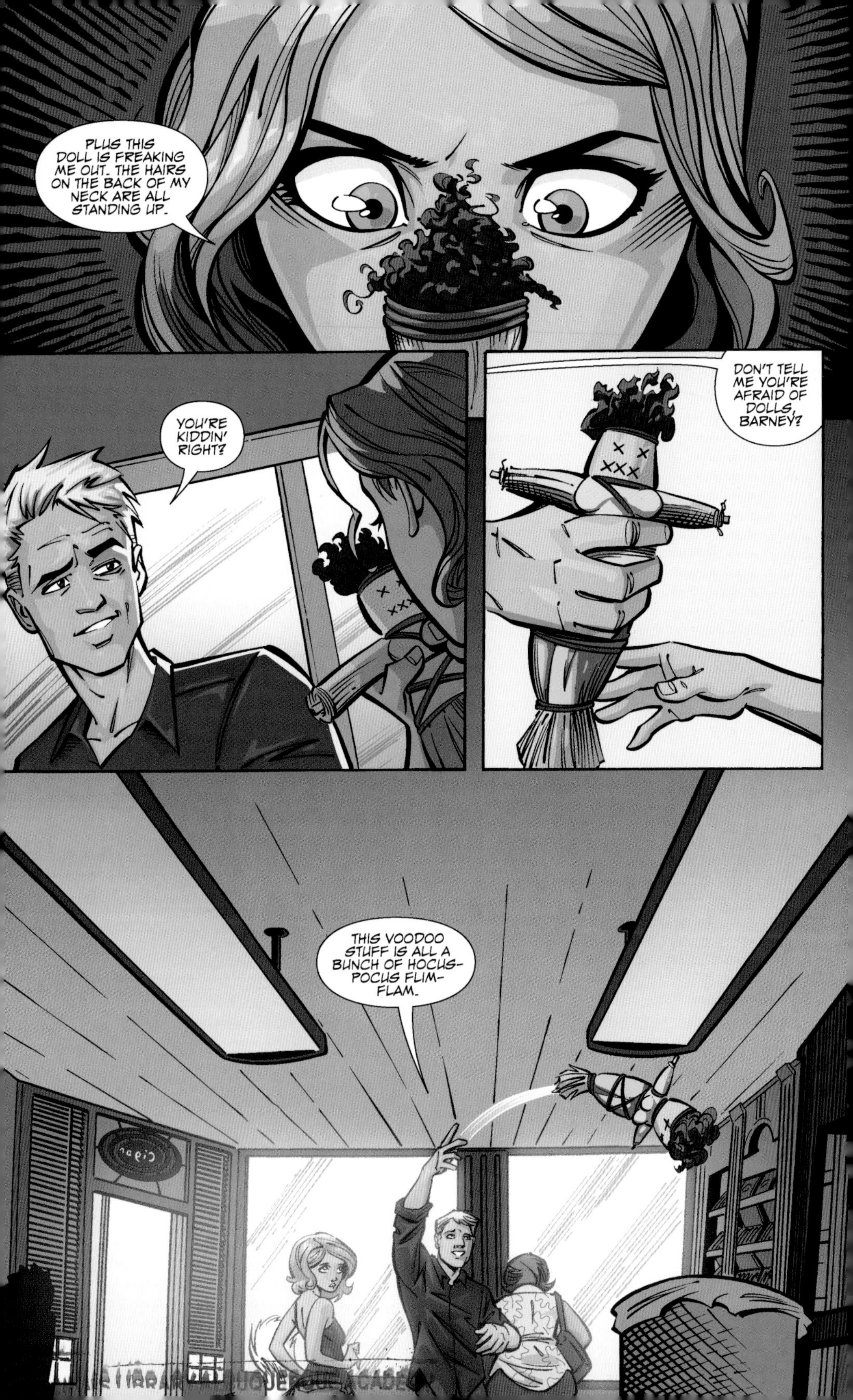
PLUS THIS DOLL IS FREAKING ME OUT. THE HAIRS ON THE BACK OF MY NECK ARE ALL STANDING UP.
YOU'RE KIDDIN' RIGHT?
DON'T TELL ME YOU'RE AFRAID OF DOLLS, BARNEY?
THIS VOODOO STUFF IS ALL A BUNCH OF HOCUS-POCUS FLIM-FLAM.

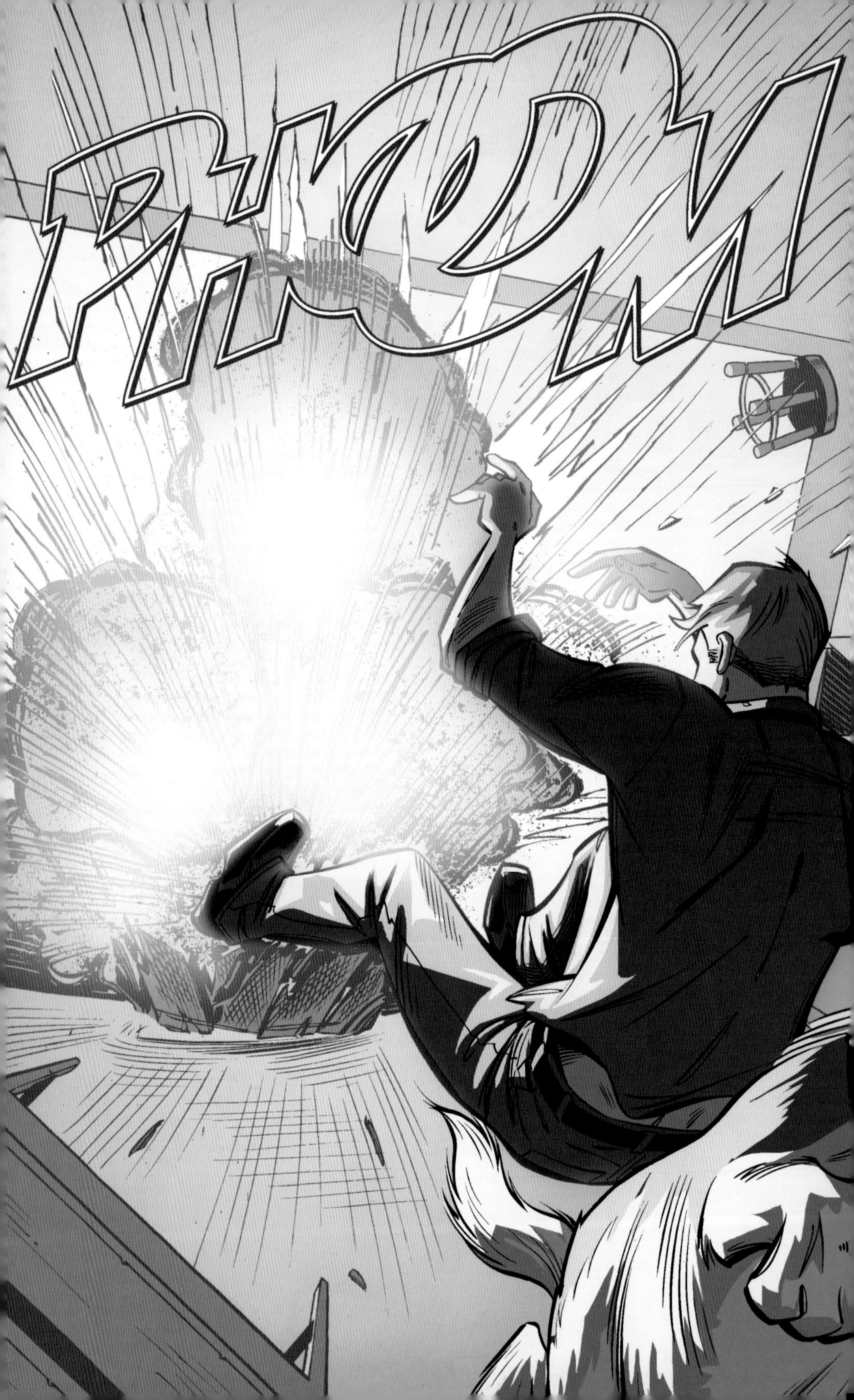
BROOM

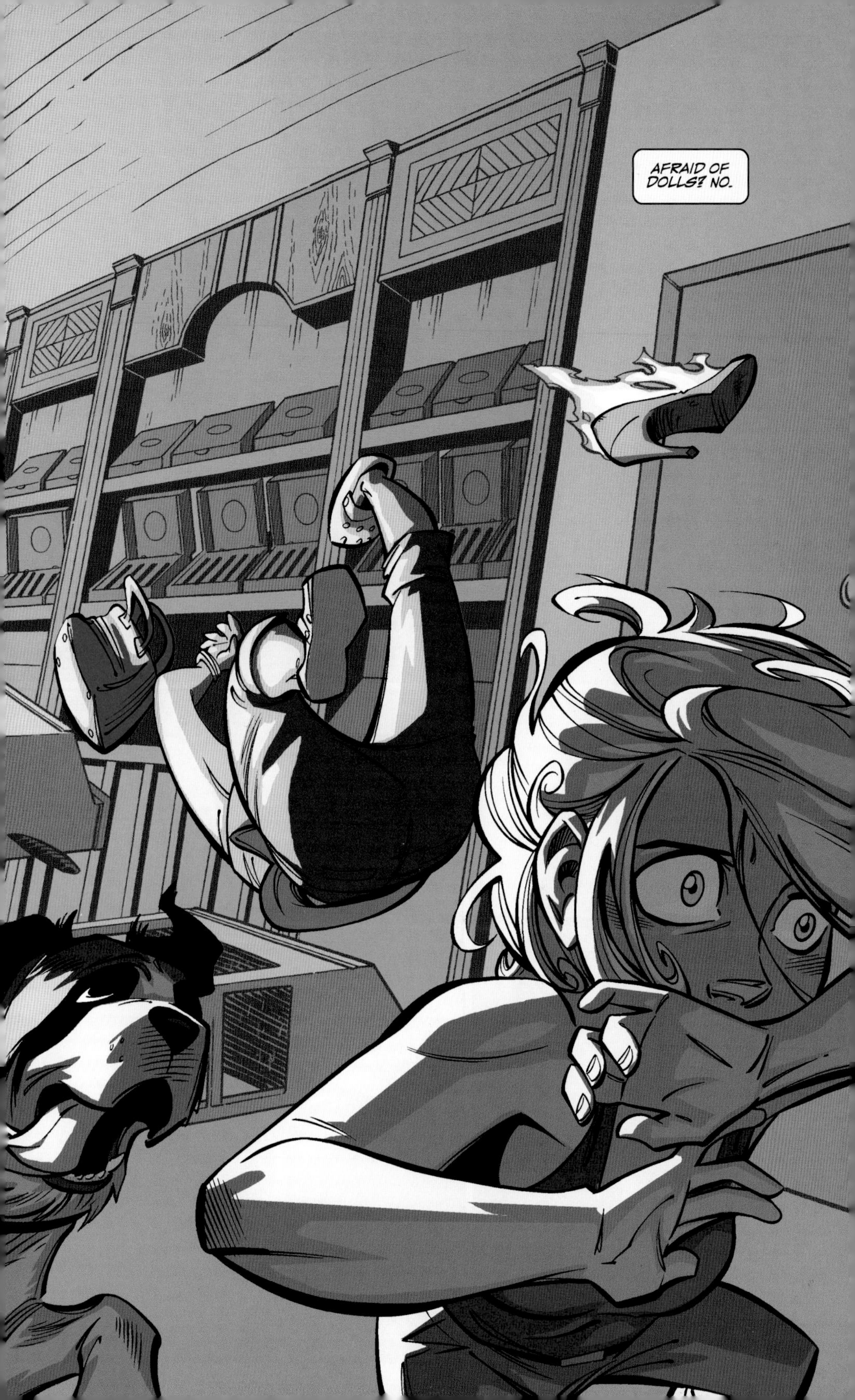
AFRAID OF DOLLS? NO.

BUT A GIRL CAN ONLY BE BLOWN UP SO MANY TIMES. IT'S HELL ON HAIR...

PSSST

...AND SHOES.

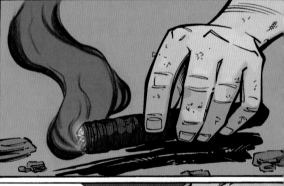

SEE, BARNEY, I TOLD YOU WE'D HAVE FUN IN MIAMI. AND YOU WANTED TO VACATION IN ARUBA.

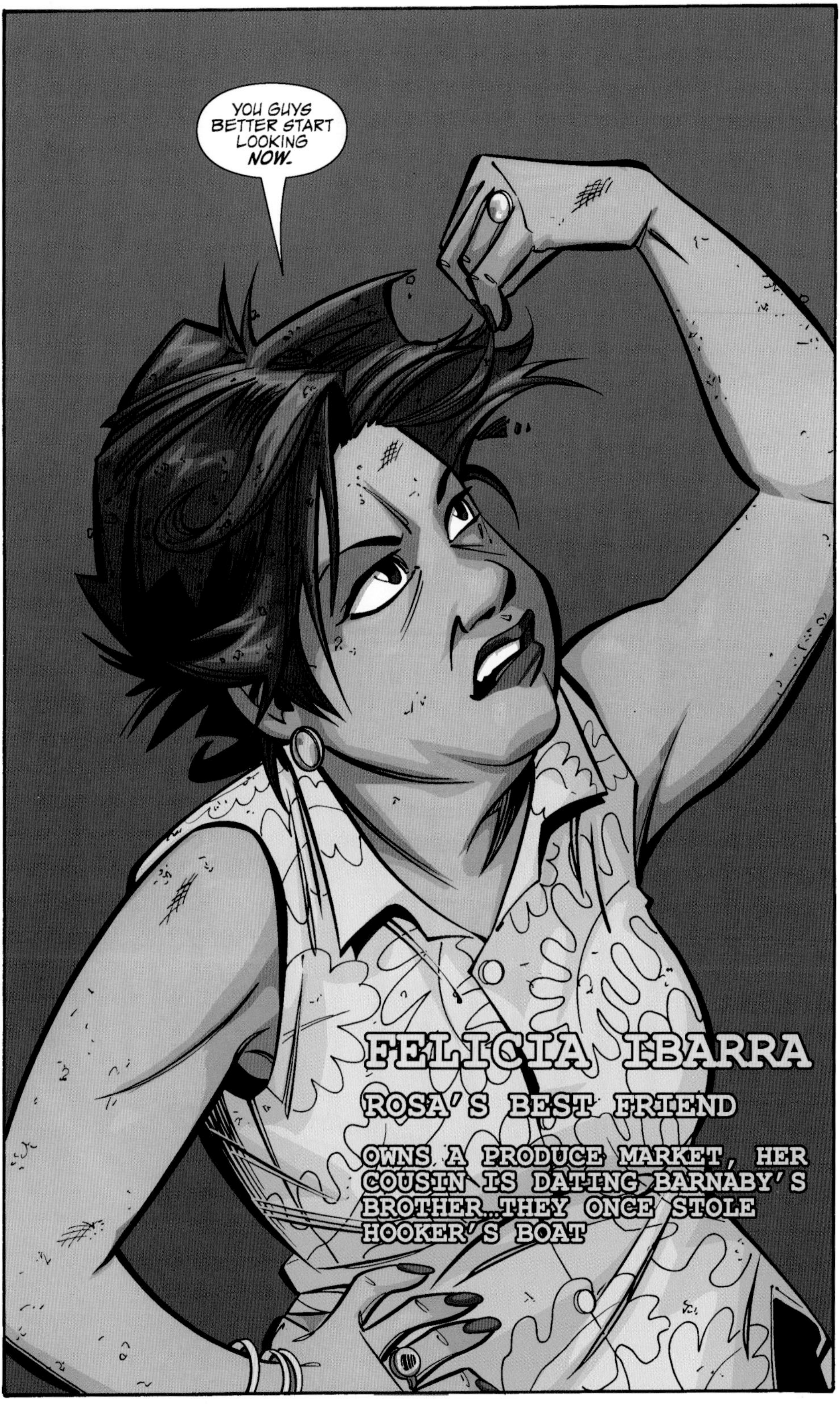
YOU GUYS BETTER START LOOKING NOW.
FELICIA IBARRA
ROSA'S BEST FRIEND
OWNS A PRODUCE MARKET, HER COUSIN IS DATING BARNABY'S BROTHER...THEY ONCE STOLE HOOKER'S BOAT

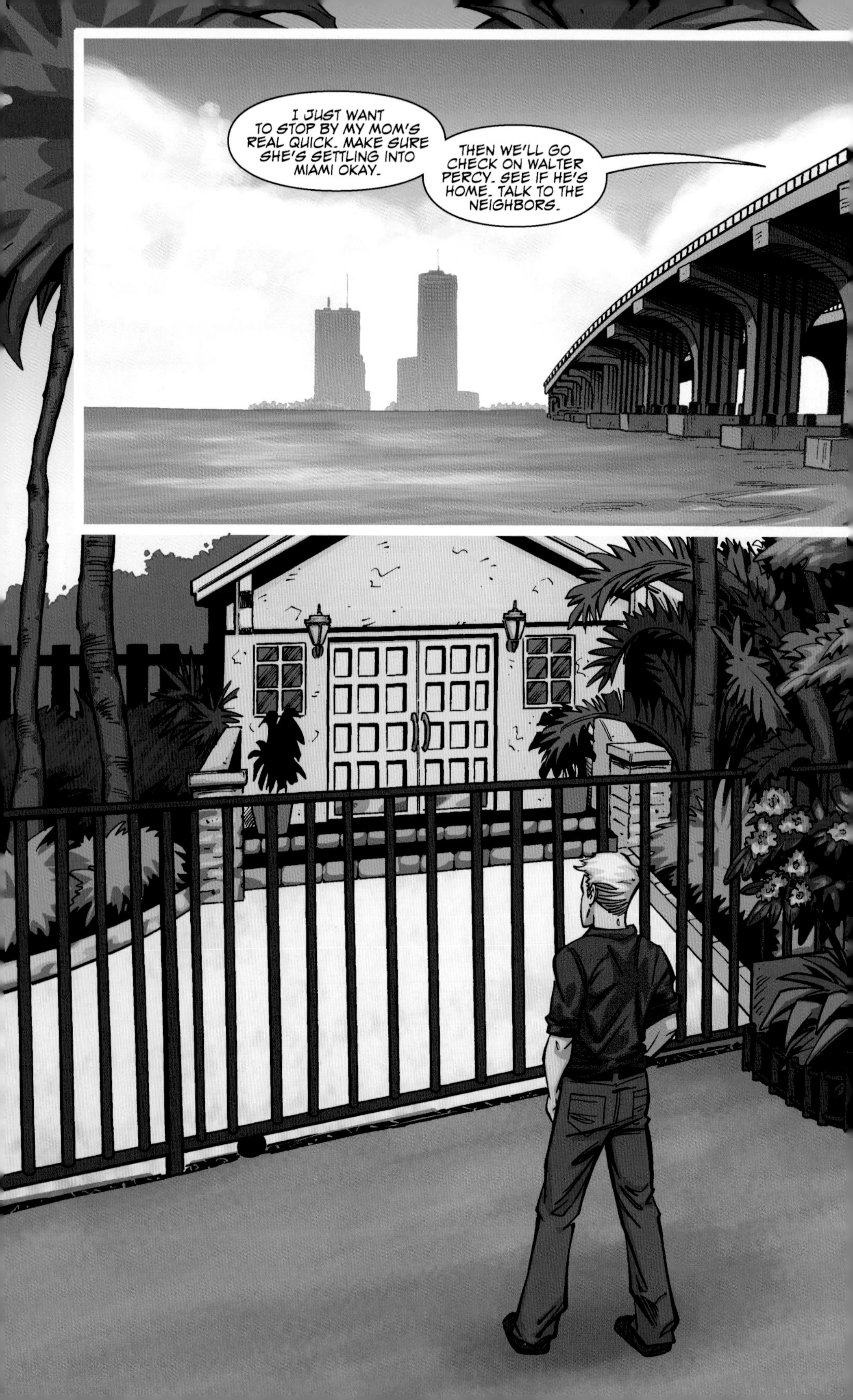
I JUST WANT TO STOP BY MY MOM'S REAL QUICK. MAKE SURE SHE'S SETTLING INTO MIAMI OKAY.
THEN WE'LL GO CHECK ON WALTER PERCY. SEE IF HE'S HOME. TALK TO THE NEIGHBORS.

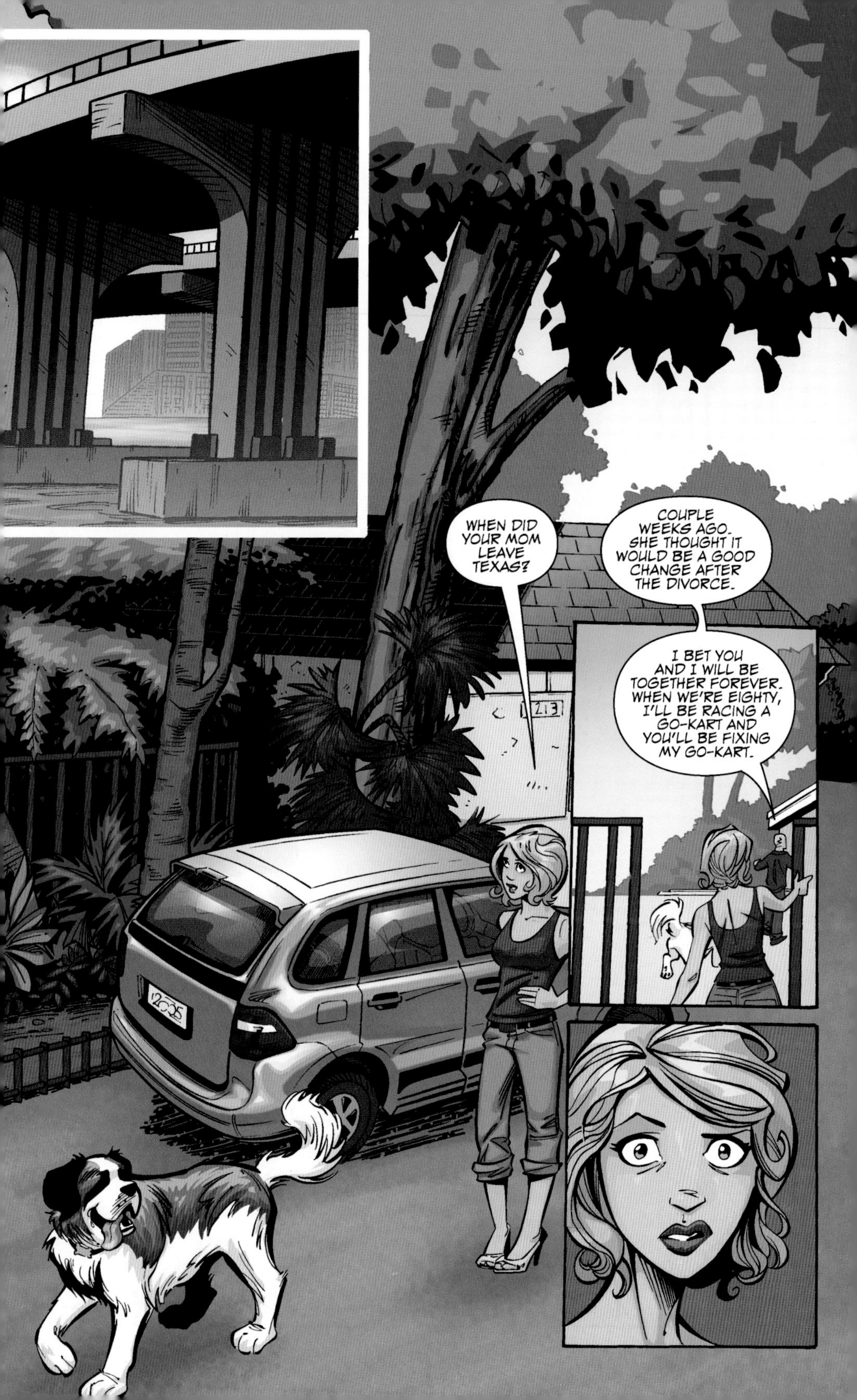
WHEN DID YOUR MOM LEAVE TEXAS?
COUPLE WEEKS AGO. SHE THOUGHT IT WOULD BE A GOOD CHANGE AFTER THE DIVORCE.
I BET YOU AND I WILL BE TOGETHER FOREVER. WHEN WE'RE EIGHTY, I'LL BE RACING A GO-KART AND YOU'LL BE FIXING MY GO-KART.

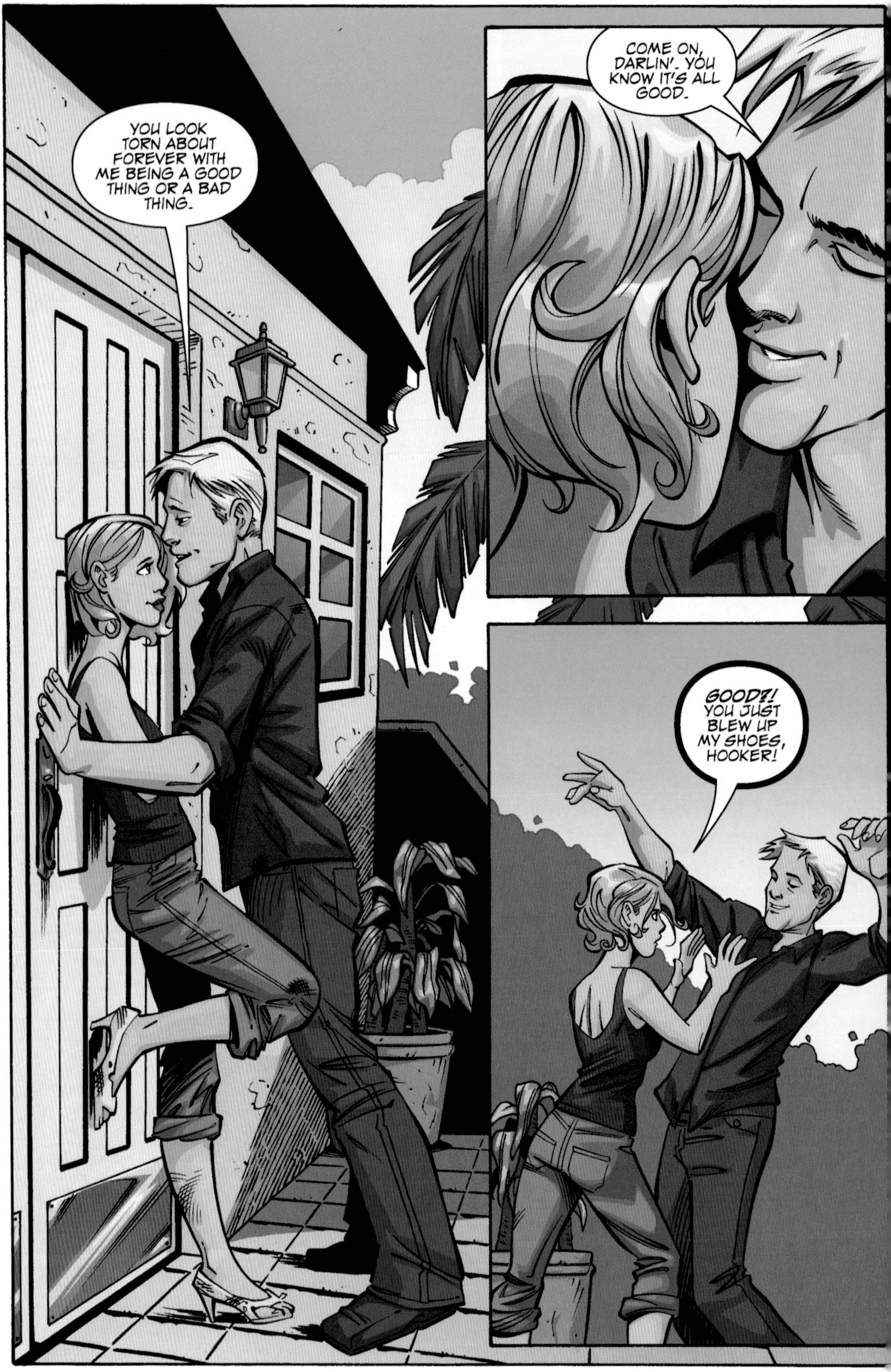
YOU LOOK TORN ABOUT FOREVER WITH ME BEING A GOOD THING OR A BAD THING.
COME ON, DARLIN'. YOU KNOW IT'S ALL GOOD.
GOOD?! YOU JUST BLEW UP MY SHOES, HOOKER!

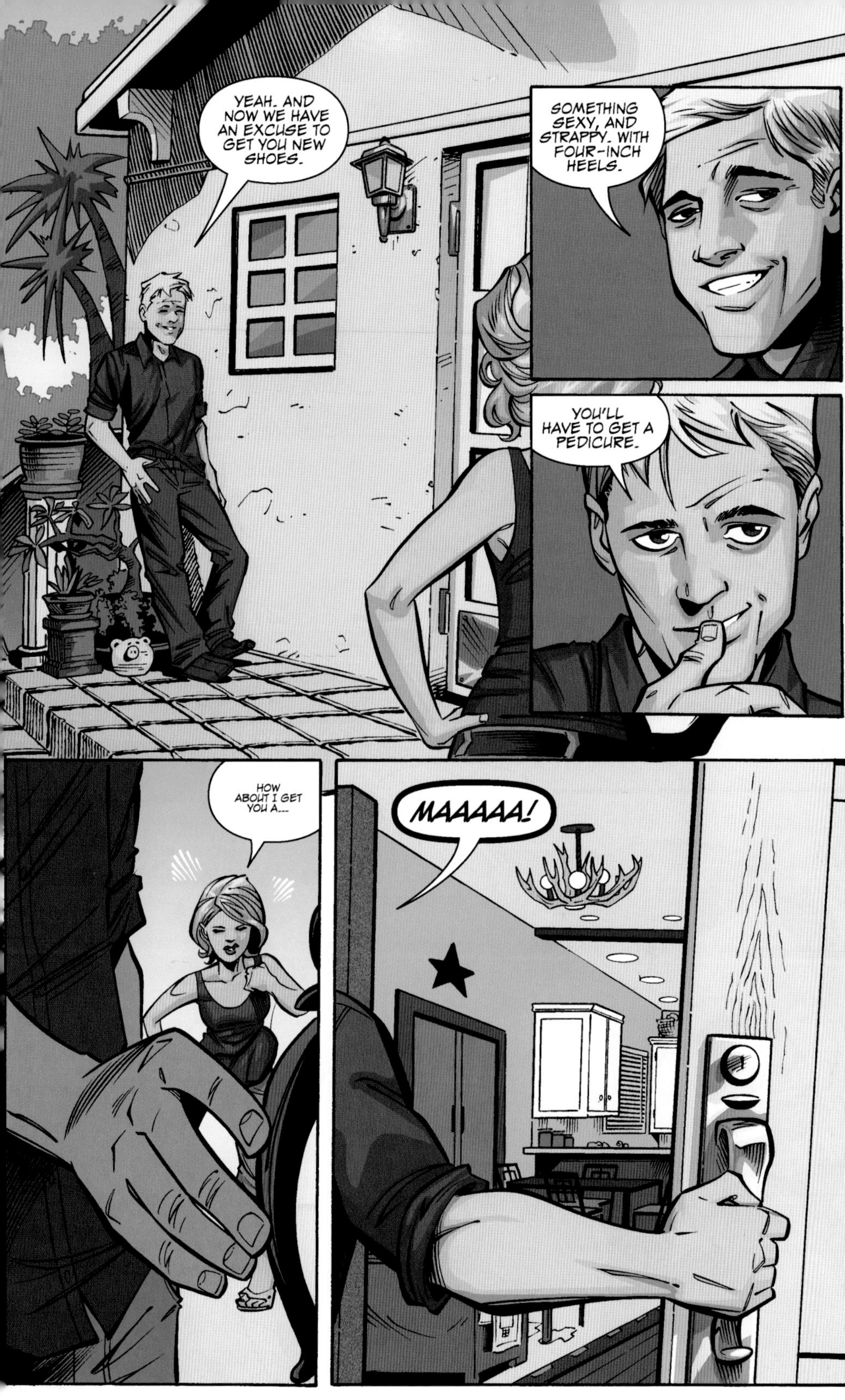
YEAH. AND NOW WE HAVE AN EXCUSE TO GET YOU NEW SHOES.
SOMETHING SEXY, AND STRAPPY. WITH FOUR-INCH HEELS.
YOU'LL HAVE TO GET A PEDICURE.
HOW ABOUT I GET YOU A...
MAAAAA!

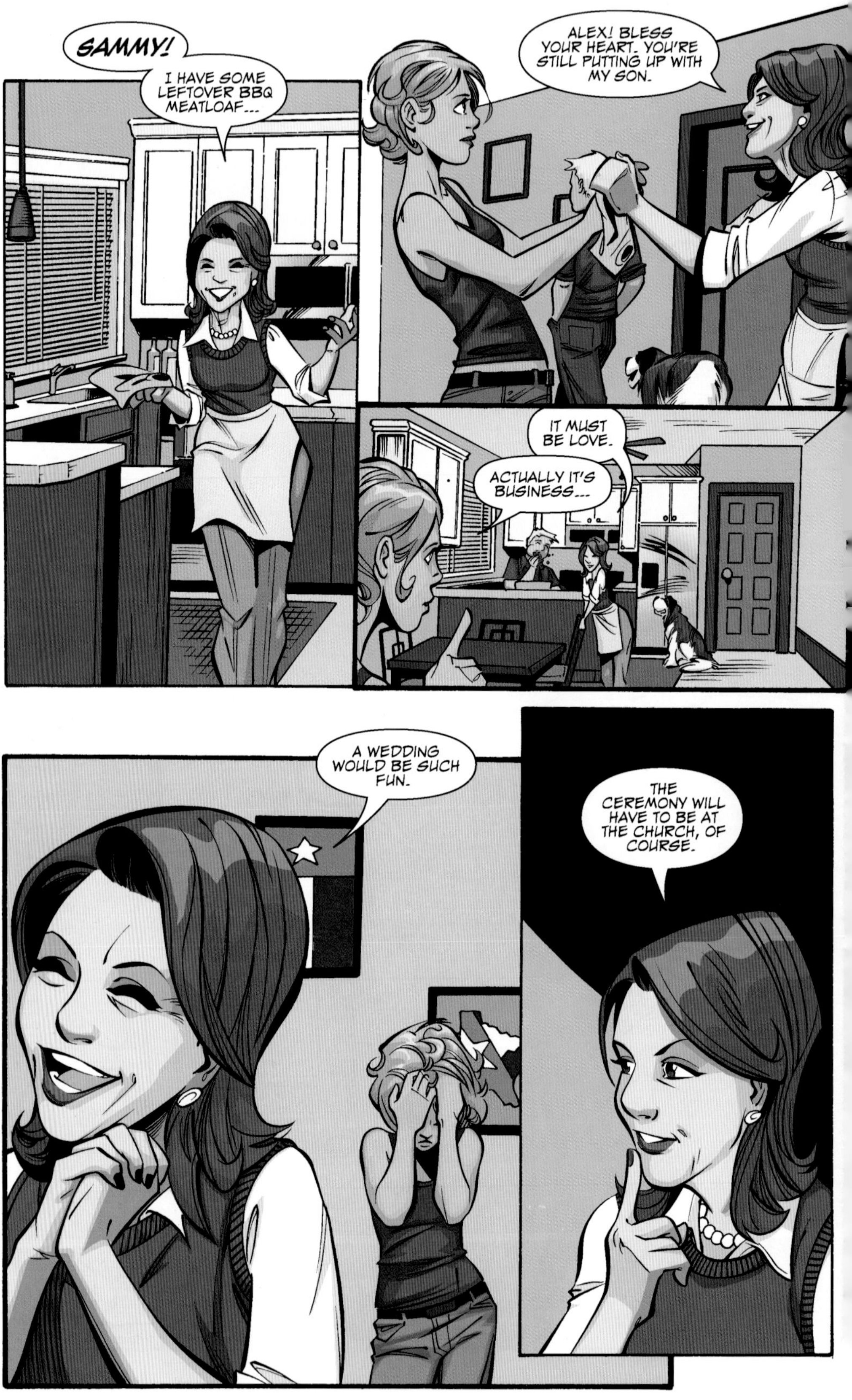
SAMMY!
I HAVE SOME LEFTOVER BBQ MEATLOAF...
ALEX! BLESS YOUR HEART. YOU'RE STILL PUTTING UP WITH MY SON.
IT MUST BE LOVE.
ACTUALLY IT'S BUSINESS...
A WEDDING WOULD BE SUCH FUN.
THE CEREMONY WILL HAVE TO BE AT THE CHURCH, OF COURSE.

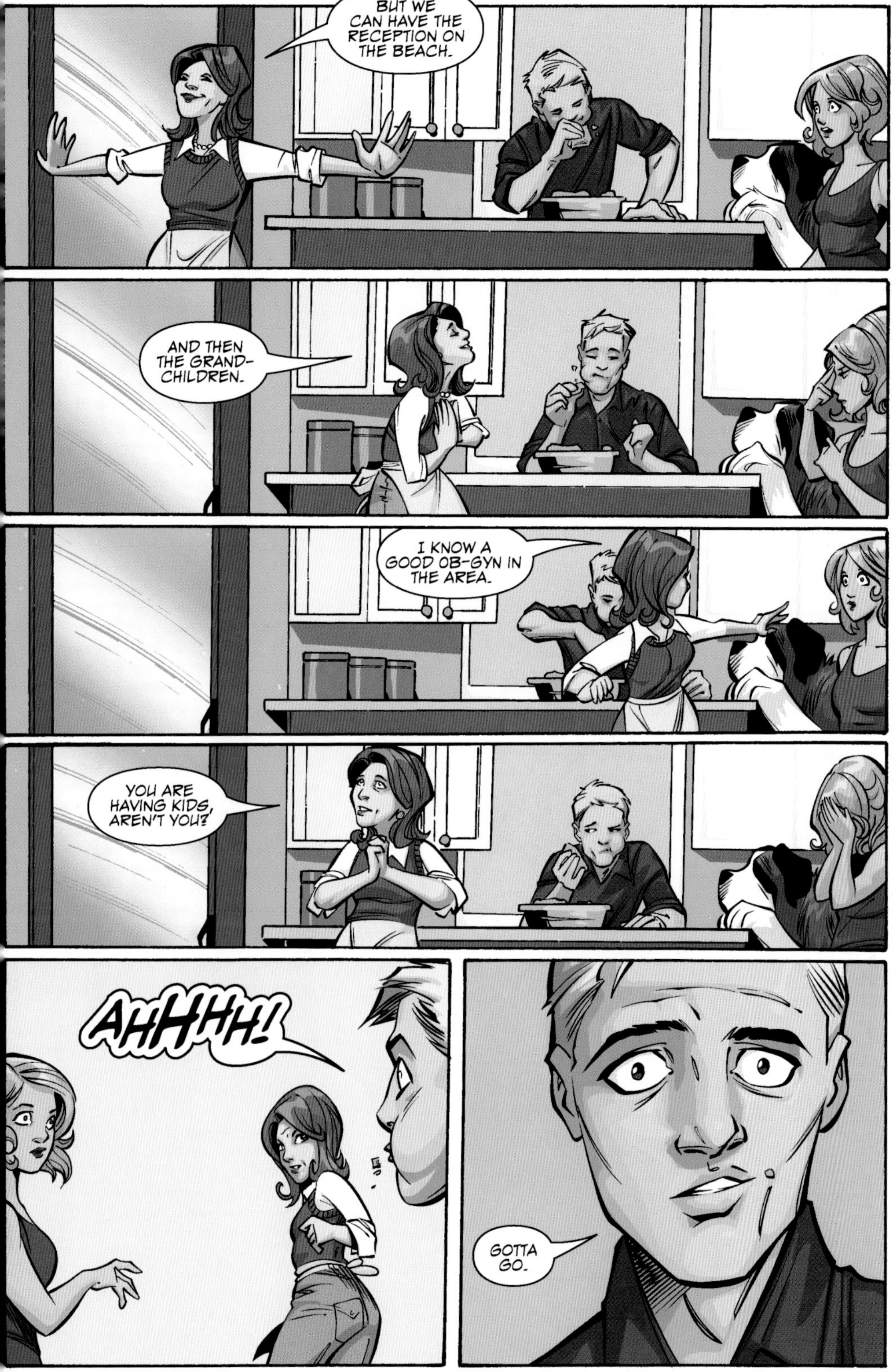
BUT WE CAN HAVE THE RECEPTION ON THE BEACH.
AND THEN THE GRAND-CHILDREN.
I KNOW A GOOD OB-GYN IN THE AREA.
YOU ARE HAVING KIDS, AREN'T YOU?
AHHHH!
GOTTA GO.

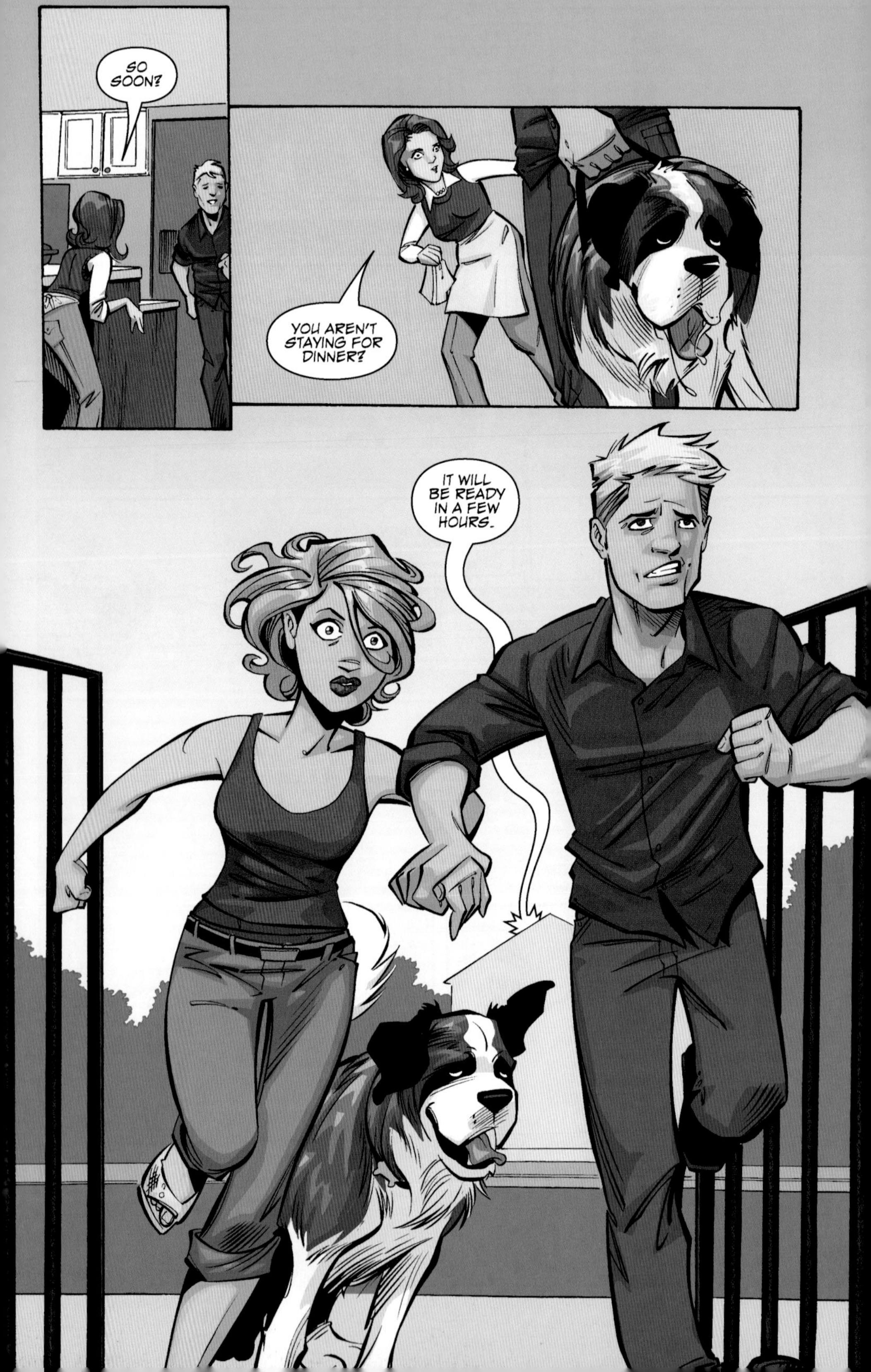
SO SOON?
YOU AREN'T STAYING FOR DINNER?
IT WILL BE READY IN A FEW HOURS.

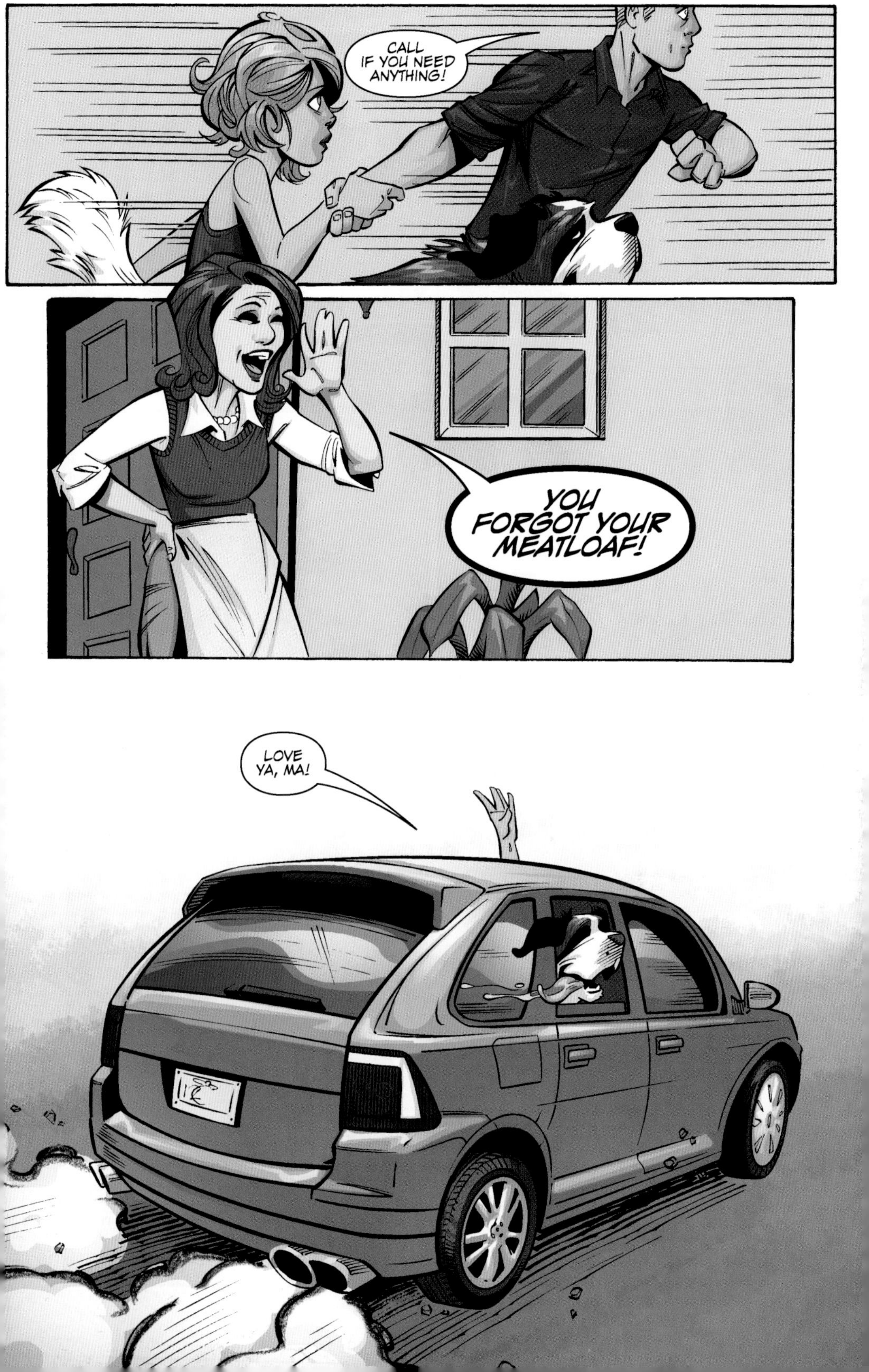
CALL IF YOU NEED ANYTHING!
YOU FORGOT YOUR MEATLOAF!
LOVE YA, MA!

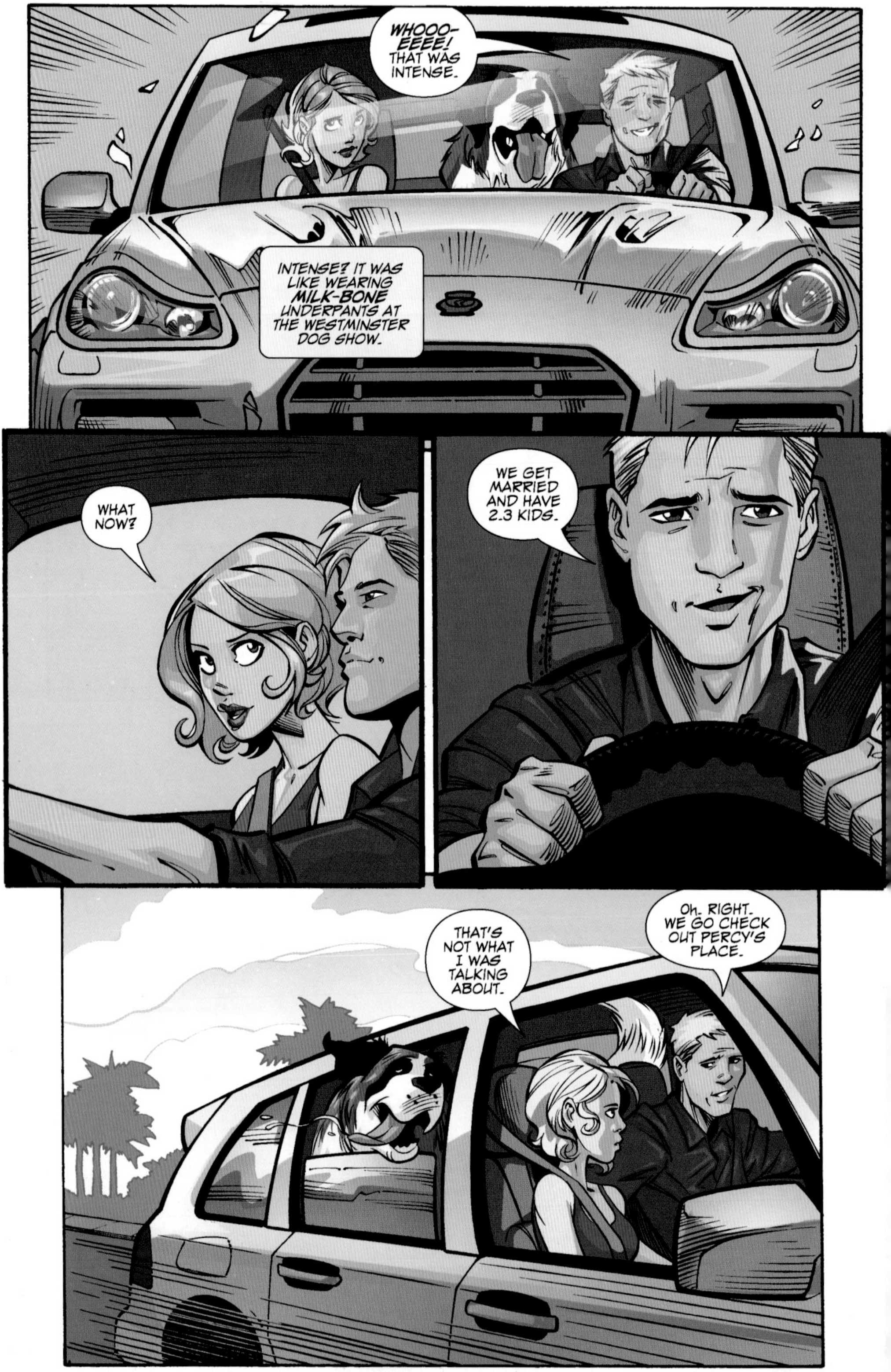
WHOOO-EEEE! THAT WAS INTENSE.
INTENSE? IT WAS LIKE WEARING MILK-BONE UNDERPANTS AT THE WESTMINSTER DOG SHOW.
WHAT NOW?
WE GET MARRIED AND HAVE 2.3 KIDS.
THAT'S NOT WHAT I WAS TALKING ABOUT.
Oh. RIGHT. WE GO CHECK OUT PERCY'S PLACE.

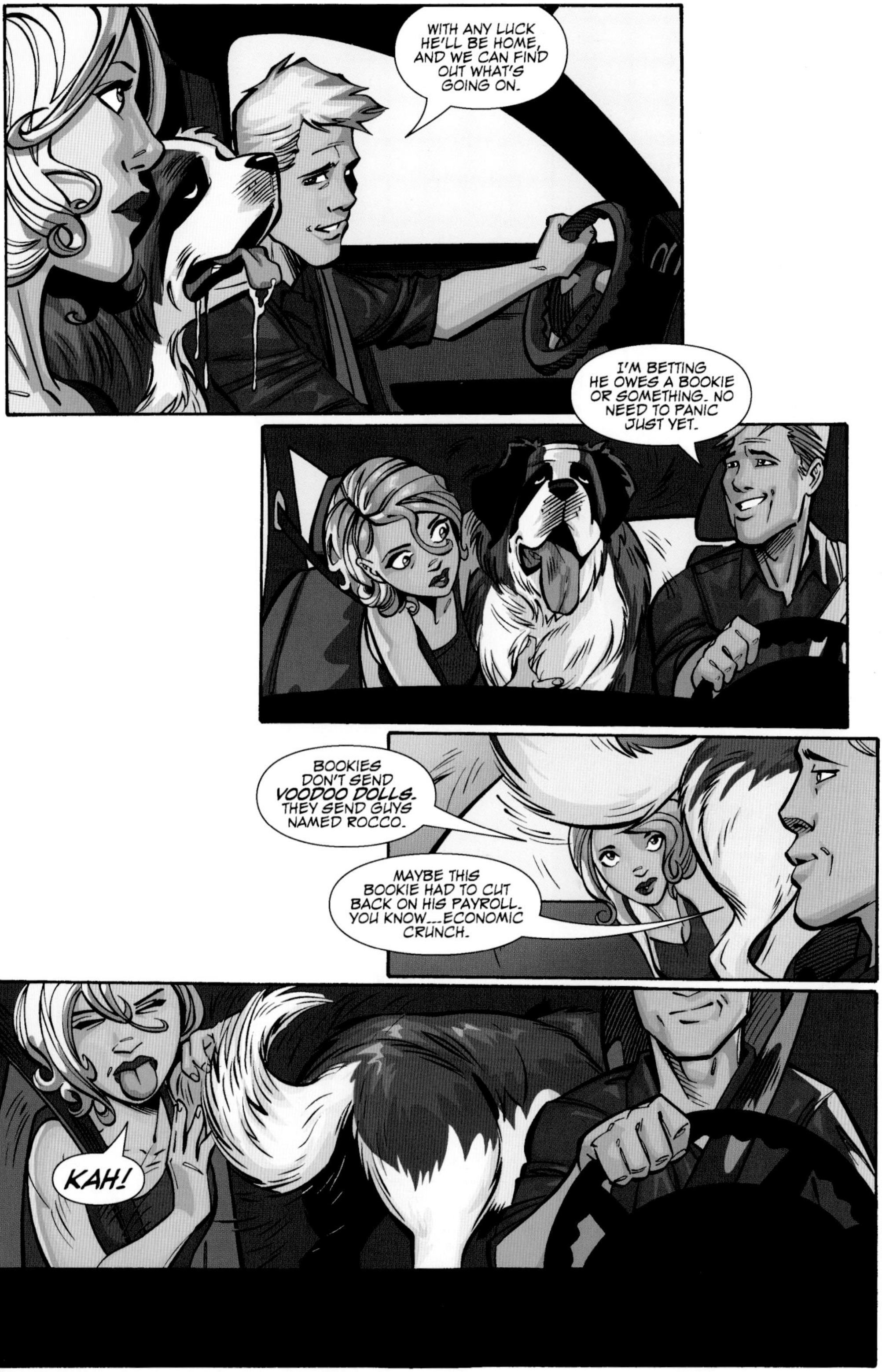
WITH ANY LUCK HE'LL BE HOME, AND WE CAN FIND OUT WHAT'S GOING ON.
I'M BETTING HE OWES A BOOKIE OR SOMETHING. NO NEED TO PANIC JUST YET.
BOOKIES DON'T SEND VOODOO DOLLS. THEY SEND GUYS NAMED ROCCO.
MAYBE THIS BOOKIE HAD TO CUT BACK ON HIS PAYROLL. YOU KNOW... ECONOMIC CRUNCH.
KAH!

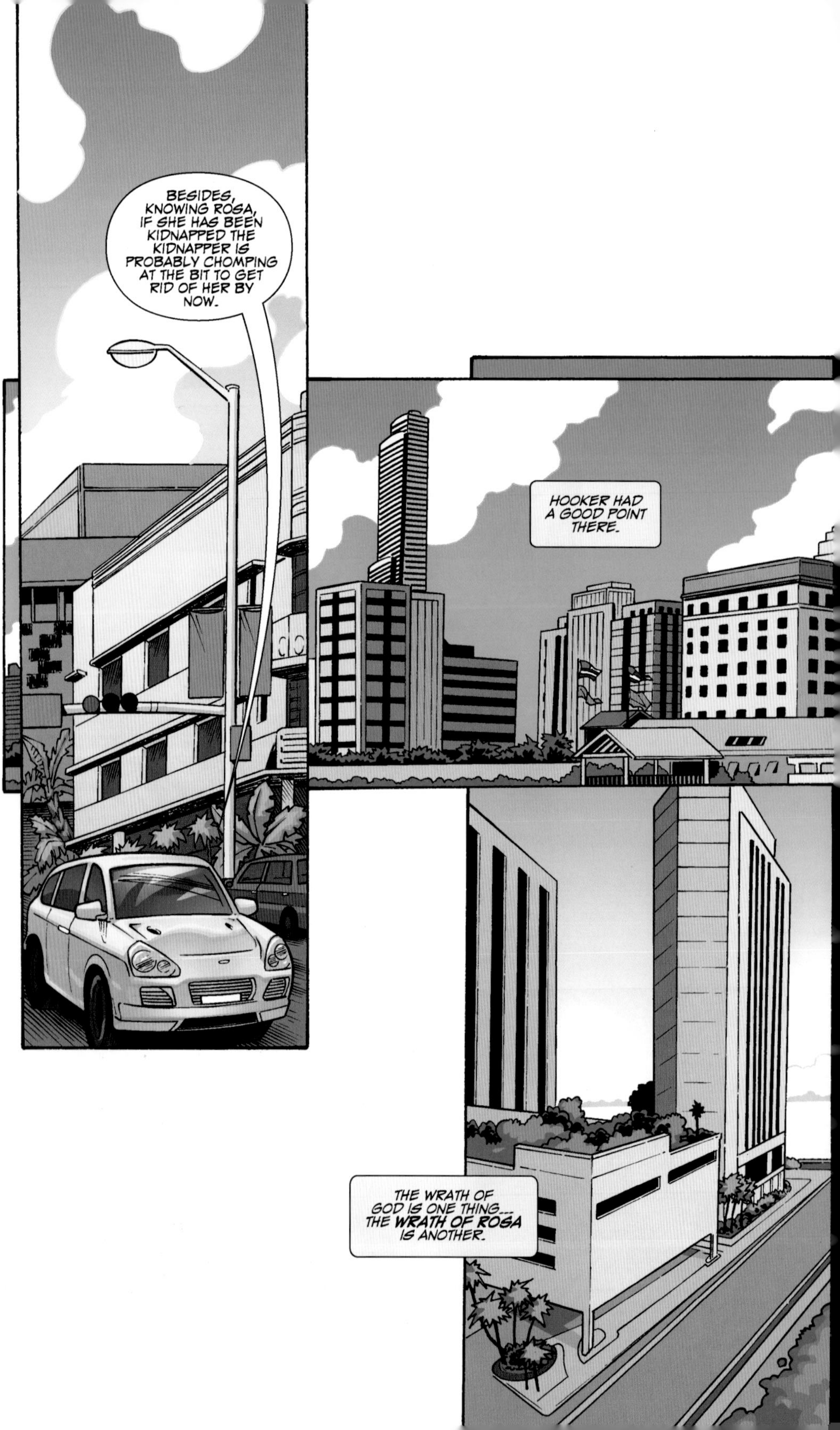
BESIDES, KNOWING ROSA, IF SHE HAS BEEN KIDNAPPED THE KIDNAPPER IS PROBABLY CHOMPING AT THE BIT TO GET RID OF HER BY NOW.
HOOKER HAD A GOOD POINT THERE.
THE WRATH OF GOD IS ONE THING... THE WRATH OF ROSA IS ANOTHER.

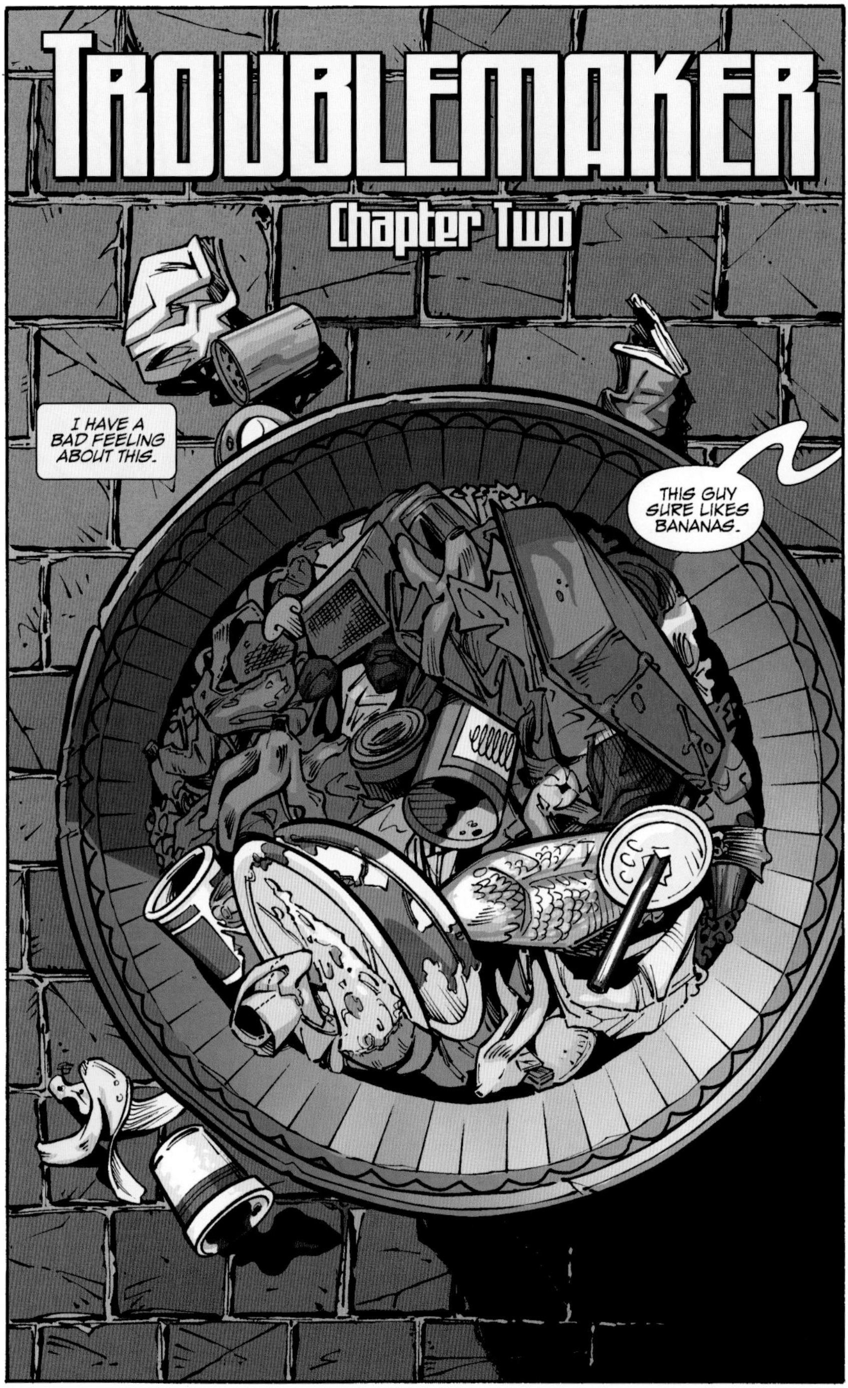
TROUBLEMAKER
Chapter Two
I HAVE A BAD FEELING ABOUT THIS.
THIS GUY SURE LIKES BANANAS.

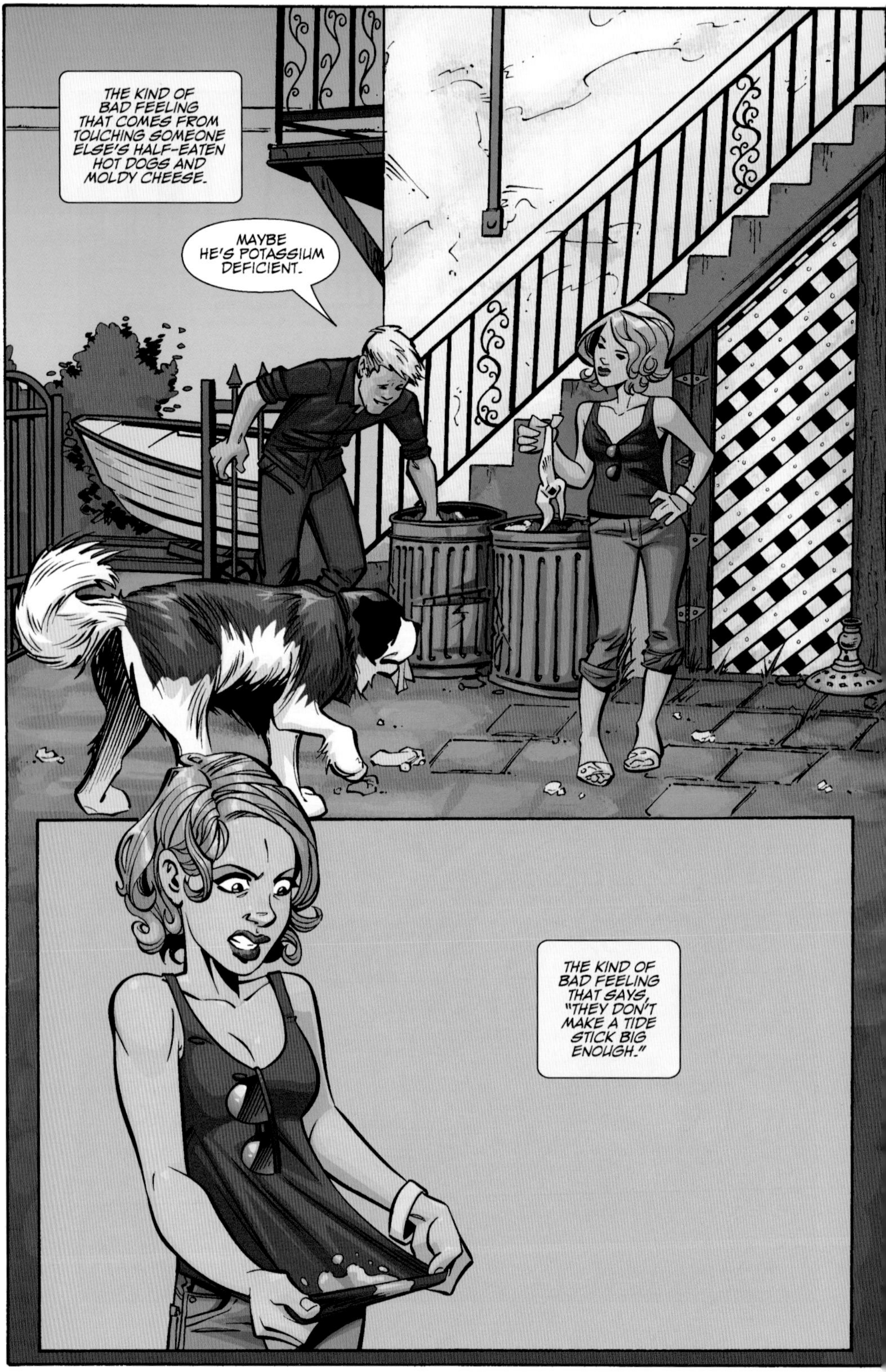
THE KIND OF BAD FEELING THAT COMES FROM TOUCHING SOMEONE ELSE'S HALF-EATEN HOT DOGS AND MOLDY CHEESE.
MAYBE HE'S POTASSIUM DEFICIENT.
THE KIND OF BAD FEELING THAT SAYS, "THEY DON'T MAKE A TIDE STICK BIG ENOUGH."

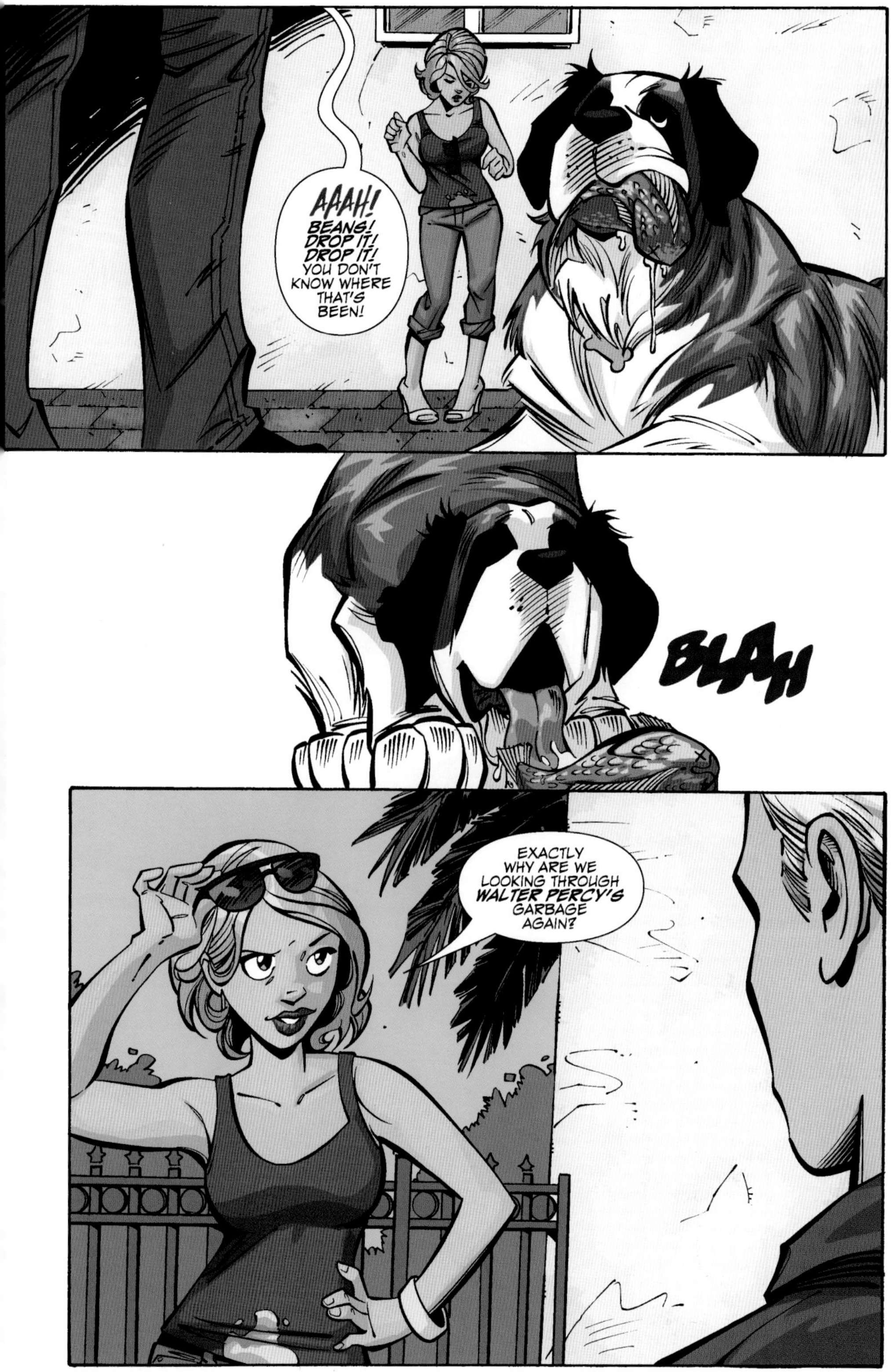
AAAH! BEANS! DROP IT! DROP IT! YOU DON'T KNOW WHERE THAT'S BEEN!
BLAH
EXACTLY WHY ARE WE LOOKING THROUGH WALTER PERCY'S GARBAGE AGAIN?

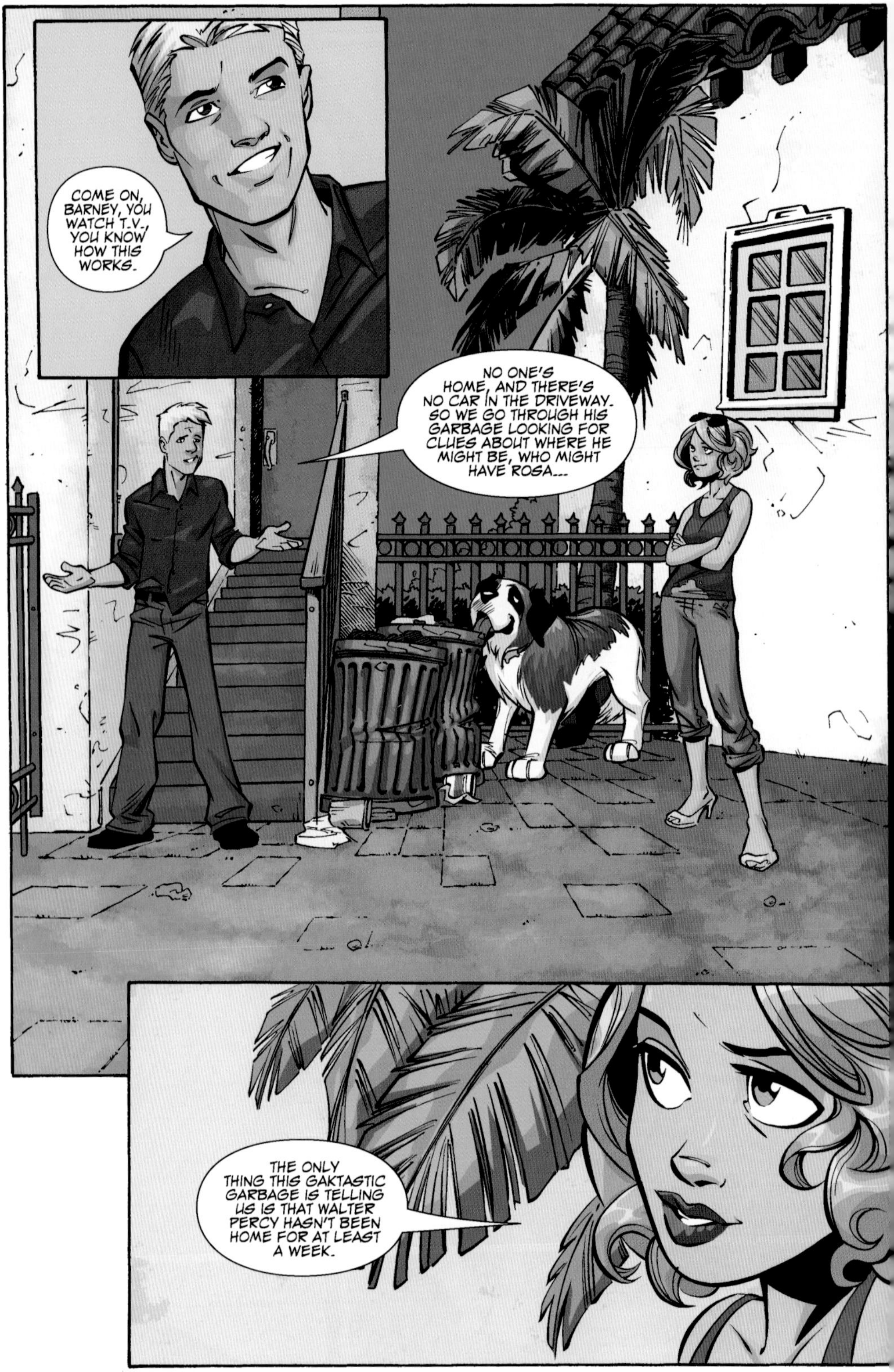
COME ON, BARNEY, YOU WATCH T.V., YOU KNOW HOW THIS WORKS.
NO ONE'S HOME, AND THERE'S NO CAR IN THE DRIVEWAY. SO WE GO THROUGH HIS GARBAGE LOOKING FOR CLUES ABOUT WHERE HE MIGHT BE, WHO MIGHT HAVE ROSA...
THE ONLY THING THIS GAKTASTIC GARBAGE IS TELLING US IS THAT WALTER PERCY HASN'T BEEN HOME FOR AT LEAST A WEEK.

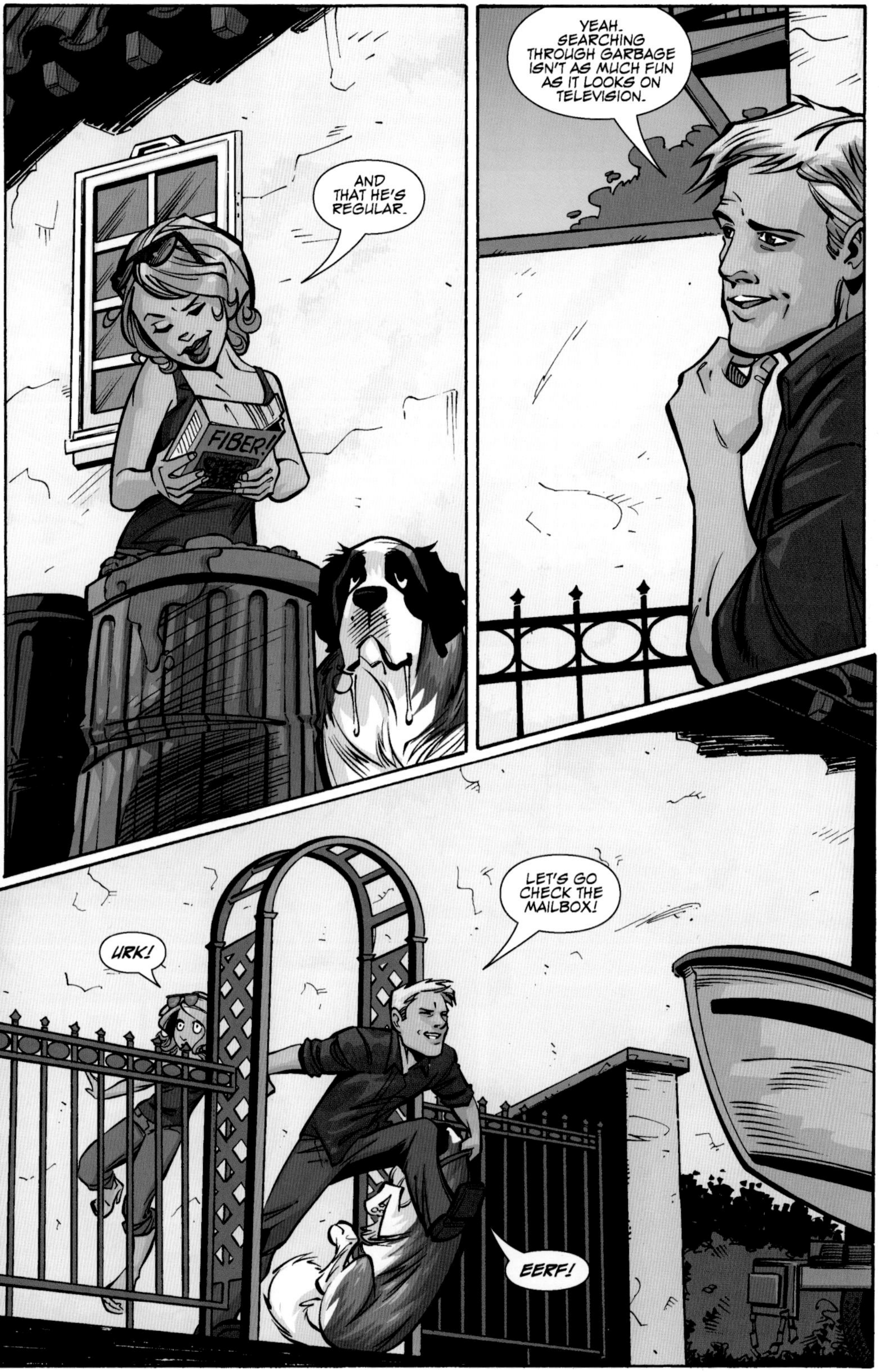

AND THAT HE'S REGULAR.
FIBER!
YEAH. SEARCHING THROUGH GARBAGE ISN'T AS MUCH FUN AS IT LOOKS ON TELEVISION.
LET'S GO CHECK THE MAILBOX!
URK!
EERF!

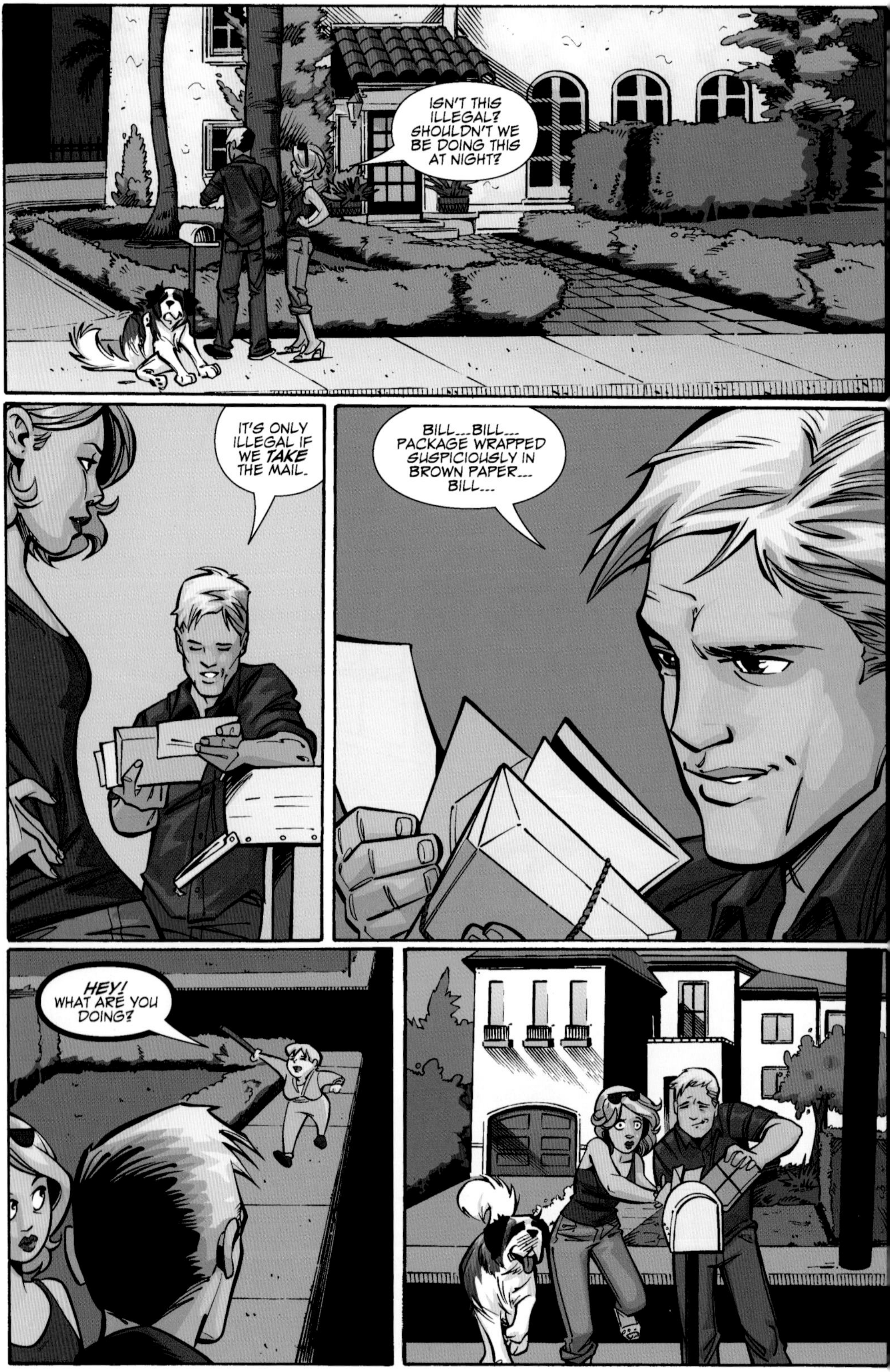
ISN'T THIS ILLEGAL? SHOULDN'T WE BE DOING THIS AT NIGHT?
IT'S ONLY ILLEGAL IF WE *TAKE* THE MAIL.
BILL... BILL... PACKAGE WRAPPED SUSPICIOUSLY IN BROWN PAPER... BILL...
HEY! WHAT ARE YOU DOING?

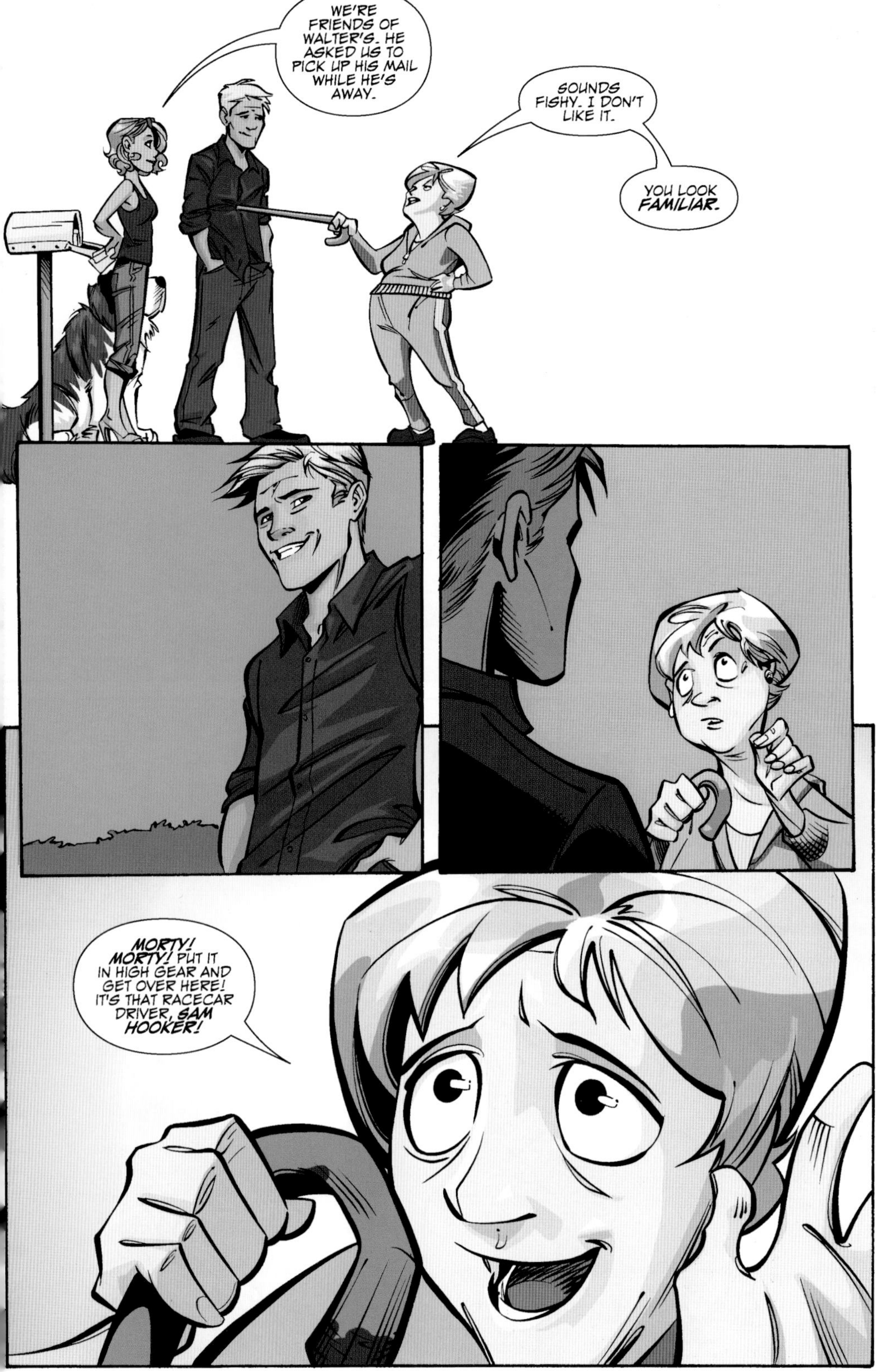
WE'RE FRIENDS OF WALTER'S. HE ASKED US TO PICK UP HIS MAIL WHILE HE'S AWAY.
SOUNDS FISHY. I DON'T LIKE IT.
YOU LOOK **FAMILIAR**.
MORTY! MORTY! PUT IT IN HIGH GEAR AND GET OVER HERE! IT'S THAT RACECAR DRIVER, **SAM HOOKER!**

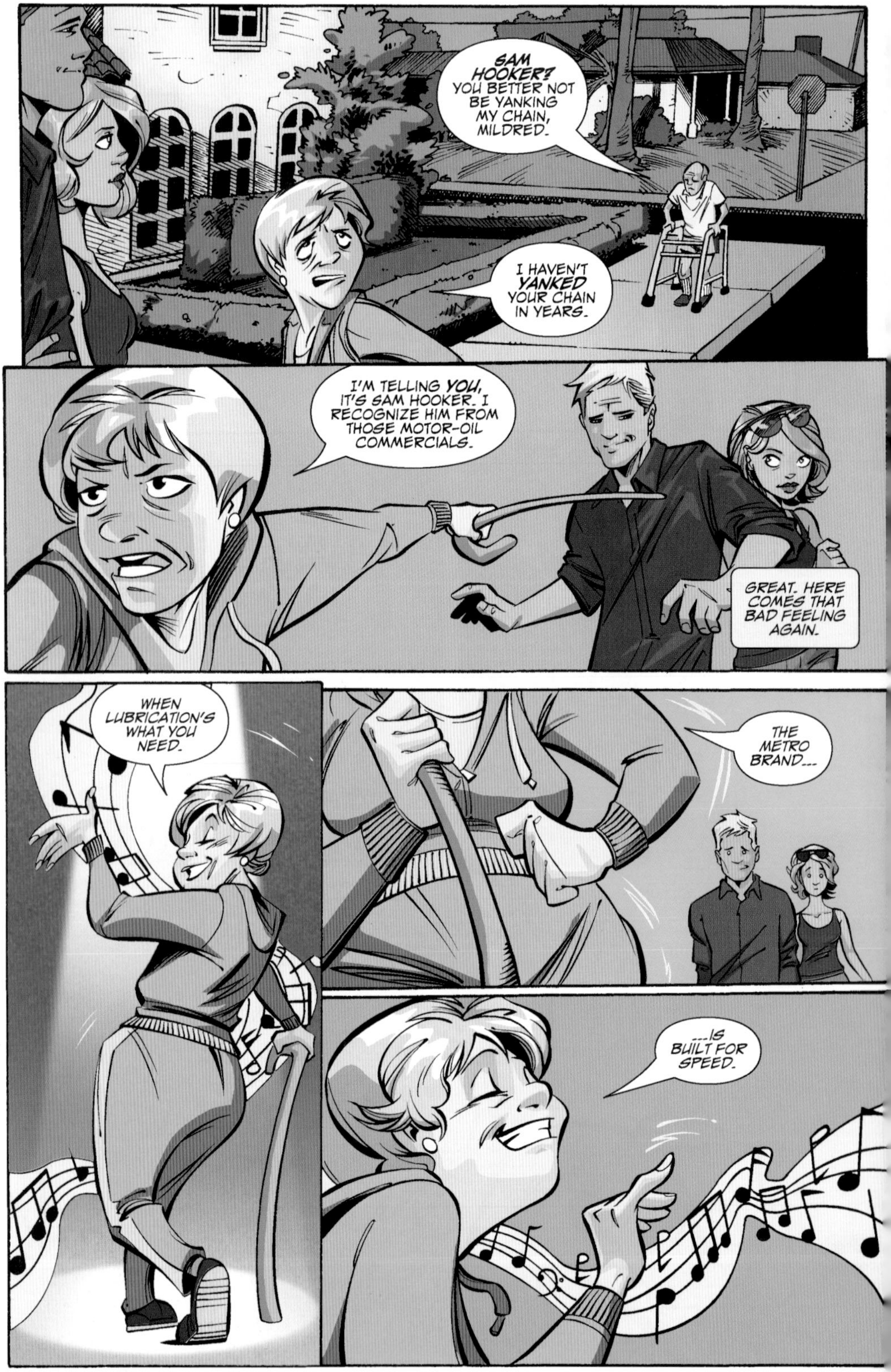
SAM HOOKER? YOU BETTER NOT BE YANKING MY CHAIN, MILDRED.
I HAVEN'T YANKED YOUR CHAIN IN YEARS.
I'M TELLING YOU, IT'S SAM HOOKER. I RECOGNIZE HIM FROM THOSE MOTOR-OIL COMMERCIALS.
GREAT. HERE COMES THAT BAD FEELING AGAIN.
WHEN LUBRICATION'S WHAT YOU NEED.
THE METRO BRAND...
...IS BUILT FOR SPEED.

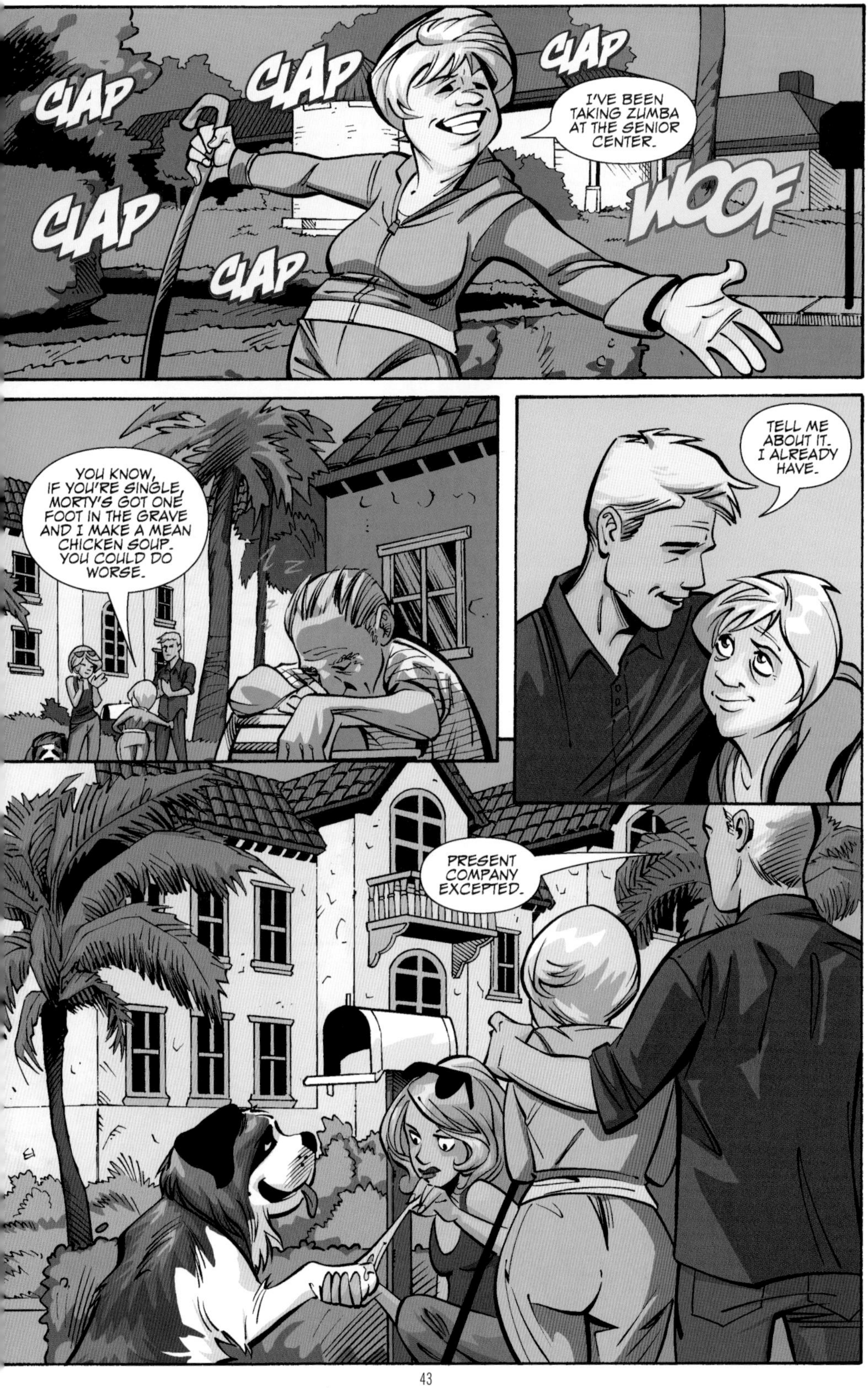
CLAP
CLAP
CLAP
CLAP
CLAP
I'VE BEEN TAKING ZUMBA AT THE SENIOR CENTER.
WOOF
YOU KNOW, IF YOU'RE SINGLE, MORTY'S GOT ONE FOOT IN THE GRAVE AND I MAKE A MEAN CHICKEN SOUP. YOU COULD DO WORSE.
TELL ME ABOUT IT. I ALREADY HAVE.
PRESENT COMPANY EXCEPTED.

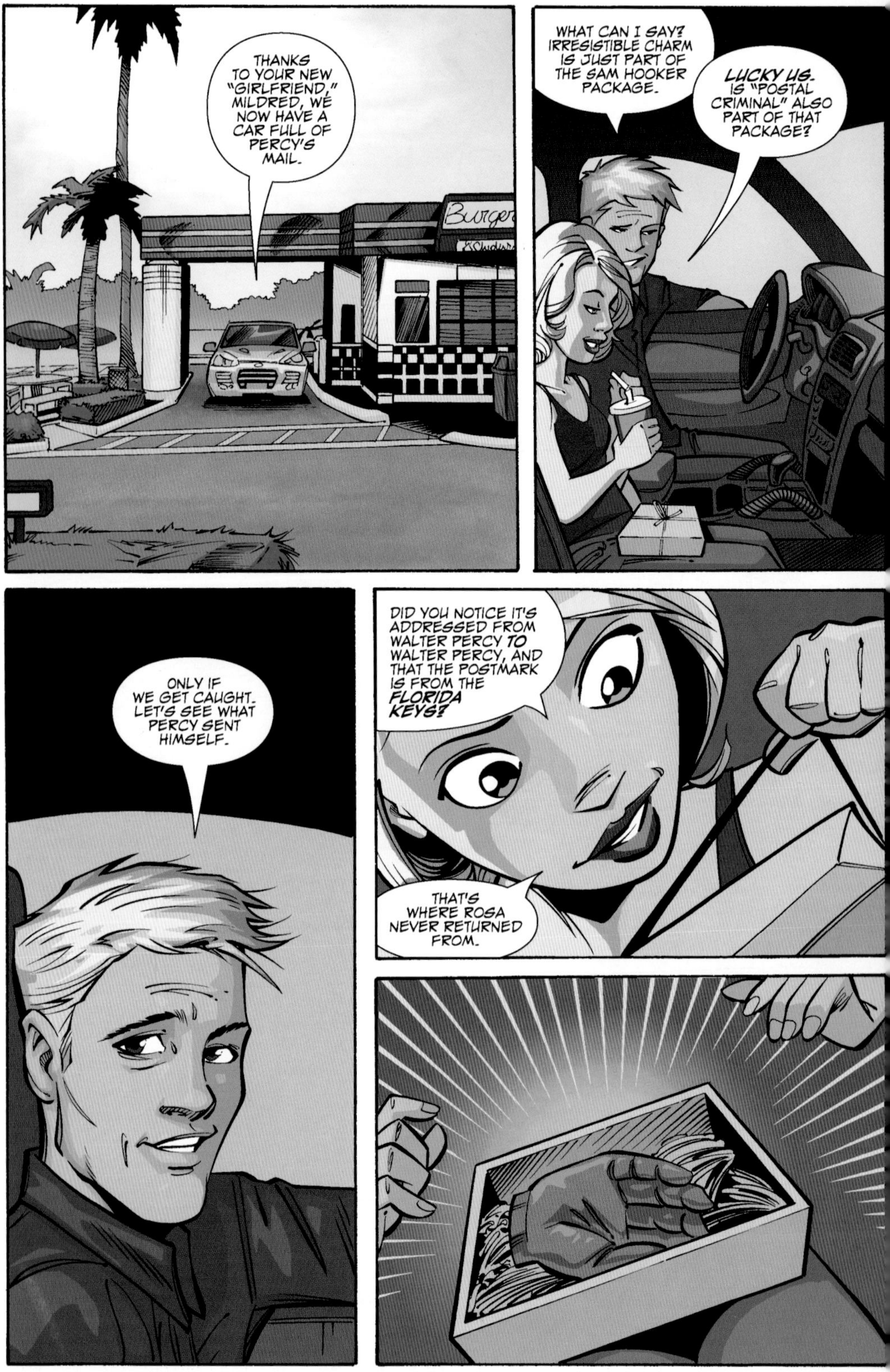
THANKS TO YOUR NEW "GIRLFRIEND," MILDRED, WE NOW HAVE A CAR FULL OF PERCY'S MAIL.
Burger
WHAT CAN I SAY? IRRESISTIBLE CHARM IS JUST PART OF THE SAM HOOKER PACKAGE.
LUCKY US. IS "POSTAL CRIMINAL" ALSO PART OF THAT PACKAGE?
ONLY IF WE GET CAUGHT. LET'S SEE WHAT PERCY SENT HIMSELF.
DID YOU NOTICE IT'S ADDRESSED FROM WALTER PERCY TO WALTER PERCY, AND THAT THE POSTMARK IS FROM THE FLORIDA KEYS?
THAT'S WHERE ROSA NEVER RETURNED FROM.

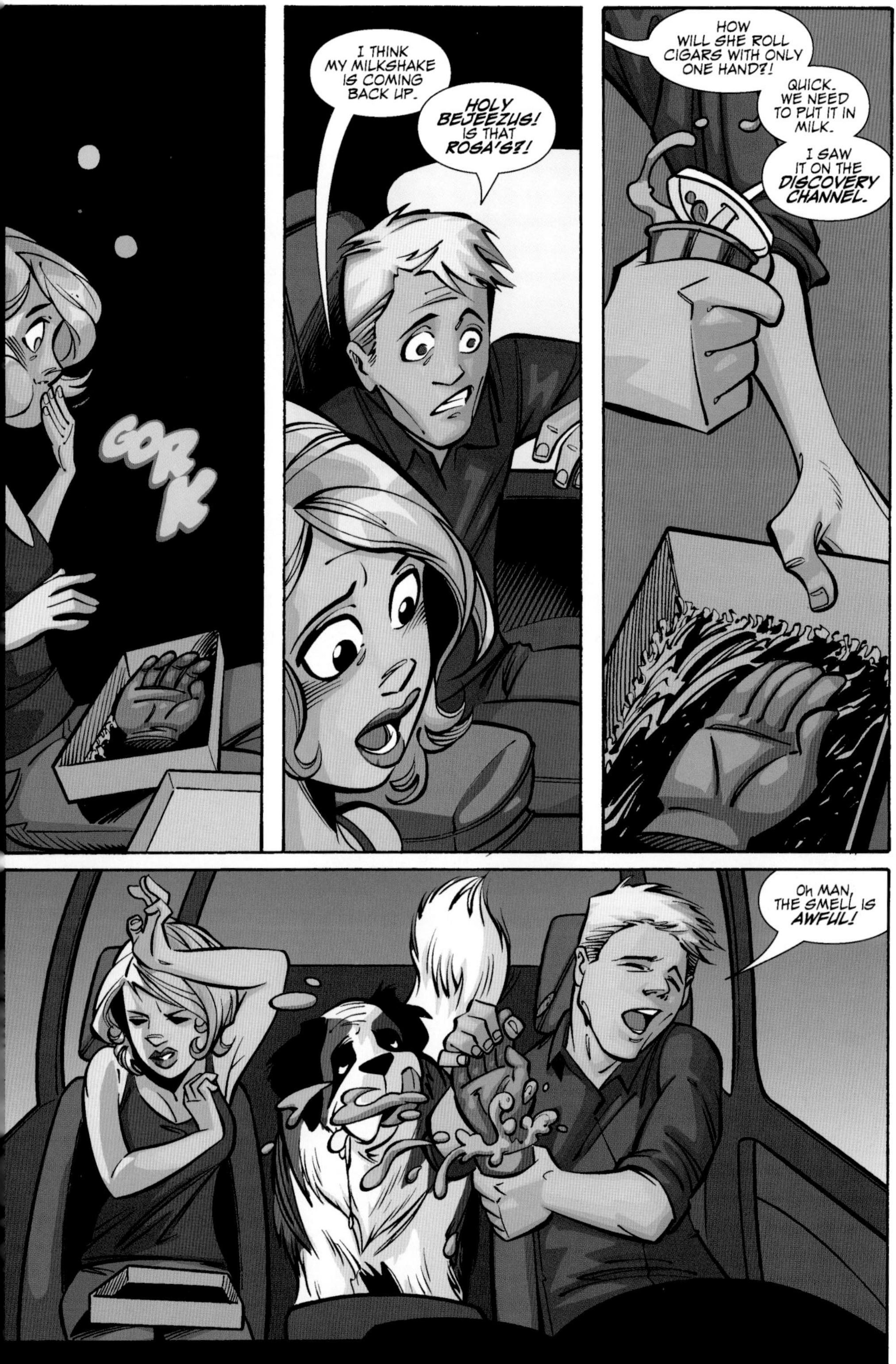
GORK
I THINK MY MILKSHAKE IS COMING BACK UP.
HOLY BEJEEZUS! IS THAT ROSA'S?!
HOW WILL SHE ROLL CIGARS WITH ONLY ONE HAND?!
QUICK. WE NEED TO PUT IT IN MILK.
I SAW IT ON THE DISCOVERY CHANNEL.
Oh MAN, THE SMELL IS AWFUL!

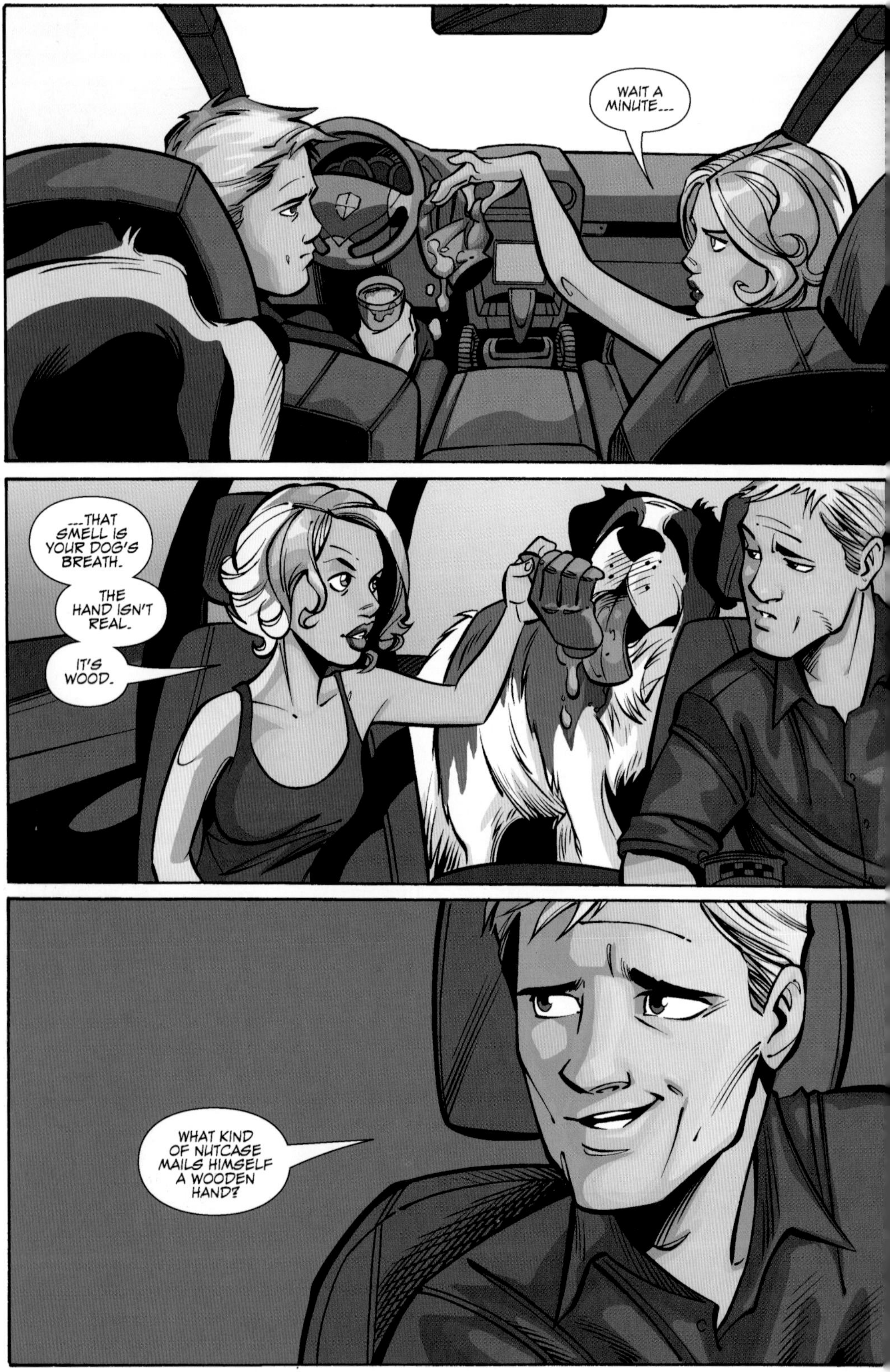
WAIT A MINUTE...
...THAT SMELL IS YOUR DOG'S BREATH.
THE HAND ISN'T REAL.
IT'S WOOD.
WHAT KIND OF NUTCASE MAILS HIMSELF A WOODEN HAND?

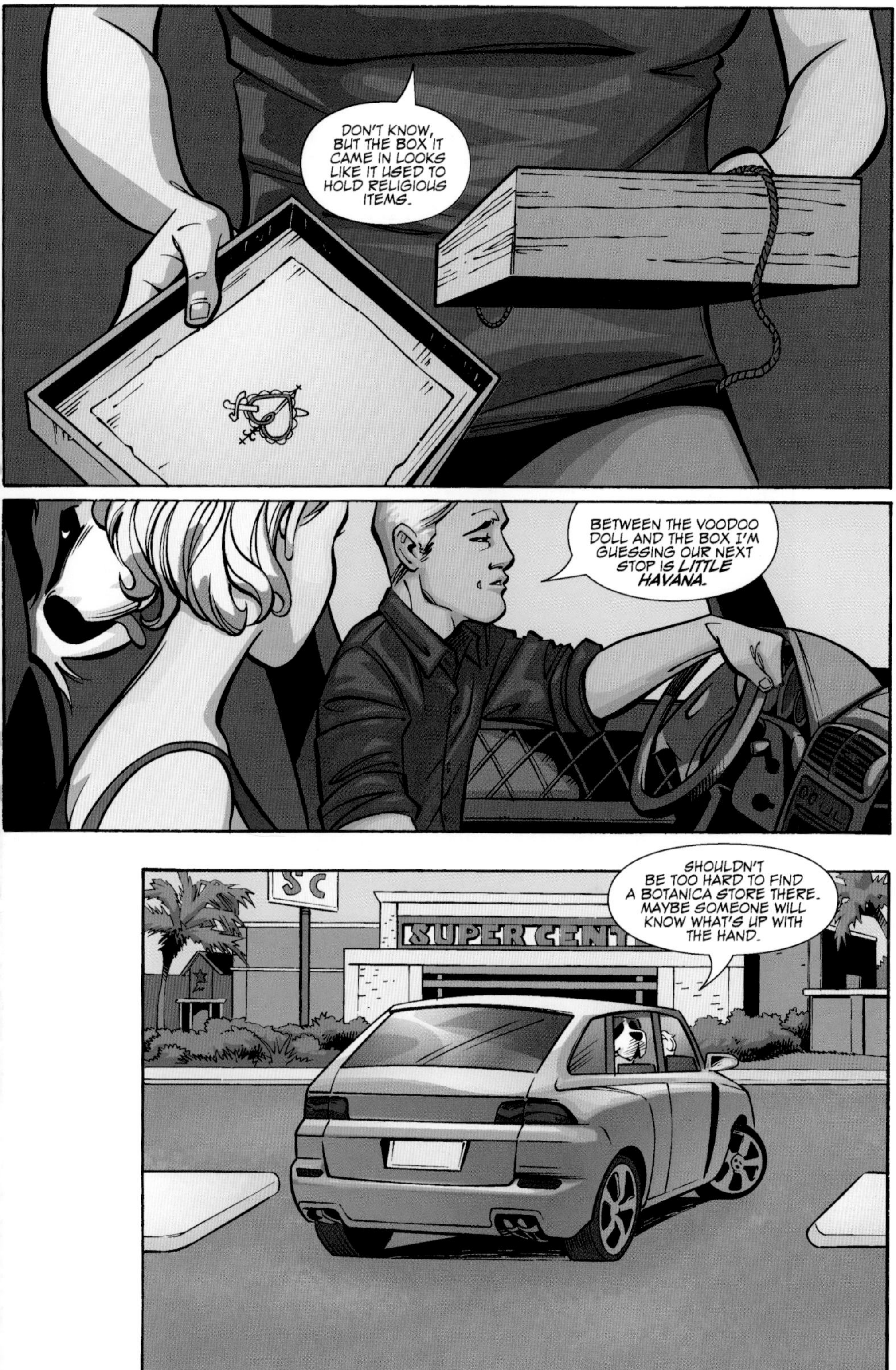
DON'T KNOW, BUT THE BOX IT CAME IN LOOKS LIKE IT USED TO HOLD RELIGIOUS ITEMS.
BETWEEN THE VOODOO DOLL AND THE BOX I'M GUESSING OUR NEXT STOP IS *LITTLE HAVANA.*
SHOULDN'T BE TOO HARD TO FIND A BOTANICA STORE THERE. MAYBE SOMEONE WILL KNOW WHAT'S UP WITH THE HAND.

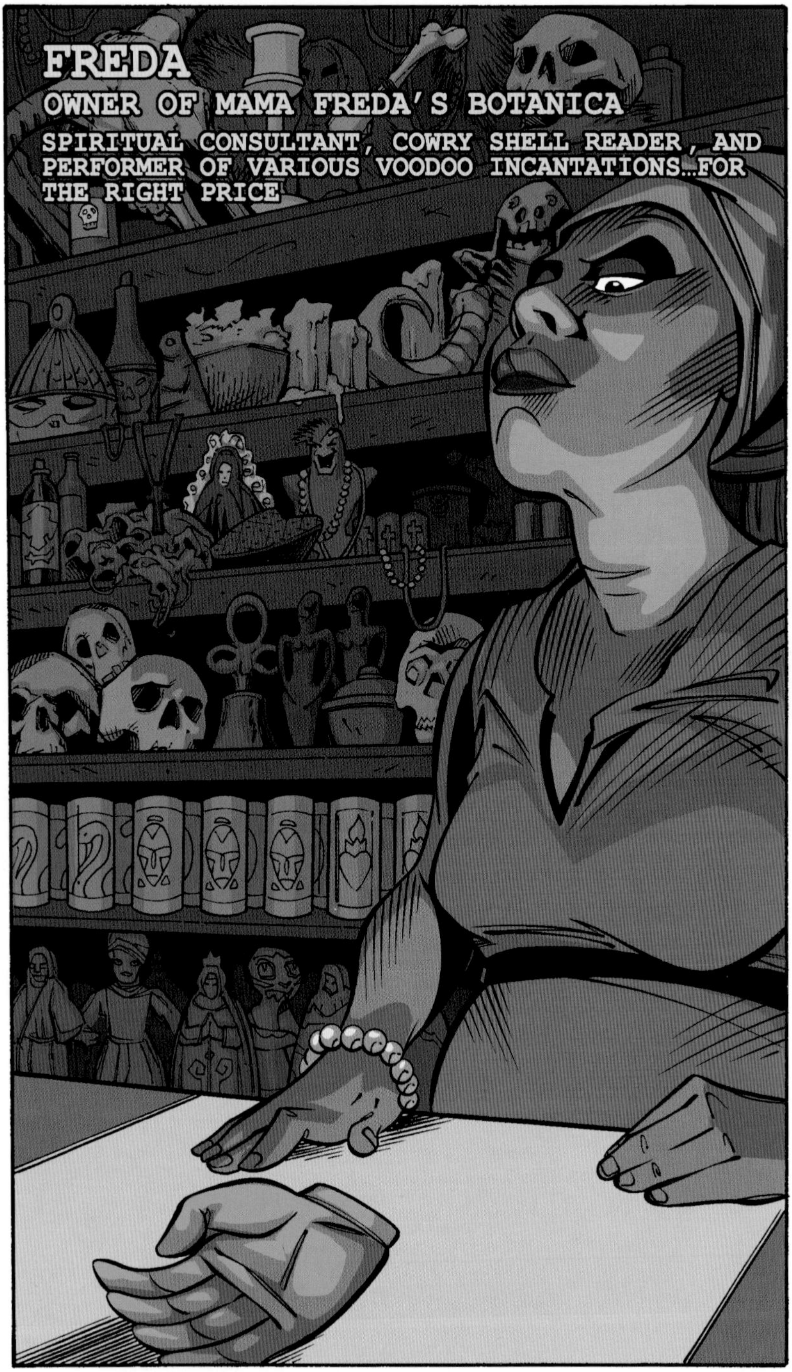
FREDA
OWNER OF MAMA FREDA'S BOTANICA
SPIRITUAL CONSULTANT, COWRY SHELL READER, AND PERFORMER OF VARIOUS VOODOO INCANTATIONS…FOR THE RIGHT PRICE

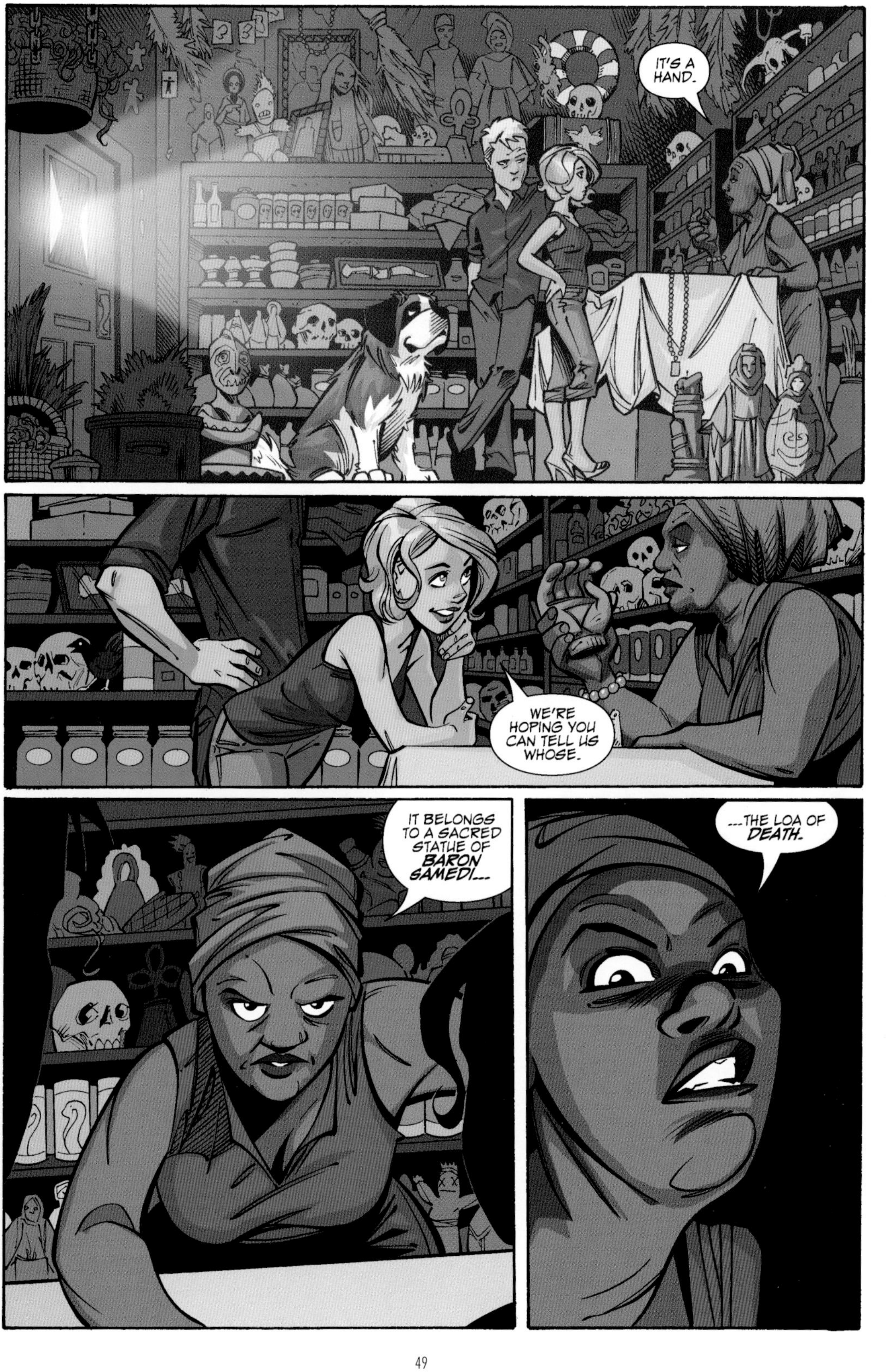
IT'S A HAND.
WE'RE HOPING YOU CAN TELL US WHOSE.
IT BELONGS TO A SACRED STATUE OF BARON SAMEDI...
...THE LOA OF DEATH.

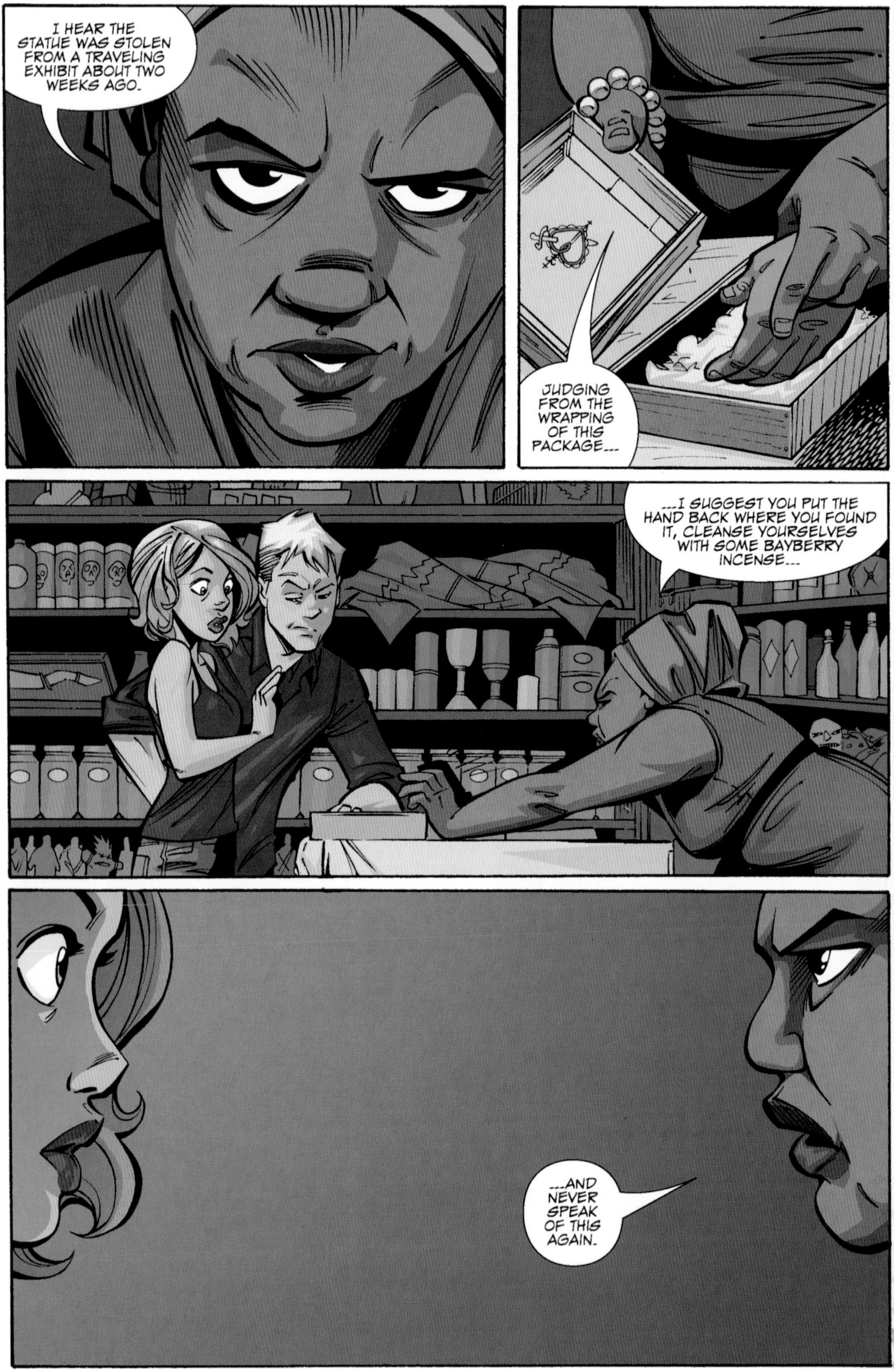
I HEAR THE STATUE WAS STOLEN FROM A TRAVELING EXHIBIT ABOUT TWO WEEKS AGO.
JUDGING FROM THE WRAPPING OF THIS PACKAGE...
...I SUGGEST YOU PUT THE HAND BACK WHERE YOU FOUND IT, CLEANSE YOURSELVES WITH SOME BAYBERRY INCENSE...
...AND NEVER SPEAK OF THIS AGAIN.

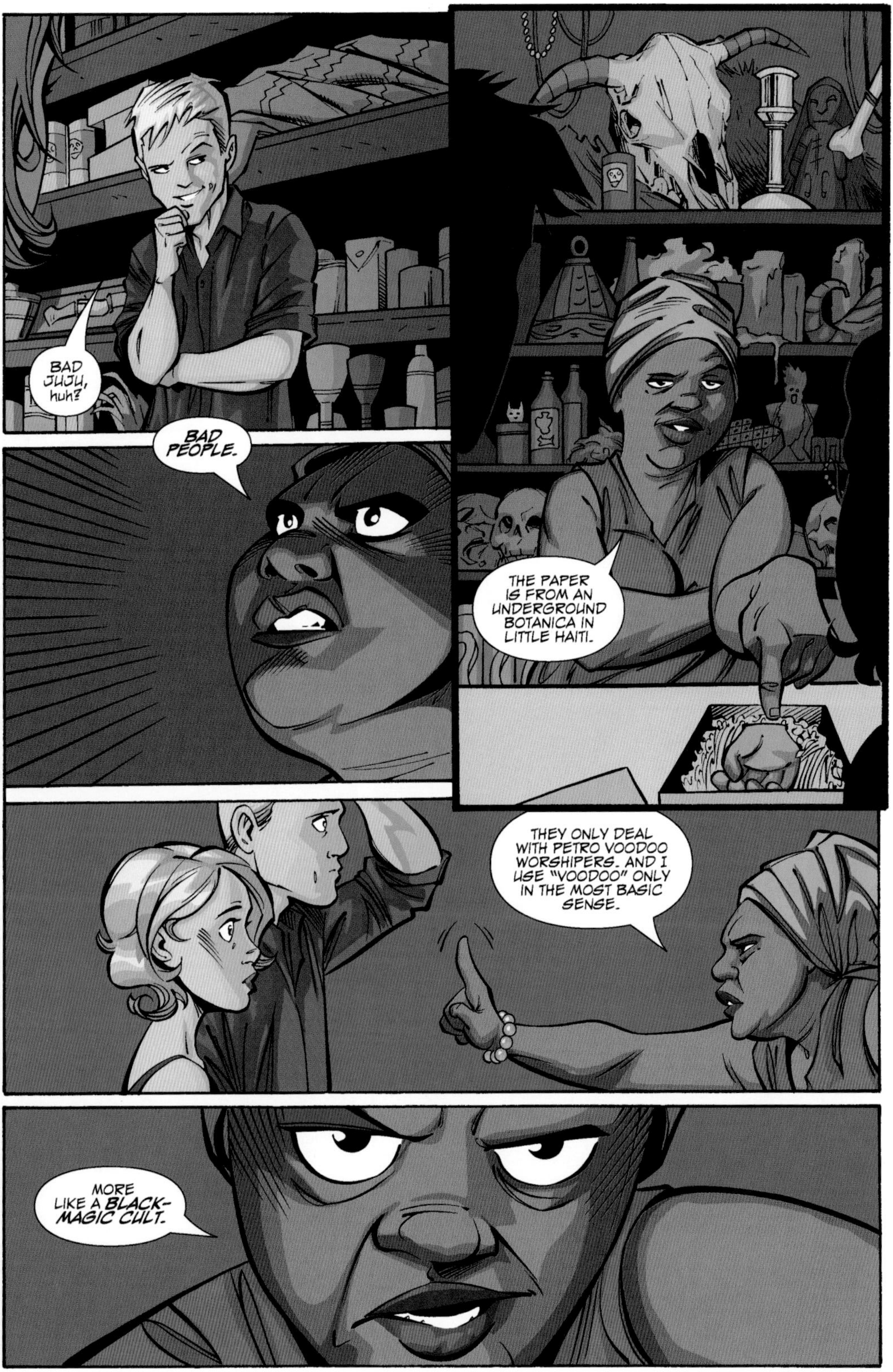
BAD JUJU, huh?
BAD PEOPLE.
THE PAPER IS FROM AN UNDERGROUND BOTANICA IN LITTLE HAITI.
THEY ONLY DEAL WITH PETRO VOODOO WORSHIPERS. AND I USE "VOODOO" ONLY IN THE MOST BASIC SENSE.
MORE LIKE A BLACK-MAGIC CULT.

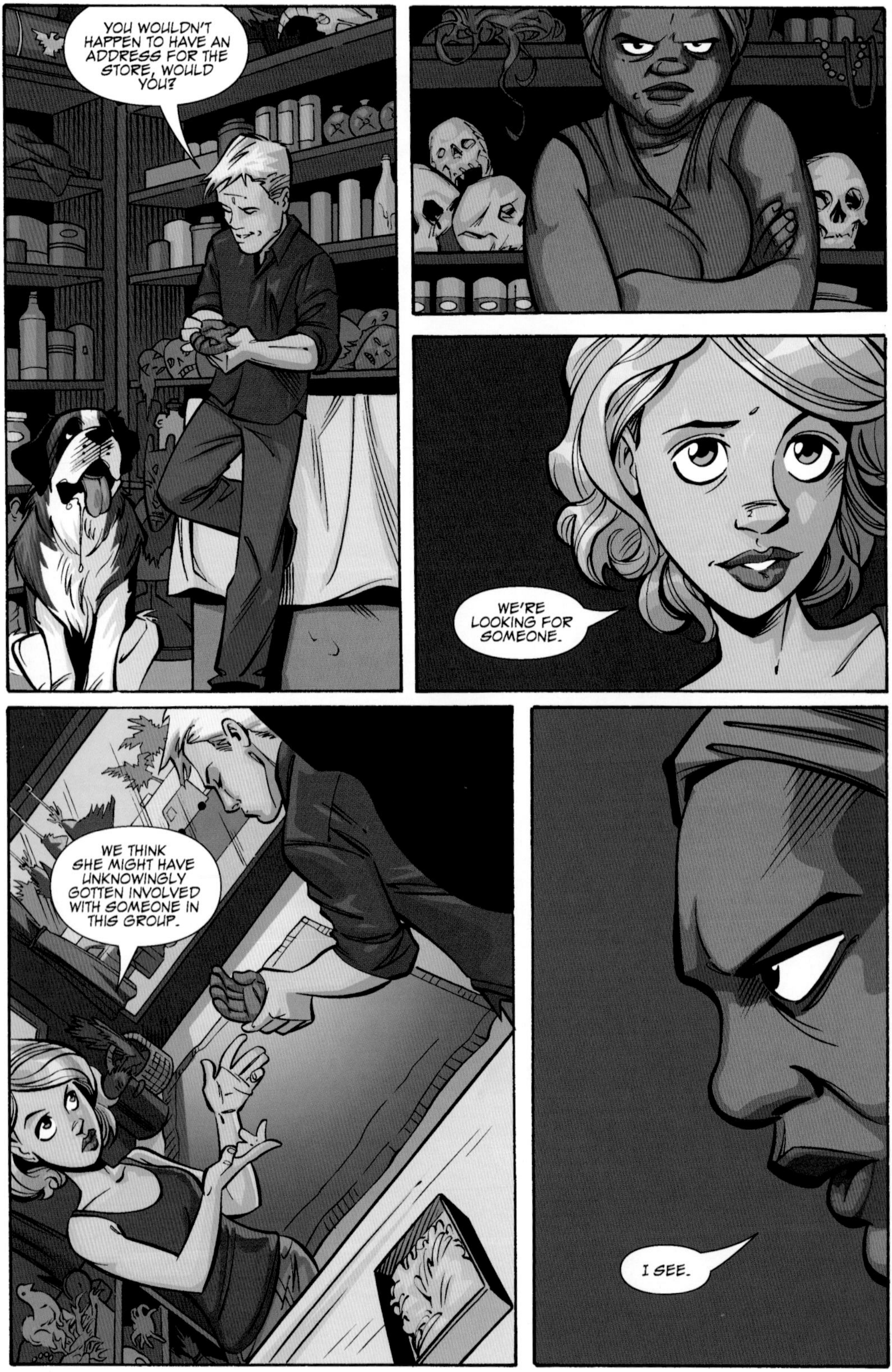

YOU WOULDN'T HAPPEN TO HAVE AN ADDRESS FOR THE STORE, WOULD YOU?
WE'RE LOOKING FOR SOMEONE.
WE THINK SHE MIGHT HAVE UNKNOWINGLY GOTTEN INVOLVED WITH SOMEONE IN THIS GROUP.
I SEE.

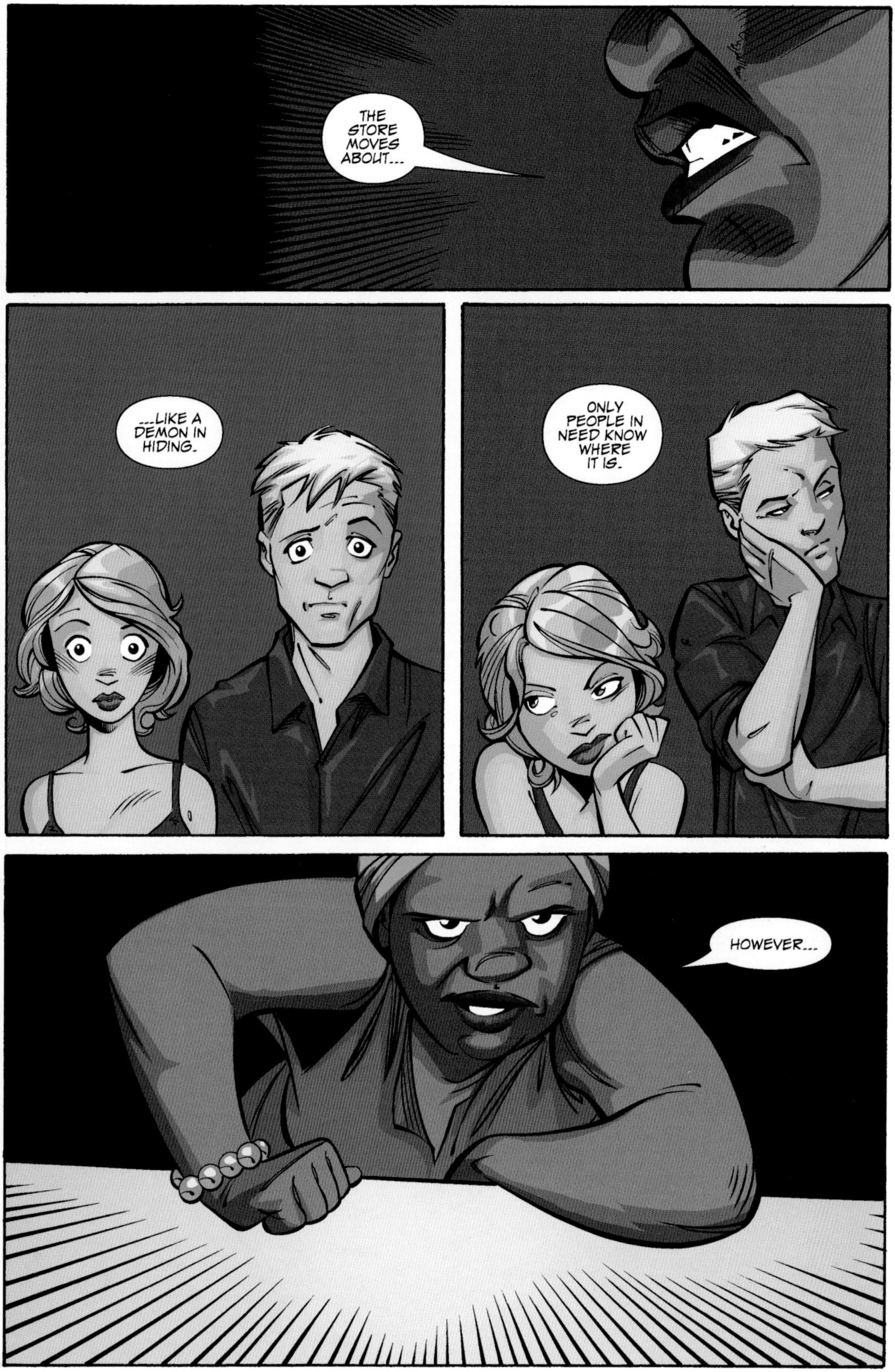
THE STORE MOVES ABOUT...
...LIKE A DEMON IN HIDING.
ONLY PEOPLE IN NEED KNOW WHERE IT IS.
HOWEVER...

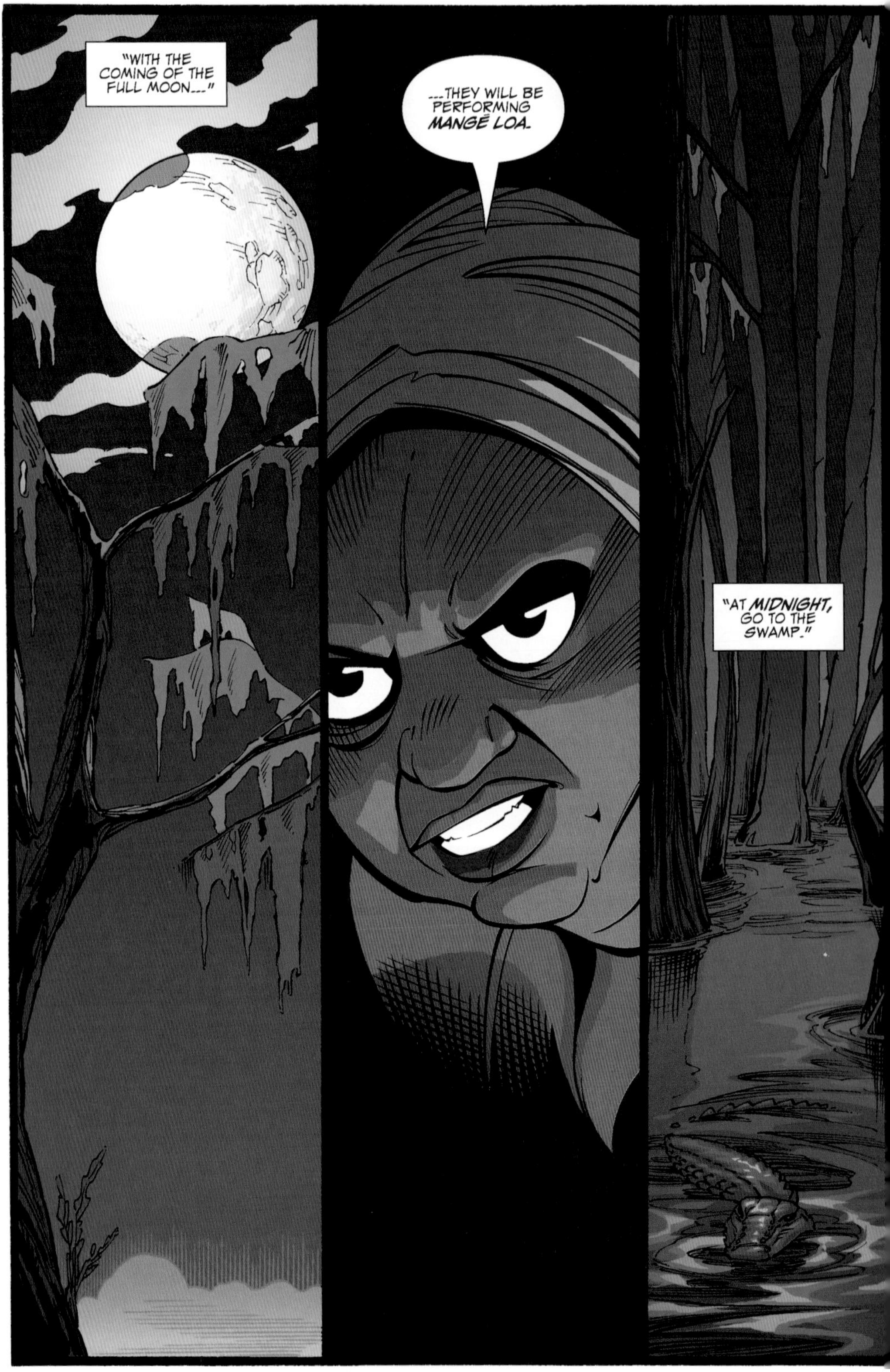

"WITH THE COMING OF THE FULL MOON..."
...THEY WILL BE PERFORMING MANGĒ LOA.
"AT MIDNIGHT, GO TO THE SWAMP."

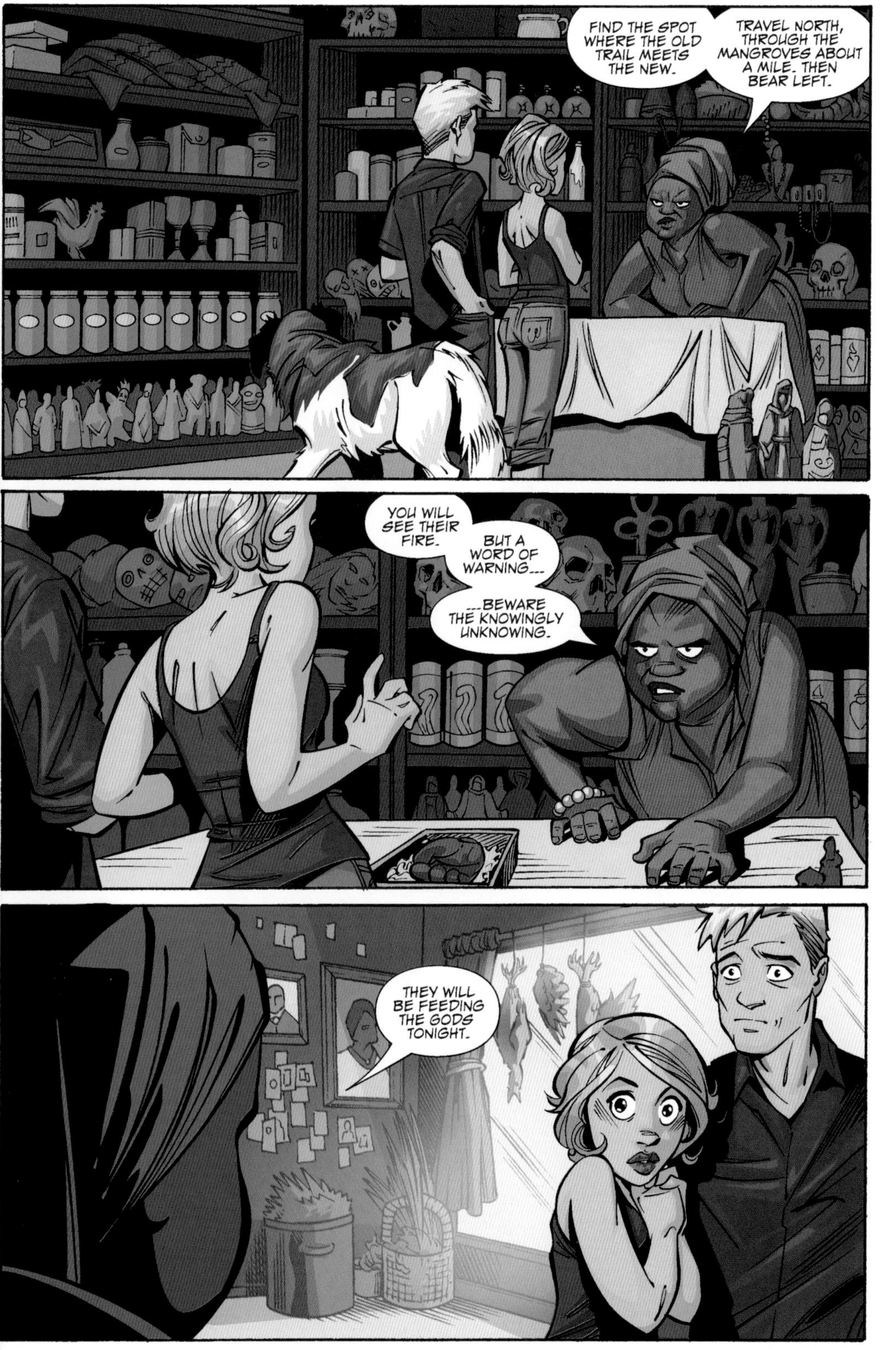

TRAVEL NORTH, THROUGH THE MANGROVES ABOUT A MILE. THEN BEAR LEFT.
FIND THE SPOT WHERE THE OLD TRAIL MEETS THE NEW.
YOU WILL SEE THEIR FIRE.
BUT A WORD OF WARNING...
...BEWARE THE KNOWINGLY UNKNOWING.
THEY WILL BE FEEDING THE GODS TONIGHT.

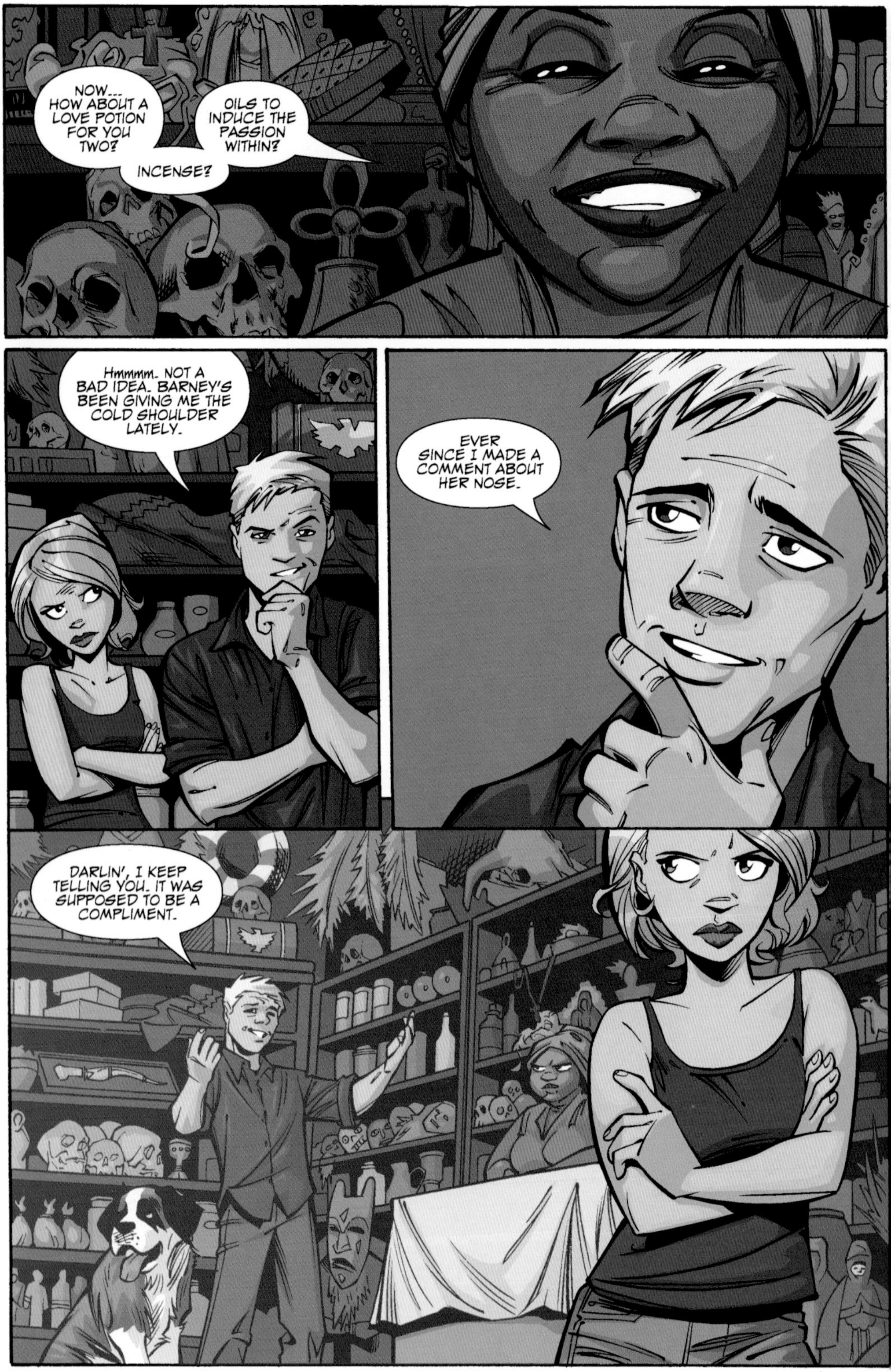
NOW... HOW ABOUT A LOVE POTION FOR YOU TWO?
INCENSE?
OILS TO INDUCE THE PASSION WITHIN?
Hmmmm. NOT A BAD IDEA. BARNEY'S BEEN GIVING ME THE COLD SHOULDER LATELY.
EVER SINCE I MADE A COMMENT ABOUT HER NOSE.
DARLIN', I KEEP TELLING YOU. IT WAS SUPPOSED TO BE A COMPLIMENT.

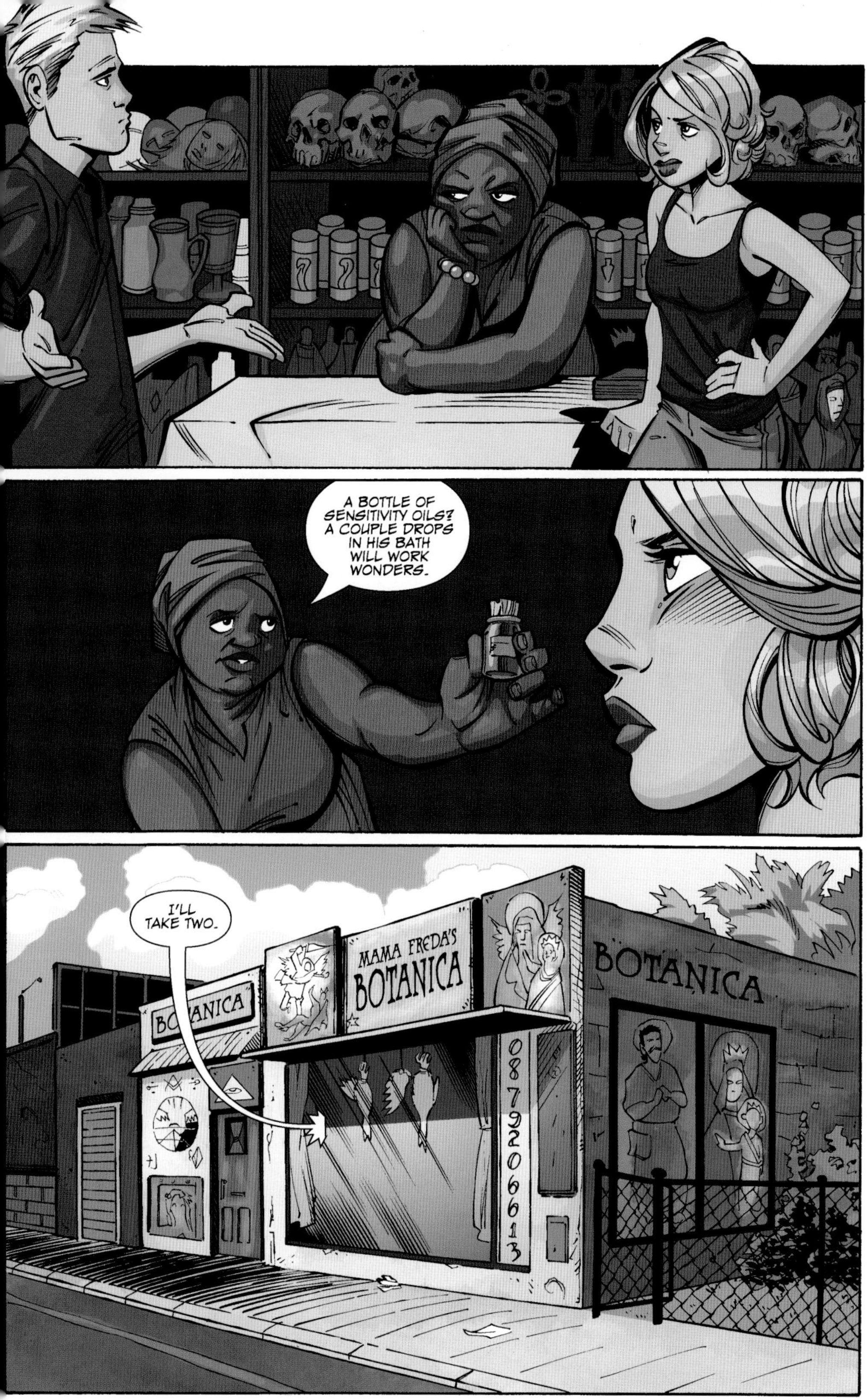
A BOTTLE OF SENSITIVITY OILS? A COUPLE DROPS IN HIS BATH WILL WORK WONDERS.
I'LL TAKE TWO.
BOTANICA
MAMA FREDA'S BOTANICA
BOTANICA
0879206613

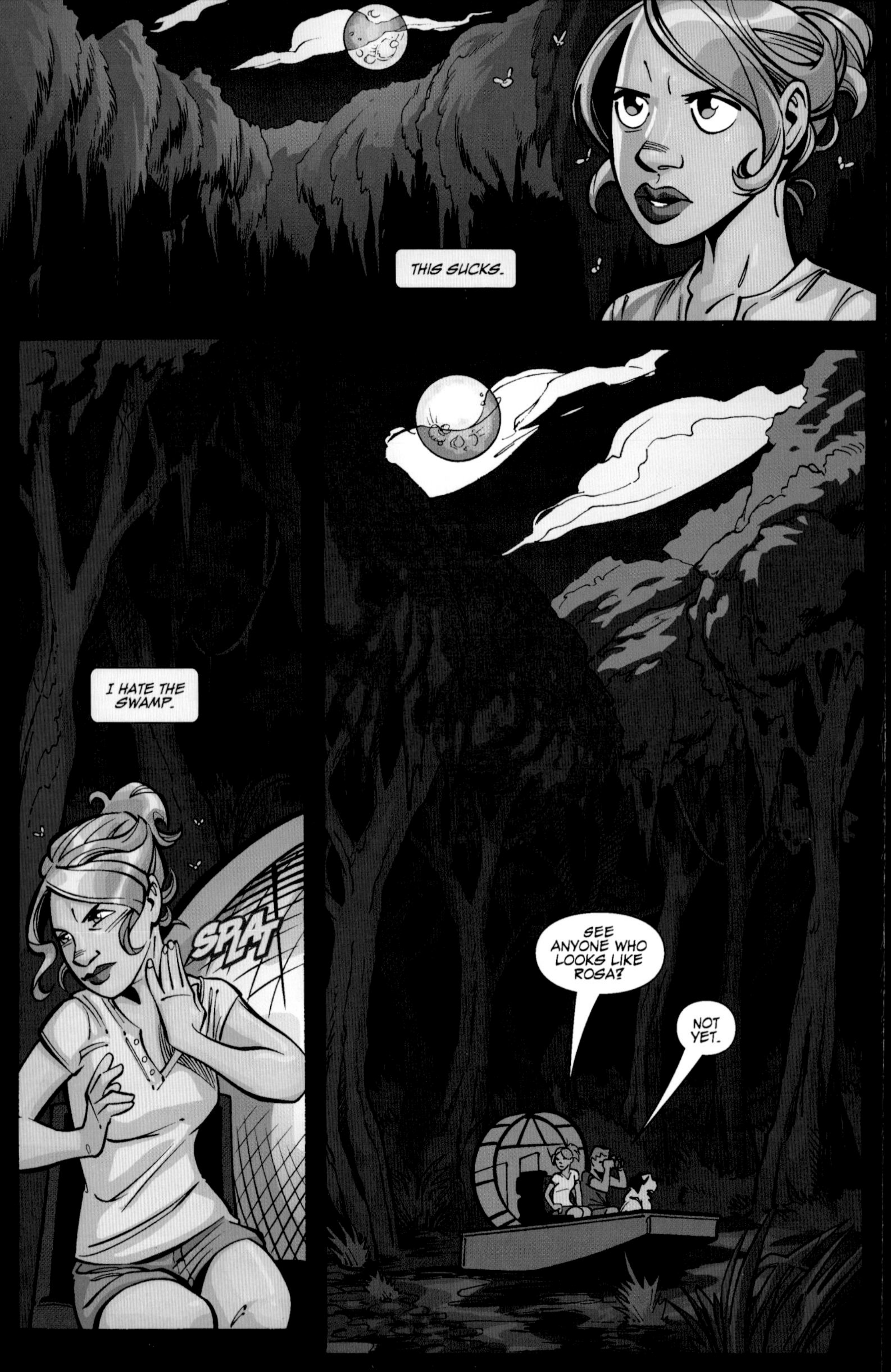
THIS SUCKS.
I HATE THE SWAMP.
SPLAT
SEE ANYONE WHO LOOKS LIKE ROSA?
NOT YET.

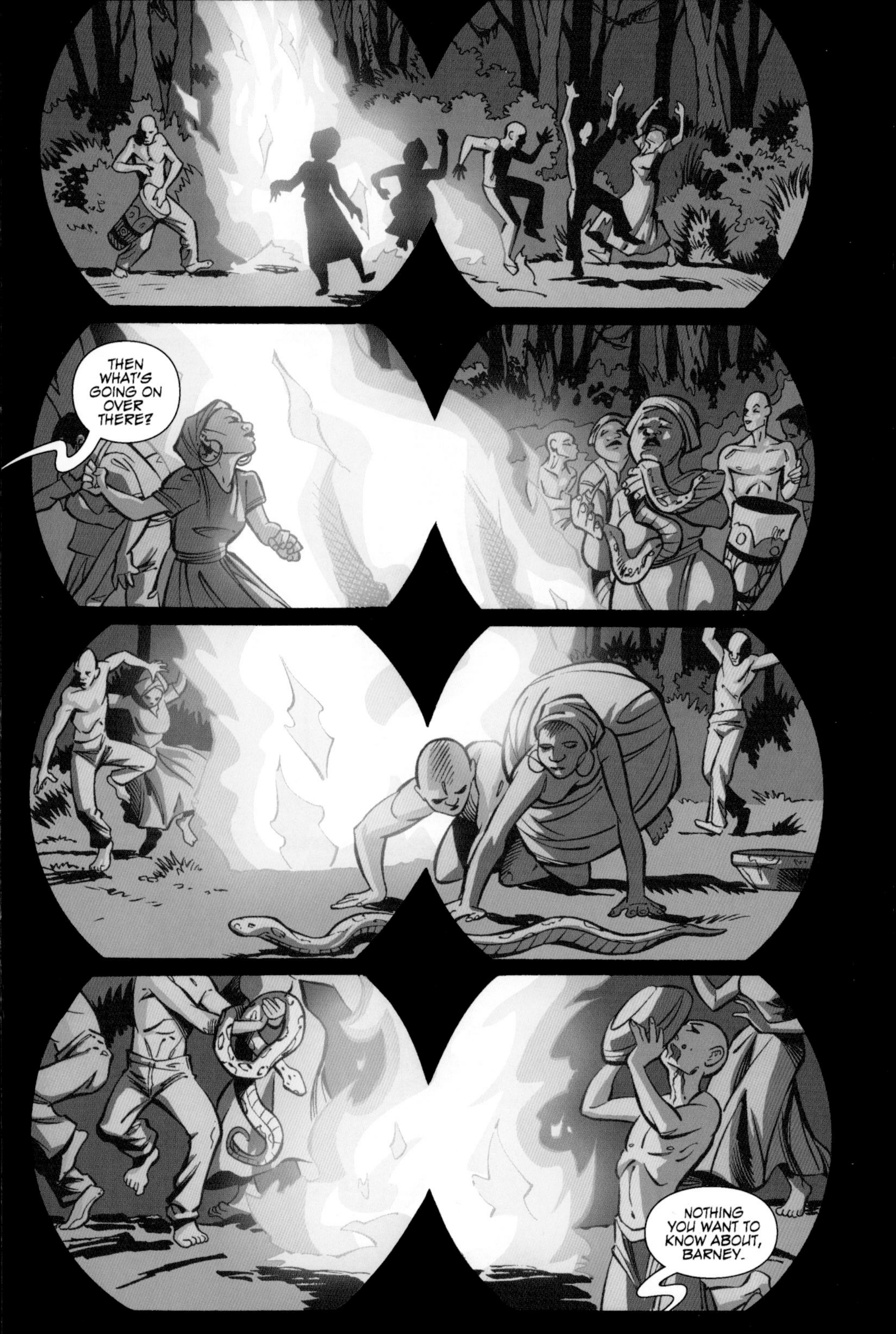
THEN WHAT'S GOING ON OVER THERE?
NOTHING YOU WANT TO KNOW ABOUT, BARNEY.

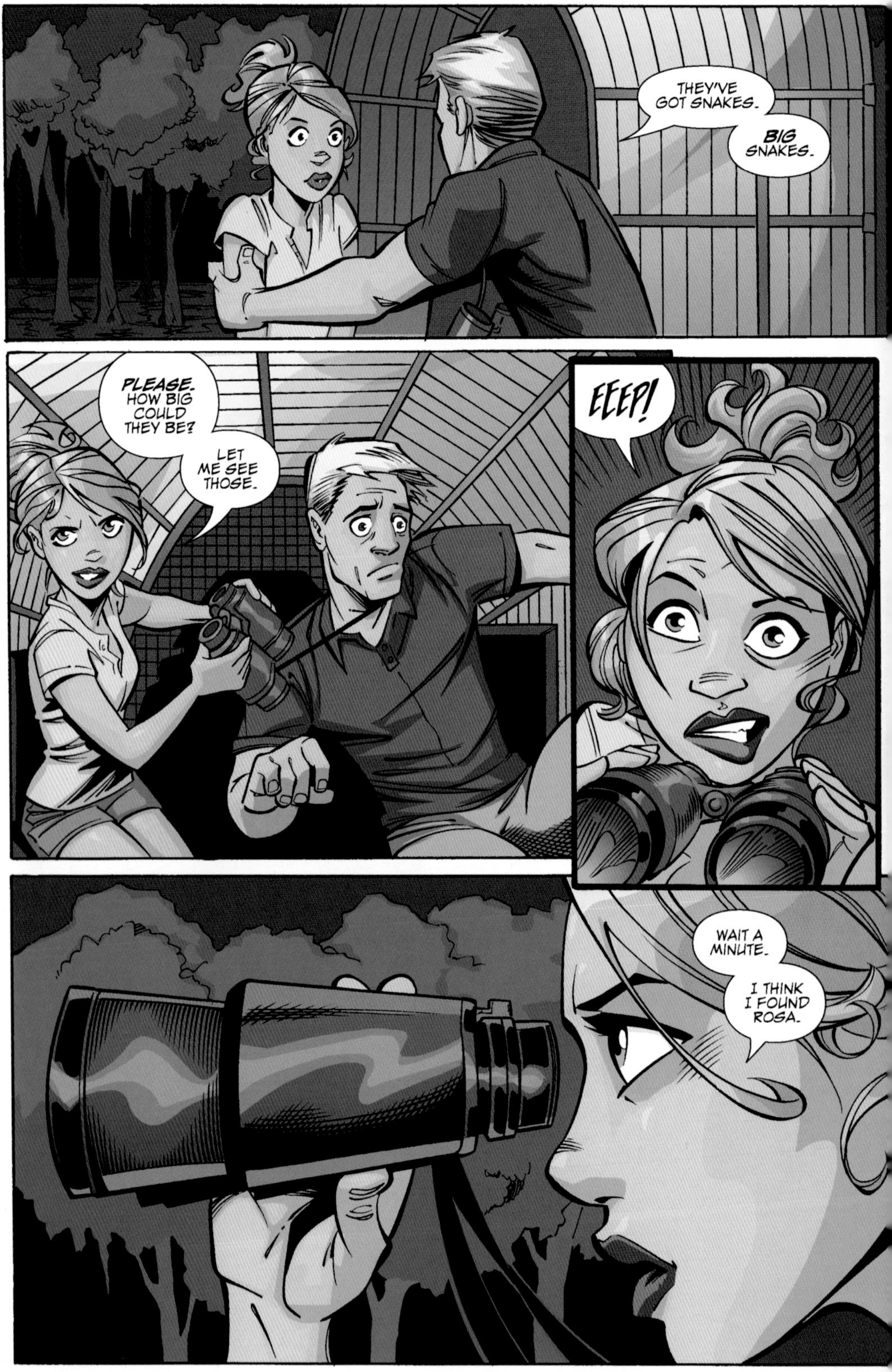
THEY'VE GOT SNAKES.
BIG SNAKES.
PLEASE. HOW BIG COULD THEY BE?
LET ME SEE THOSE.
EEEP!
WAIT A MINUTE.
I THINK I FOUND ROSA.

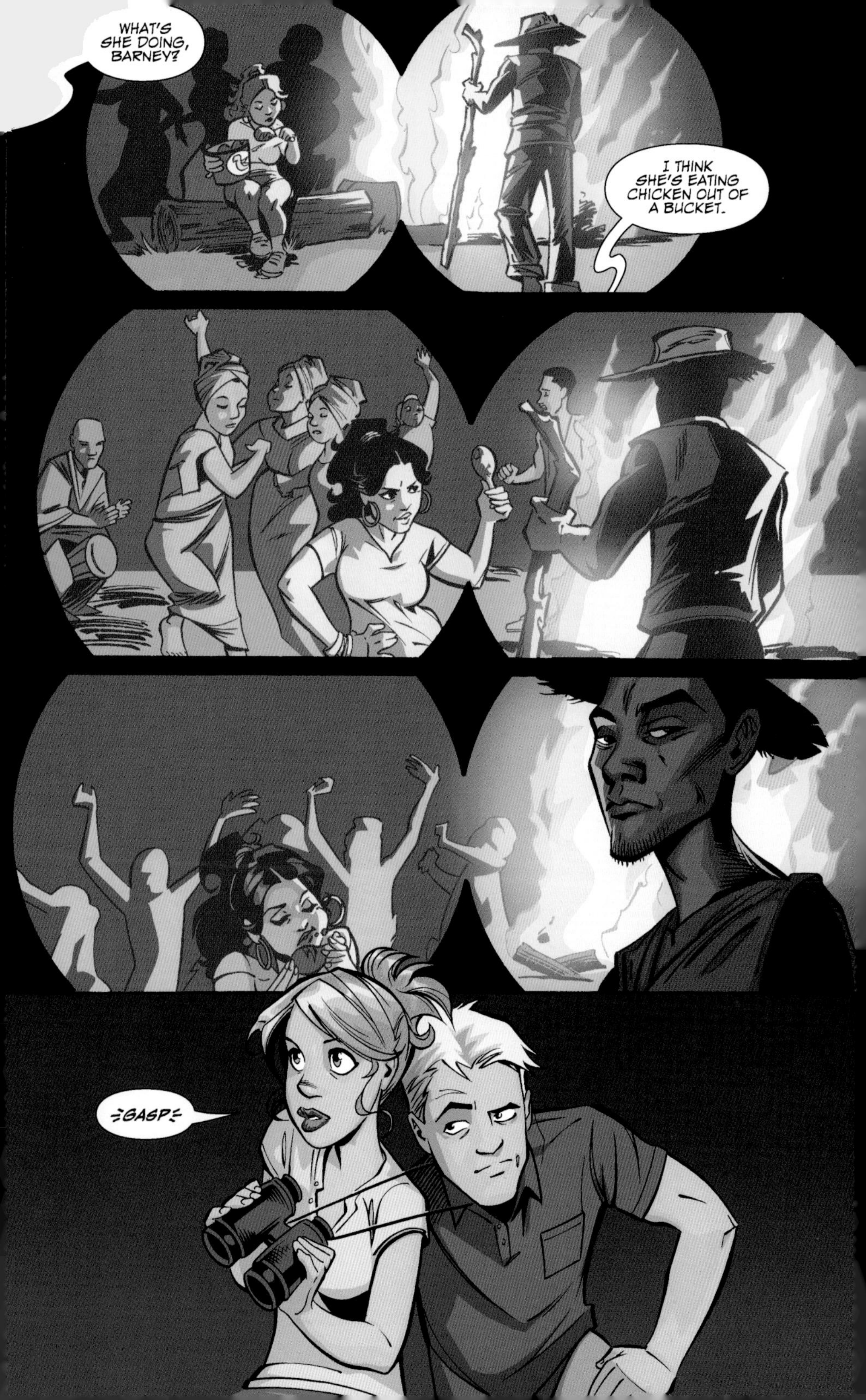
WHAT'S SHE DOING, BARNEY?
I THINK SHE'S EATING CHICKEN OUT OF A BUCKET.
GASP

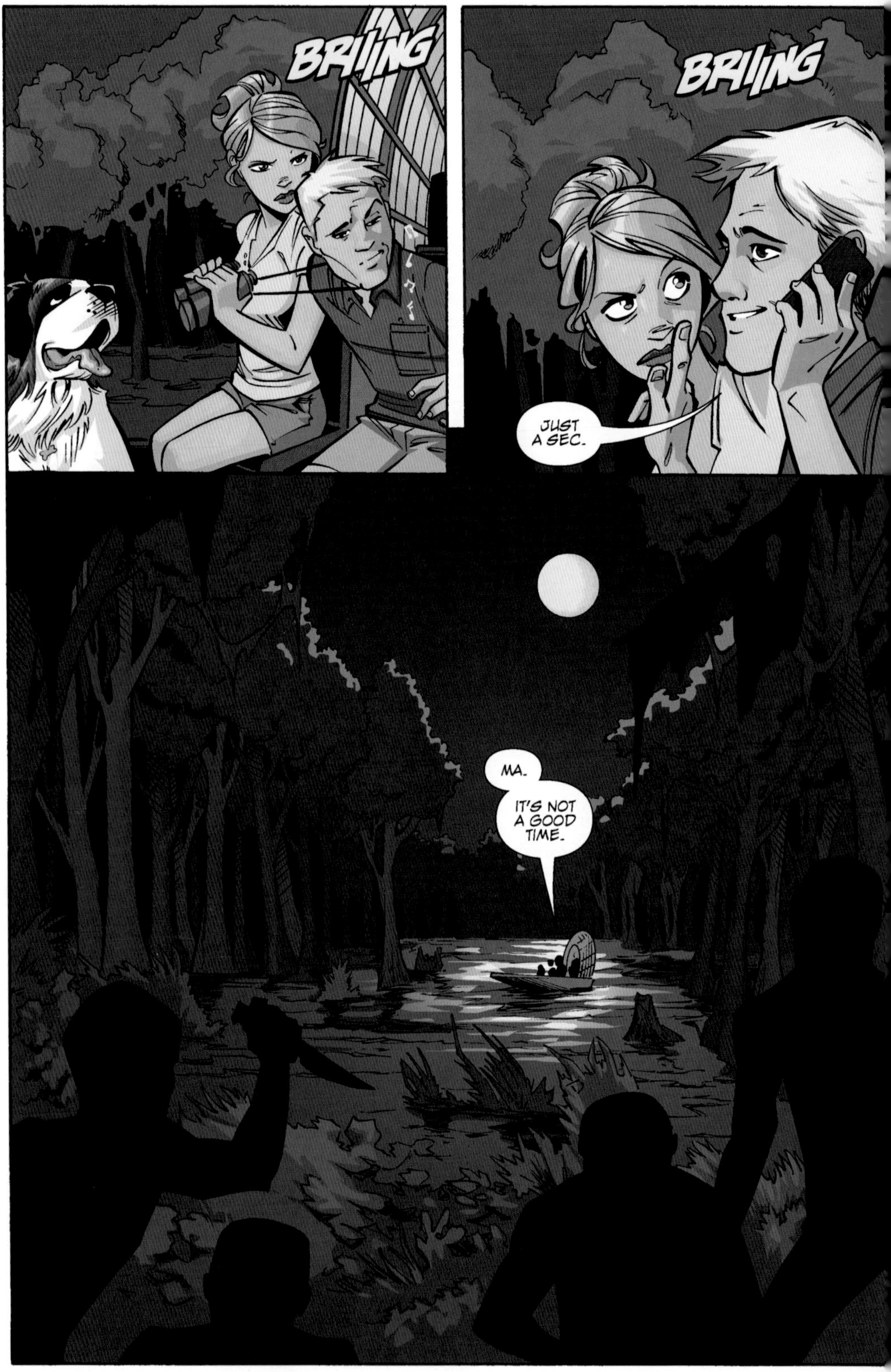
BRIIING
BRIIING
JUST A SEC.
MA.
IT'S NOT A GOOD TIME.

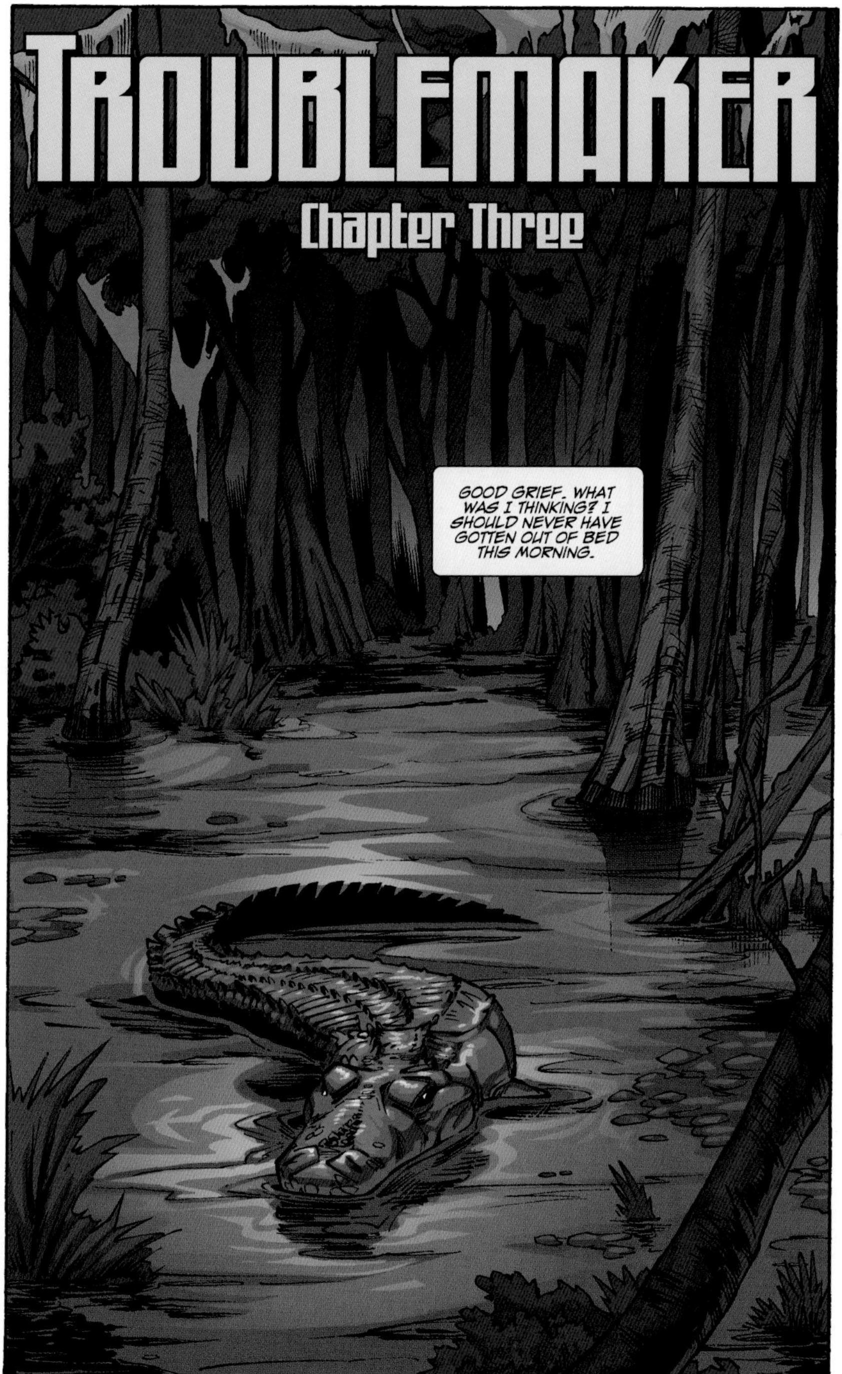
TROUBLEMAKER
Chapter Three
GOOD GRIEF. WHAT WAS I THINKING? I SHOULD NEVER HAVE GOTTEN OUT OF BED THIS MORNING.

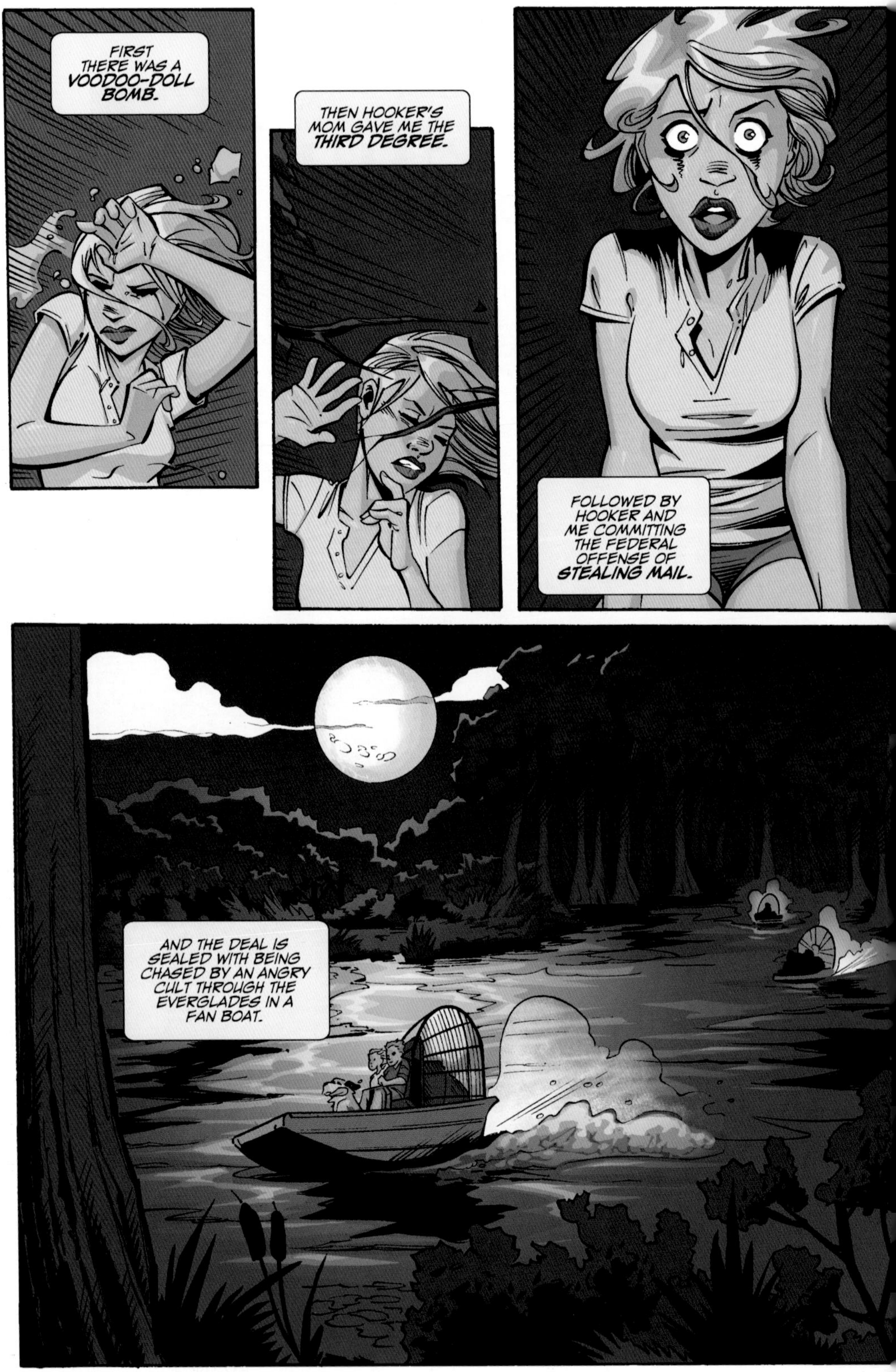
FIRST THERE WAS A VOODOO-DOLL BOMB.
THEN HOOKER'S MOM GAVE ME THE THIRD DEGREE.
FOLLOWED BY HOOKER AND ME COMMITTING THE FEDERAL OFFENSE OF STEALING MAIL.
AND THE DEAL IS SEALED WITH BEING CHASED BY AN ANGRY CULT THROUGH THE EVERGLADES IN A FAN BOAT.

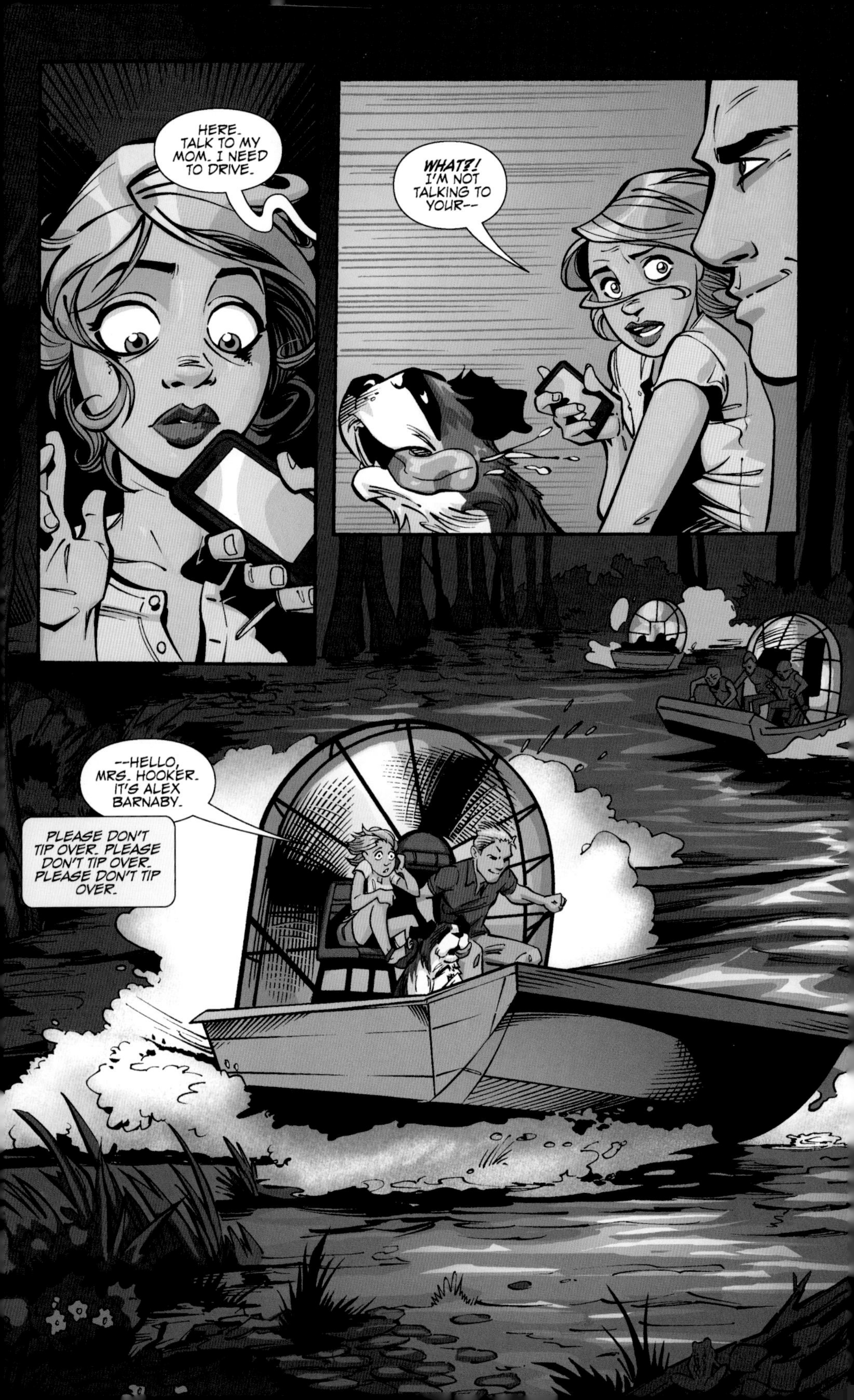
HERE. TALK TO MY MOM. I NEED TO DRIVE.
WHAT?! I'M NOT TALKING TO YOUR--
--HELLO, MRS. HOOKER. IT'S ALEX BARNABY.
PLEASE DON'T TIP OVER. PLEASE DON'T TIP OVER. PLEASE DON'T TIP OVER.

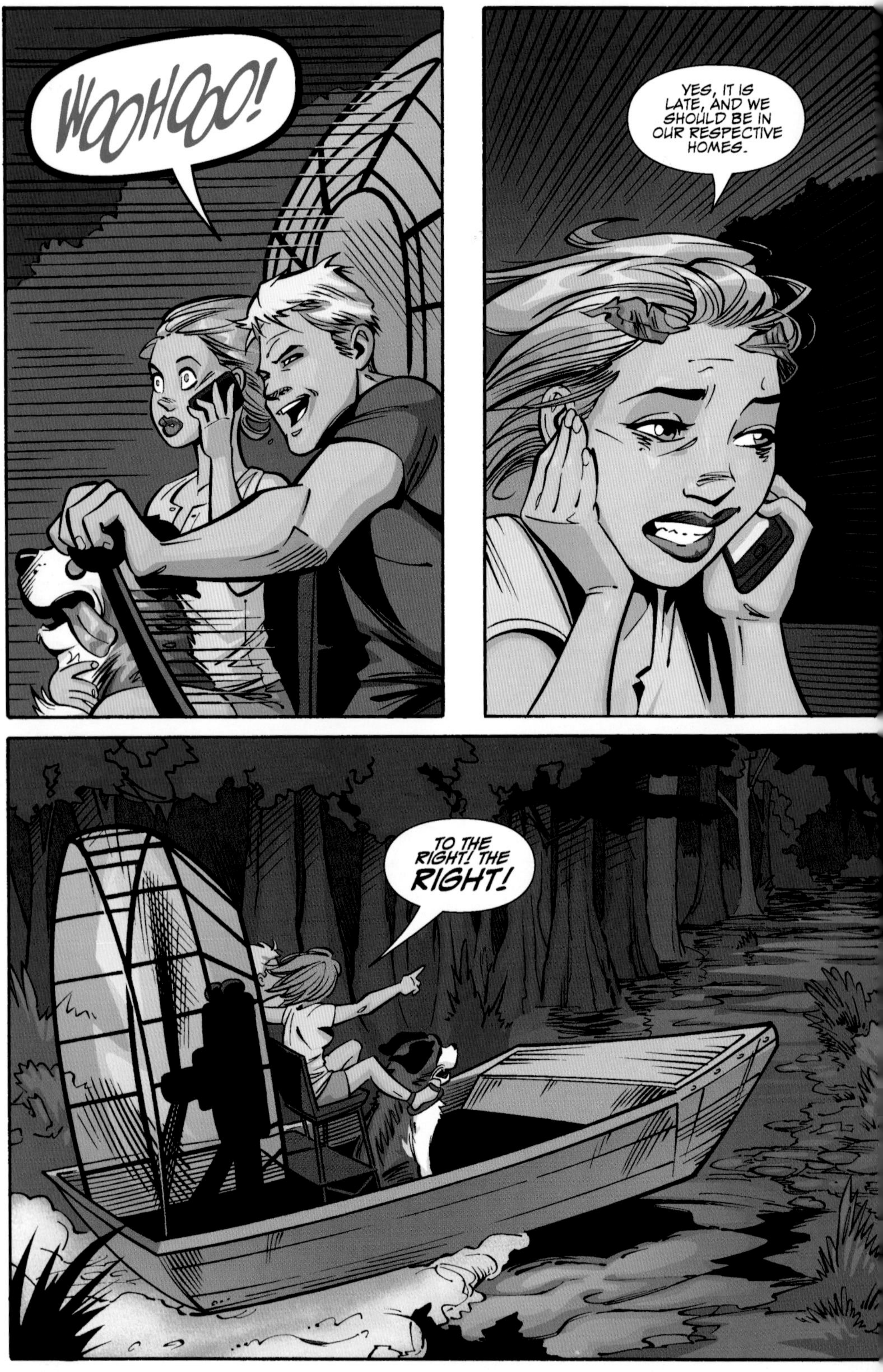
WOOHOO!
YES, IT IS LATE, AND WE SHOULD BE IN OUR RESPECTIVE HOMES.
TO THE RIGHT! THE RIGHT!

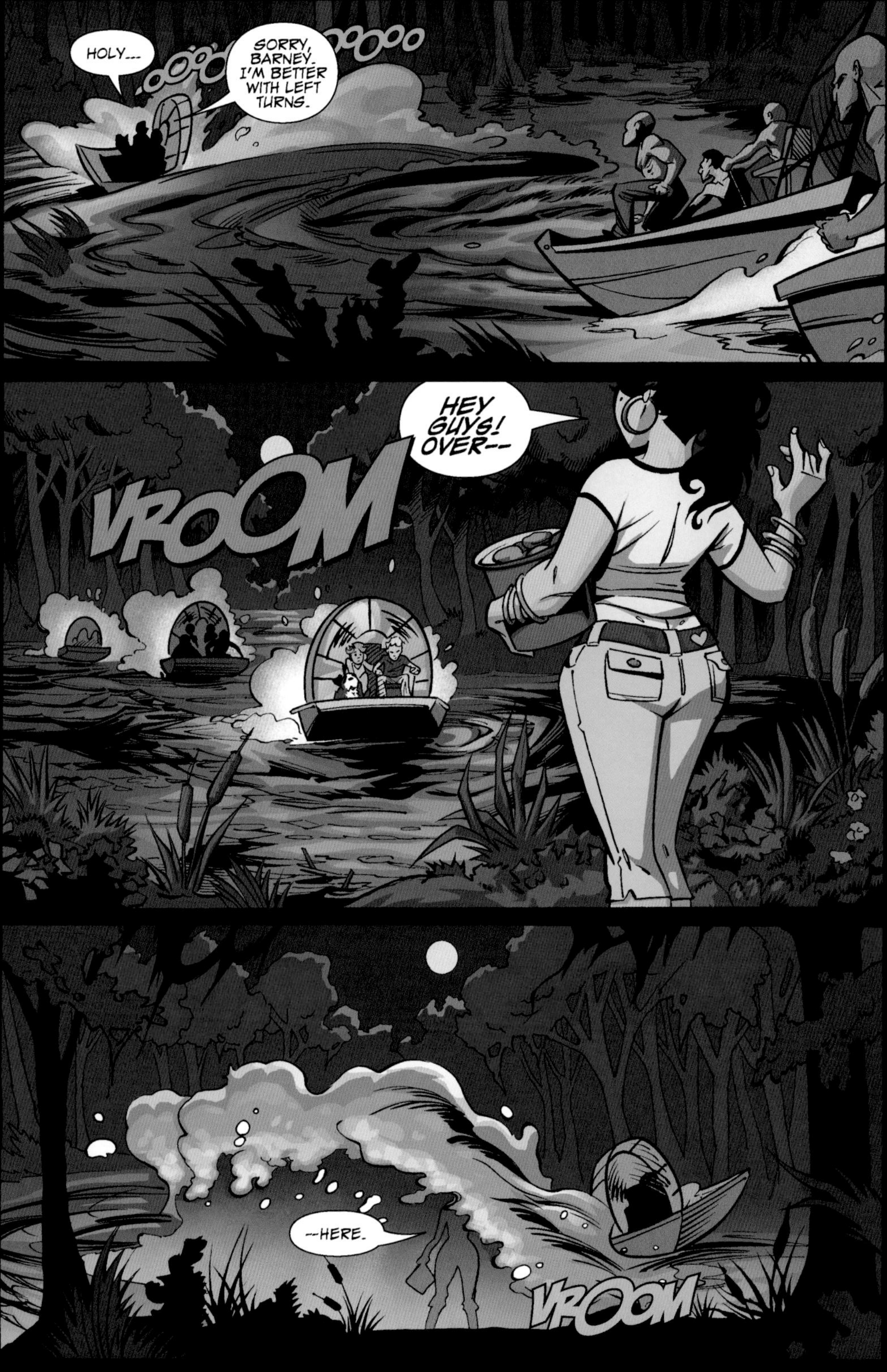
HOLY...
SORRY, BARNEY. I'M BETTER WITH LEFT TURNS.
OOOOOOOOO
HEY GUYS! OVER--
VROOM
--HERE.
VROOM

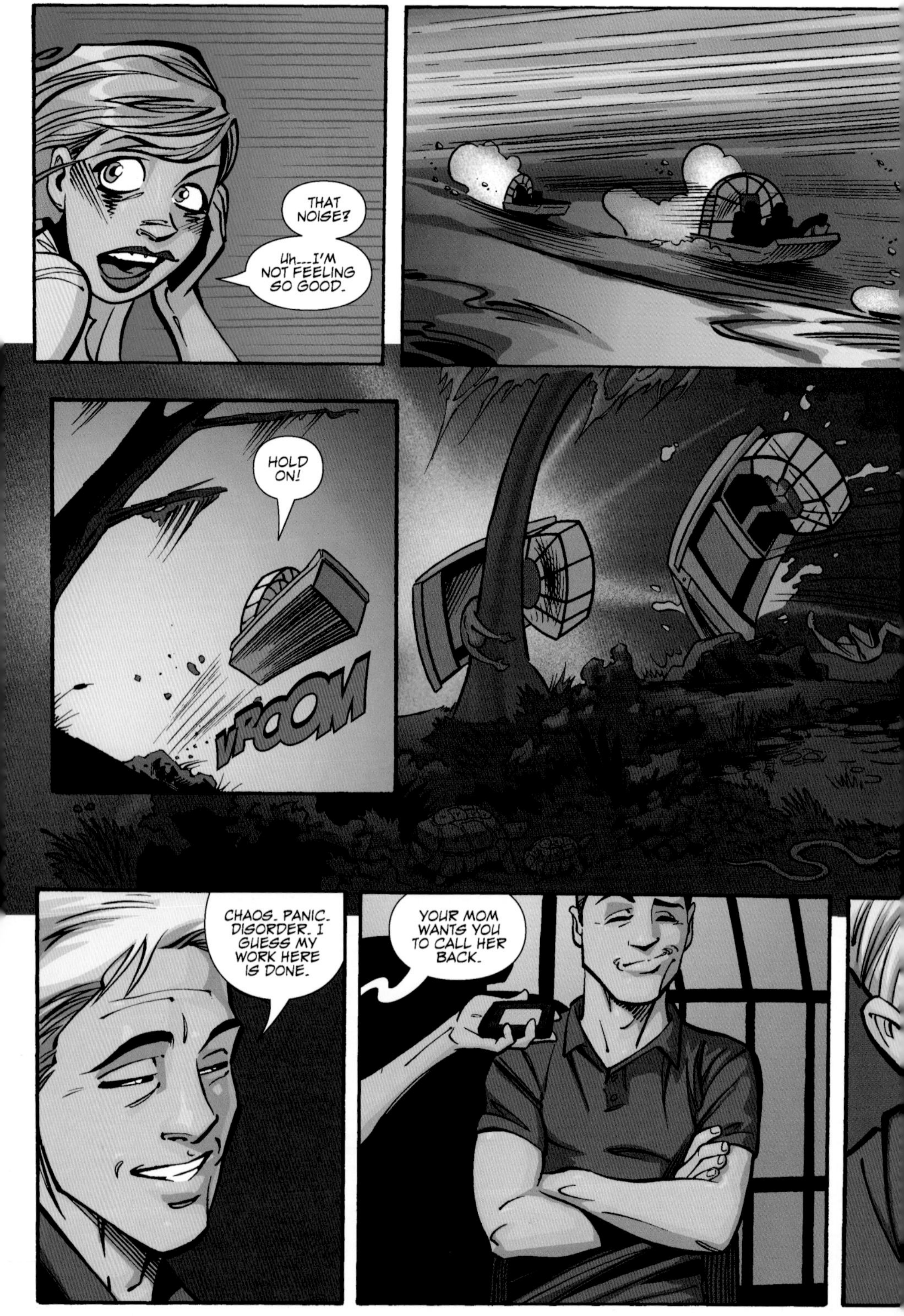
THAT NOISE?
Uh...I'M NOT FEELING SO GOOD.
HOLD ON!
VROOM
CHAOS. PANIC. DISORDER. I GUESS MY WORK HERE IS DONE.
YOUR MOM WANTS YOU TO CALL HER BACK.

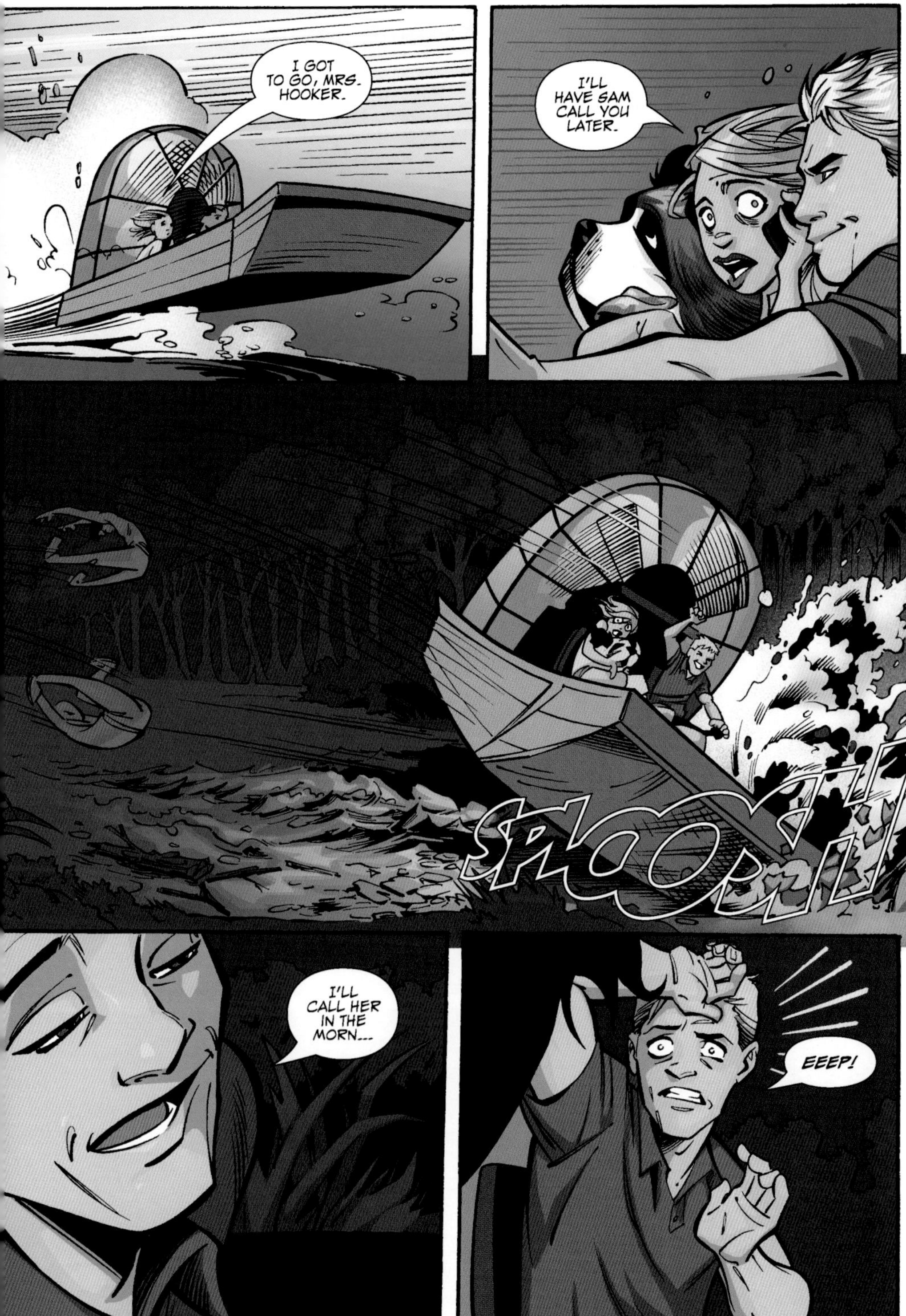
I GOT TO GO, MRS. HOOKER.
I'LL HAVE SAM CALL YOU LATER.
SPLOOSH!!
I'LL CALL HER IN THE MORN...
EEEP!

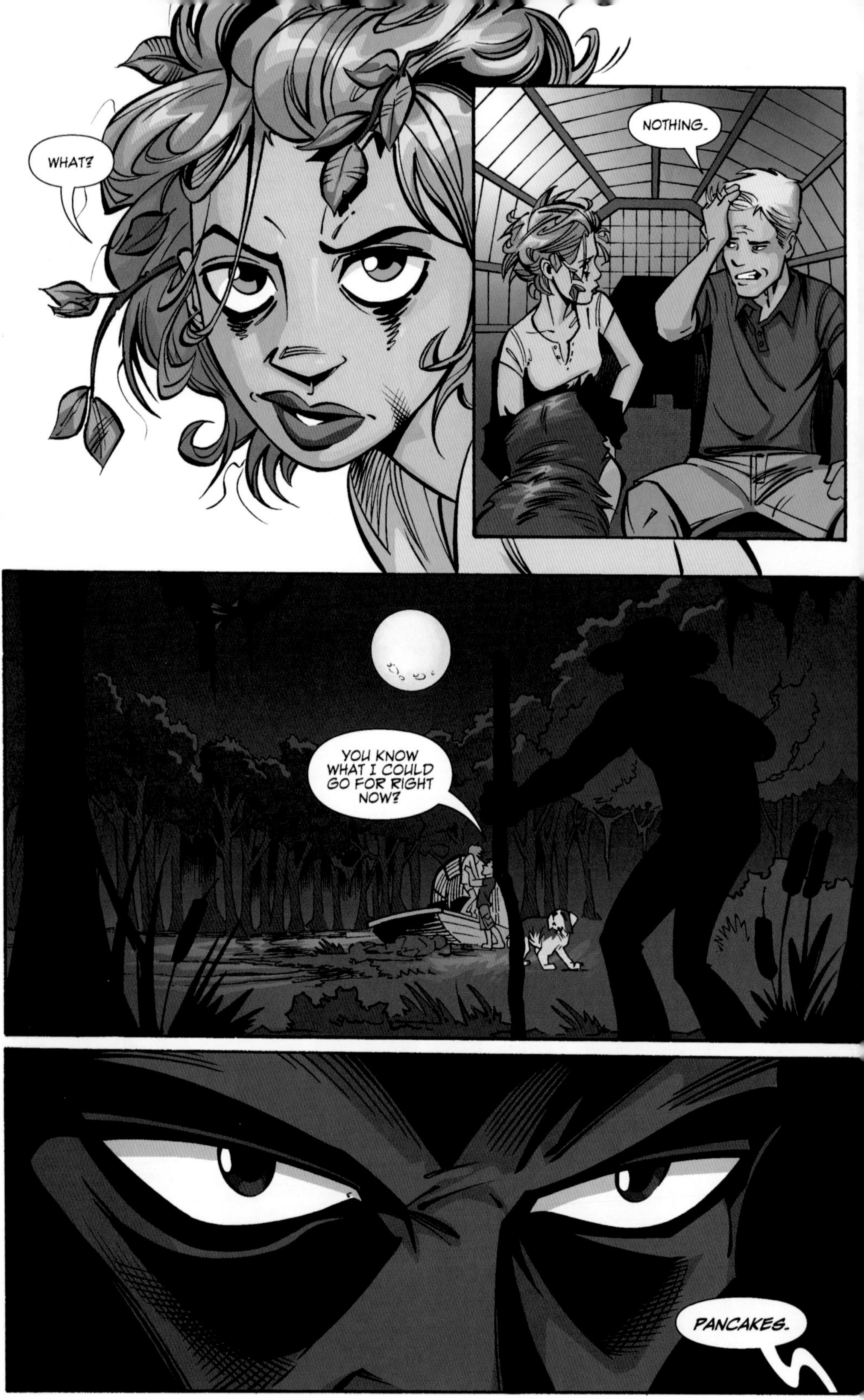
WHAT?
NOTHING.
YOU KNOW WHAT I COULD GO FOR RIGHT NOW?
PANCAKES.

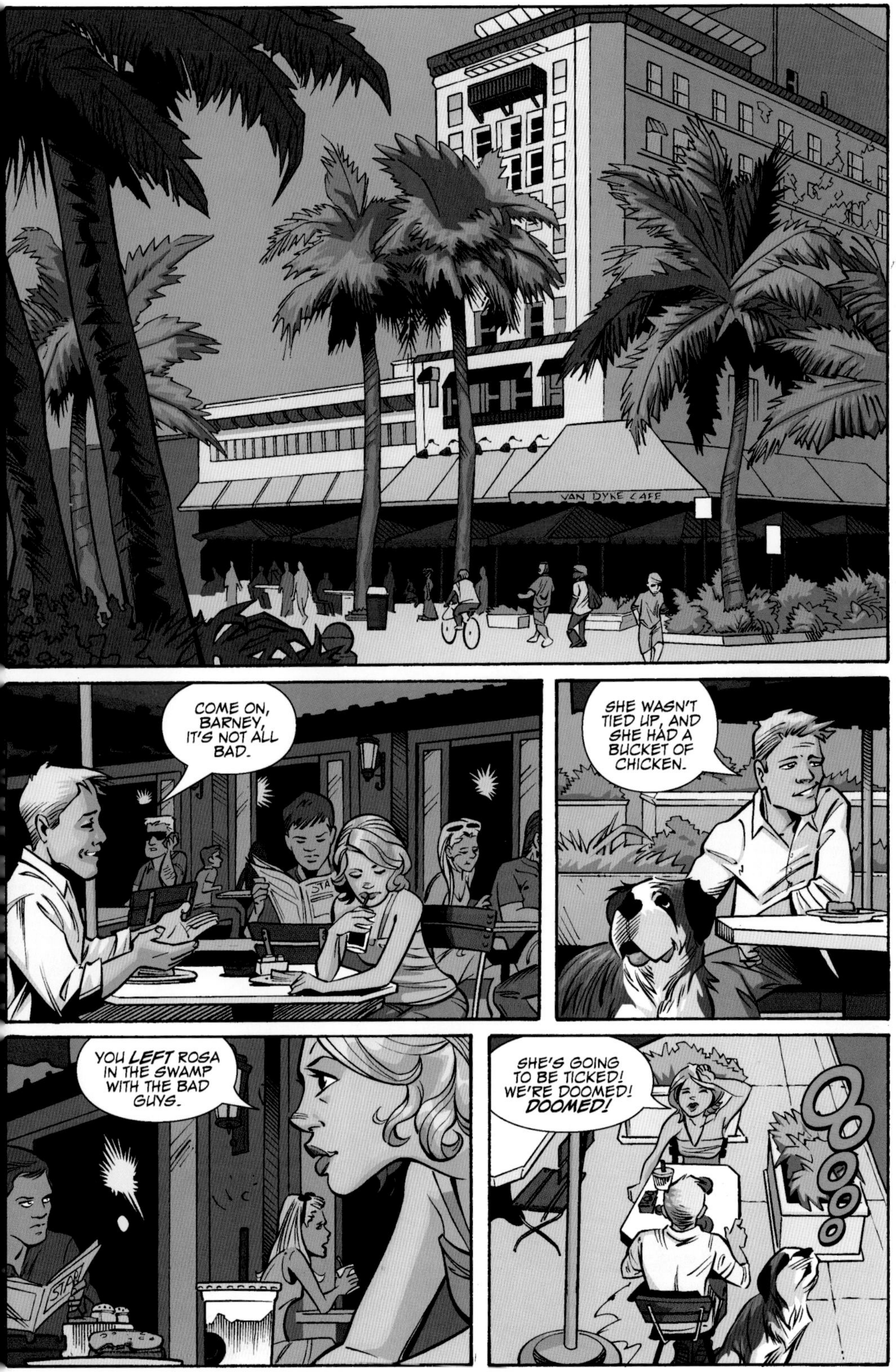
VAN DYKE CAFE
COME ON, BARNEY, IT'S NOT ALL BAD.
SHE WASN'T TIED UP, AND SHE HAD A BUCKET OF CHICKEN.
YOU LEFT ROSA IN THE SWAMP WITH THE BAD GUYS.
SHE'S GOING TO BE TICKED! WE'RE DOOMED! DOOMED!

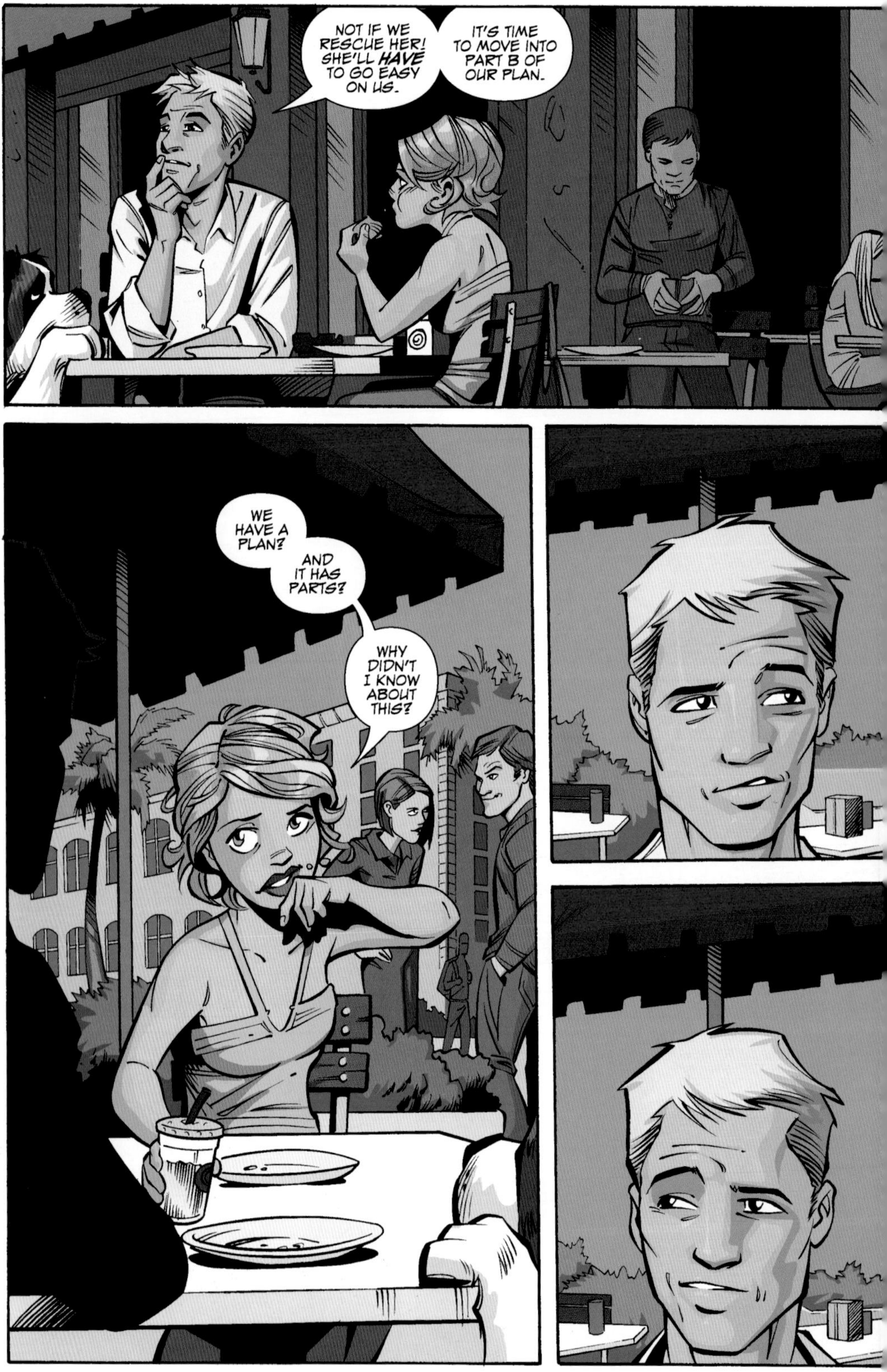
NOT IF WE RESCUE HER! SHE'LL ***HAVE*** TO GO EASY ON US.
IT'S TIME TO MOVE INTO PART B OF OUR PLAN.
WE HAVE A PLAN?
AND IT HAS PARTS?
WHY DIDN'T I KNOW ABOUT THIS?

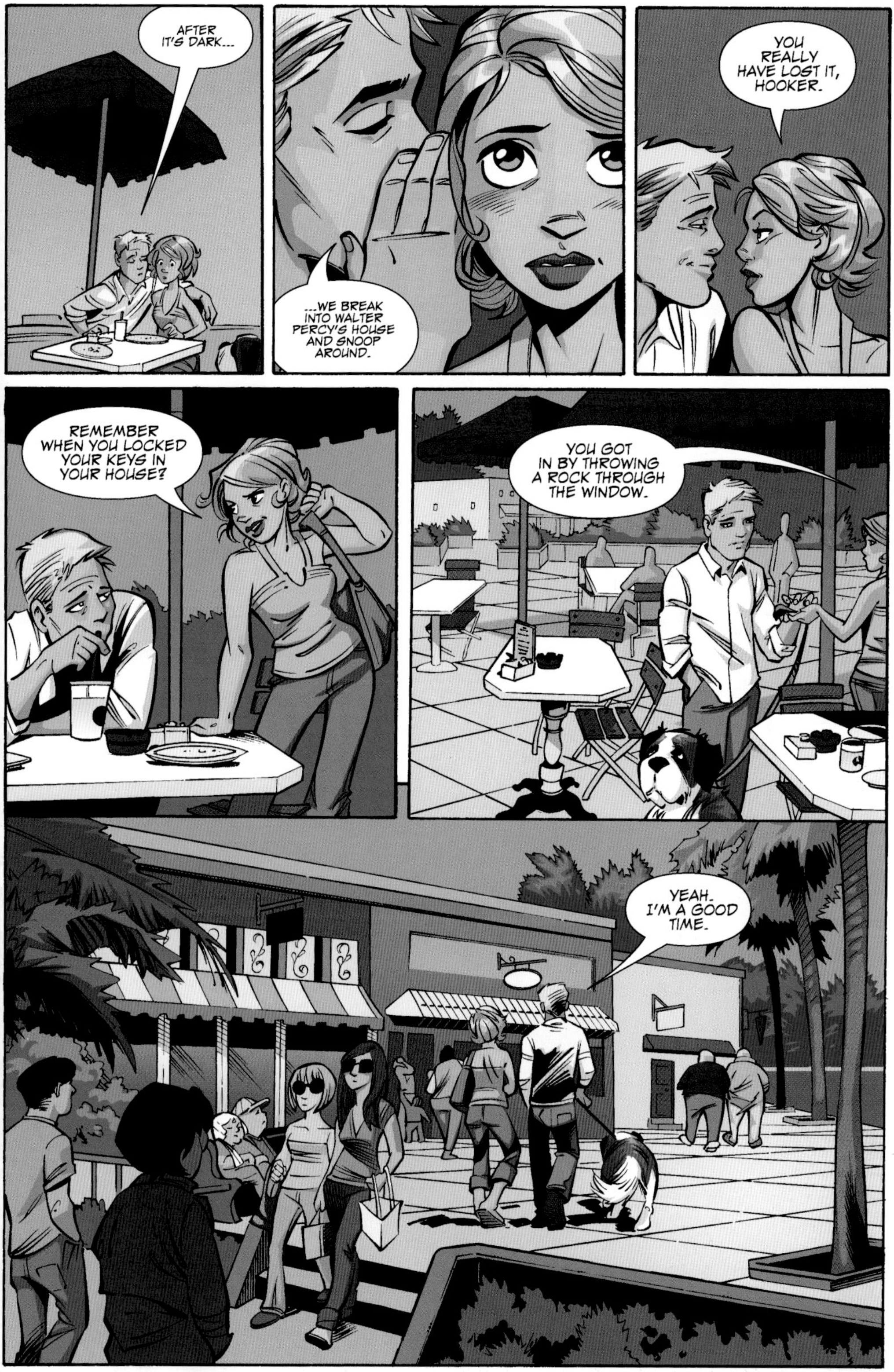
AFTER IT'S DARK...
...WE BREAK INTO WALTER PERCY'S HOUSE AND SNOOP AROUND.
YOU REALLY HAVE LOST IT, HOOKER.
REMEMBER WHEN YOU LOCKED YOUR KEYS IN YOUR HOUSE?
YOU GOT IN BY THROWING A ROCK THROUGH THE WINDOW.
YEAH. I'M A GOOD TIME.

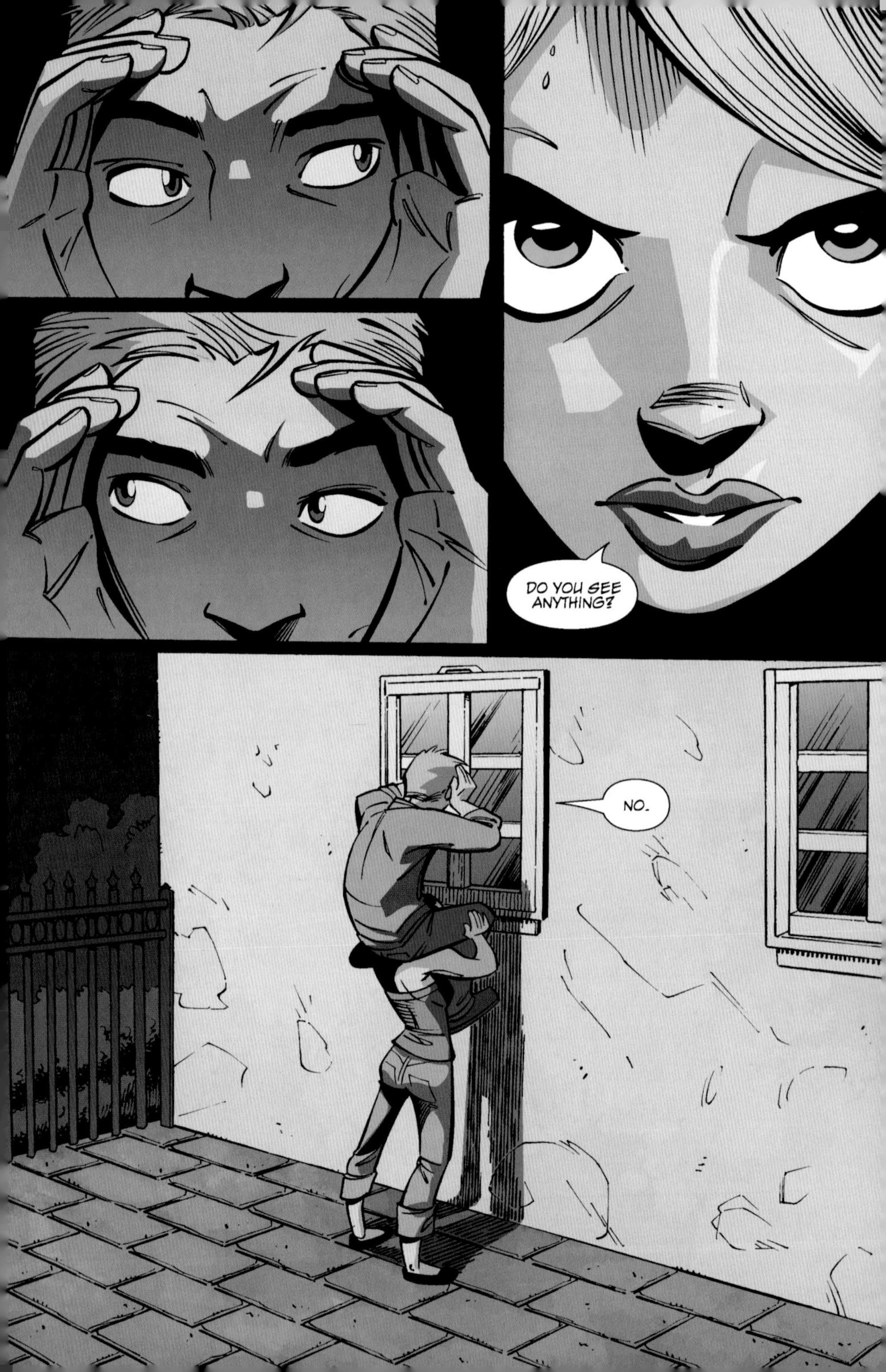
DO YOU SEE ANYTHING?
NO.

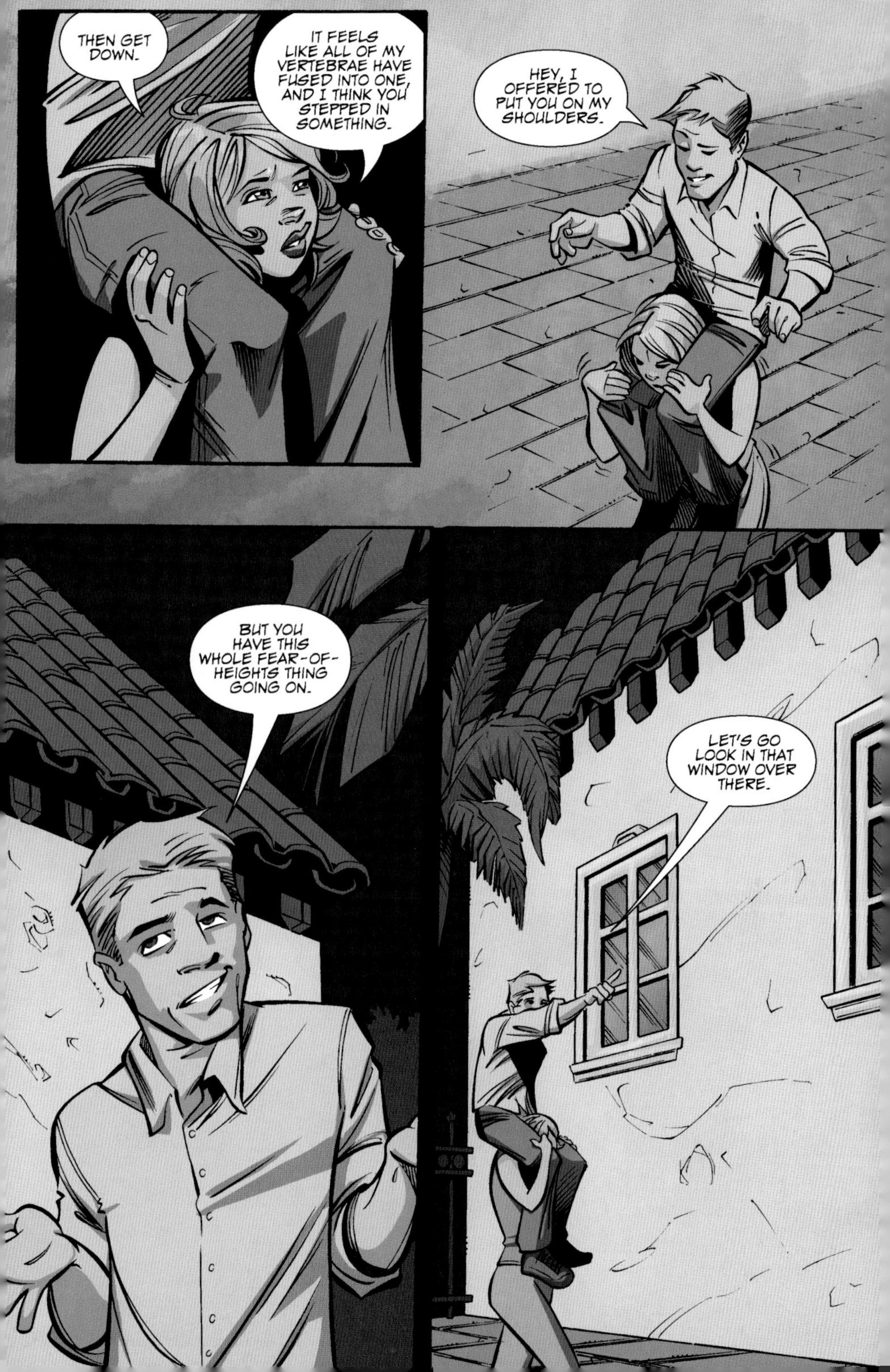
THEN GET DOWN.
IT FEELS LIKE ALL OF MY VERTEBRAE HAVE FUSED INTO ONE, AND I THINK YOU STEPPED IN SOMETHING.
HEY, I OFFERED TO PUT YOU ON MY SHOULDERS.
BUT YOU HAVE THIS WHOLE FEAR-OF-HEIGHTS THING GOING ON.
LET'S GO LOOK IN THAT WINDOW OVER THERE.

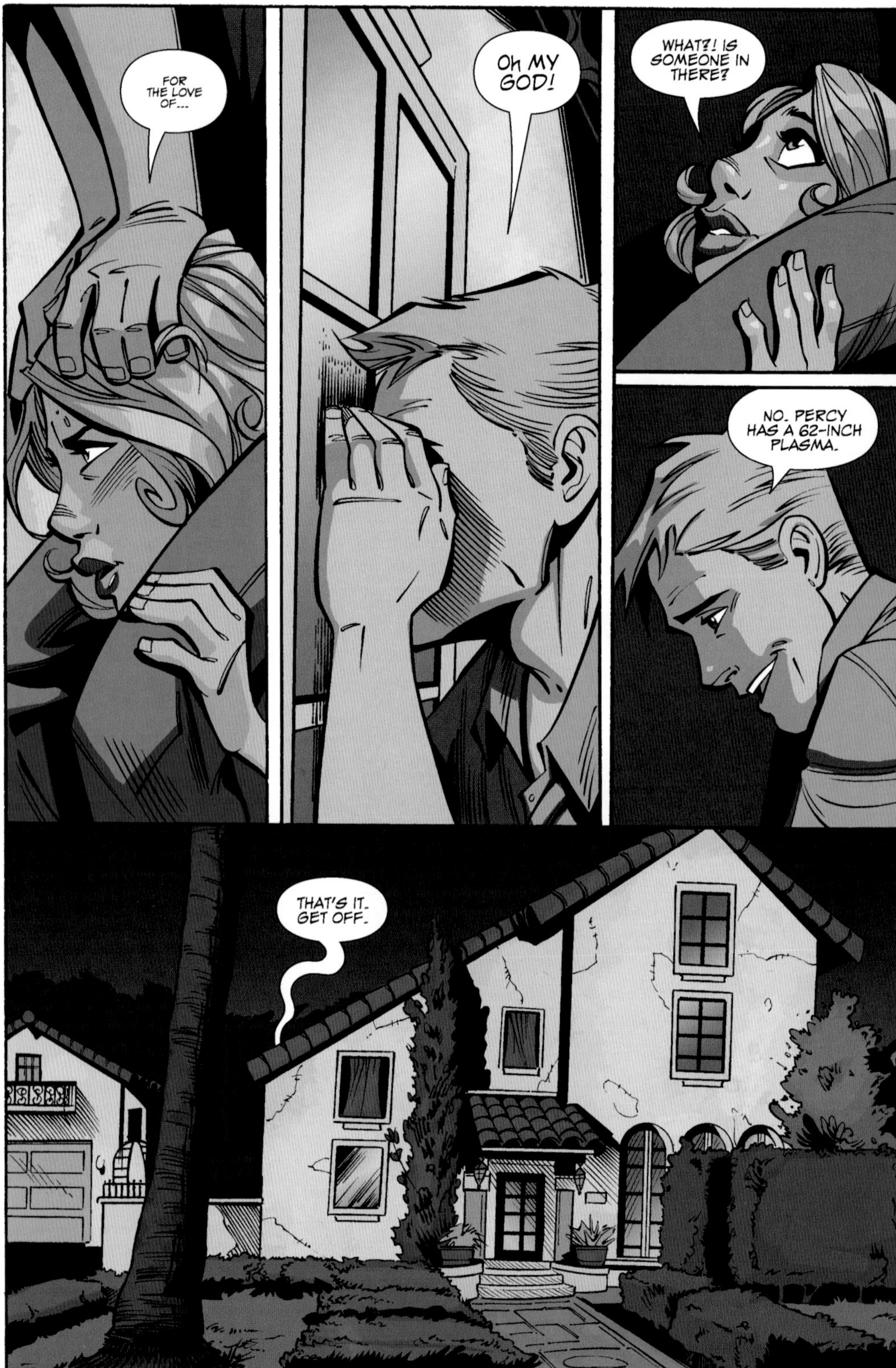
FOR THE LOVE OF...
Oh MY GOD!
WHAT?! IS SOMEONE IN THERE?
NO. PERCY HAS A 62-INCH PLASMA.
THAT'S IT. GET OFF.

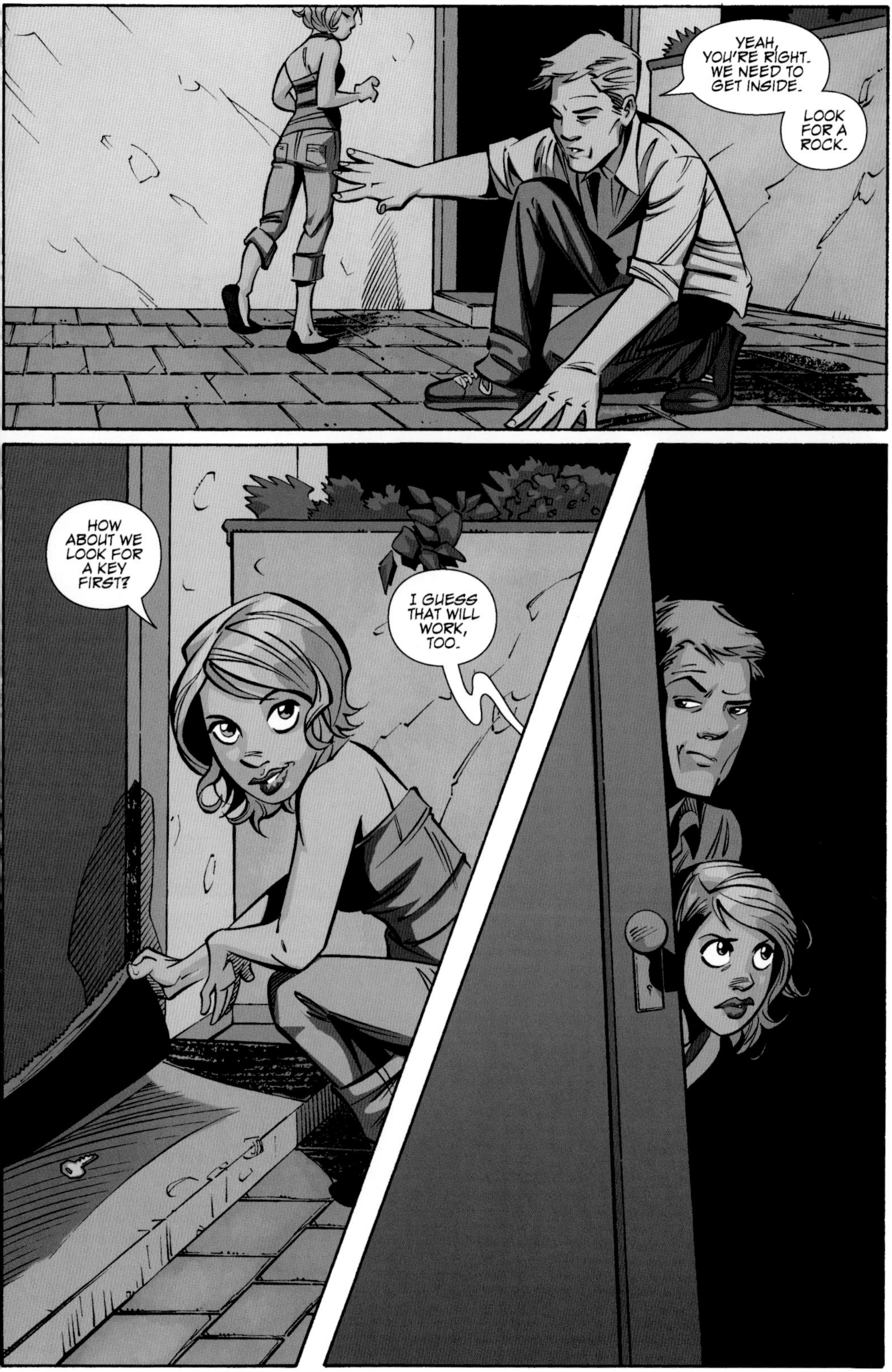

YEAH, YOU'RE RIGHT. WE NEED TO GET INSIDE.
LOOK FOR A ROCK.
HOW ABOUT WE LOOK FOR A KEY FIRST?
I GUESS THAT WILL WORK, TOO.

OVER THE YEARS I'VE LEARNED THAT THERE ARE A COUPLE REASONS, OTHER THAN "BEING NOSY IS FUN," TO SNOOP IN A MISSING PERSON'S HOUSE.

I'LL CHECK UPSTAIRS.

ONE IS TO SEE IF THE PERSON LEFT WILLINGLY.

TOOTHBRUSH AND SHAVING STUFF STILL HERE. DISAPPEARING WASN'T PLANNED.

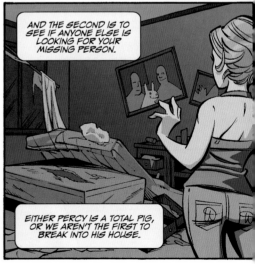

AND THE SECOND IS TO SEE IF ANYONE ELSE IS LOOKING FOR YOUR MISSING PERSON.

EITHER PERCY IS A TOTAL PIG, OR WE AREN'T THE FIRST TO BREAK INTO HIS HOUSE.

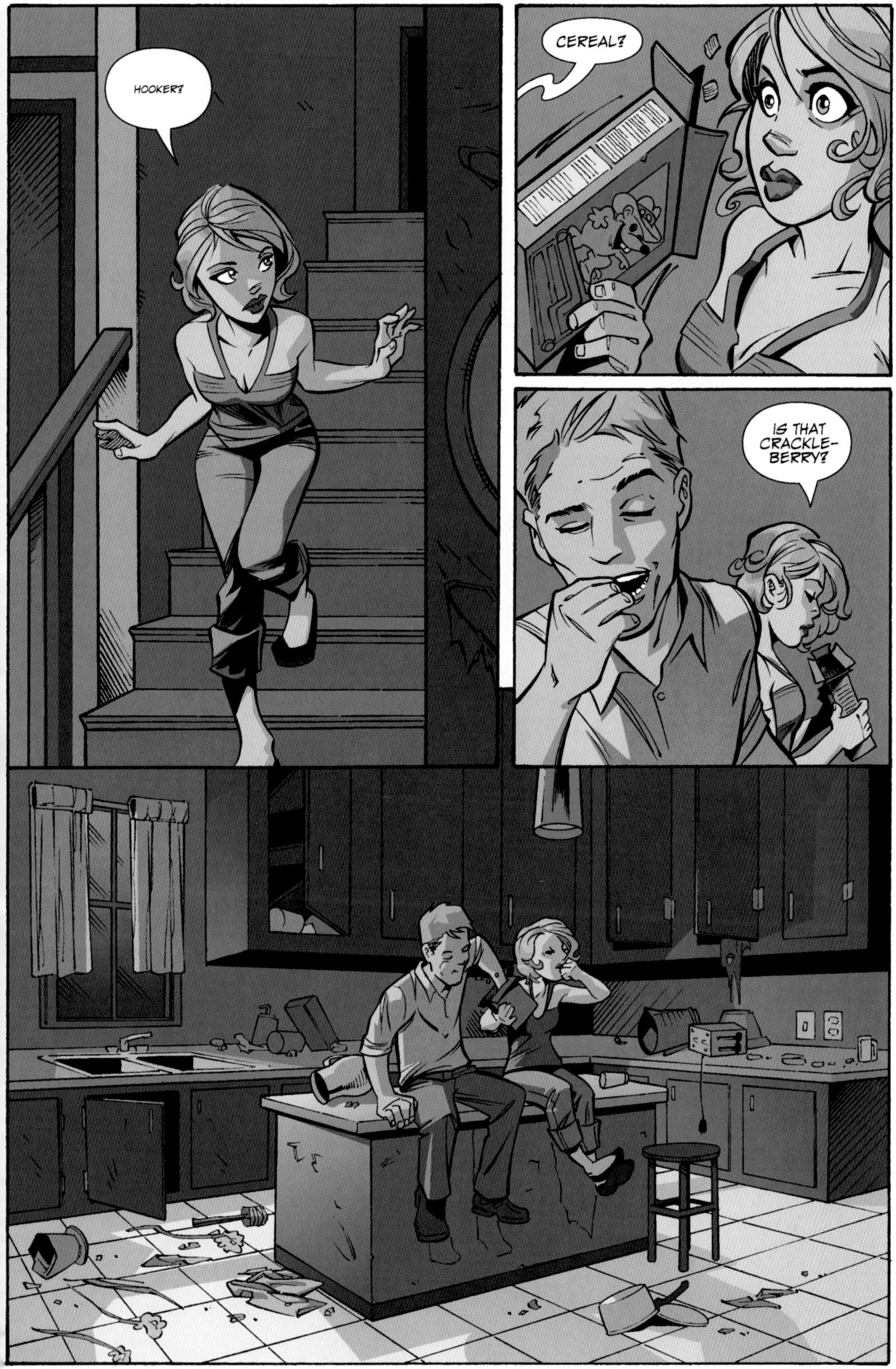
HOOKER?
CEREAL?
IS THAT CRACKLE-BERRY?

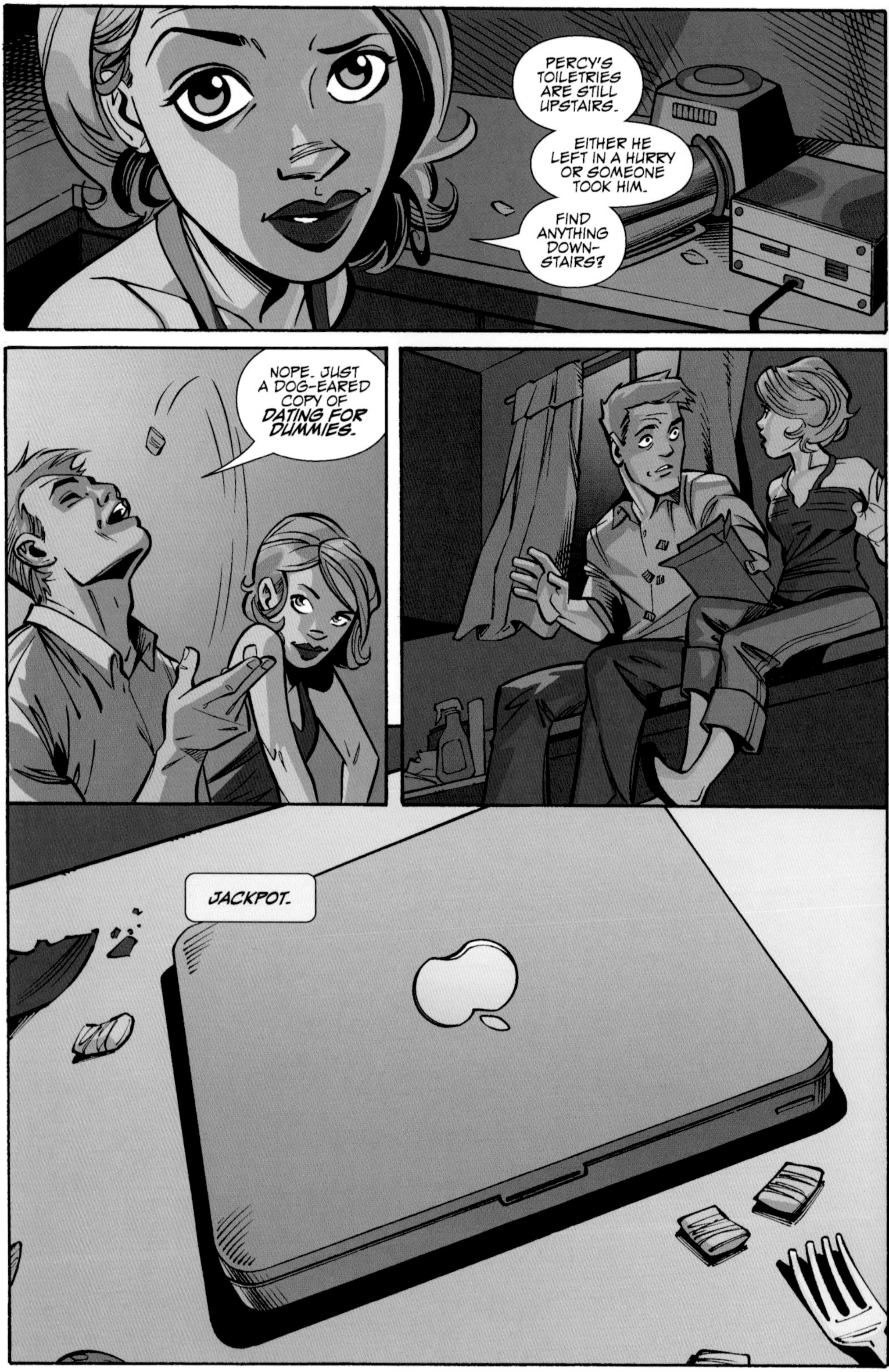
PERCY'S TOILETRIES ARE STILL UPSTAIRS.
EITHER HE LEFT IN A HURRY OR SOMEONE TOOK HIM.
FIND ANYTHING DOWN-STAIRS?
NOPE. JUST A DOG-EARED COPY OF *DATING FOR DUMMIES.*
JACKPOT.

NO E-MAIL. NO CALENDAR. NO BOOKMARKS. IT'S LIKE IT'S BEEN CLEANED OUT.

NO WONDER WHOEVER TRASHED THIS PLACE DIDN'T TAKE IT.

NOW WHAT?

BING

• NITRO: About time you surfaced. Come get your broad, and bring the goods. You better not stand me up again tonight.

CAN YOU REPLY TO HIM, HOOKER? FIND OUT WHEN AND WHERE?

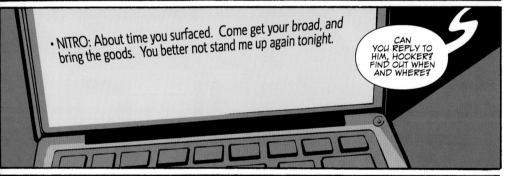

• NITRO: About time you surfaced. bring the goods. You better not stand me up again tonight.

• PERCINATOR: Just tell me when and where.

• NITRO: Same as always. Back of the Domino. Under the canopy. Don't be late.

TIME TO BREAK OUT THE LITTLE BLACK DRESS. LOOKS LIKE WE'RE GOING CLUBBING.

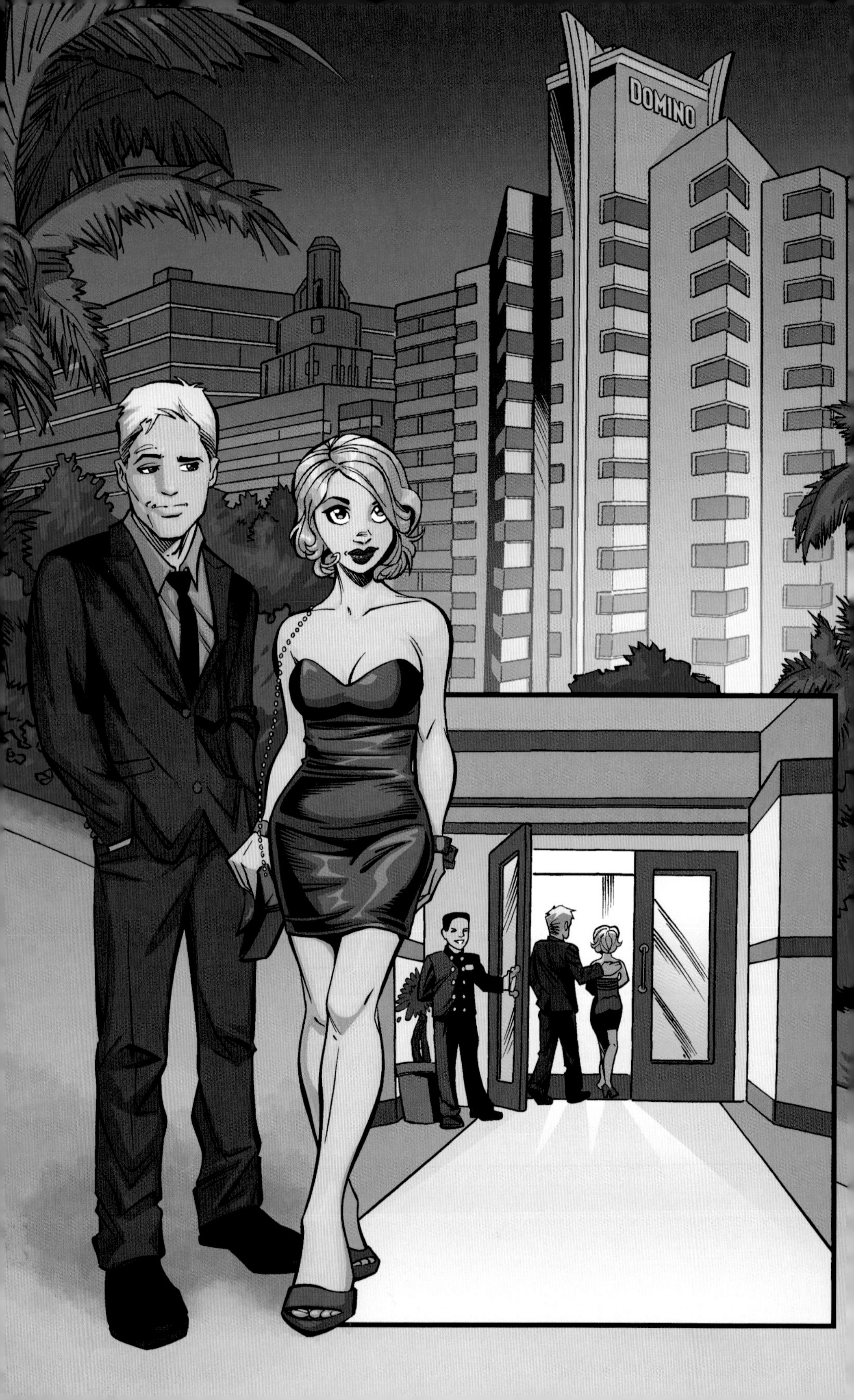
DOMINO

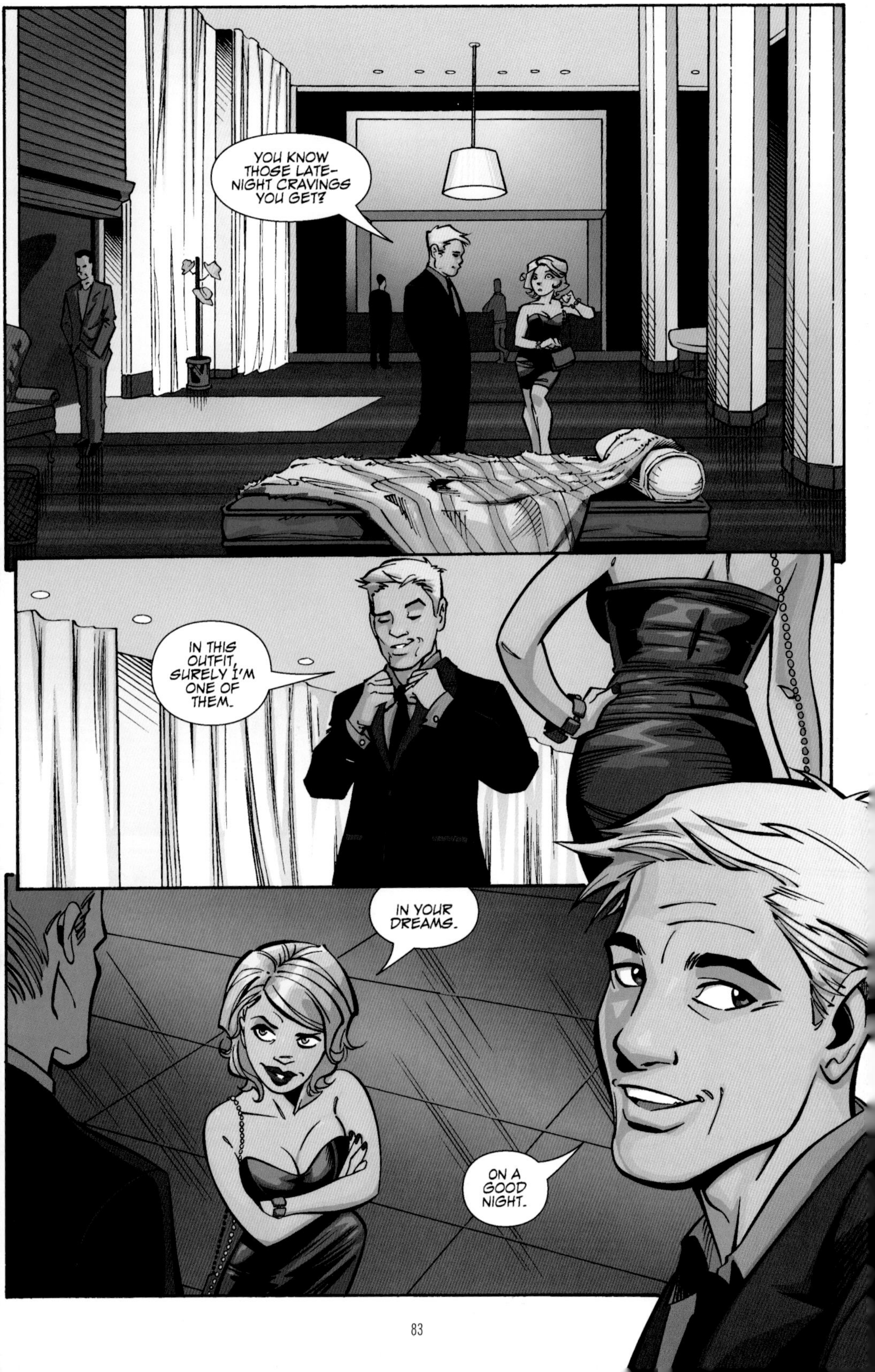
YOU KNOW THOSE LATE-NIGHT CRAVINGS YOU GET?
IN THIS OUTFIT, SURELY I'M ONE OF THEM.
IN YOUR DREAMS.
ON A GOOD NIGHT.

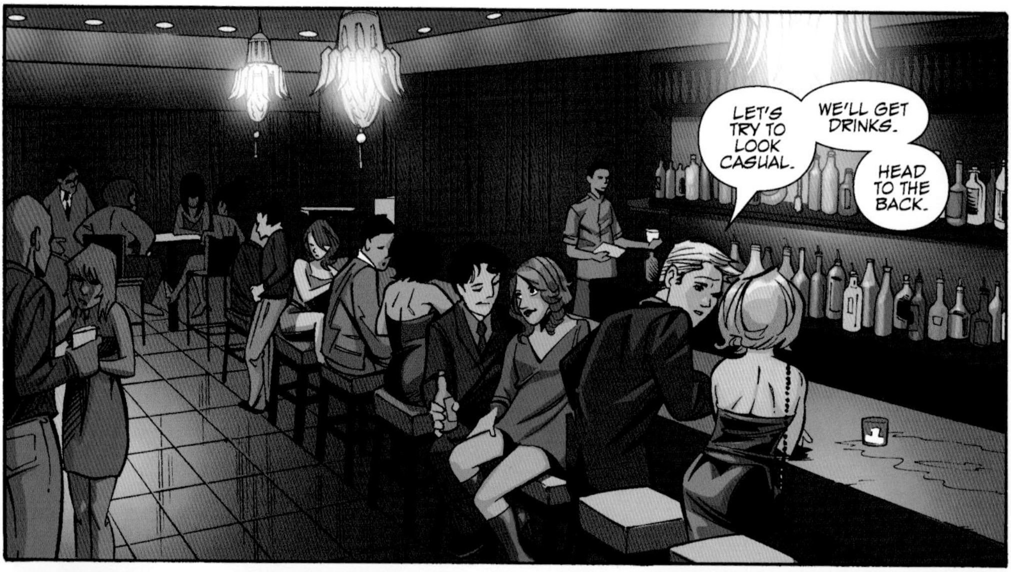
LET'S TRY TO LOOK CASUAL.
WE'LL GET DRINKS.
HEAD TO THE BACK.

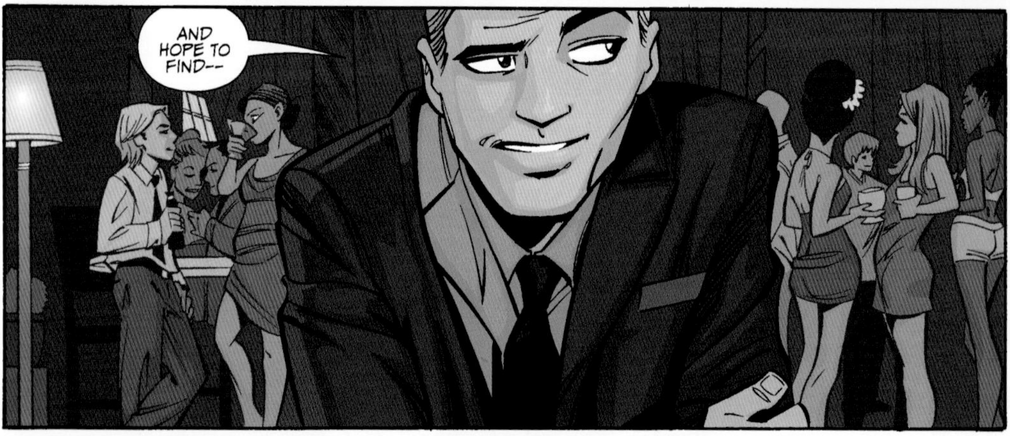
AND HOPE TO FIND--

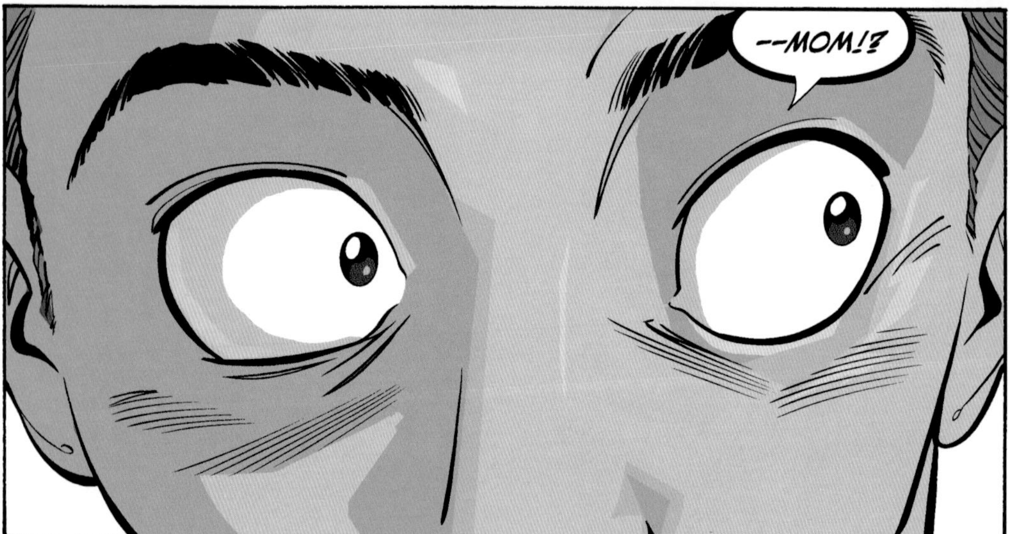
--MOM!?

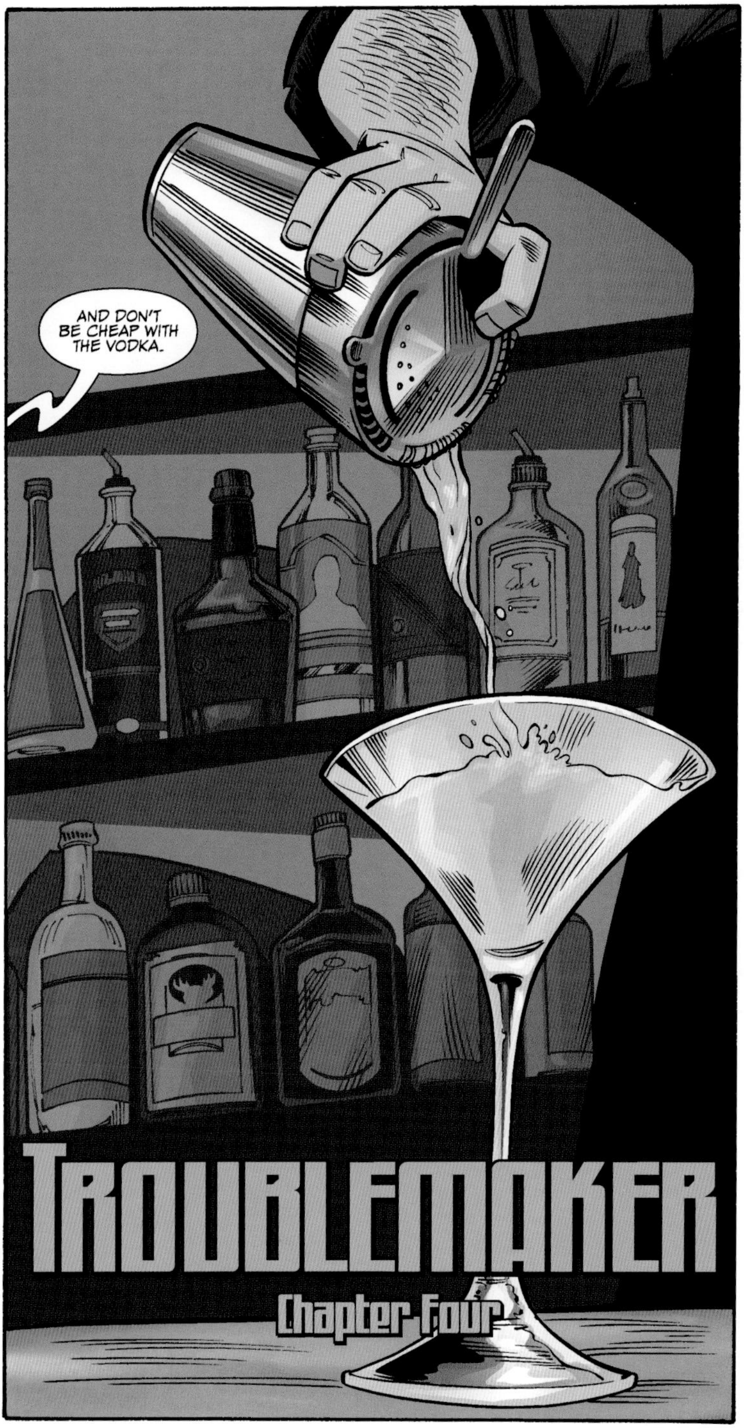
AND DON'T BE CHEAP WITH THE VODKA.
TROUBLEMAKER
Chapter Four

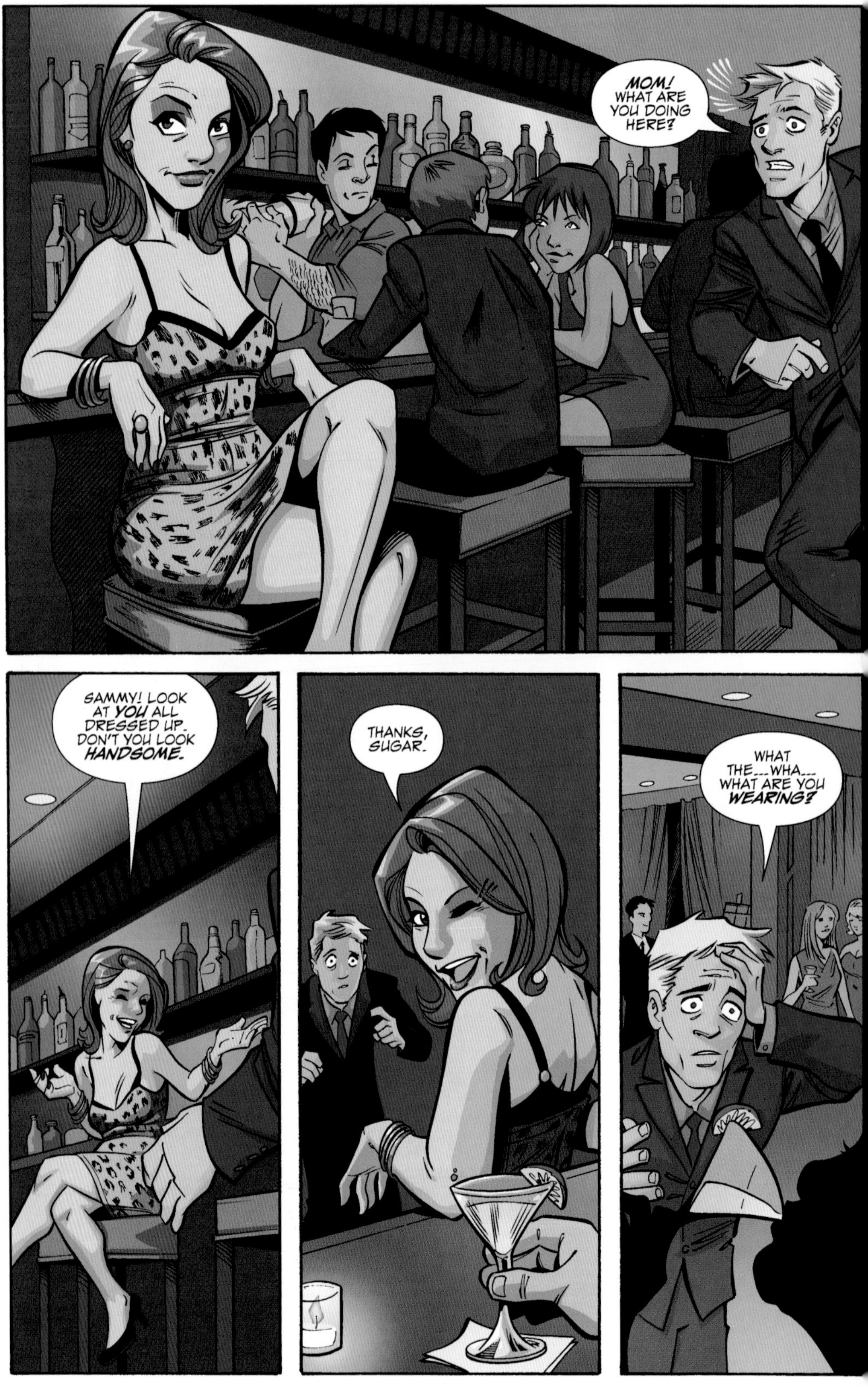
MOM! WHAT ARE YOU DOING HERE?
SAMMY! LOOK AT YOU ALL DRESSED UP. DON'T YOU LOOK HANDSOME.
THANKS, SUGAR.
WHAT THE...WHA... WHAT ARE YOU WEARING?

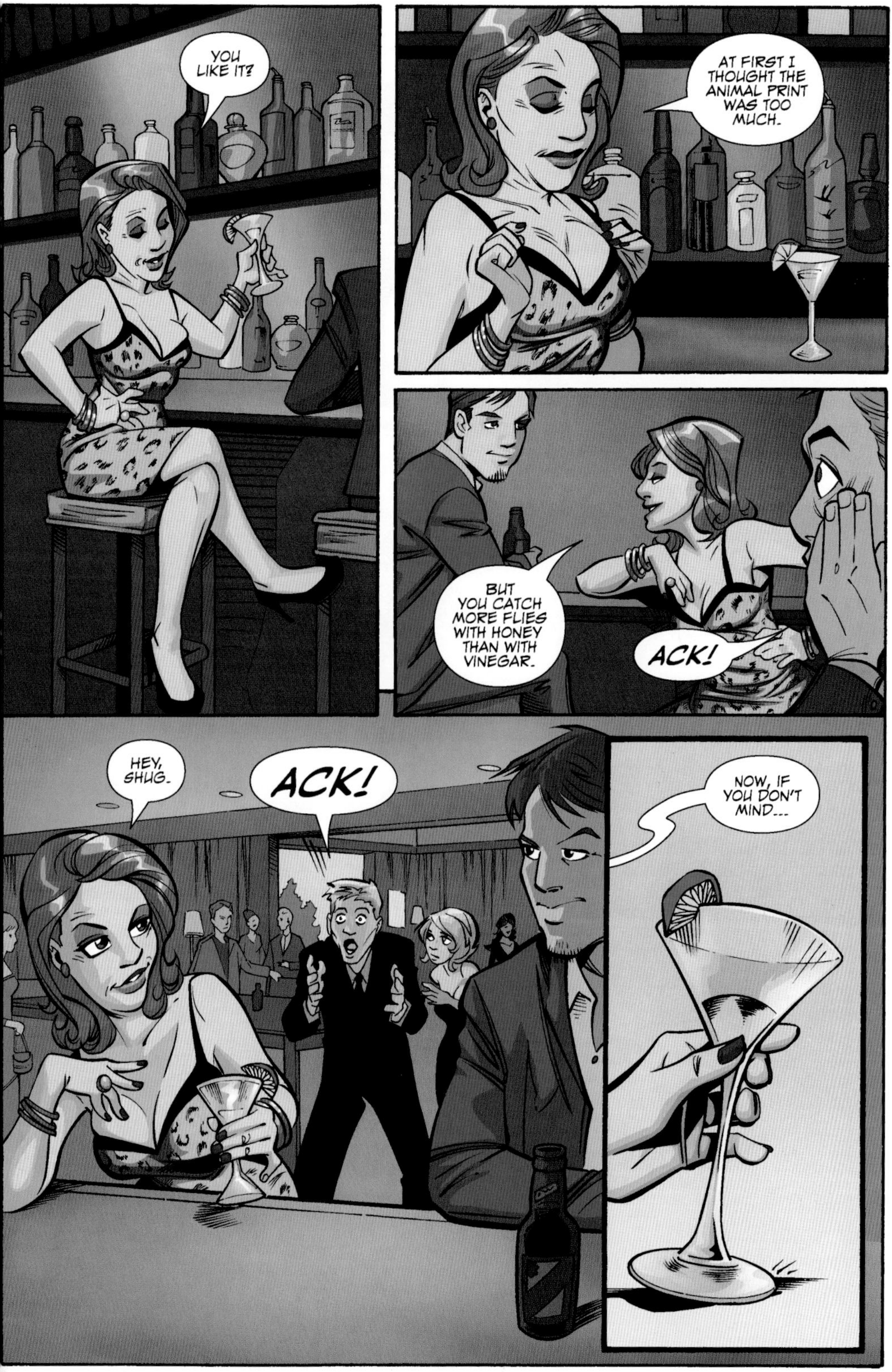
YOU LIKE IT?
AT FIRST I THOUGHT THE ANIMAL PRINT WAS TOO MUCH.
BUT YOU CATCH MORE FLIES WITH HONEY THAN WITH VINEGAR.
ACK!
HEY, SHUG.
ACK!
NOW, IF YOU DON'T MIND...

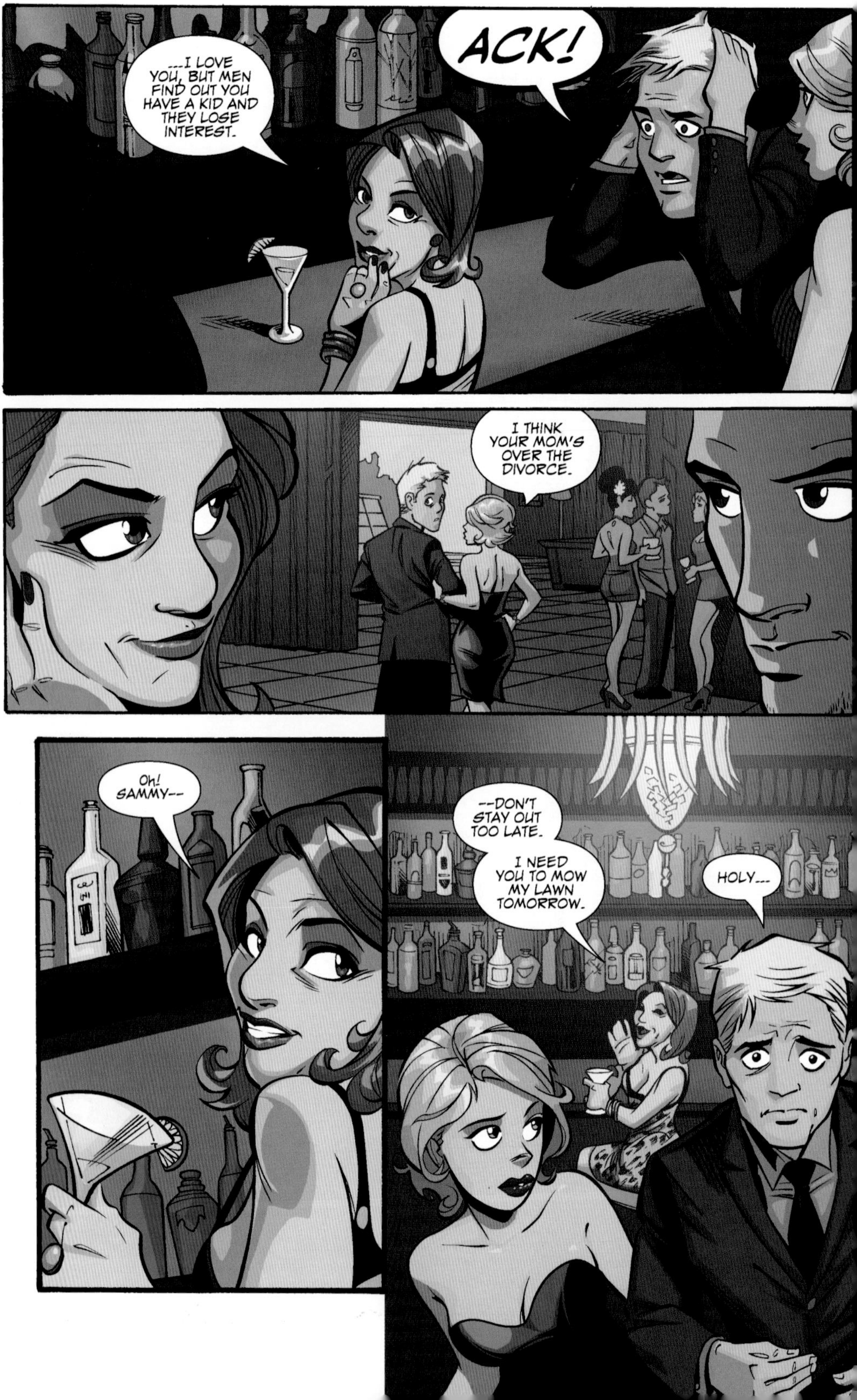
---I LOVE YOU, BUT MEN FIND OUT YOU HAVE A KID AND THEY LOSE INTEREST.
ACK!
I THINK YOUR MOM'S OVER THE DIVORCE.
Oh! SAMMY--
--DON'T STAY OUT TOO LATE.
I NEED YOU TO MOW MY LAWN TOMORROW.
HOLY---

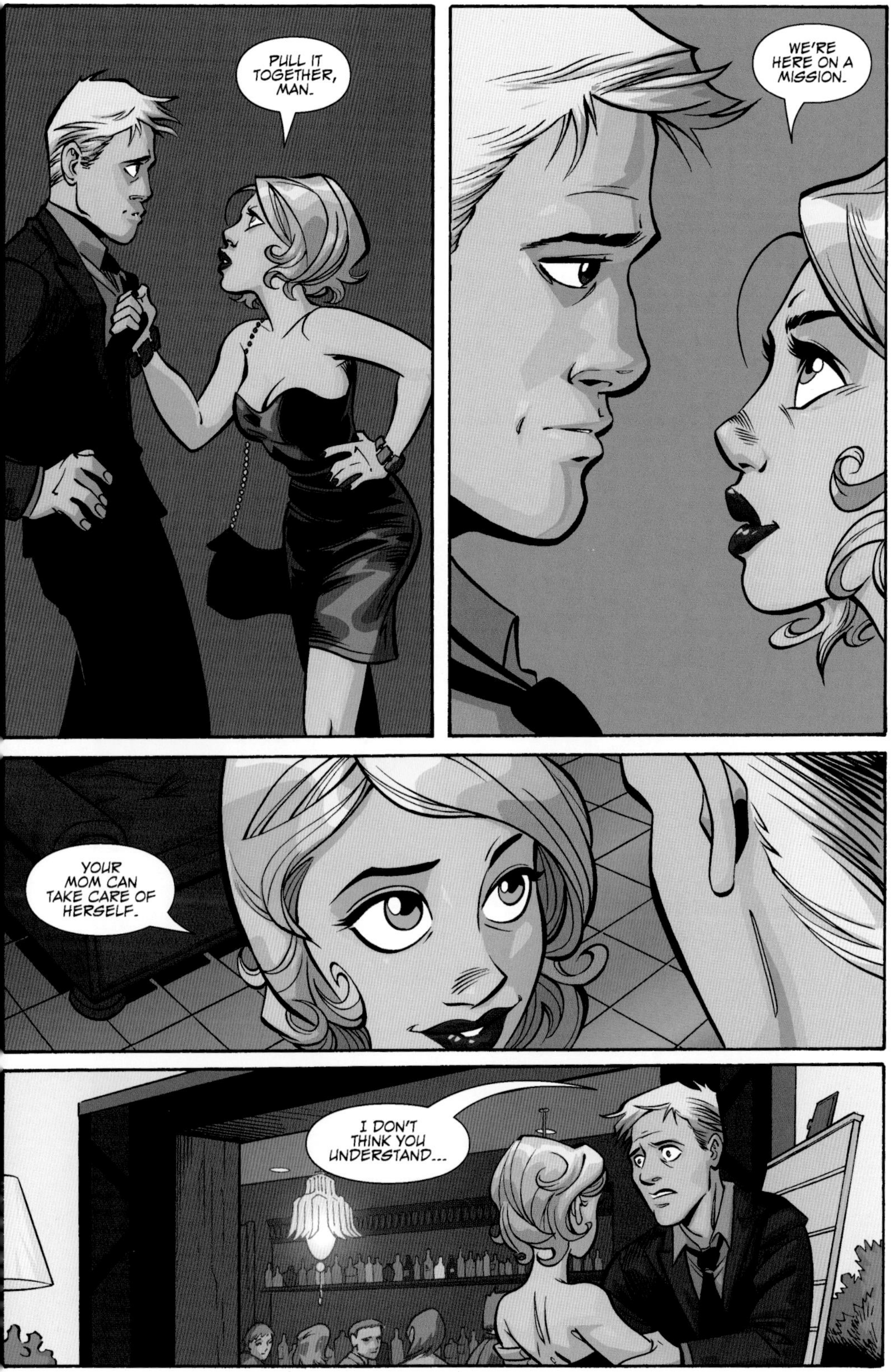
PULL IT TOGETHER, MAN.
WE'RE HERE ON A MISSION.
YOUR MOM CAN TAKE CARE OF HERSELF.
I DON'T THINK YOU UNDERSTAND...

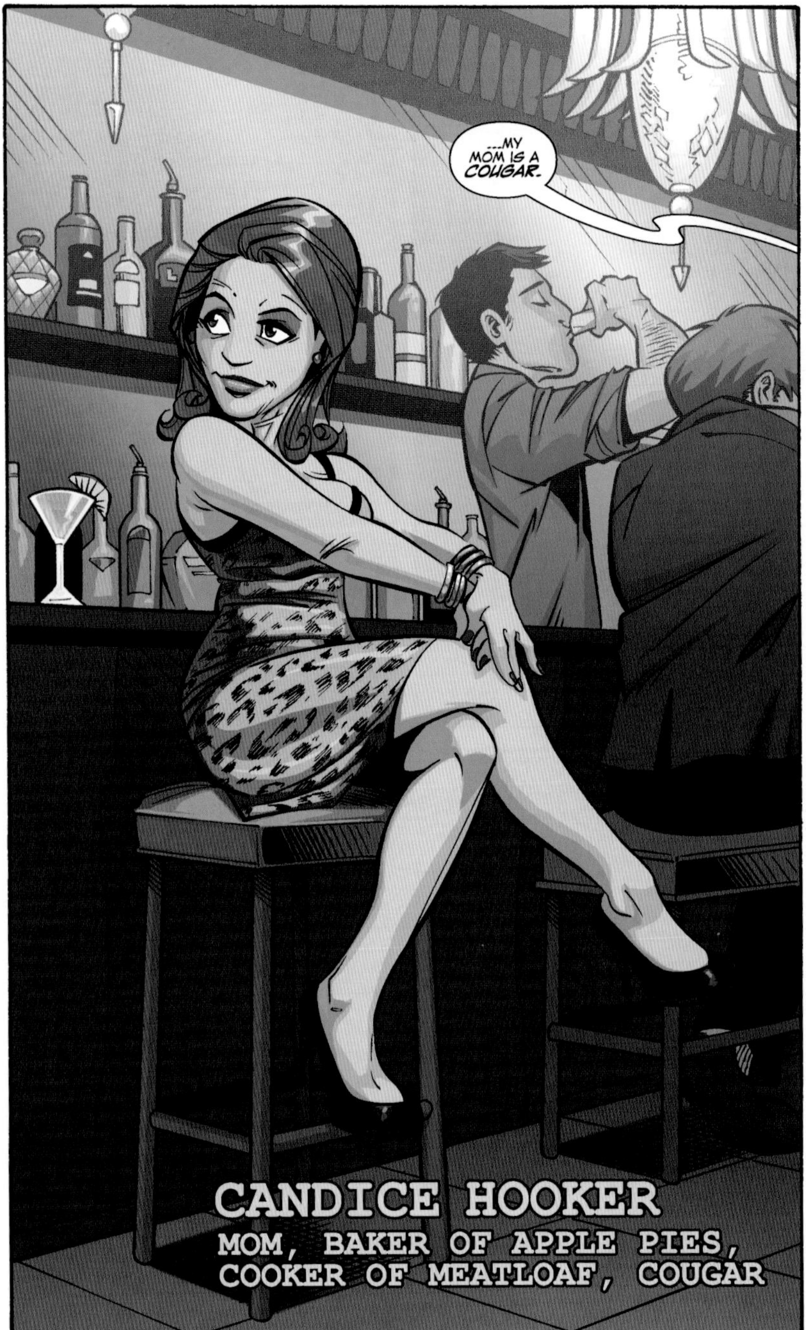
...MY MOM IS A COUGAR.
CANDICE HOOKER
MOM, BAKER OF APPLE PIES, COOKER OF MEATLOAF, COUGAR

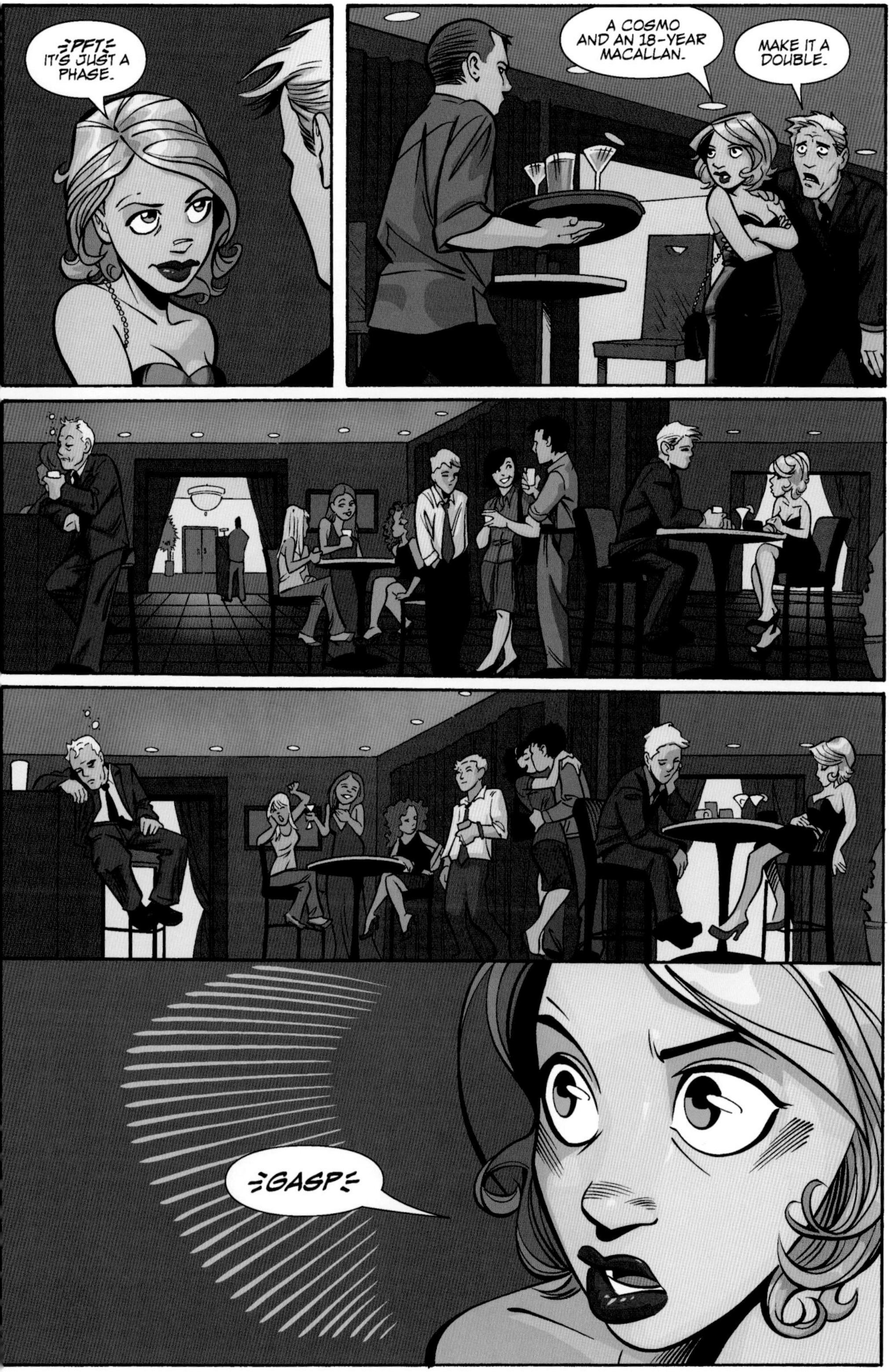

=PFT= IT'S JUST A PHASE.
A COSMO AND AN 18-YEAR MACALLAN.
MAKE IT A DOUBLE.
=GASP=

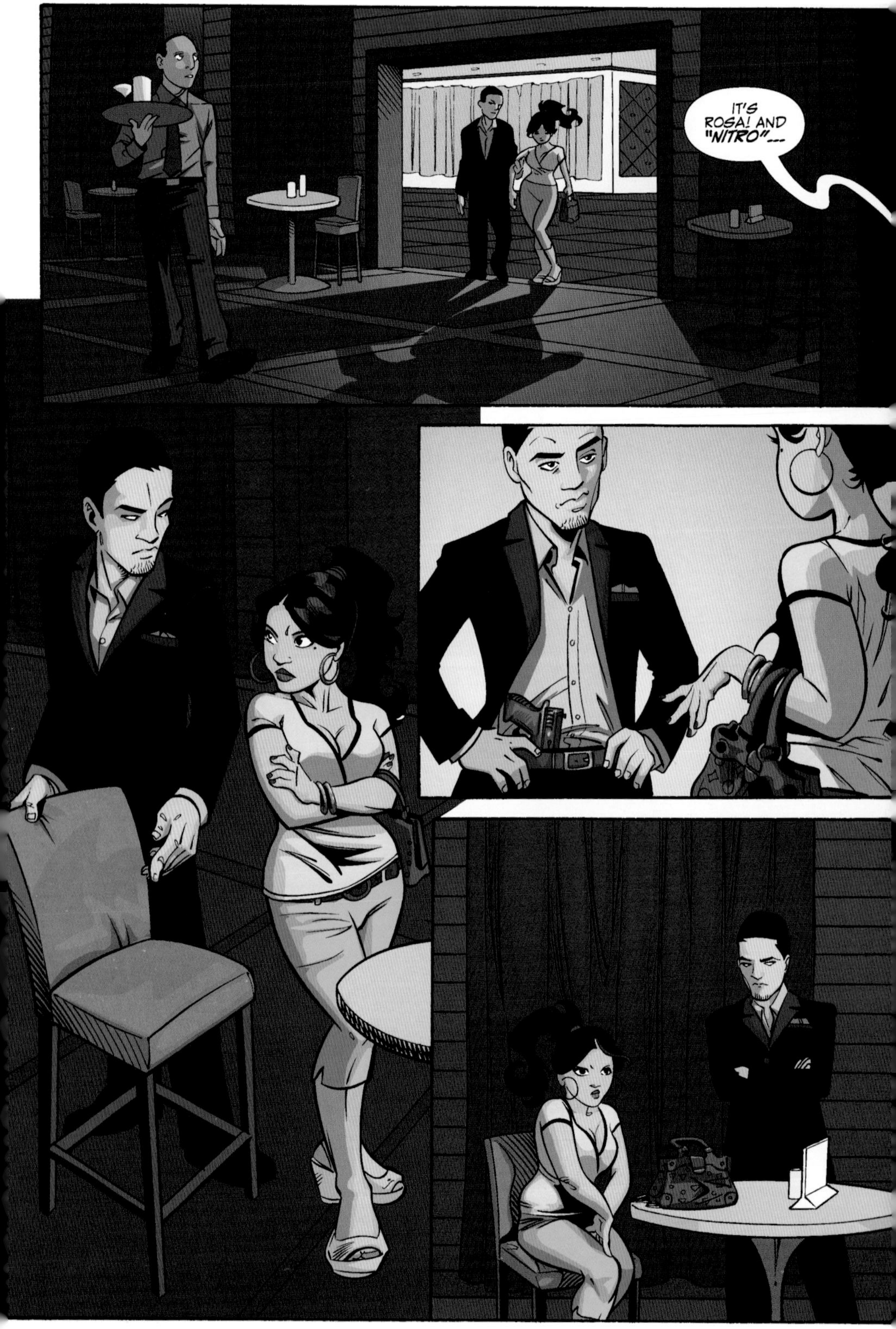
IT'S ROSA! AND "NITRO"...

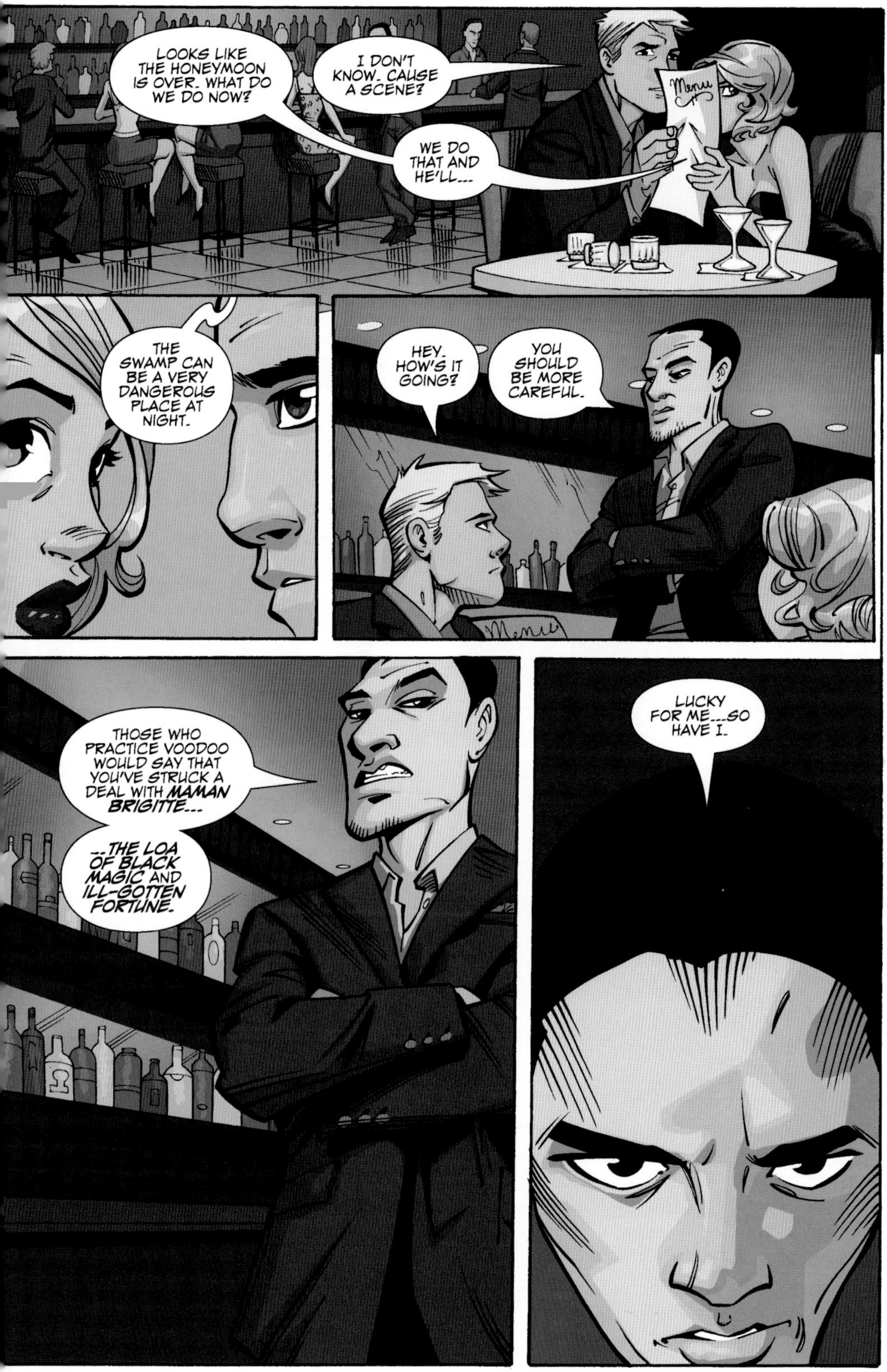

LOOKS LIKE THE HONEYMOON IS OVER. WHAT DO WE DO NOW?
I DON'T KNOW. CAUSE A SCENE?
WE DO THAT AND HE'LL...
Menu
THE SWAMP CAN BE A VERY DANGEROUS PLACE AT NIGHT.
HEY. HOW'S IT GOING?
YOU SHOULD BE MORE CAREFUL.
Menu
THOSE WHO PRACTICE VOODOO WOULD SAY THAT YOU'VE STRUCK A DEAL WITH MAMAN BRIGITTE...
...THE LOA OF BLACK MAGIC AND ILL-GOTTEN FORTUNE.
LUCKY FOR ME...SO HAVE I.

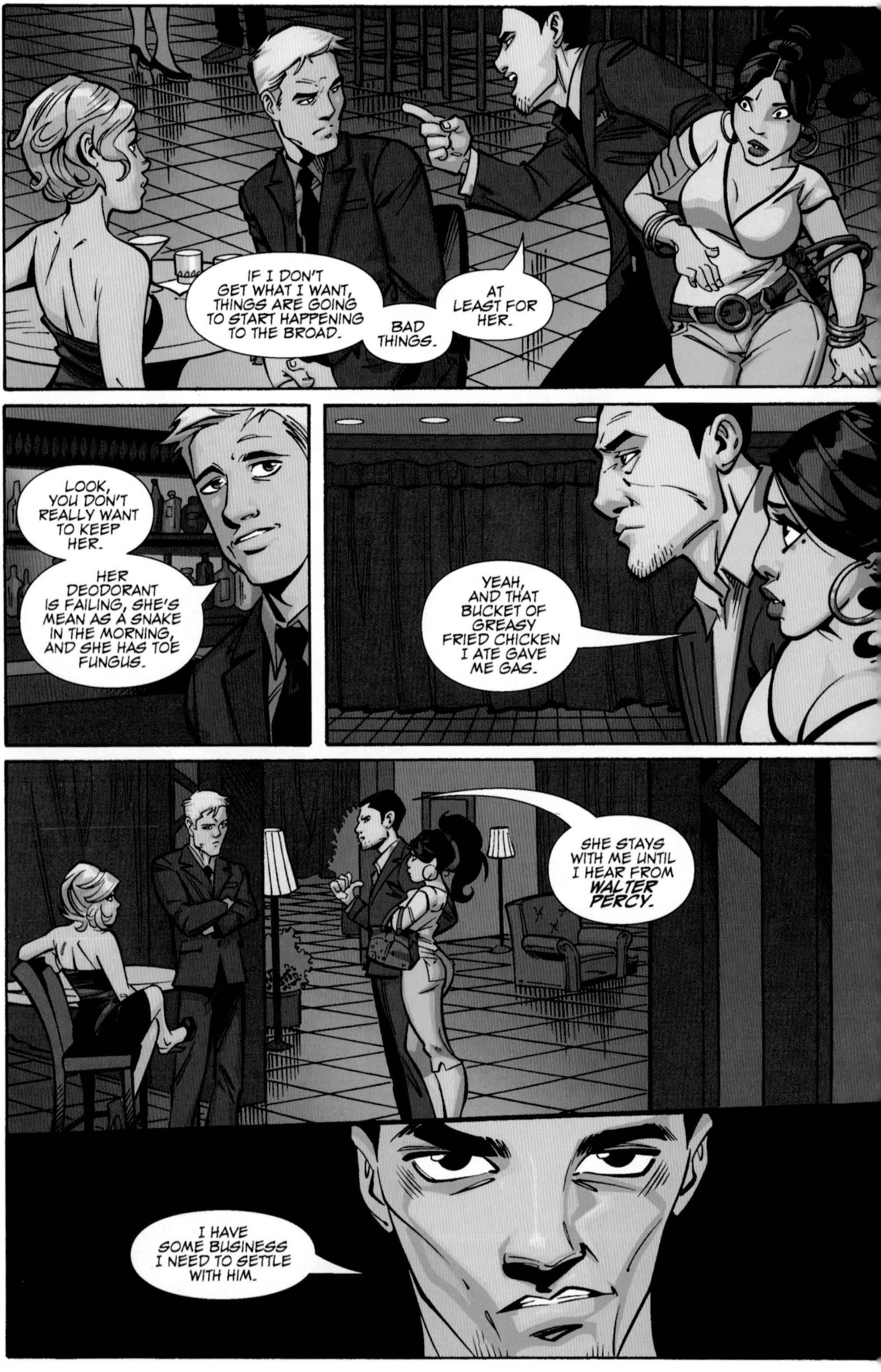
IF I DON'T GET WHAT I WANT, THINGS ARE GOING TO START HAPPENING TO THE BROAD.
BAD THINGS.
AT LEAST FOR HER.
LOOK, YOU DON'T REALLY WANT TO KEEP HER.
HER DEODORANT IS FAILING, SHE'S MEAN AS A SNAKE IN THE MORNING, AND SHE HAS TOE FUNGUS.
YEAH, AND THAT BUCKET OF GREASY FRIED CHICKEN I ATE GAVE ME GAS.
SHE STAYS WITH ME UNTIL I HEAR FROM WALTER PERCY.
I HAVE SOME BUSINESS I NEED TO SETTLE WITH HIM.

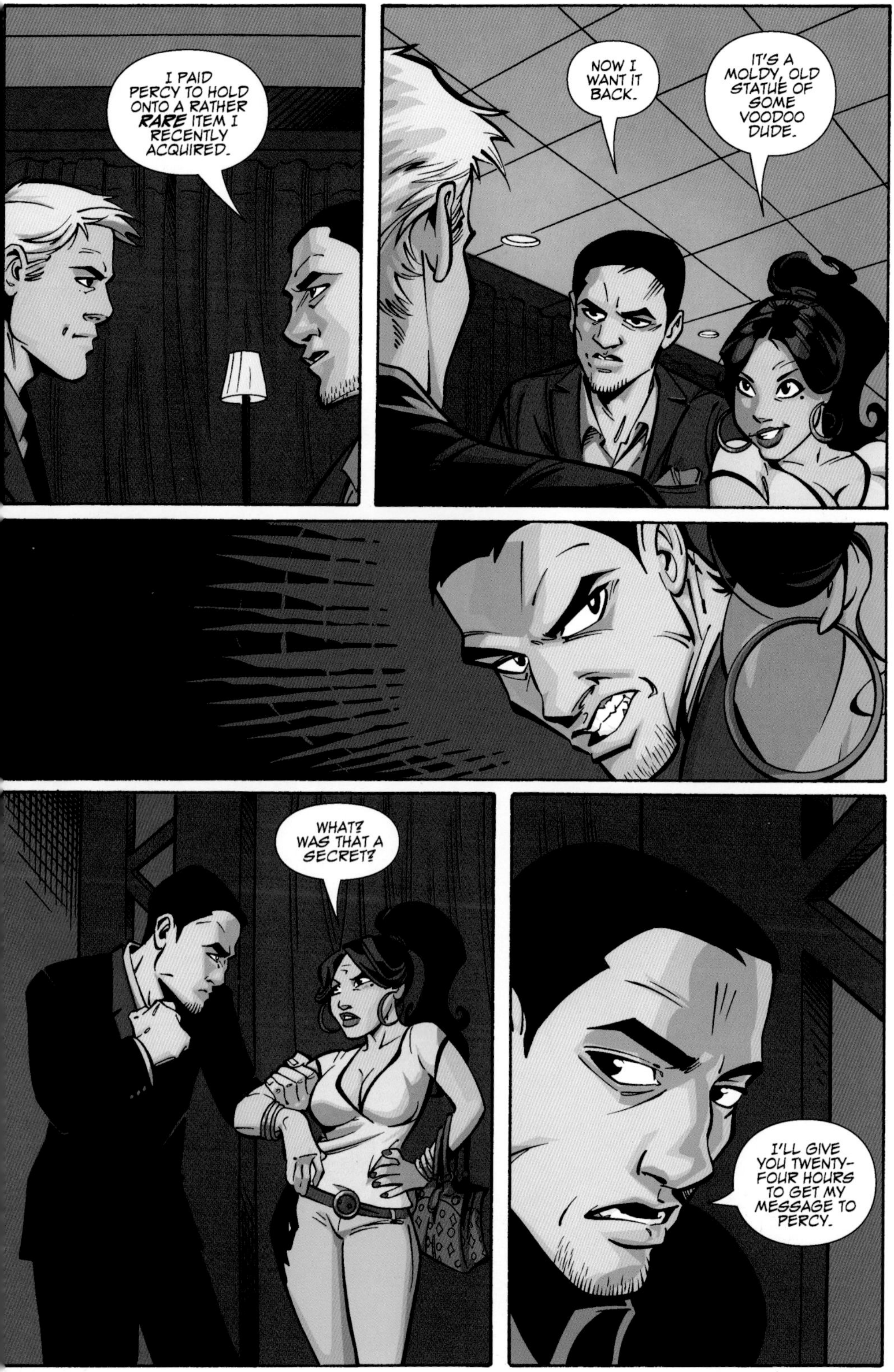
I PAID PERCY TO HOLD ONTO A RATHER **RARE** ITEM I RECENTLY ACQUIRED.
NOW I WANT IT BACK.
IT'S A MOLDY, OLD STATUE OF SOME VOODOO DUDE.
WHAT? WAS THAT A SECRET?
I'LL GIVE YOU TWENTY-FOUR HOURS TO GET MY MESSAGE TO PERCY.

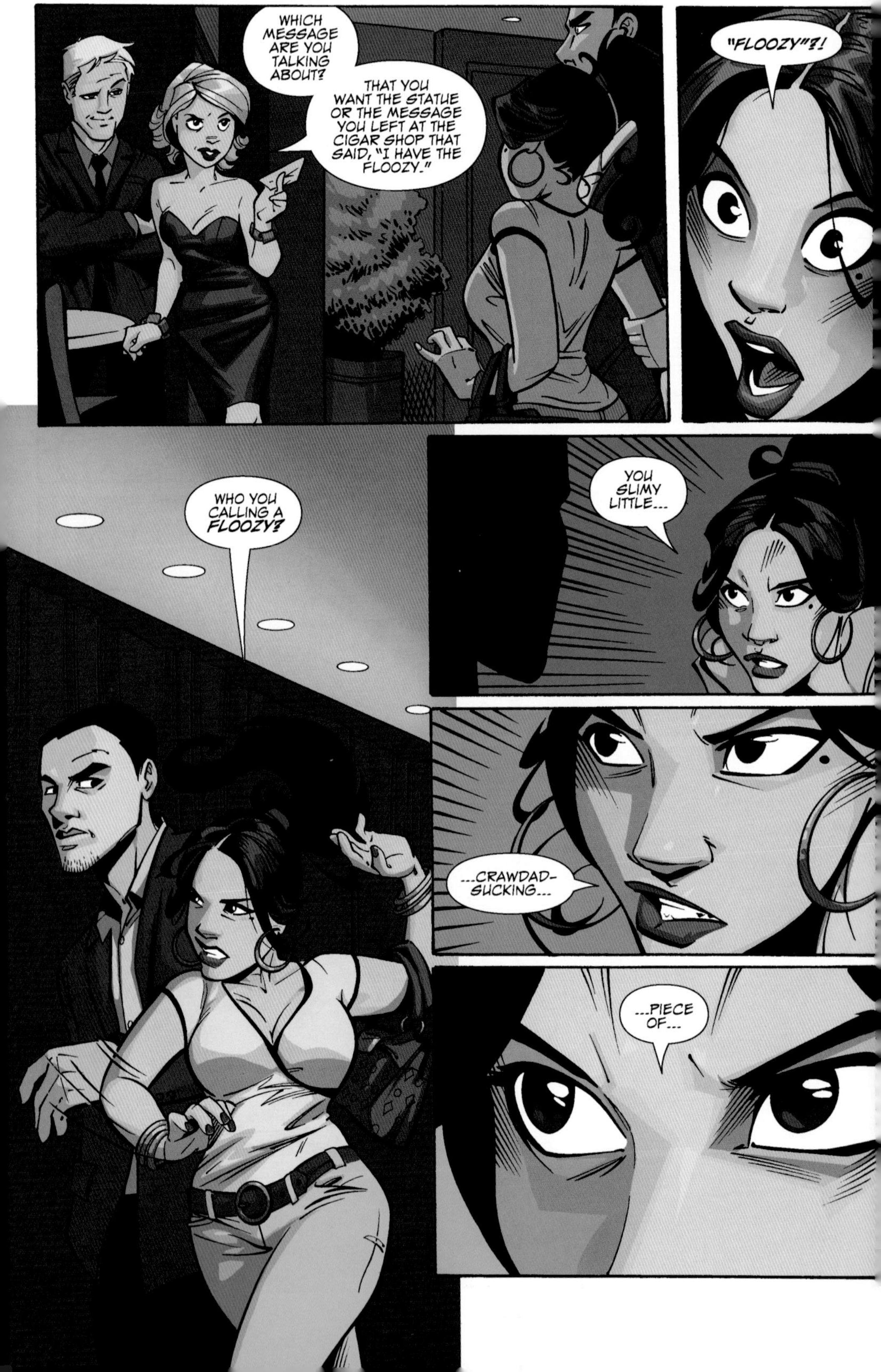
WHICH MESSAGE ARE YOU TALKING ABOUT?
THAT YOU WANT THE STATUE OR THE MESSAGE YOU LEFT AT THE CIGAR SHOP THAT SAID, "I HAVE THE FLOOZY."
"FLOOZY"?!
WHO YOU CALLING A *FLOOZY*?
YOU SLIMY LITTLE...
...CRAWDAD-SUCKING...
...PIECE OF...

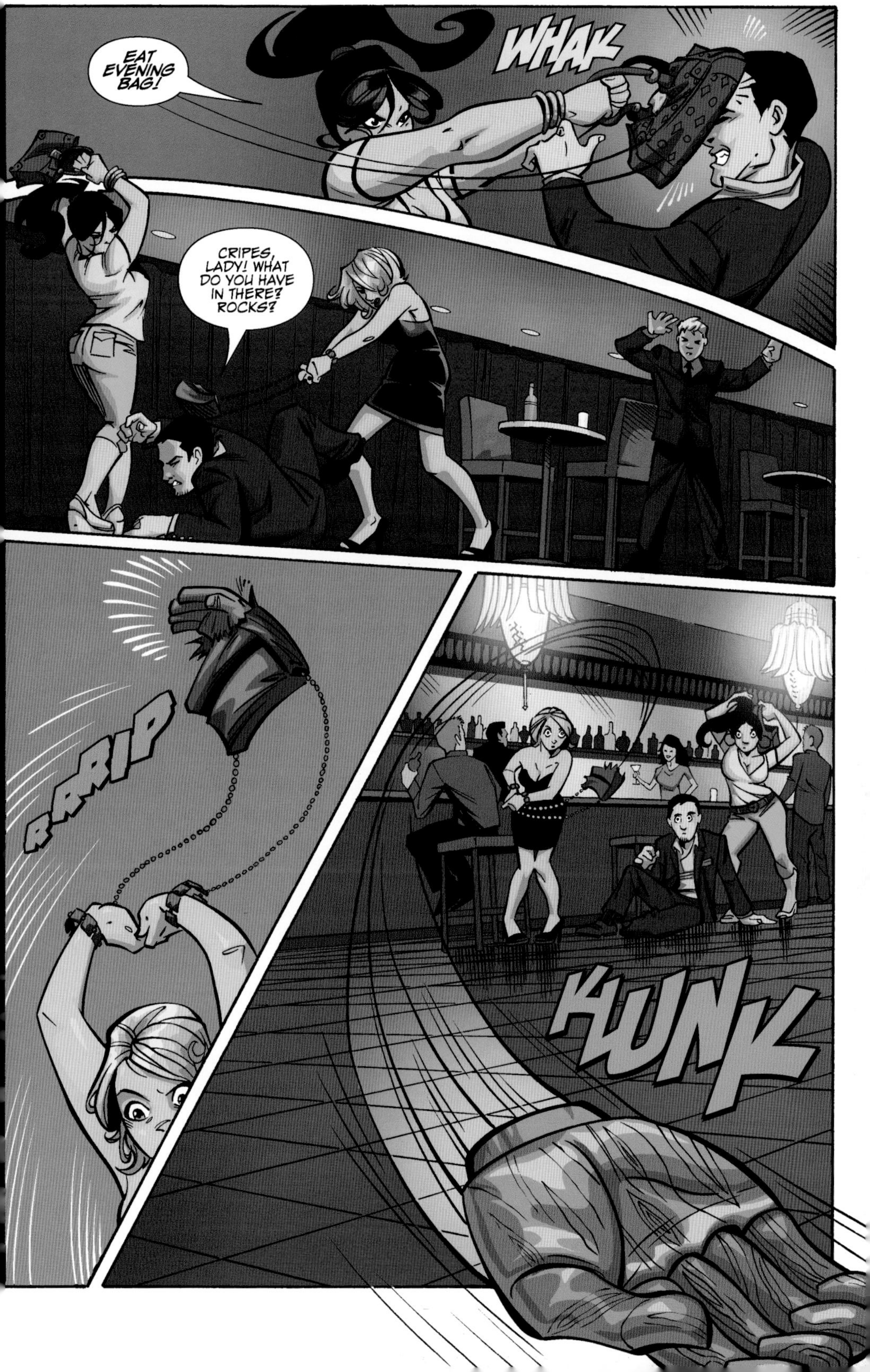
EAT EVENING BAG!
WHAK
CRIPES, LADY! WHAT DO YOU HAVE IN THERE? ROCKS?
RRRIP
KUNK

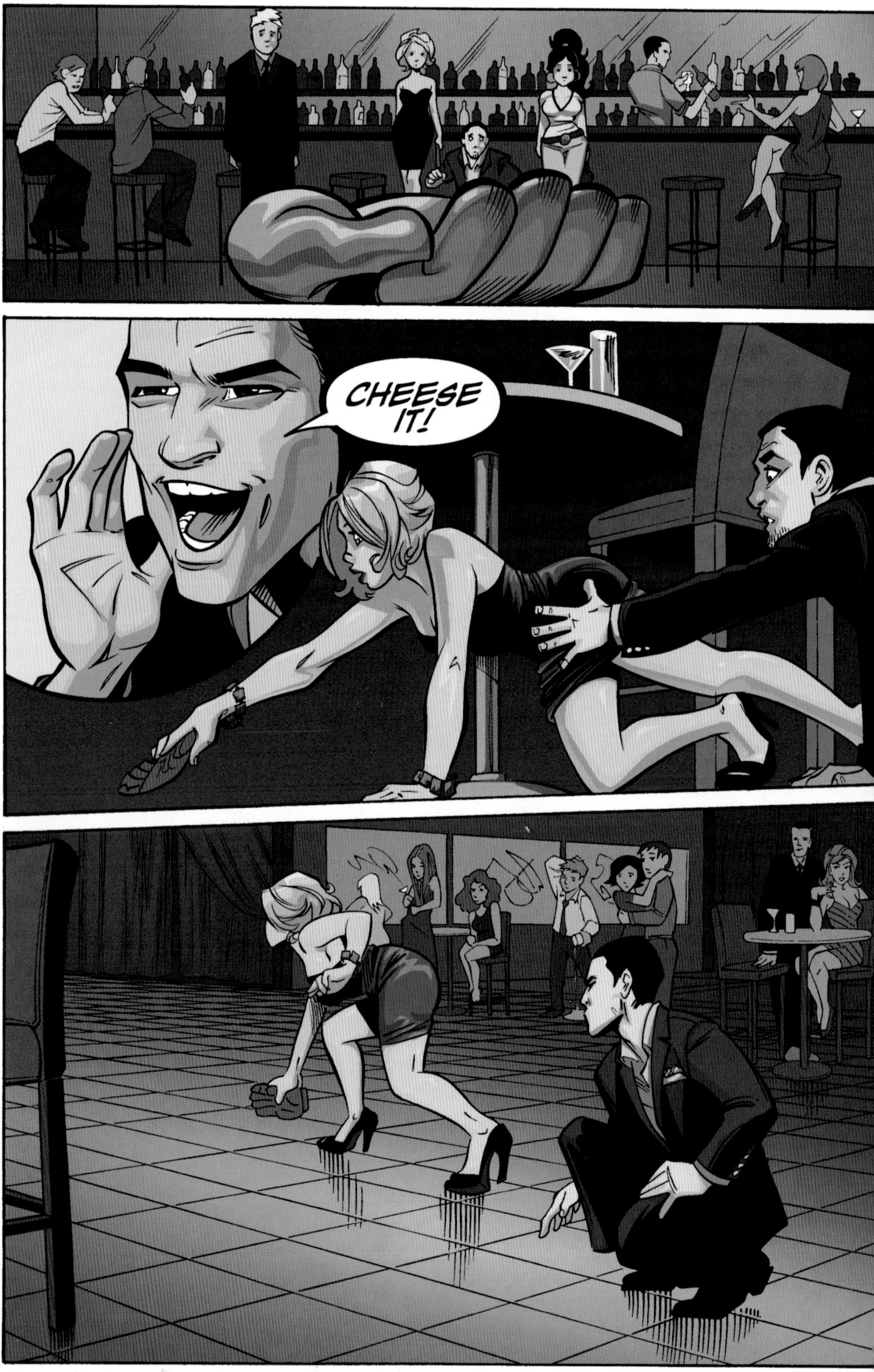
CHEESE IT!

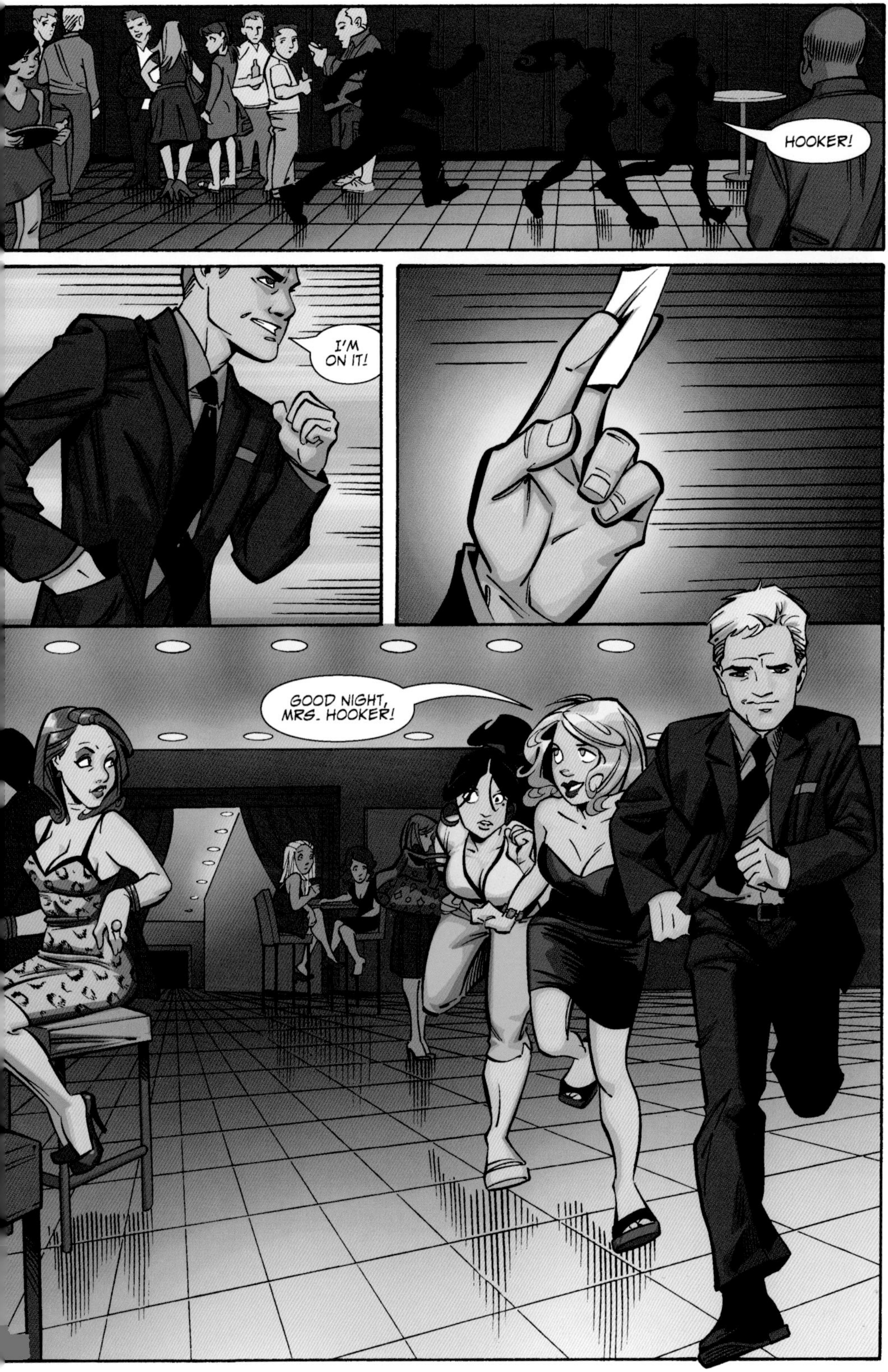
HOOKER!
I'M ON IT!
GOOD NIGHT, MRS. HOOKER!

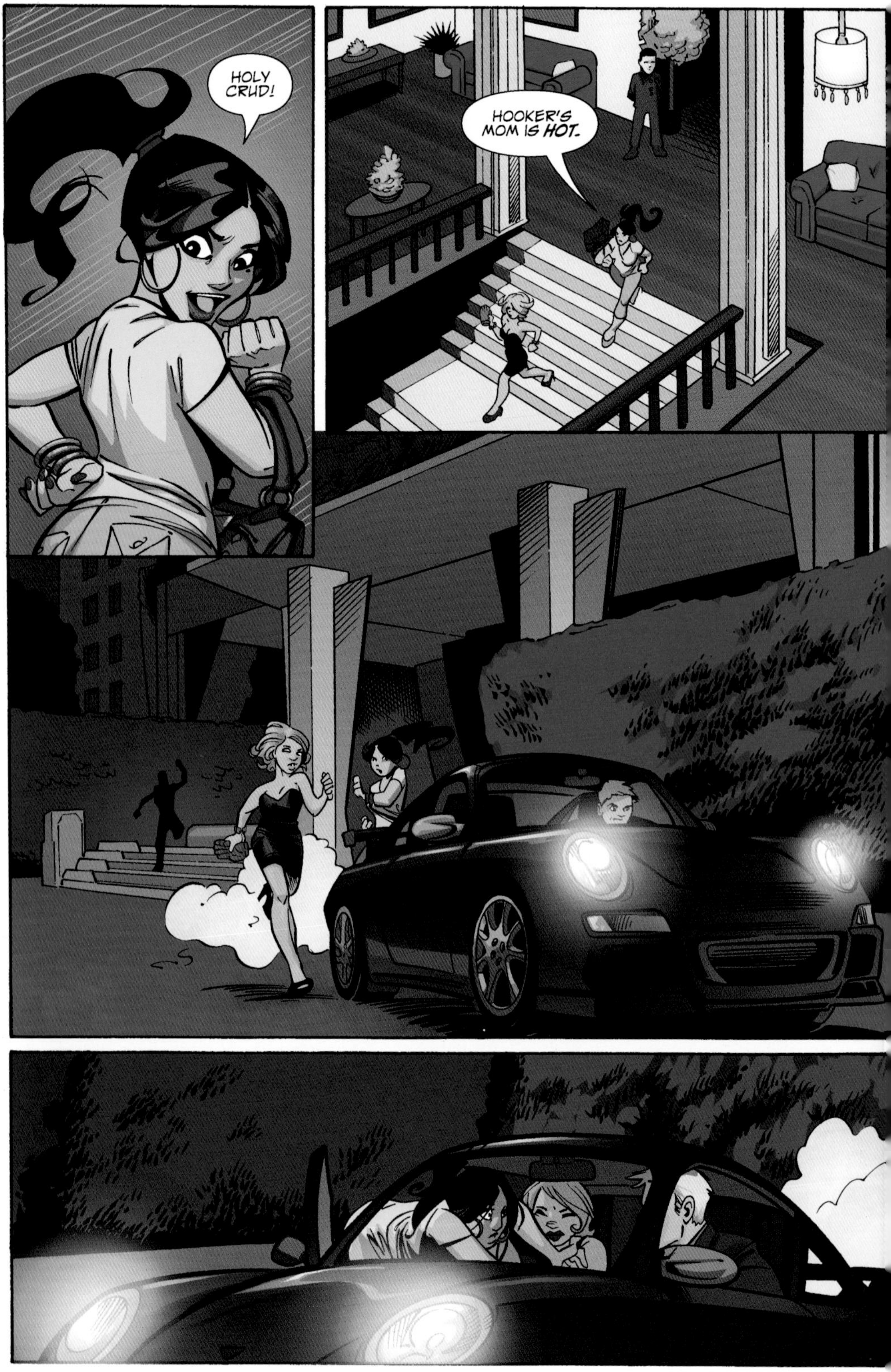
HOLY CRUD!
HOOKER'S MOM IS HOT.

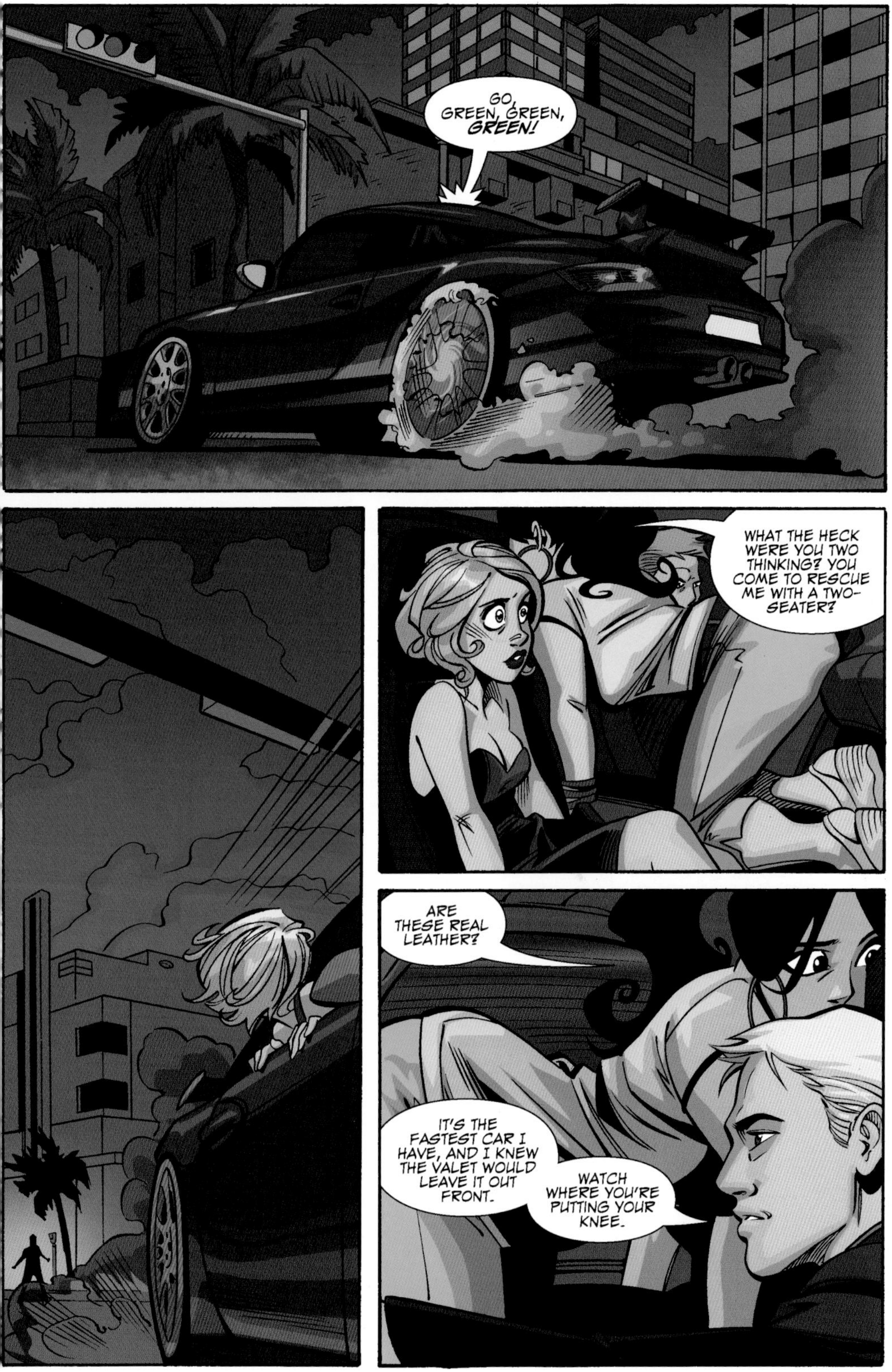
GO, GREEN, GREEN, GREEN!
WHAT THE HECK WERE YOU TWO THINKING? YOU COME TO RESCUE ME WITH A TWO-SEATER?
ARE THESE REAL LEATHER?
IT'S THE FASTEST CAR I HAVE, AND I KNEW THE VALET WOULD LEAVE IT OUT FRONT.
WATCH WHERE YOU'RE PUTTING YOUR KNEE.

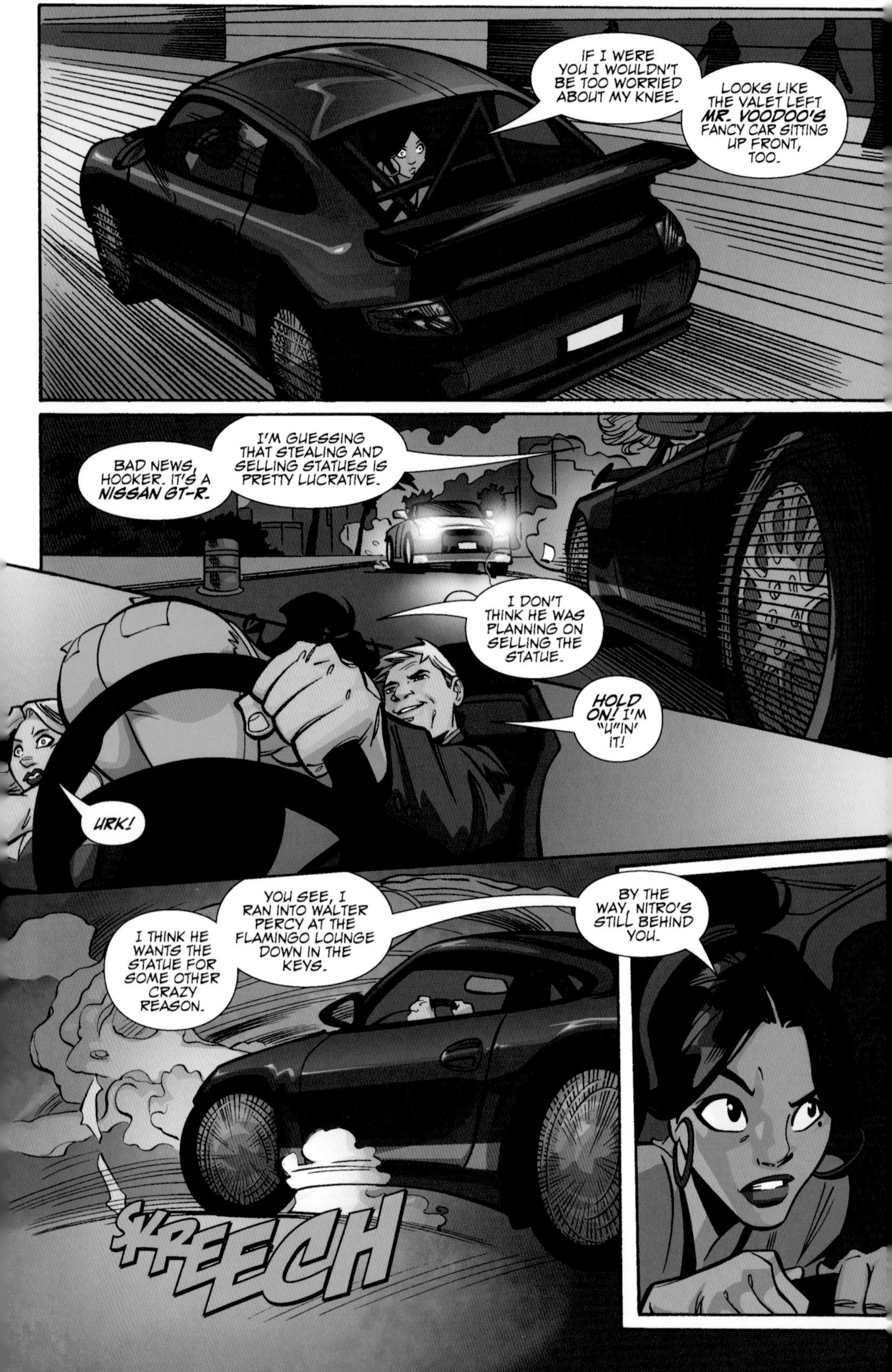
IF I WERE YOU I WOULDN'T BE TOO WORRIED ABOUT MY KNEE.
LOOKS LIKE THE VALET LEFT **MR. VOODOO'S** FANCY CAR SITTING UP FRONT, TOO.
BAD NEWS, HOOKER. IT'S A **NISSAN GT-R.**
I'M GUESSING THAT STEALING AND SELLING STATUES IS PRETTY LUCRATIVE.
I DON'T THINK HE WAS PLANNING ON SELLING THE STATUE.
HOLD ON! I'M "U"IN' IT!
URK!
I THINK HE WANTS THE STATUE FOR SOME OTHER CRAZY REASON.
YOU SEE, I RAN INTO WALTER PERCY AT THE FLAMINGO LOUNGE DOWN IN THE KEYS.
BY THE WAY, NITRO'S STILL BEHIND YOU.
SKREECH

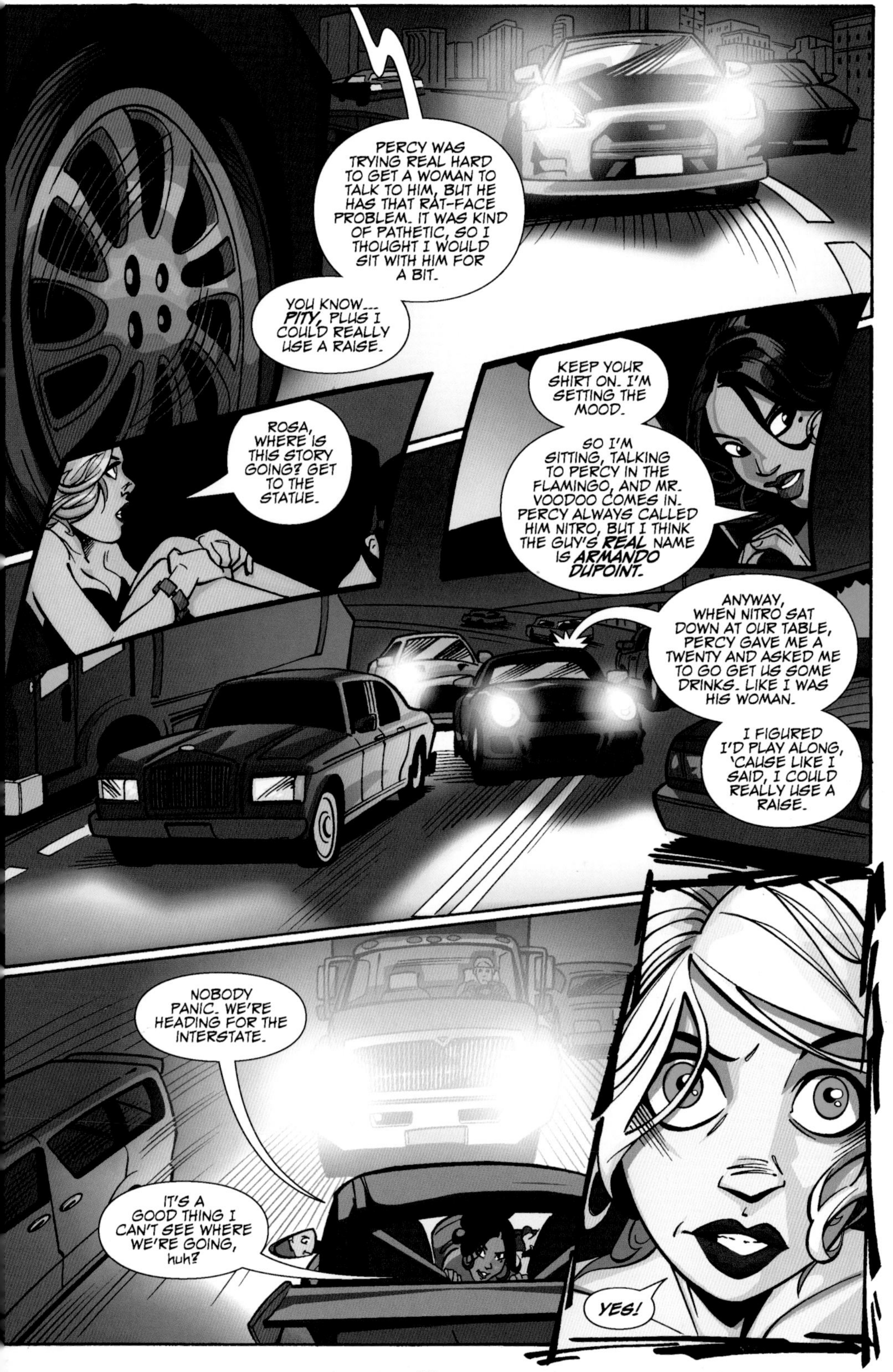
PERCY WAS TRYING REAL HARD TO GET A WOMAN TO TALK TO HIM, BUT HE HAS THAT RAT-FACE PROBLEM. IT WAS KIND OF PATHETIC, SO I THOUGHT I WOULD SIT WITH HIM FOR A BIT.
YOU KNOW... PITY, PLUS I COULD REALLY USE A RAISE.
ROSA, WHERE IS THIS STORY GOING? GET TO THE STATUE.
KEEP YOUR SHIRT ON. I'M SETTING THE MOOD.
SO I'M SITTING, TALKING TO PERCY IN THE FLAMINGO, AND MR. VOODOO COMES IN. PERCY ALWAYS CALLED HIM NITRO, BUT I THINK THE GUY'S REAL NAME IS ARMANDO DUPOINT.
ANYWAY, WHEN NITRO SAT DOWN AT OUR TABLE, PERCY GAVE ME A TWENTY AND ASKED ME TO GO GET US SOME DRINKS. LIKE I WAS HIS WOMAN.
I FIGURED I'D PLAY ALONG, 'CAUSE LIKE I SAID, I COULD REALLY USE A RAISE.
NOBODY PANIC. WE'RE HEADING FOR THE INTERSTATE.
IT'S A GOOD THING I CAN'T SEE WHERE WE'RE GOING, huh?
YES!

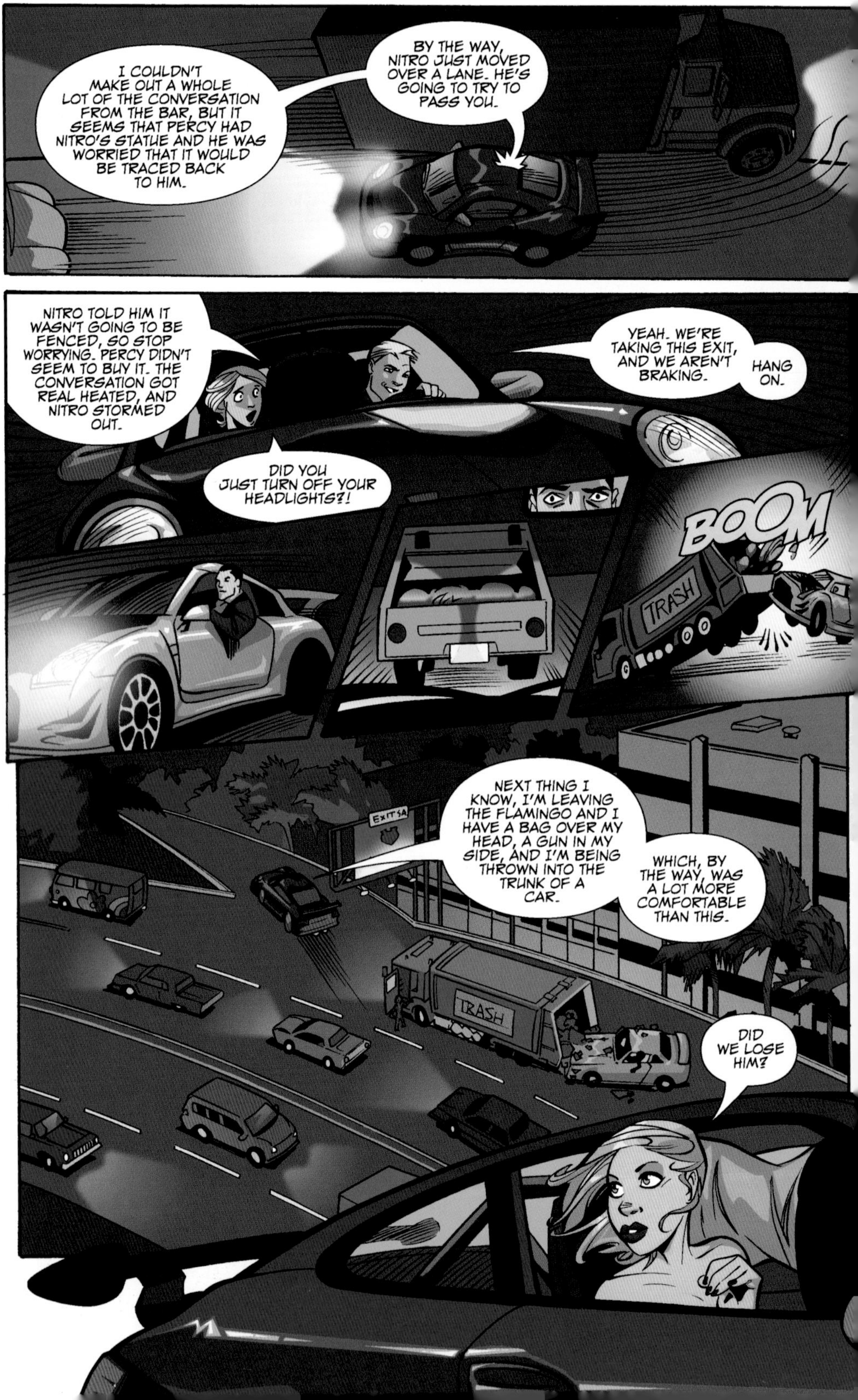
I COULDN'T MAKE OUT A WHOLE LOT OF THE CONVERSATION FROM THE BAR, BUT IT SEEMS THAT PERCY HAD NITRO'S STATUE AND HE WAS WORRIED THAT IT WOULD BE TRACED BACK TO HIM.
BY THE WAY, NITRO JUST MOVED OVER A LANE. HE'S GOING TO TRY TO PASS YOU.
NITRO TOLD HIM IT WASN'T GOING TO BE FENCED, SO STOP WORRYING. PERCY DIDN'T SEEM TO BUY IT. THE CONVERSATION GOT REAL HEATED, AND NITRO STORMED OUT.
YEAH. WE'RE TAKING THIS EXIT, AND WE AREN'T BRAKING.
HANG ON.
DID YOU JUST TURN OFF YOUR HEADLIGHTS?!
BOOM
TRASH
NEXT THING I KNOW, I'M LEAVING THE FLAMINGO AND I HAVE A BAG OVER MY HEAD, A GUN IN MY SIDE, AND I'M BEING THROWN INTO THE TRUNK OF A CAR.
WHICH, BY THE WAY, WAS A LOT MORE COMFORTABLE THAN THIS.
TRASH
DID WE LOSE HIM?

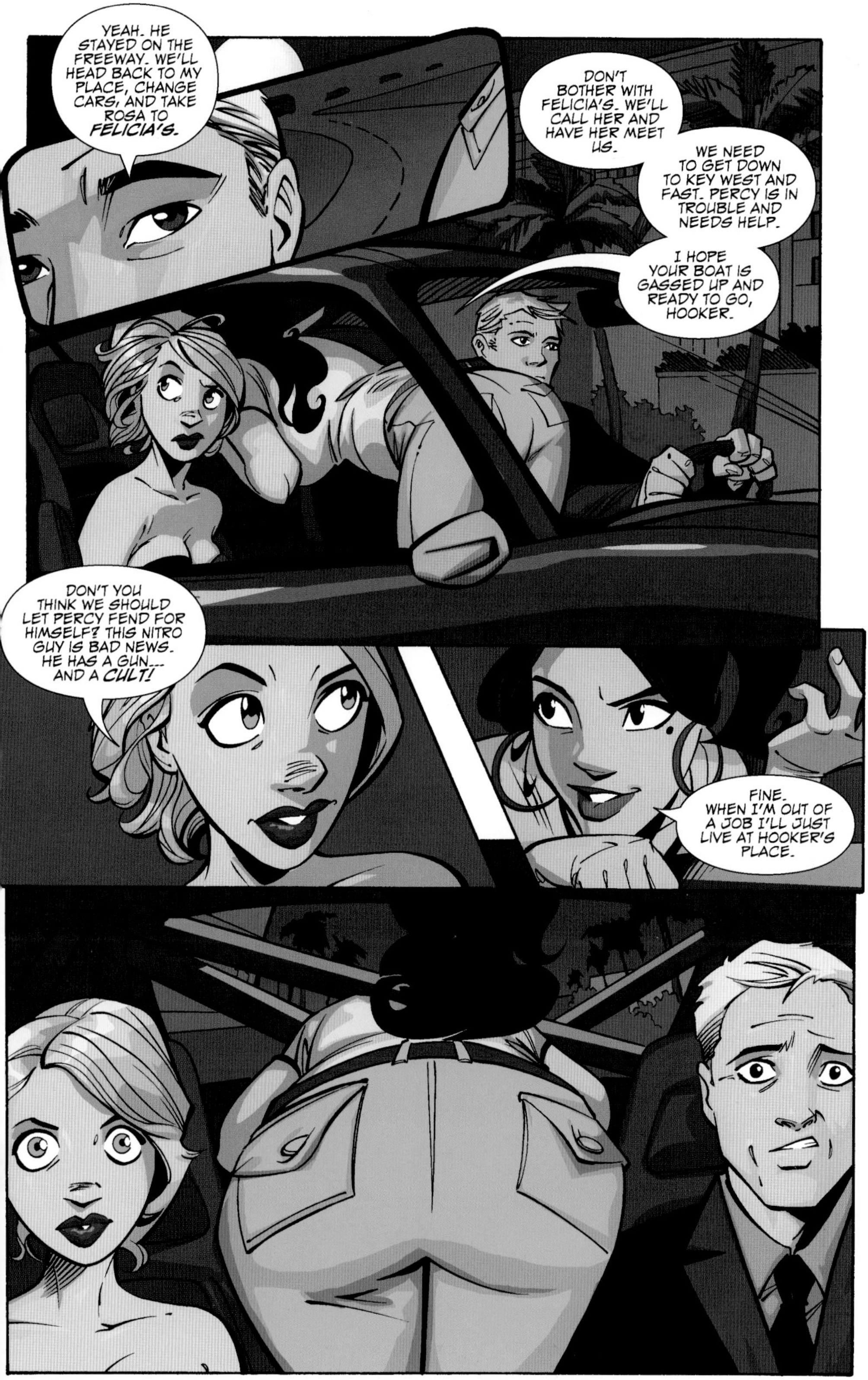
YEAH. HE STAYED ON THE FREEWAY. WE'LL HEAD BACK TO MY PLACE, CHANGE CARS, AND TAKE ROSA TO *FELICIA'S.*
DON'T BOTHER WITH FELICIA'S. WE'LL CALL HER AND HAVE HER MEET US.
WE NEED TO GET DOWN TO KEY WEST AND FAST. PERCY IS IN TROUBLE AND NEEDS HELP.
I HOPE YOUR BOAT IS GASSED UP AND READY TO GO, HOOKER.
DON'T YOU THINK WE SHOULD LET PERCY FEND FOR HIMSELF? THIS NITRO GUY IS BAD NEWS. HE HAS A GUN... AND A *CULT!*
FINE. WHEN I'M OUT OF A JOB I'LL JUST LIVE AT HOOKER'S PLACE.

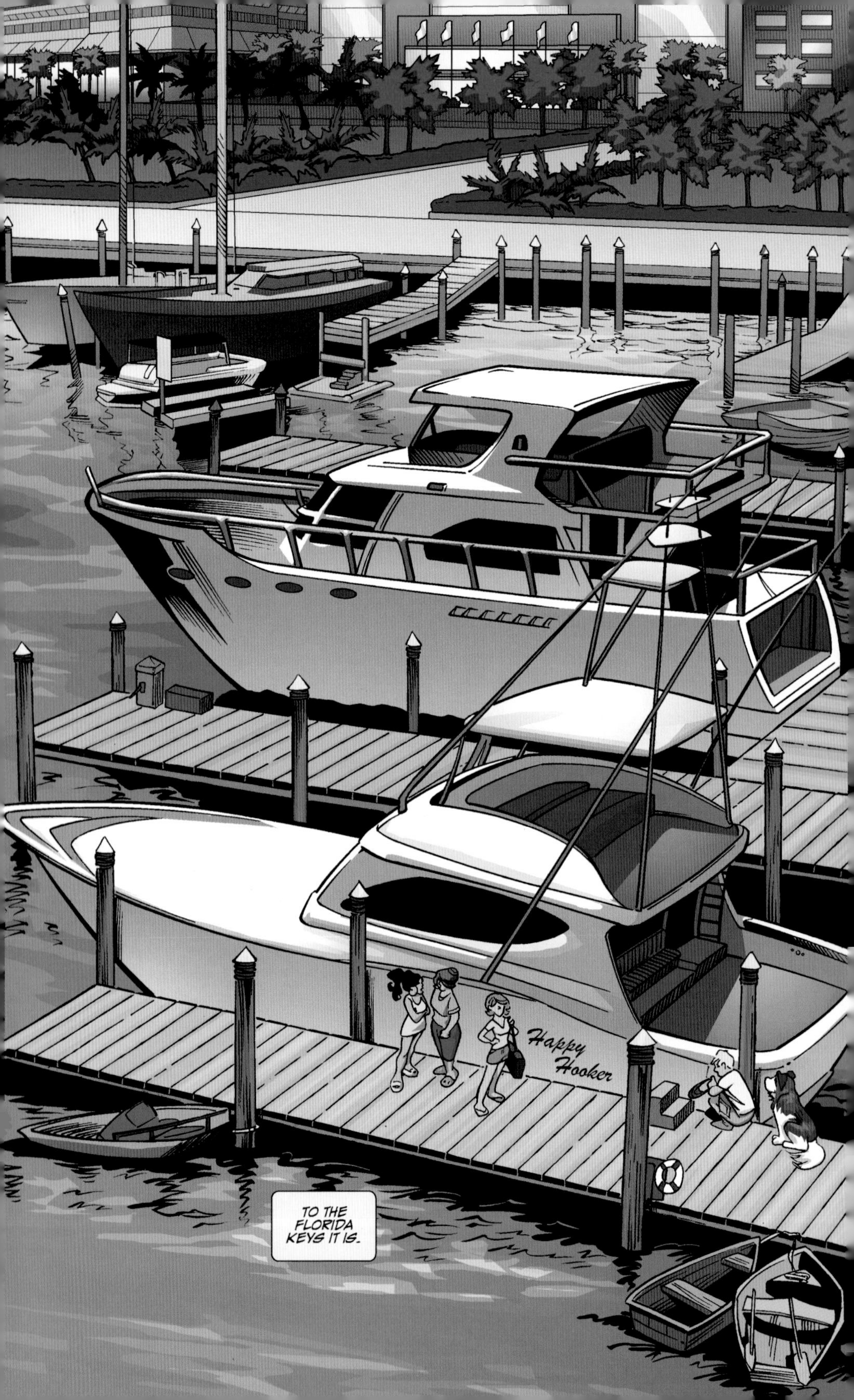
Happy Hooker
TO THE FLORIDA KEYS IT IS.

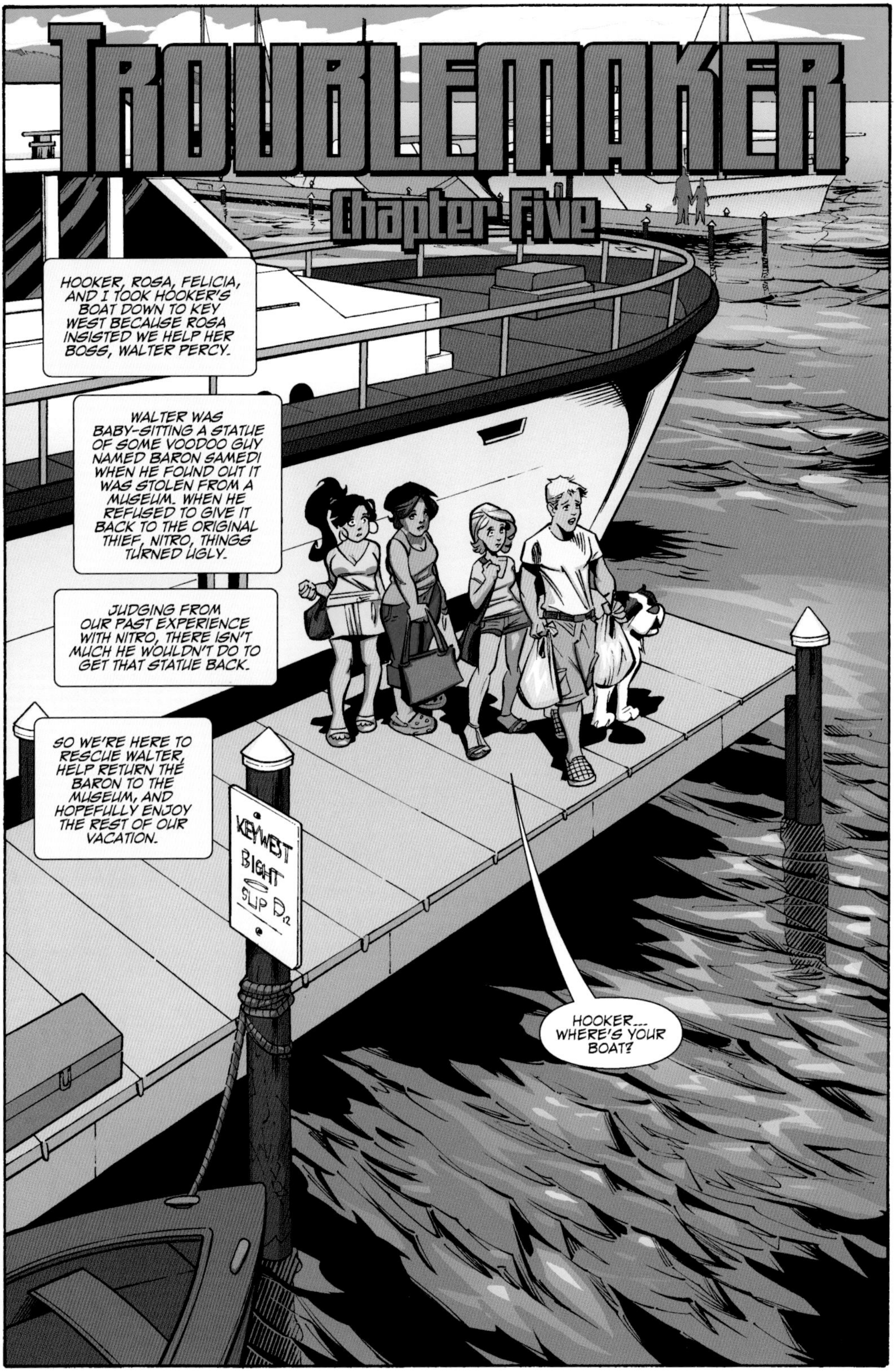
TROUBLEMAKER
Chapter Five
HOOKER, ROSA, FELICIA, AND I TOOK HOOKER'S BOAT DOWN TO KEY WEST BECAUSE ROSA INSISTED WE HELP HER BOSS, WALTER PERCY.
WALTER WAS BABY-SITTING A STATUE OF SOME VOODOO GUY NAMED BARON SAMEDI WHEN HE FOUND OUT IT WAS STOLEN FROM A MUSEUM. WHEN HE REFUSED TO GIVE IT BACK TO THE ORIGINAL THIEF, NITRO, THINGS TURNED UGLY.
JUDGING FROM OUR PAST EXPERIENCE WITH NITRO, THERE ISN'T MUCH HE WOULDN'T DO TO GET THAT STATUE BACK.
SO WE'RE HERE TO RESCUE WALTER, HELP RETURN THE BARON TO THE MUSEUM, AND HOPEFULLY ENJOY THE REST OF OUR VACATION.
KEYWEST BIGHT SLIP D12
HOOKER... WHERE'S YOUR BOAT?

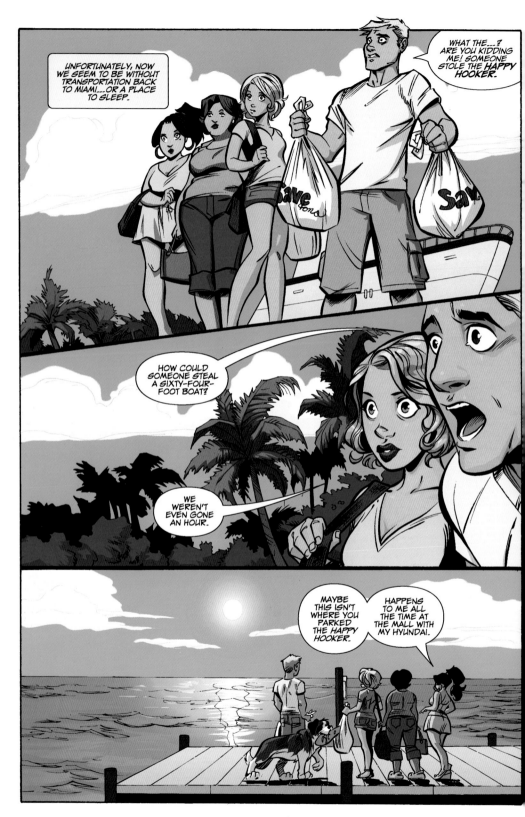

UNFORTUNATELY, NOW WE SEEM TO BE WITHOUT TRANSPORTATION BACK TO MIAMI....OR A PLACE TO SLEEP.

WHAT THE...? ARE YOU KIDDING ME! SOMEONE STOLE THE *HAPPY HOOKER.*

HOW COULD SOMEONE STEAL A SIXTY-FOUR-FOOT BOAT?

WE WEREN'T EVEN GONE AN HOUR.

MAYBE THIS ISN'T WHERE YOU PARKED THE *HAPPY HOOKER.*

HAPPENS TO ME ALL THE TIME AT THE MALL WITH MY HYUNDAI.

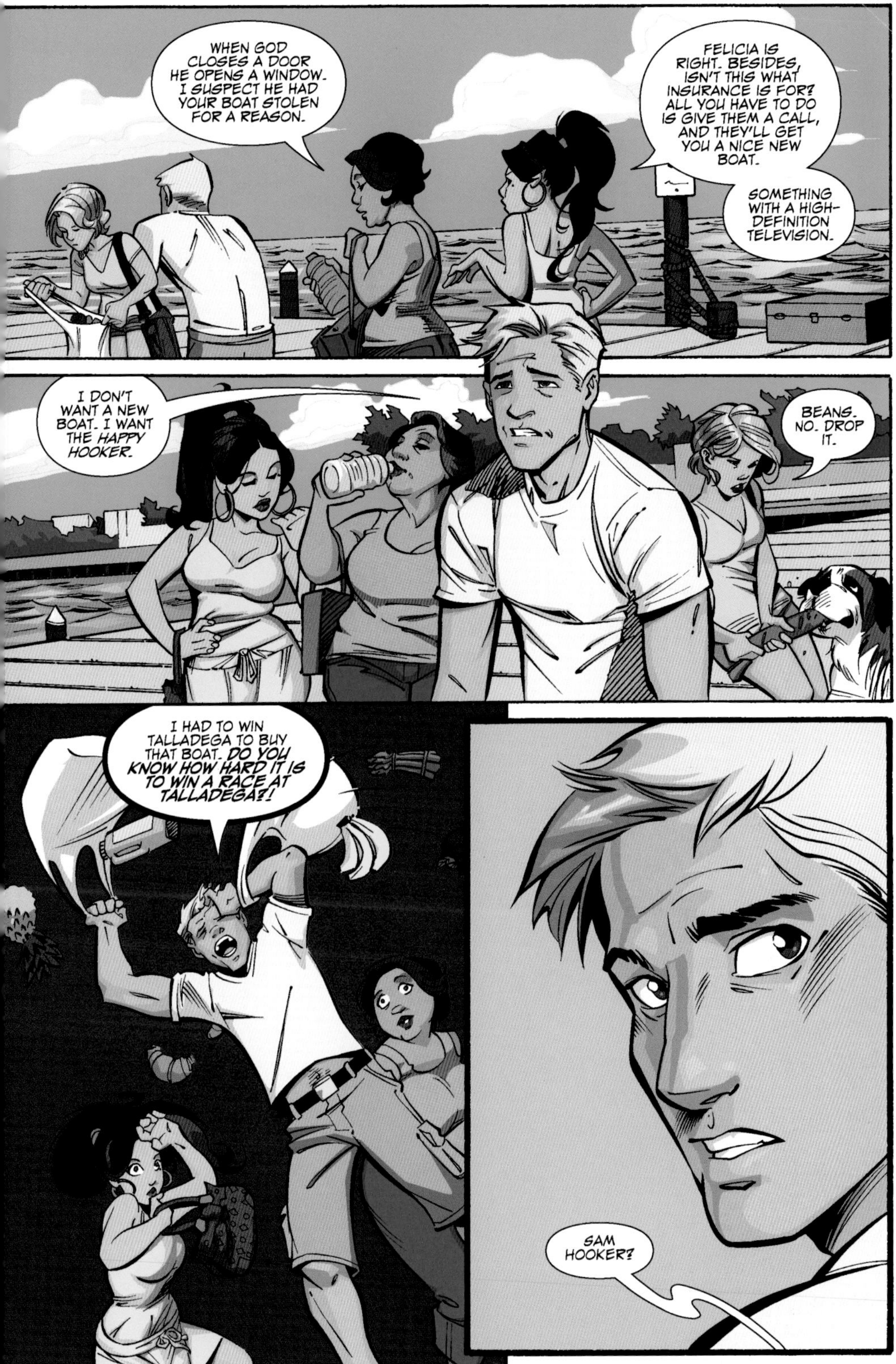
WHEN GOD CLOSES A DOOR HE OPENS A WINDOW. I SUSPECT HE HAD YOUR BOAT STOLEN FOR A REASON.
FELICIA IS RIGHT. BESIDES, ISN'T THIS WHAT INSURANCE IS FOR? ALL YOU HAVE TO DO IS GIVE THEM A CALL, AND THEY'LL GET YOU A NICE NEW BOAT.
SOMETHING WITH A HIGH-DEFINITION TELEVISION.
I DON'T WANT A NEW BOAT. I WANT THE *HAPPY HOOKER*.
BEANS. NO. DROP IT.
I HAD TO WIN TALLADEGA TO BUY THAT BOAT. ***DO YOU KNOW HOW HARD IT IS TO WIN A RACE AT TALLADEGA?!***
SAM HOOKER?

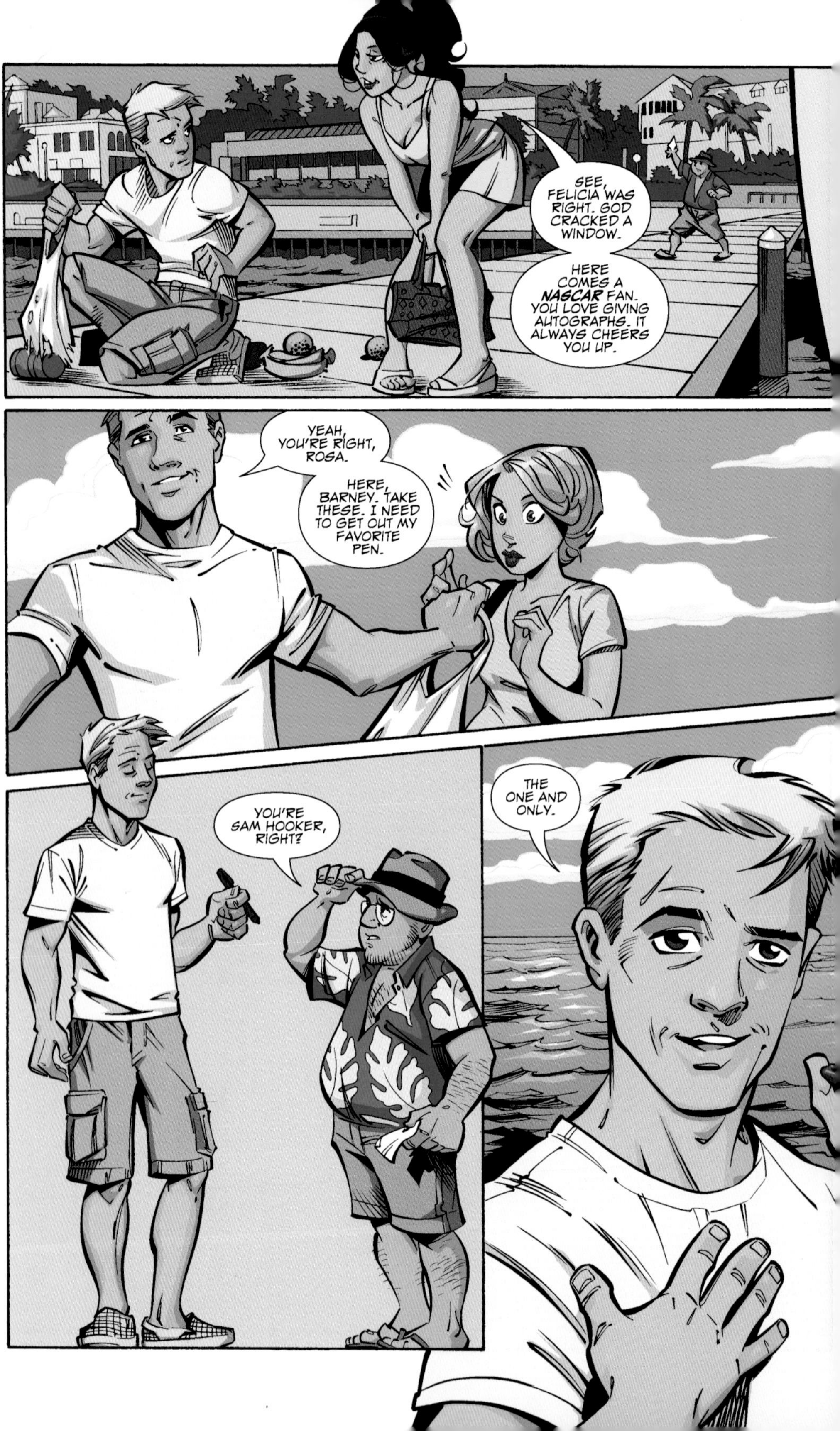
SEE, FELICIA WAS RIGHT. GOD CRACKED A WINDOW.
HERE COMES A **NASCAR** FAN. YOU LOVE GIVING AUTOGRAPHS. IT ALWAYS CHEERS YOU UP.
YEAH, YOU'RE RIGHT, ROSA.
HERE, BARNEY. TAKE THESE. I NEED TO GET OUT MY FAVORITE PEN.
YOU'RE SAM HOOKER, RIGHT?
THE ONE AND ONLY.

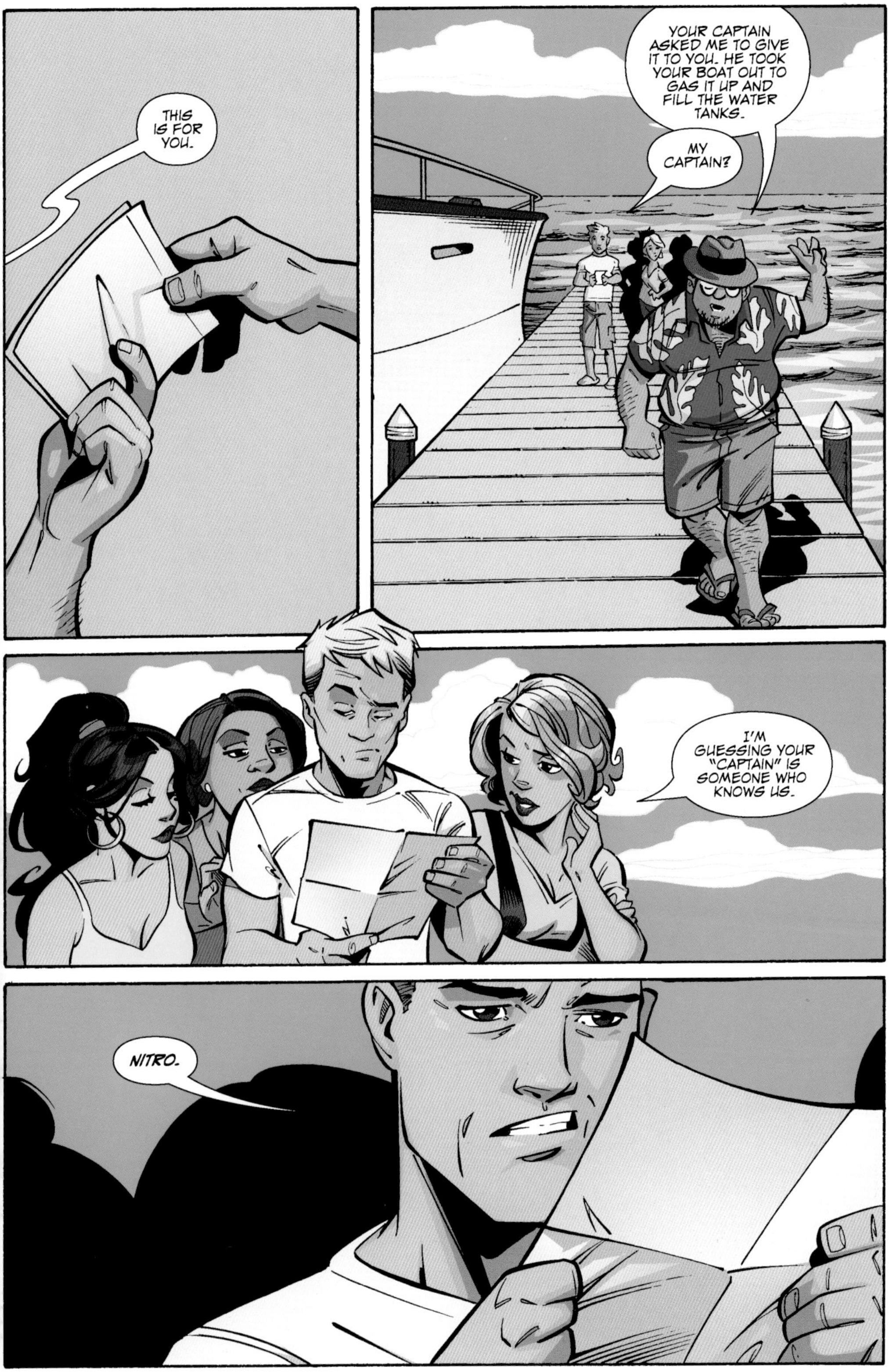
THIS IS FOR YOU.
YOUR CAPTAIN ASKED ME TO GIVE IT TO YOU. HE TOOK YOUR BOAT OUT TO GAS IT UP AND FILL THE WATER TANKS.
MY CAPTAIN?
I'M GUESSING YOUR "CAPTAIN" IS SOMEONE WHO KNOWS US.
NITRO.

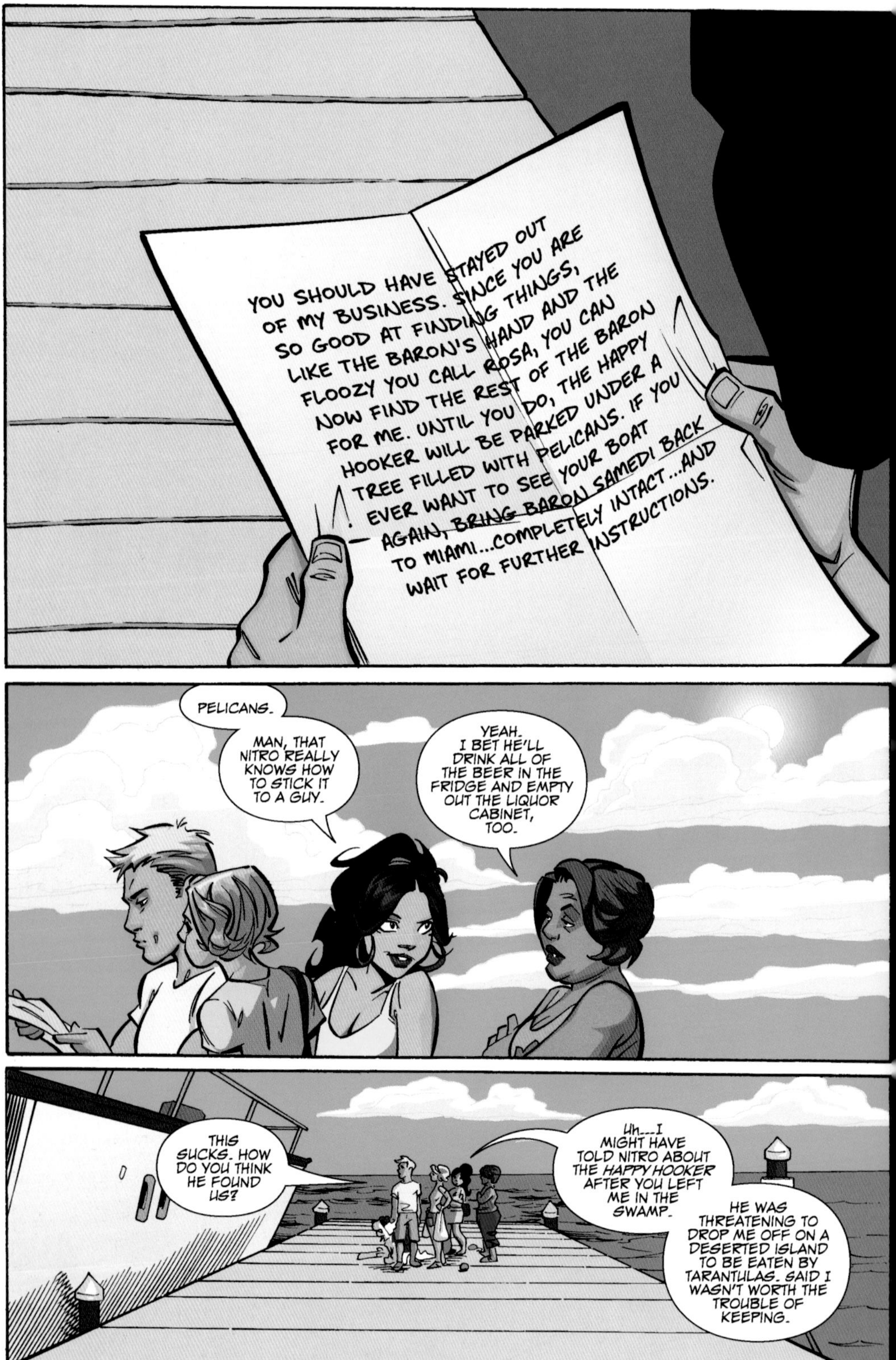
YOU SHOULD HAVE STAYED OUT OF MY BUSINESS. SINCE YOU ARE SO GOOD AT FINDING THINGS, LIKE THE BARON'S HAND AND THE FLOOZY YOU CALL ROSA, YOU CAN NOW FIND THE REST OF THE BARON FOR ME. UNTIL YOU DO, THE HAPPY HOOKER WILL BE PARKED UNDER A TREE FILLED WITH PELICANS. IF YOU EVER WANT TO SEE YOUR BOAT AGAIN, BRING BARON SAMEDI BACK TO MIAMI...COMPLETELY INTACT...AND WAIT FOR FURTHER INSTRUCTIONS.
PELICANS.
MAN, THAT NITRO REALLY KNOWS HOW TO STICK IT TO A GUY.
YEAH. I BET HE'LL DRINK ALL OF THE BEER IN THE FRIDGE AND EMPTY OUT THE LIQUOR CABINET, TOO.
THIS SUCKS. HOW DO YOU THINK HE FOUND US?
UH...I MIGHT HAVE TOLD NITRO ABOUT THE *HAPPY HOOKER* AFTER YOU LEFT ME IN THE SWAMP.
HE WAS THREATENING TO DROP ME OFF ON A DESERTED ISLAND TO BE EATEN BY TARANTULAS. SAID I WASN'T WORTH THE TROUBLE OF KEEPING.

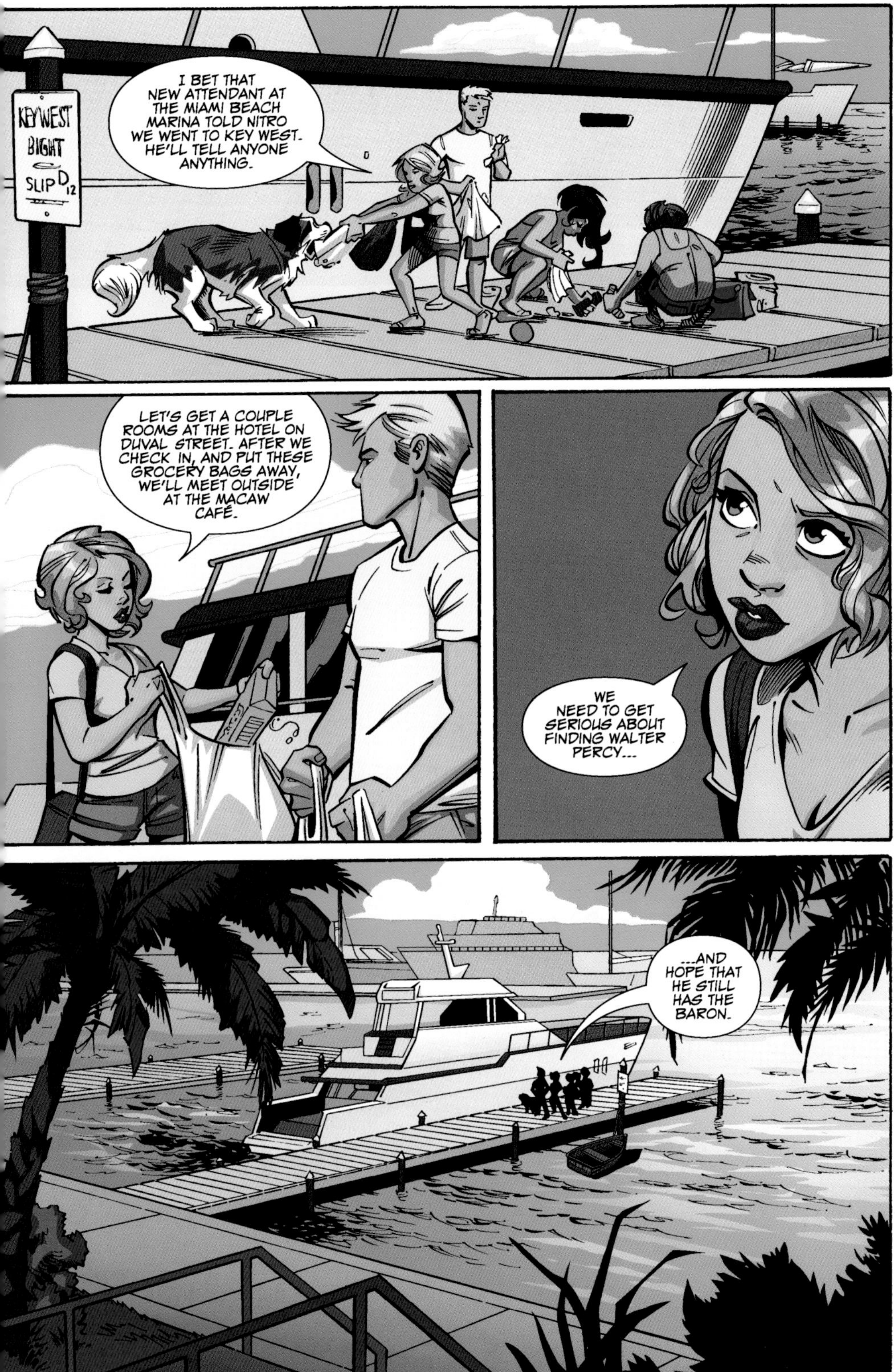
KEY WEST
BIGHT
SLIP D 12
I BET THAT NEW ATTENDANT AT THE MIAMI BEACH MARINA TOLD NITRO WE WENT TO KEY WEST. HE'LL TELL ANYONE ANYTHING.
LET'S GET A COUPLE ROOMS AT THE HOTEL ON DUVAL STREET. AFTER WE CHECK IN, AND PUT THESE GROCERY BAGS AWAY, WE'LL MEET OUTSIDE AT THE MACAW CAFÉ.
WE NEED TO GET SERIOUS ABOUT FINDING WALTER PERCY...
...AND HOPE THAT HE STILL HAS THE BARON.

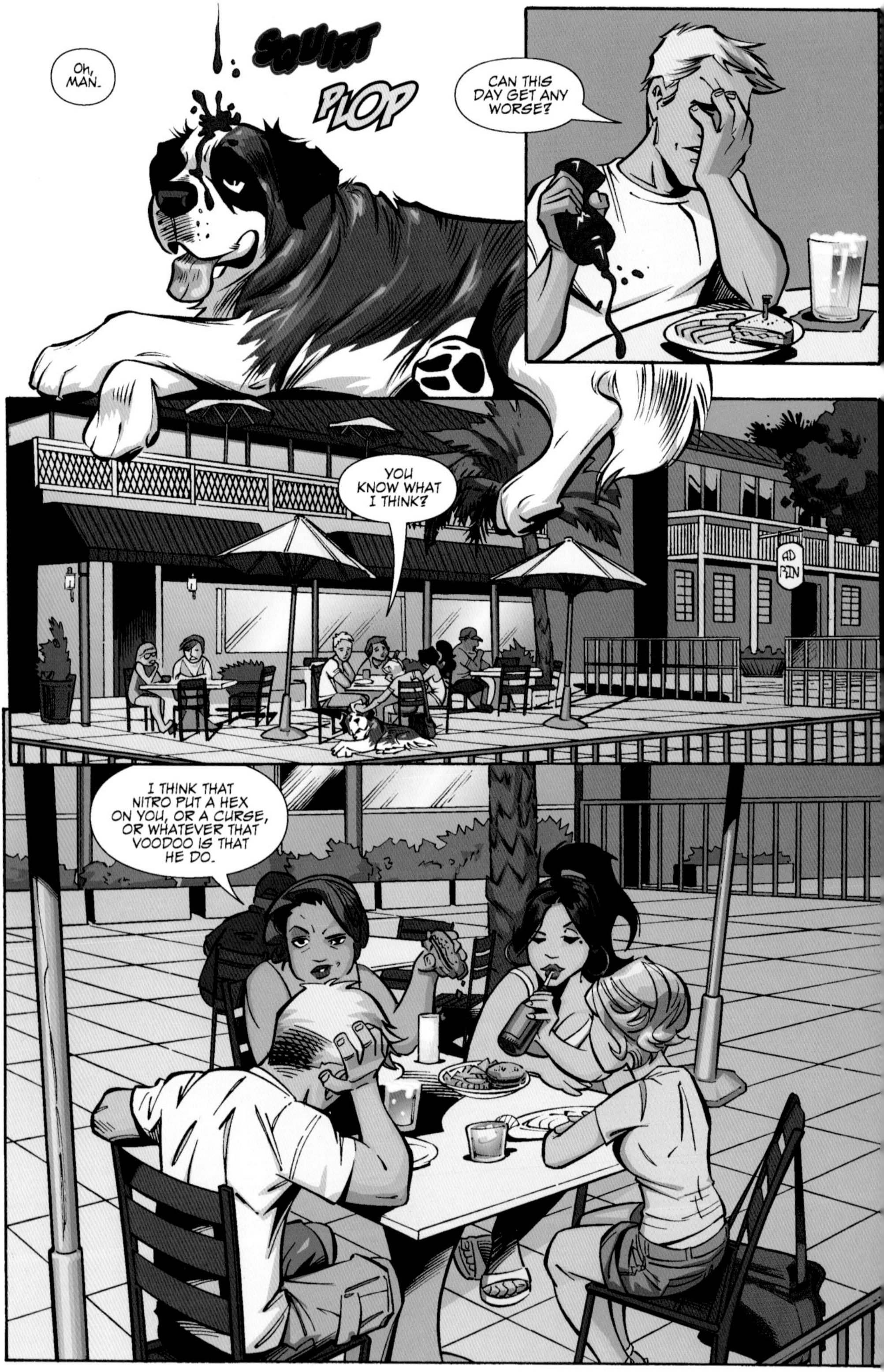
Oh, MAN.
SQUIRT
PLOP
CAN THIS DAY GET ANY WORSE?
YOU KNOW WHAT I THINK?
I THINK THAT NITRO PUT A HEX ON YOU, OR A CURSE, OR WHATEVER THAT VOODOO IS THAT HE DO.

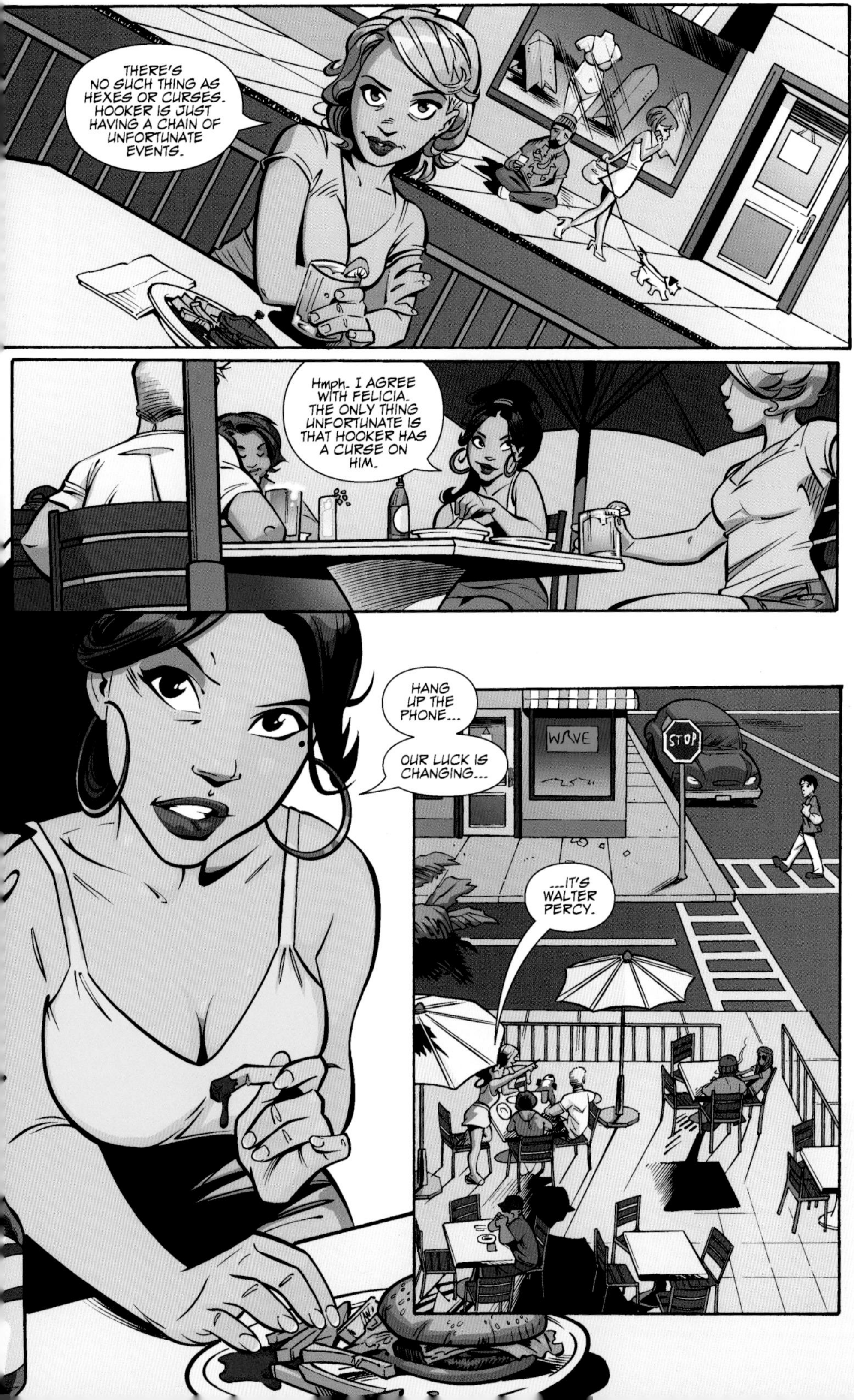
THERE'S NO SUCH THING AS HEXES OR CURSES. HOOKER IS JUST HAVING A CHAIN OF UNFORTUNATE EVENTS.
Hmph. I AGREE WITH FELICIA. THE ONLY THING UNFORTUNATE IS THAT HOOKER HAS A CURSE ON HIM.
HANG UP THE PHONE...
OUR LUCK IS CHANGING...
...IT'S WALTER PERCY.
STOP

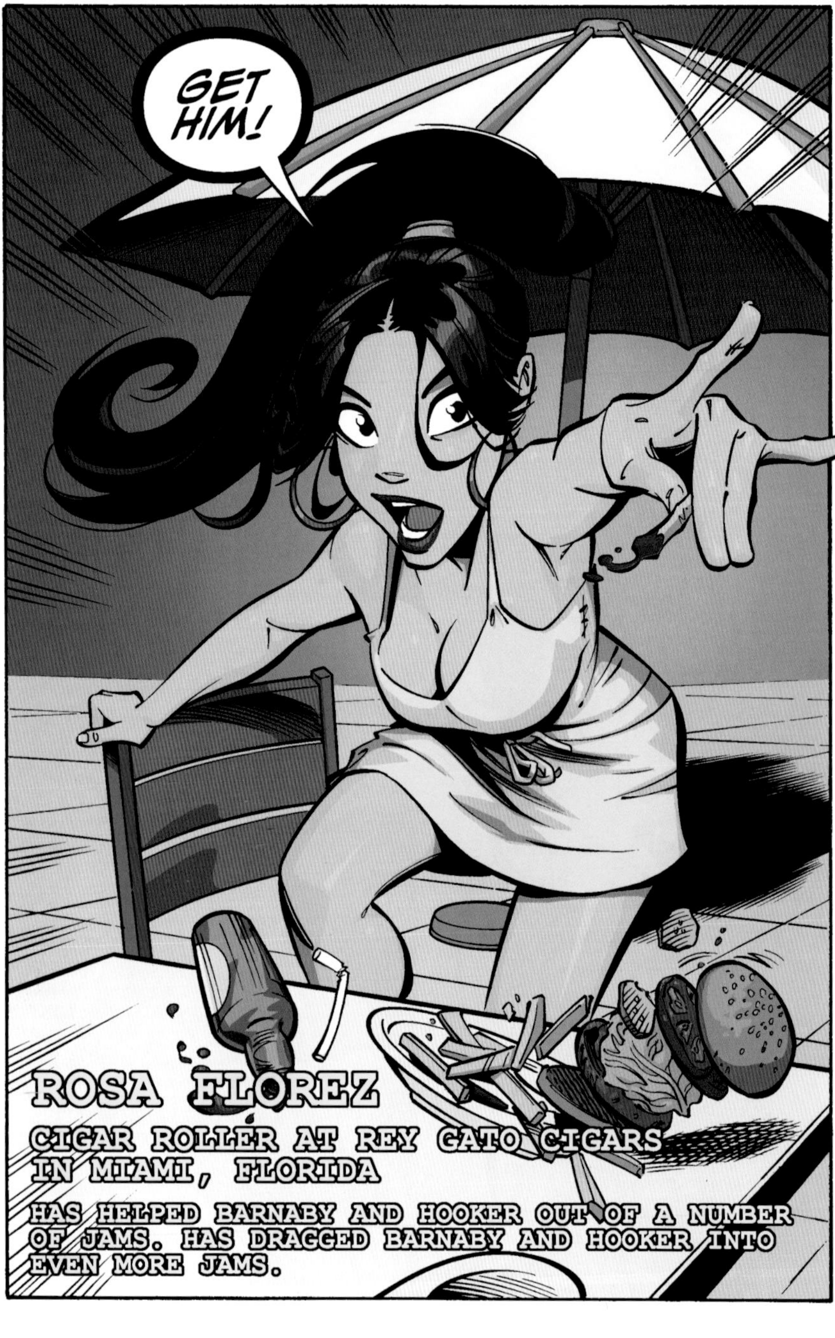
GET HIM!
ROSA FLOREZ
CIGAR ROLLER AT REY GATO CIGARS IN MIAMI, FLORIDA
HAS HELPED BARNABY AND HOOKER OUT OF A NUMBER OF JAMS. HAS DRAGGED BARNABY AND HOOKER INTO EVEN MORE JAMS.

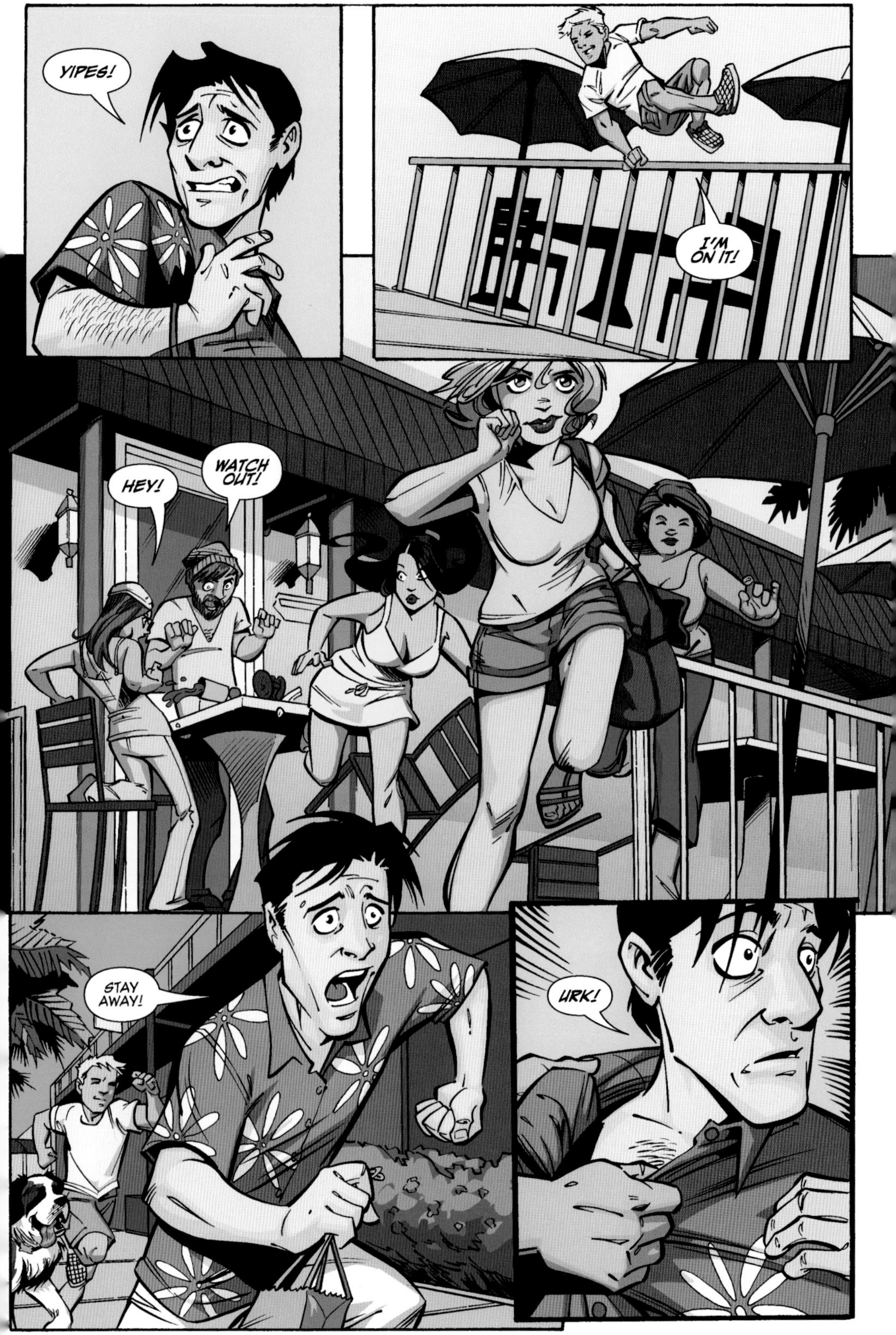
YIPES!
I'M ON IT!
HEY!
WATCH OUT!
STAY AWAY!
URK!

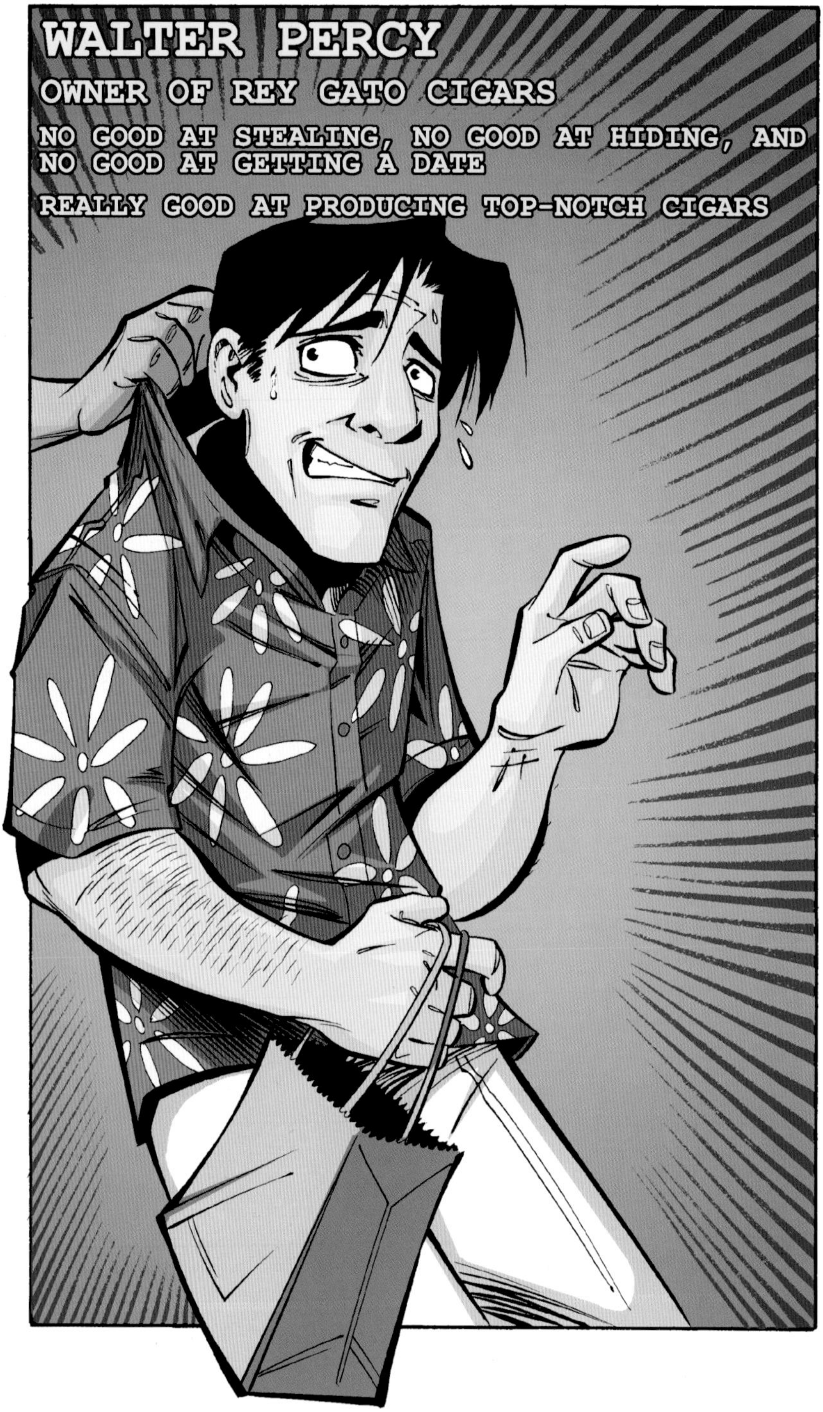
WALTER PERCY
OWNER OF REY GATO CIGARS
NO GOOD AT STEALING, NO GOOD AT HIDING, AND NO GOOD AT GETTING A DATE
REALLY GOOD AT PRODUCING TOP-NOTCH CIGARS

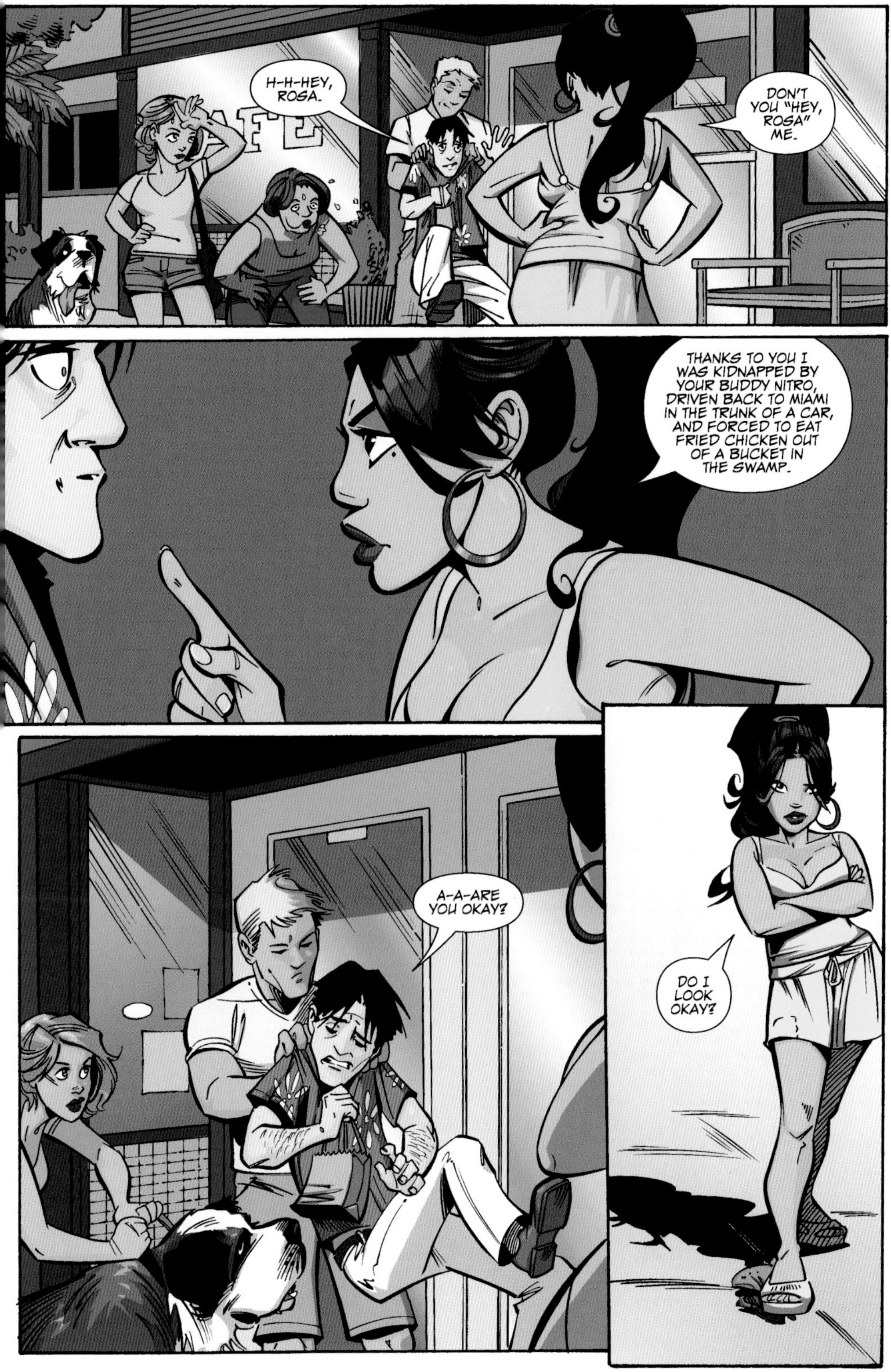
H-H-HEY, ROSA.
DON'T YOU "HEY, ROSA" ME.
THANKS TO YOU I WAS KIDNAPPED BY YOUR BUDDY NITRO, DRIVEN BACK TO MIAMI IN THE TRUNK OF A CAR, AND FORCED TO EAT FRIED CHICKEN OUT OF A BUCKET IN THE SWAMP.
A-A-ARE YOU OKAY?
DO I LOOK OKAY?

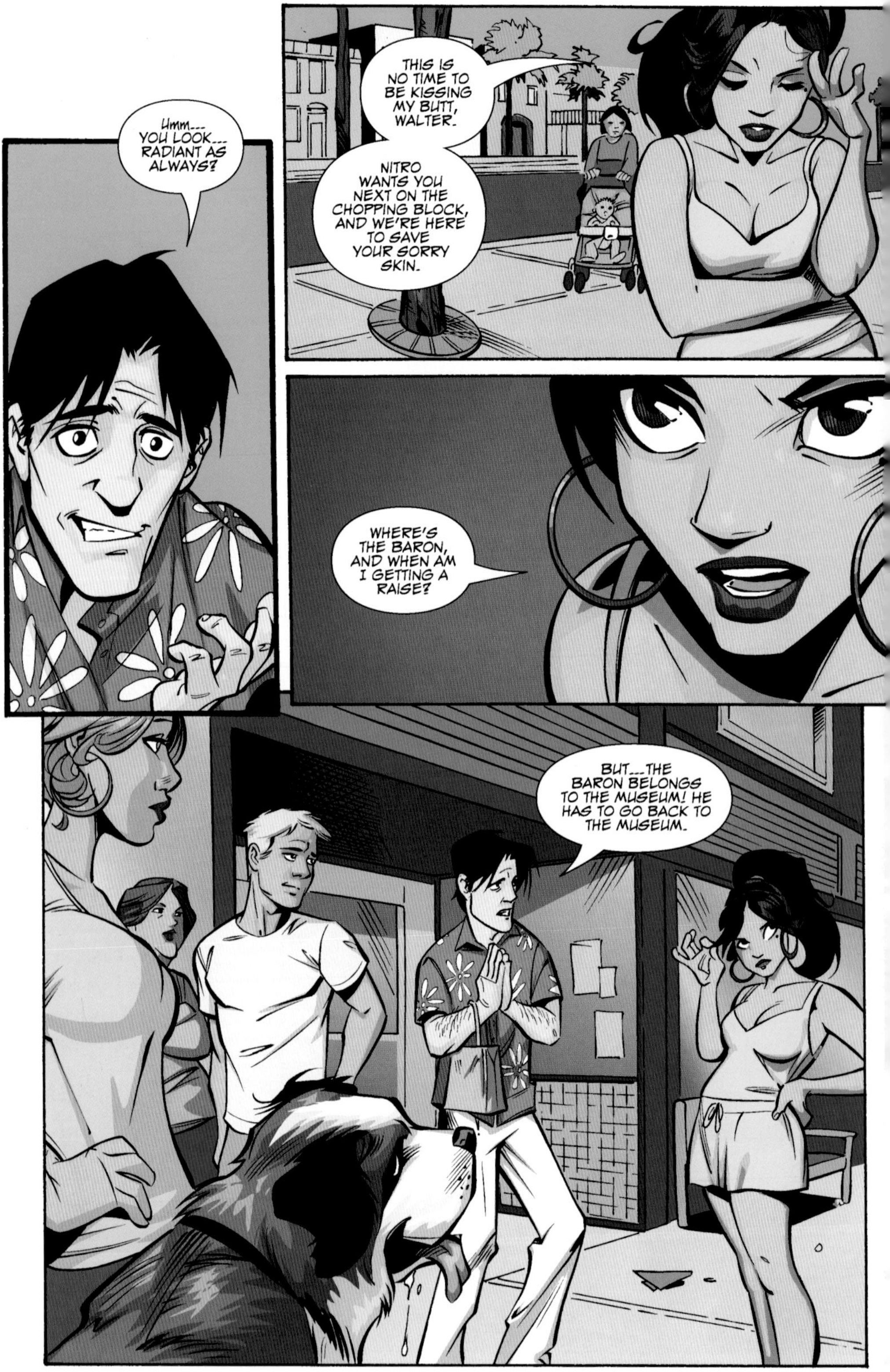
THIS IS NO TIME TO BE KISSING MY BUTT, WALTER.
NITRO WANTS YOU NEXT ON THE CHOPPING BLOCK, AND WE'RE HERE TO SAVE YOUR SORRY SKIN.
UMM... YOU LOOK... RADIANT AS ALWAYS?
WHERE'S THE BARON, AND WHEN AM I GETTING A RAISE?
BUT... THE BARON BELONGS TO THE MUSEUM! HE HAS TO GO BACK TO THE MUSEUM.

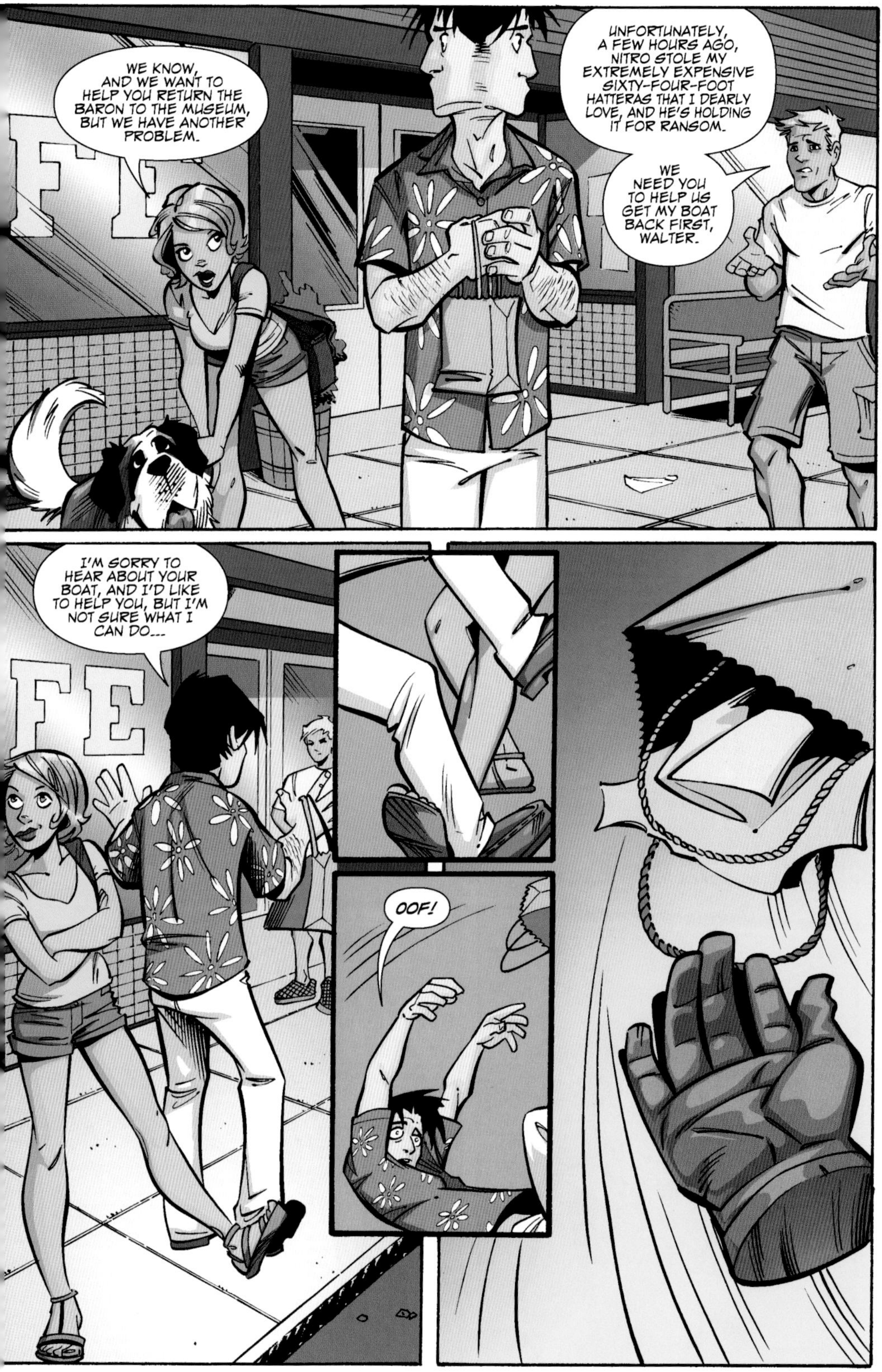
WE KNOW, AND WE WANT TO HELP YOU RETURN THE BARON TO THE MUSEUM, BUT WE HAVE ANOTHER PROBLEM.
UNFORTUNATELY, A FEW HOURS AGO, NITRO STOLE MY EXTREMELY EXPENSIVE SIXTY-FOUR-FOOT HATTERAS THAT I DEARLY LOVE, AND HE'S HOLDING IT FOR RANSOM.
WE NEED YOU TO HELP US GET MY BOAT BACK FIRST, WALTER.
I'M SORRY TO HEAR ABOUT YOUR BOAT, AND I'D LIKE TO HELP YOU, BUT I'M NOT SURE WHAT I CAN DO...
OOF!

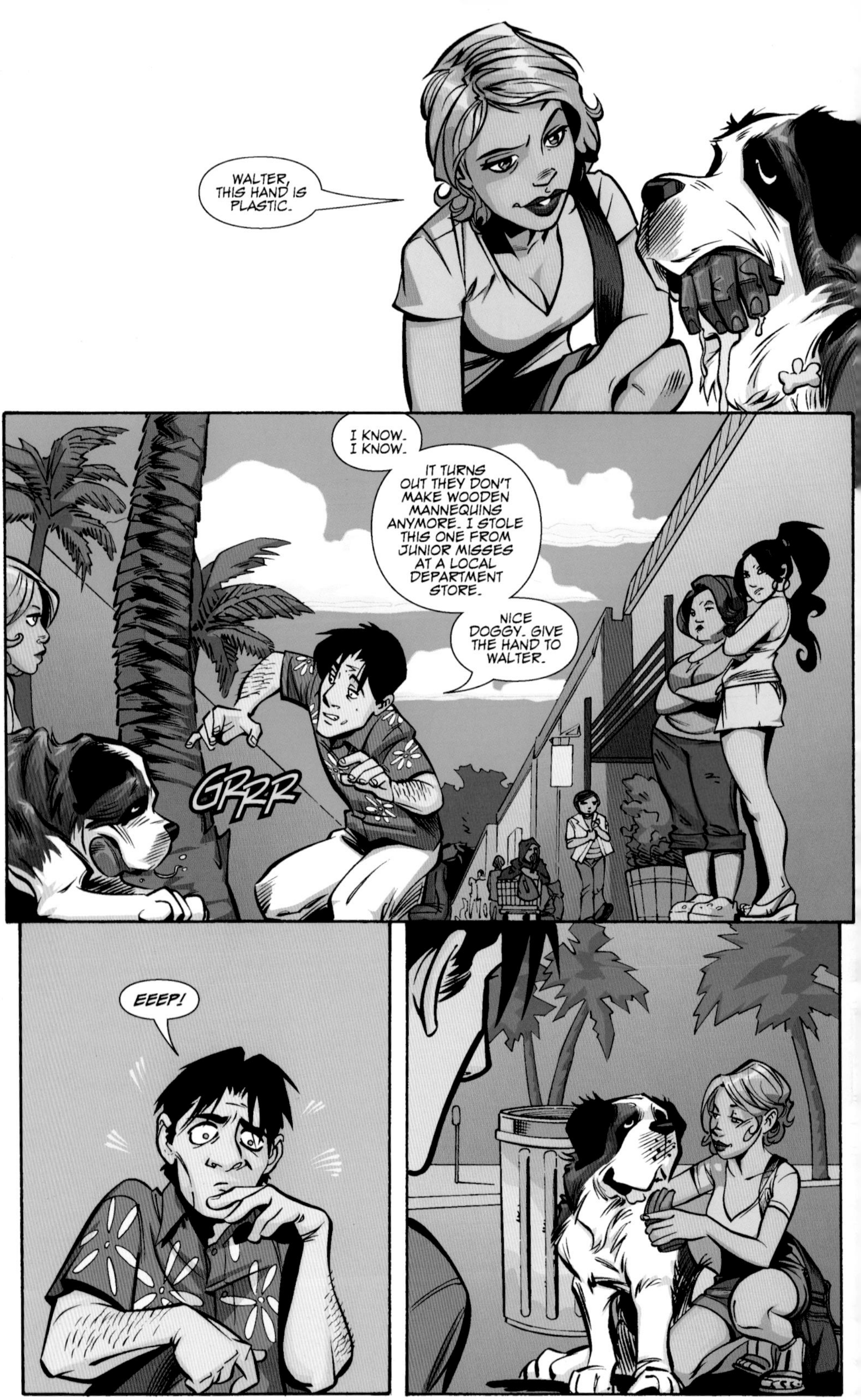
WALTER, THIS HAND IS PLASTIC.
I KNOW. I KNOW.
IT TURNS OUT THEY DON'T MAKE WOODEN MANNEQUINS ANYMORE. I STOLE THIS ONE FROM JUNIOR MISSES AT A LOCAL DEPARTMENT STORE.
NICE DOGGY. GIVE THE HAND TO WALTER.
GRRR
EEEP!

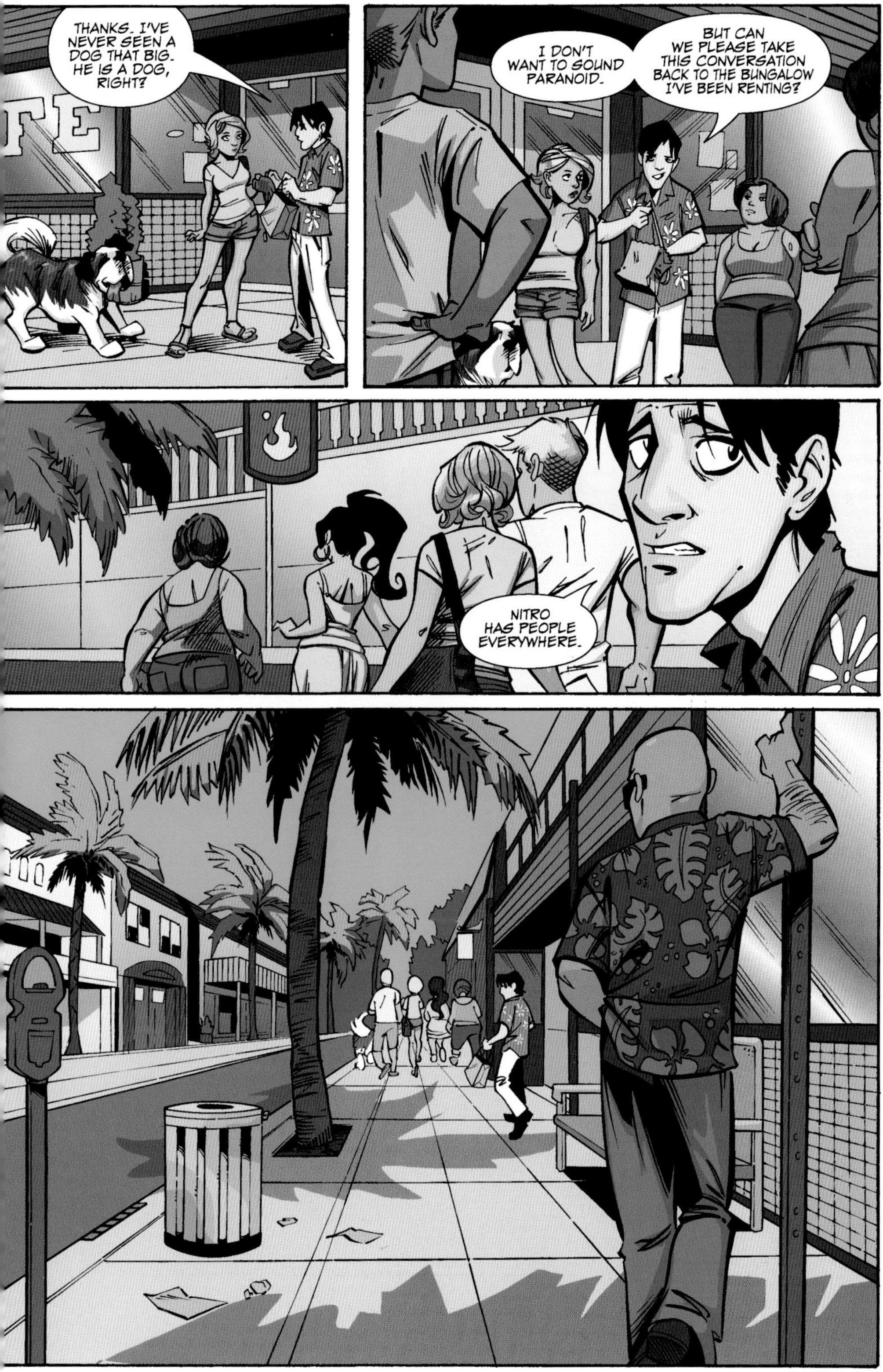
THANKS. I'VE NEVER SEEN A DOG THAT BIG. HE IS A DOG, RIGHT?
I DON'T WANT TO SOUND PARANOID.
BUT CAN WE PLEASE TAKE THIS CONVERSATION BACK TO THE BUNGALOW I'VE BEEN RENTING?
NITRO HAS PEOPLE EVERYWHERE.

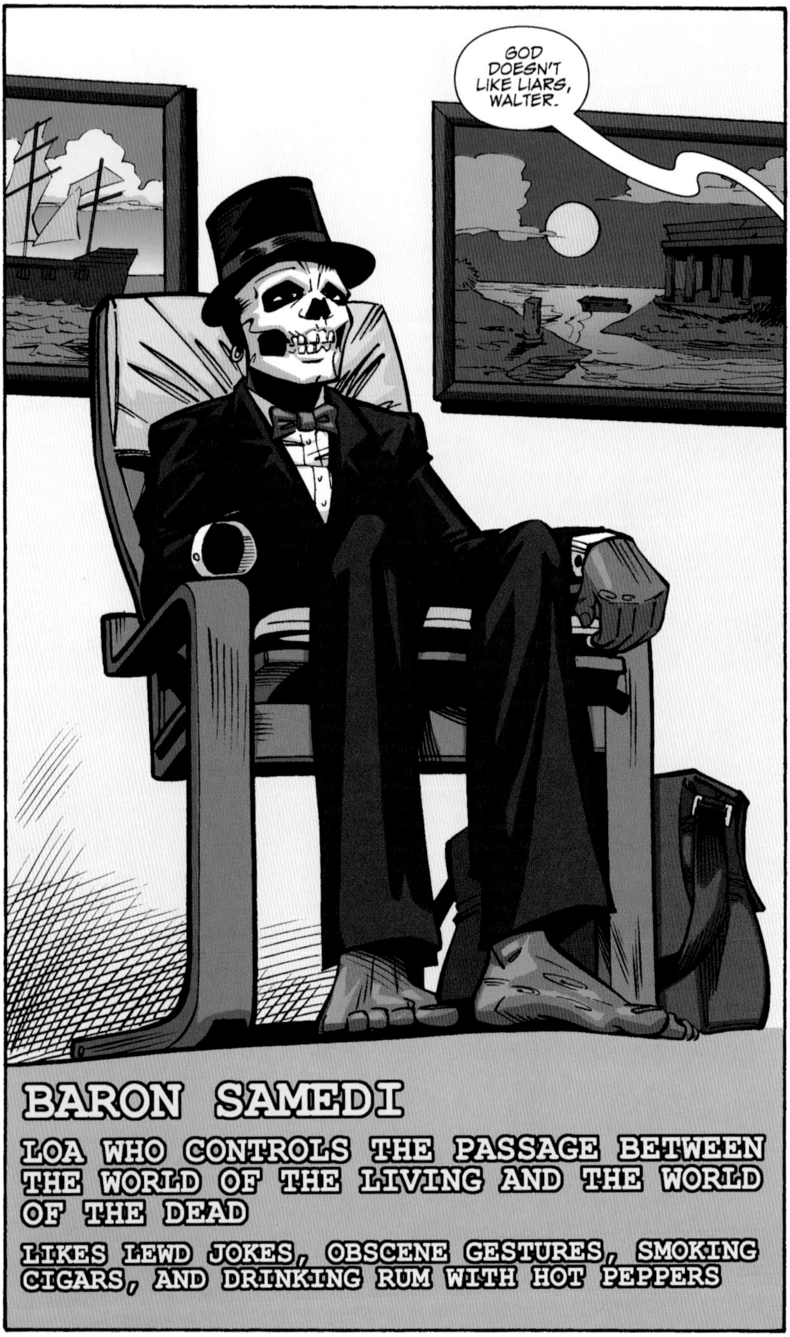
GOD DOESN'T LIKE LIARS, WALTER.
BARON SAMEDI
LOA WHO CONTROLS THE PASSAGE BETWEEN THE WORLD OF THE LIVING AND THE WORLD OF THE DEAD
LIKES LEWD JOKES, OBSCENE GESTURES, SMOKING CIGARS, AND DRINKING RUM WITH HOT PEPPERS

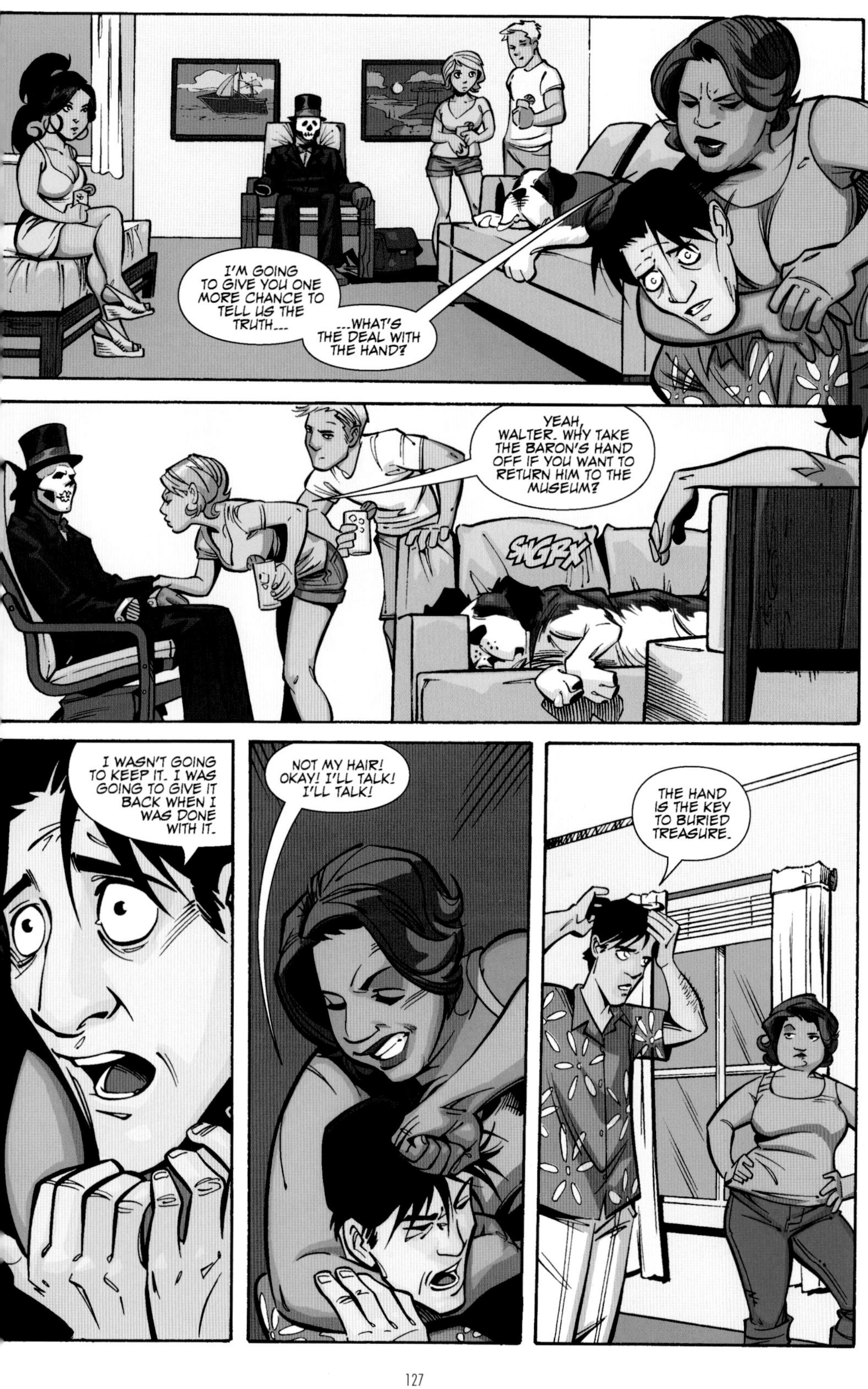
I'M GOING TO GIVE YOU ONE MORE CHANCE TO TELL US THE TRUTH---
---WHAT'S THE DEAL WITH THE HAND?
YEAH, WALTER. WHY TAKE THE BARON'S HAND OFF IF YOU WANT TO RETURN HIM TO THE MUSEUM?
SNGRX
I WASN'T GOING TO KEEP IT. I WAS GOING TO GIVE IT BACK WHEN I WAS DONE WITH IT.
NOT MY HAIR! OKAY! I'LL TALK! I'LL TALK!
THE HAND IS THE KEY TO BURIED TREASURE.

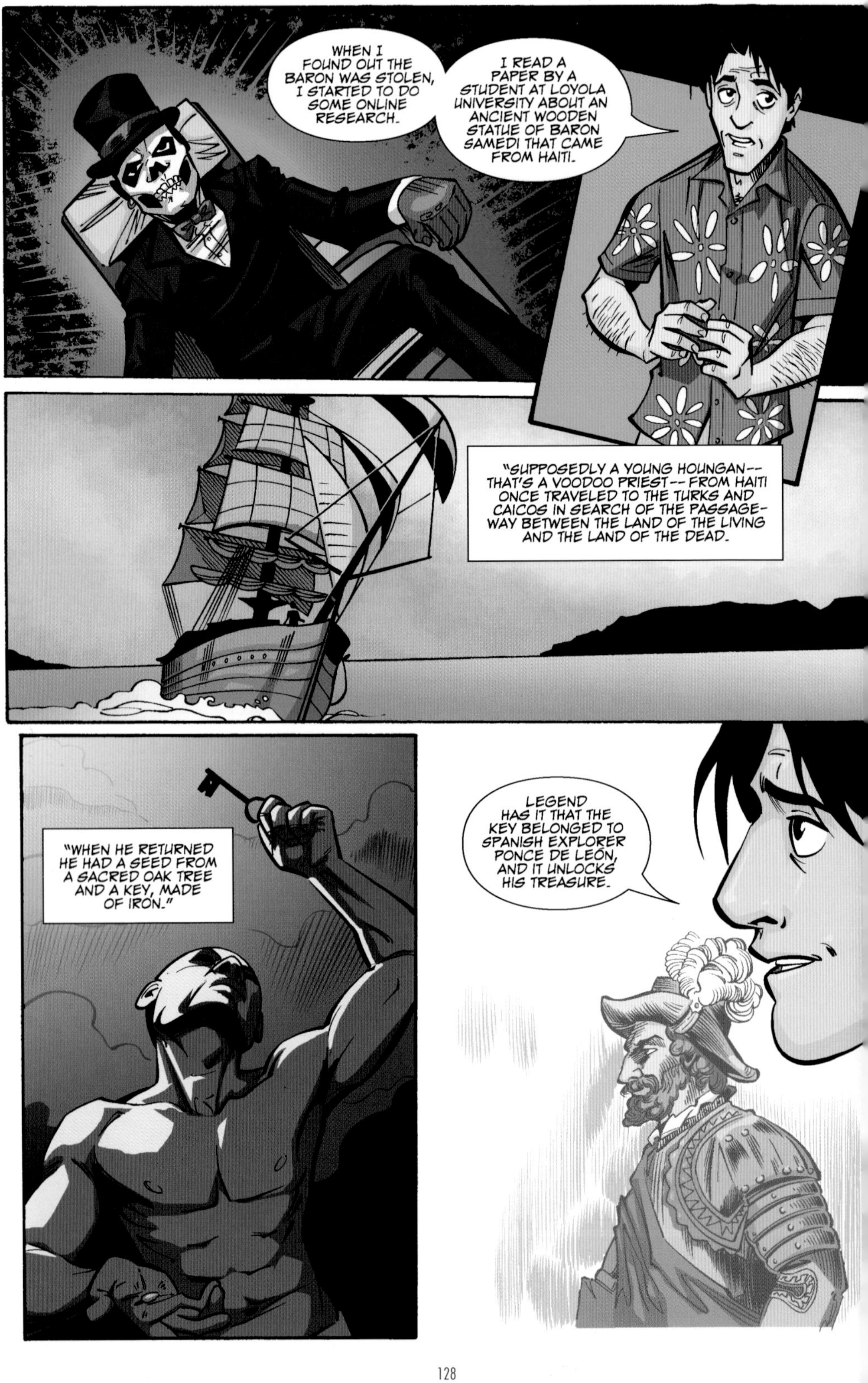
WHEN I FOUND OUT THE BARON WAS STOLEN, I STARTED TO DO SOME ONLINE RESEARCH.
I READ A PAPER BY A STUDENT AT LOYOLA UNIVERSITY ABOUT AN ANCIENT WOODEN STATUE OF BARON SAMEDI THAT CAME FROM HAITI.
"SUPPOSEDLY A YOUNG HOUNGAN-- THAT'S A VOODOO PRIEST-- FROM HAITI ONCE TRAVELED TO THE TURKS AND CAICOS IN SEARCH OF THE PASSAGEWAY BETWEEN THE LAND OF THE LIVING AND THE LAND OF THE DEAD.
"WHEN HE RETURNED HE HAD A SEED FROM A SACRED OAK TREE AND A KEY, MADE OF IRON."
LEGEND HAS IT THAT THE KEY BELONGED TO SPANISH EXPLORER PONCE DE LEÓN, AND IT UNLOCKS HIS TREASURE.

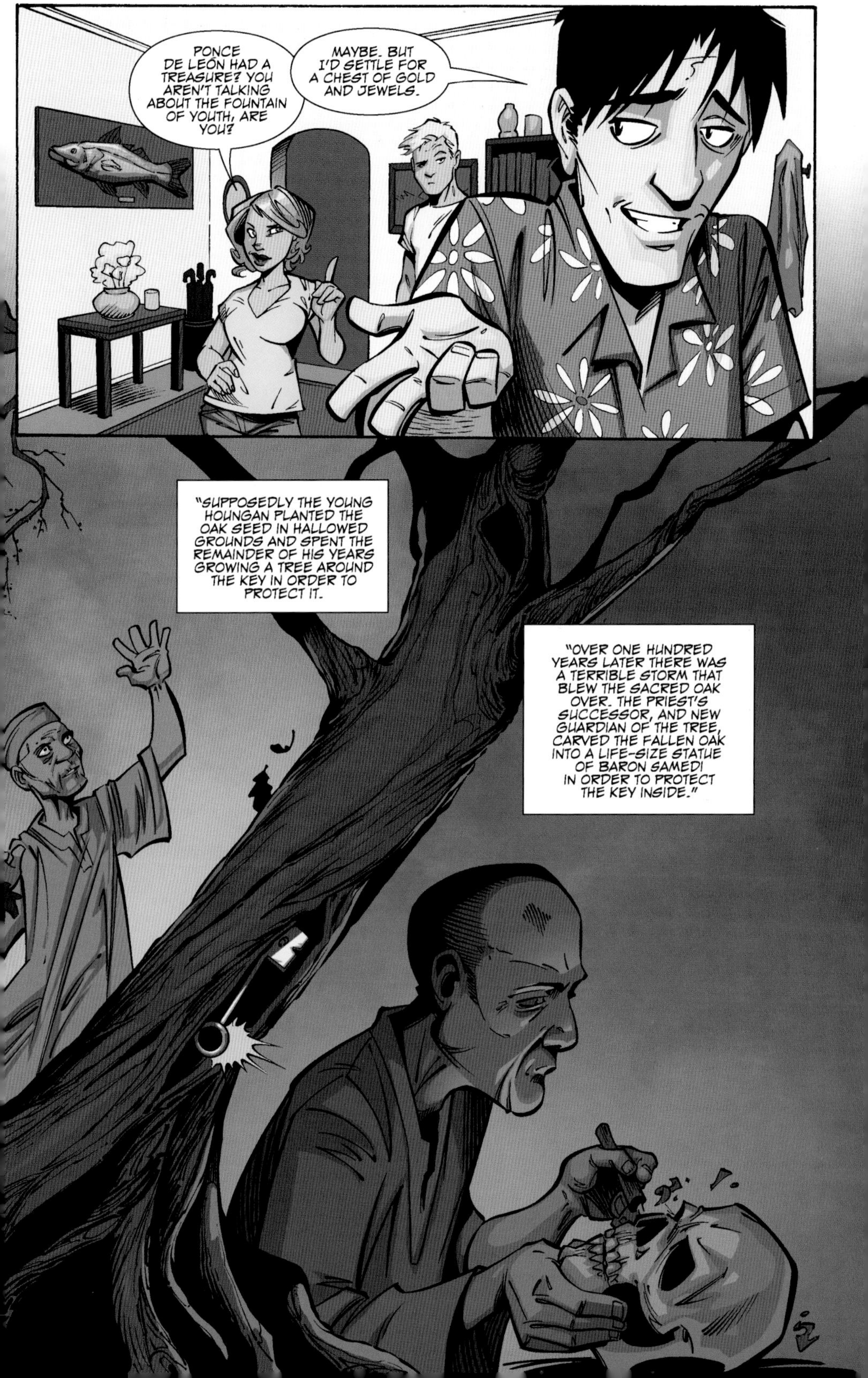
PONCE DE LEÓN HAD A TREASURE? YOU AREN'T TALKING ABOUT THE FOUNTAIN OF YOUTH, ARE YOU?
MAYBE. BUT I'D SETTLE FOR A CHEST OF GOLD AND JEWELS.
"SUPPOSEDLY THE YOUNG HOUNGAN PLANTED THE OAK SEED IN HALLOWED GROUNDS AND SPENT THE REMAINDER OF HIS YEARS GROWING A TREE AROUND THE KEY IN ORDER TO PROTECT IT.
"OVER ONE HUNDRED YEARS LATER THERE WAS A TERRIBLE STORM THAT BLEW THE SACRED OAK OVER. THE PRIEST'S SUCCESSOR, AND NEW GUARDIAN OF THE TREE, CARVED THE FALLEN OAK INTO A LIFE-SIZE STATUE OF BARON SAMEDI IN ORDER TO PROTECT THE KEY INSIDE."

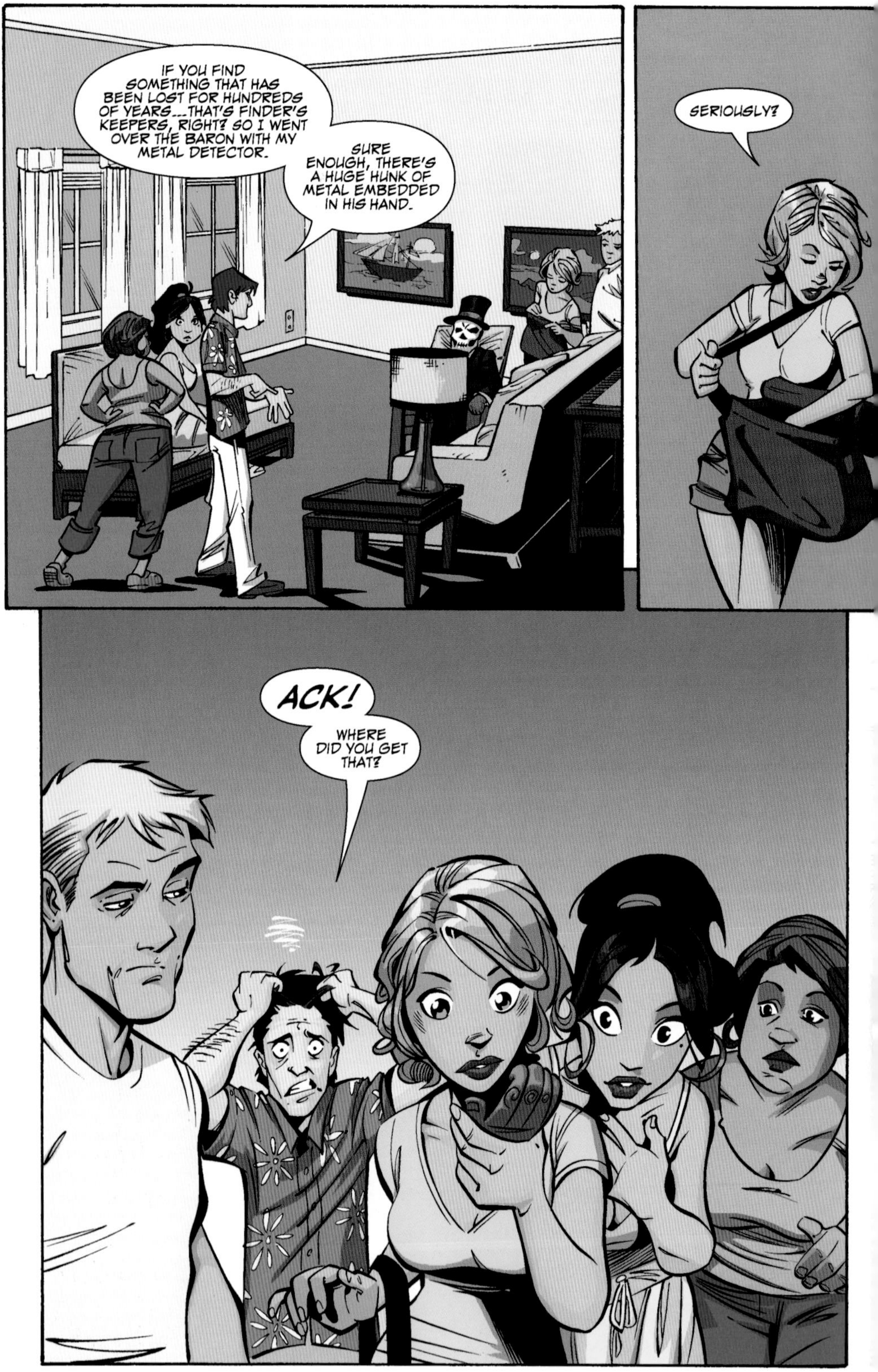

IF YOU FIND SOMETHING THAT HAS BEEN LOST FOR HUNDREDS OF YEARS...THAT'S FINDER'S KEEPERS, RIGHT? SO I WENT OVER THE BARON WITH MY METAL DETECTOR.
SURE ENOUGH, THERE'S A HUGE HUNK OF METAL EMBEDDED IN HIS HAND.
SERIOUSLY?
ACK!
WHERE DID YOU GET THAT?

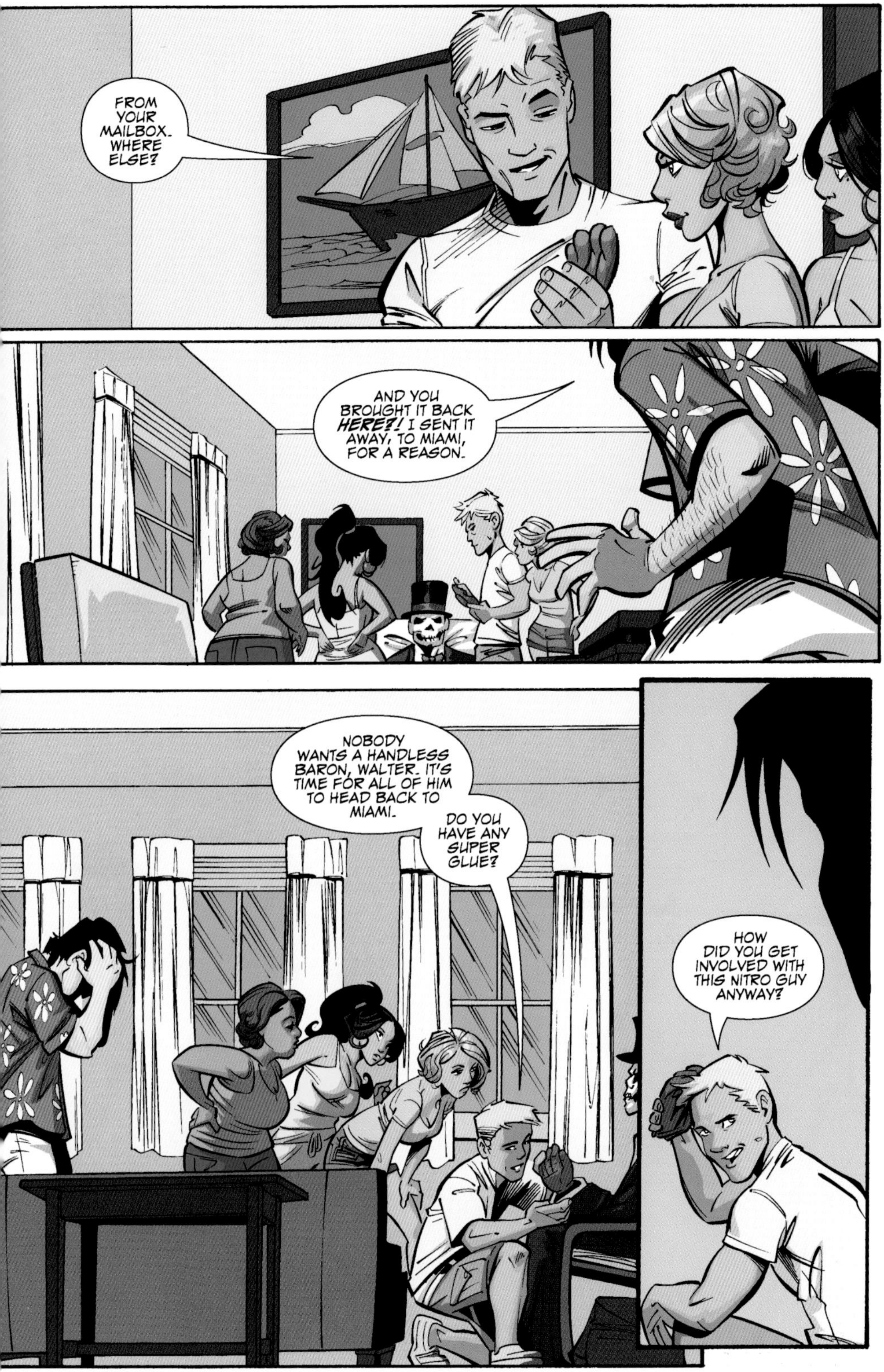
FROM YOUR MAILBOX. WHERE ELSE?
AND YOU BROUGHT IT BACK *HERE?!* I SENT IT AWAY, TO MIAMI, FOR A REASON.
NOBODY WANTS A HANDLESS BARON, WALTER. IT'S TIME FOR ALL OF HIM TO HEAD BACK TO MIAMI.
DO YOU HAVE ANY SUPER GLUE?
HOW DID YOU GET INVOLVED WITH THIS NITRO GUY ANYWAY?

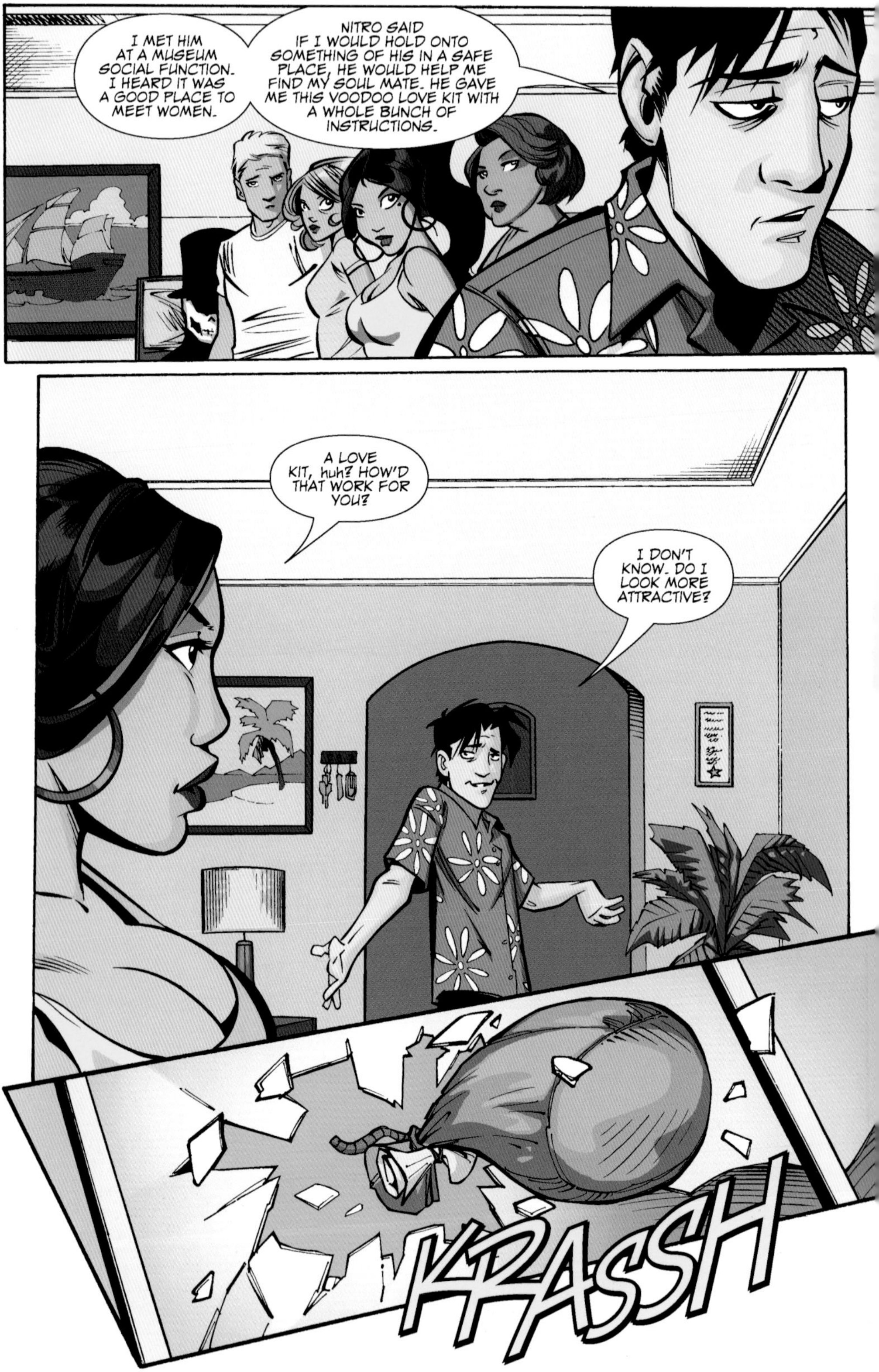
I MET HIM AT A MUSEUM SOCIAL FUNCTION. I HEARD IT WAS A GOOD PLACE TO MEET WOMEN.
NITRO SAID IF I WOULD HOLD ONTO SOMETHING OF HIS IN A SAFE PLACE, HE WOULD HELP ME FIND MY SOUL MATE. HE GAVE ME THIS VOODOO LOVE KIT WITH A WHOLE BUNCH OF INSTRUCTIONS.
A LOVE KIT, huh? HOW'D THAT WORK FOR YOU?
I DON'T KNOW. DO I LOOK MORE ATTRACTIVE?
KRASSH

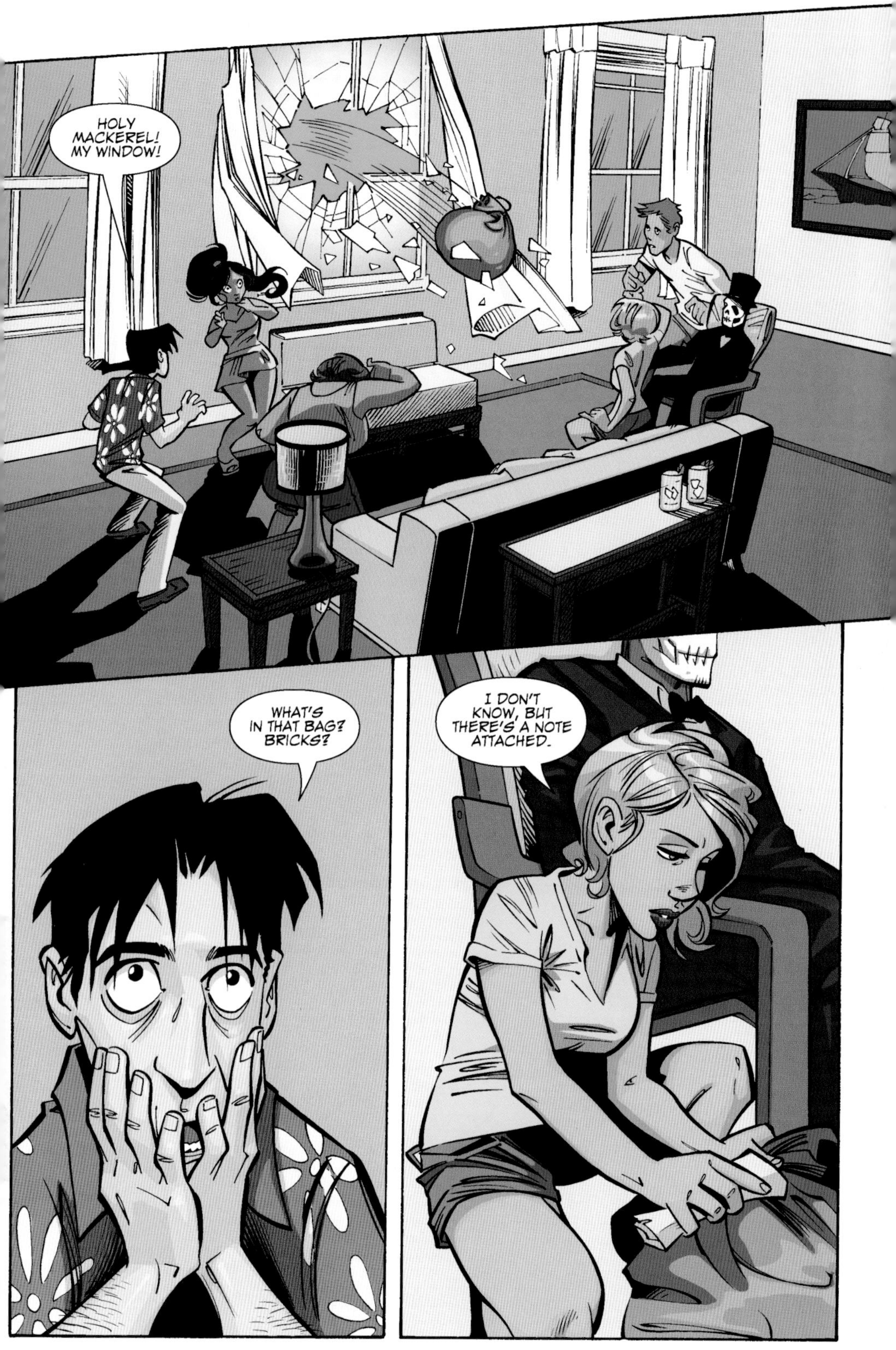
HOLY MACKEREL! MY WINDOW!
WHAT'S IN THAT BAG? BRICKS?
I DON'T KNOW, BUT THERE'S A NOTE ATTACHED.

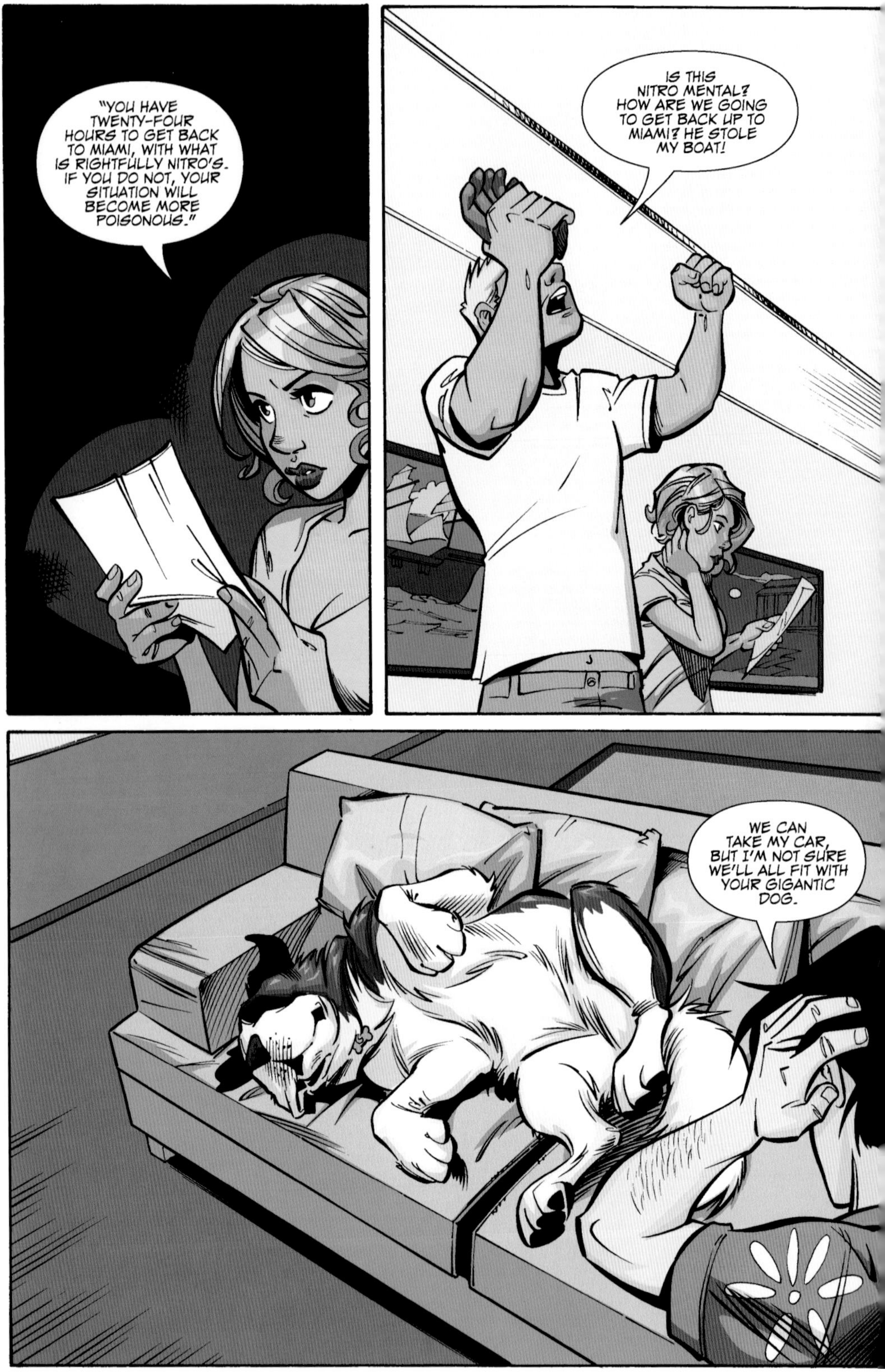
"YOU HAVE TWENTY-FOUR HOURS TO GET BACK TO MIAMI, WITH WHAT IS RIGHTFULLY NITRO'S. IF YOU DO NOT, YOUR SITUATION WILL BECOME MORE POISONOUS."
IS THIS NITRO MENTAL? HOW ARE WE GOING TO GET BACK UP TO MIAMI? HE STOLE MY BOAT!
WE CAN TAKE MY CAR, BUT I'M NOT SURE WE'LL ALL FIT WITH YOUR GIGANTIC DOG.

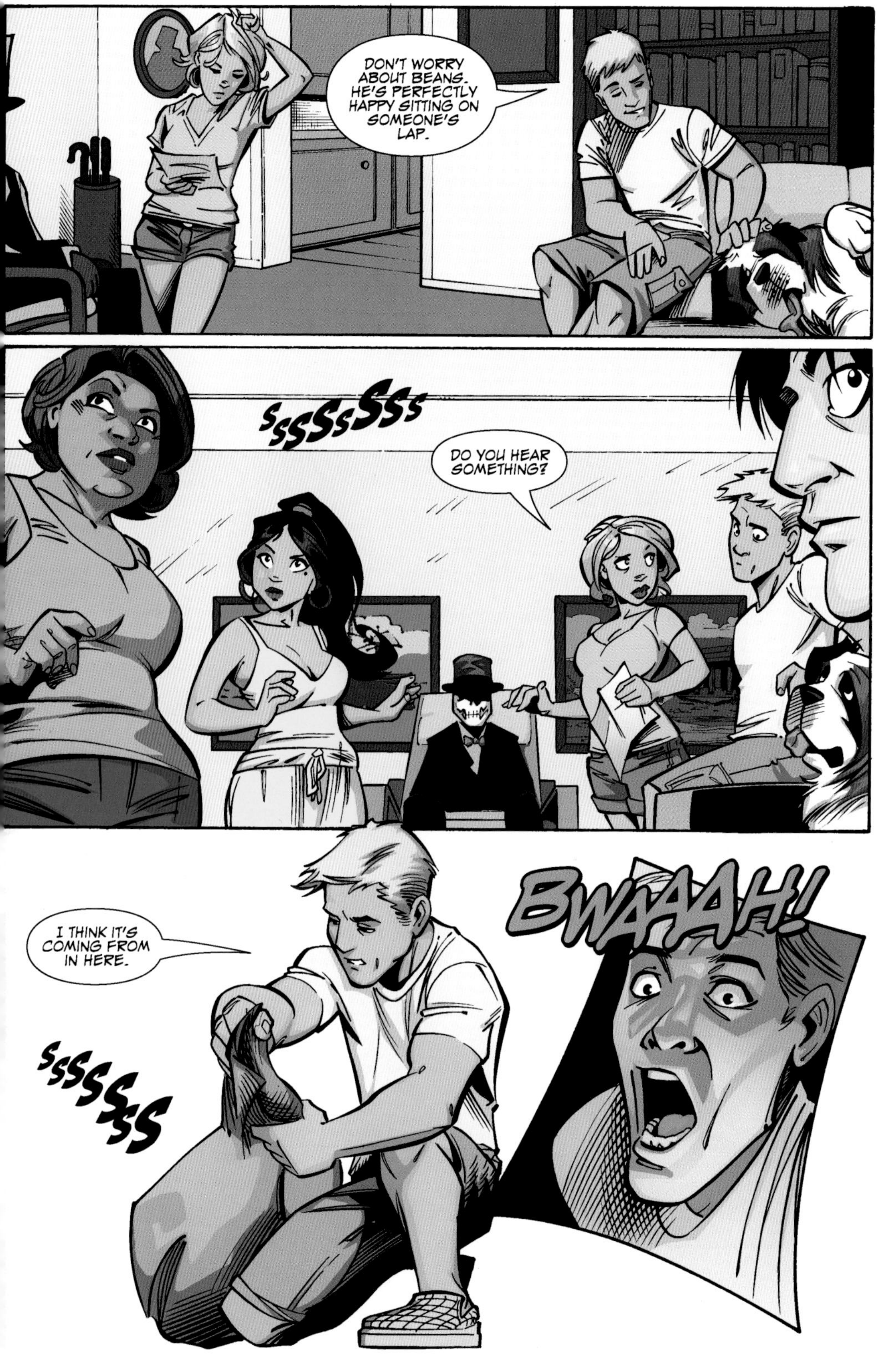
DON'T WORRY ABOUT BEANS. HE'S PERFECTLY HAPPY SITTING ON SOMEONE'S LAP.
SSSSSSSS
DO YOU HEAR SOMETHING?
I THINK IT'S COMING FROM IN HERE.
SSSSSSS
BWAAAH!

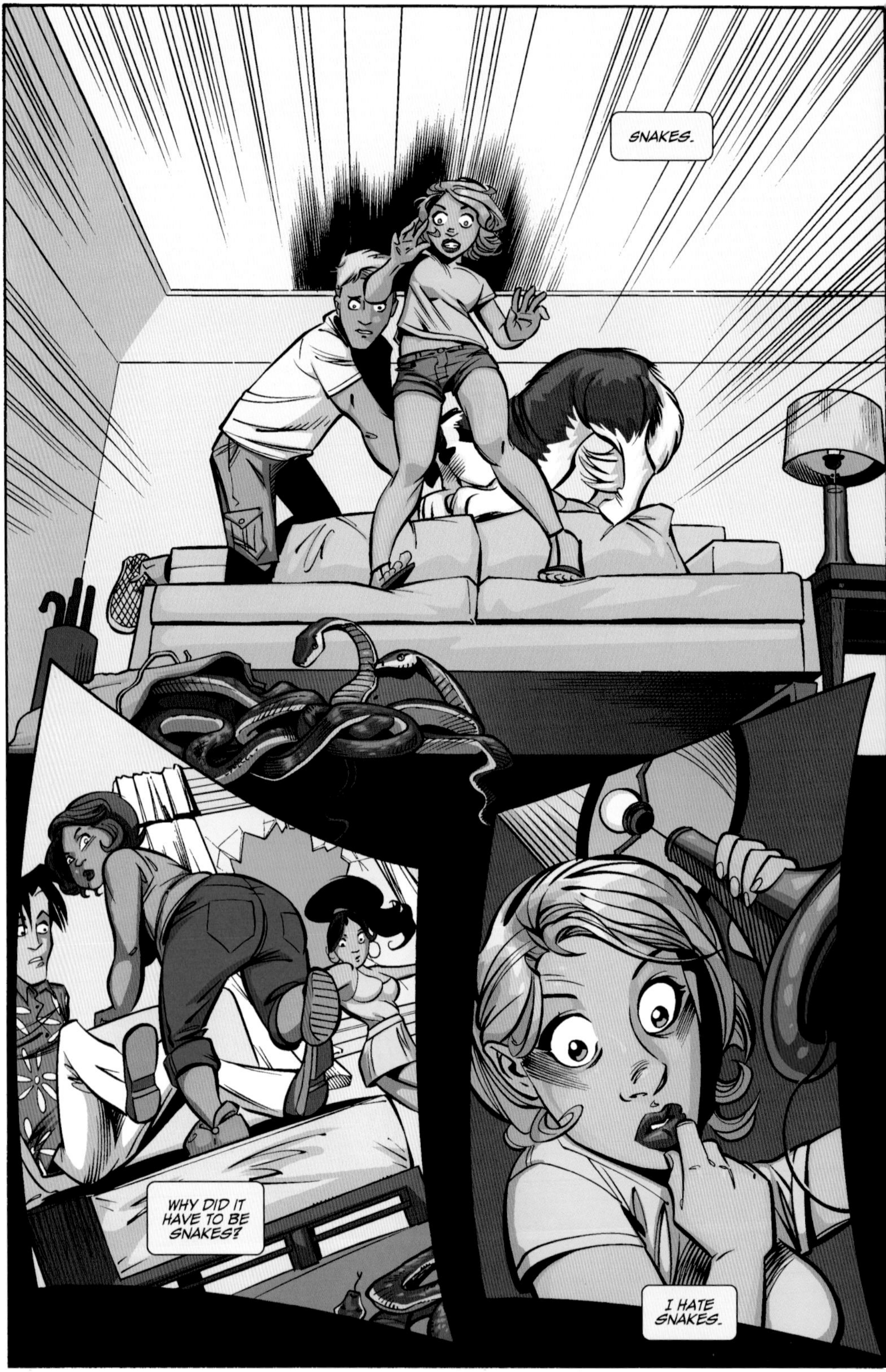
SNAKES.
WHY DID IT HAVE TO BE SNAKES?
I HATE SNAKES.

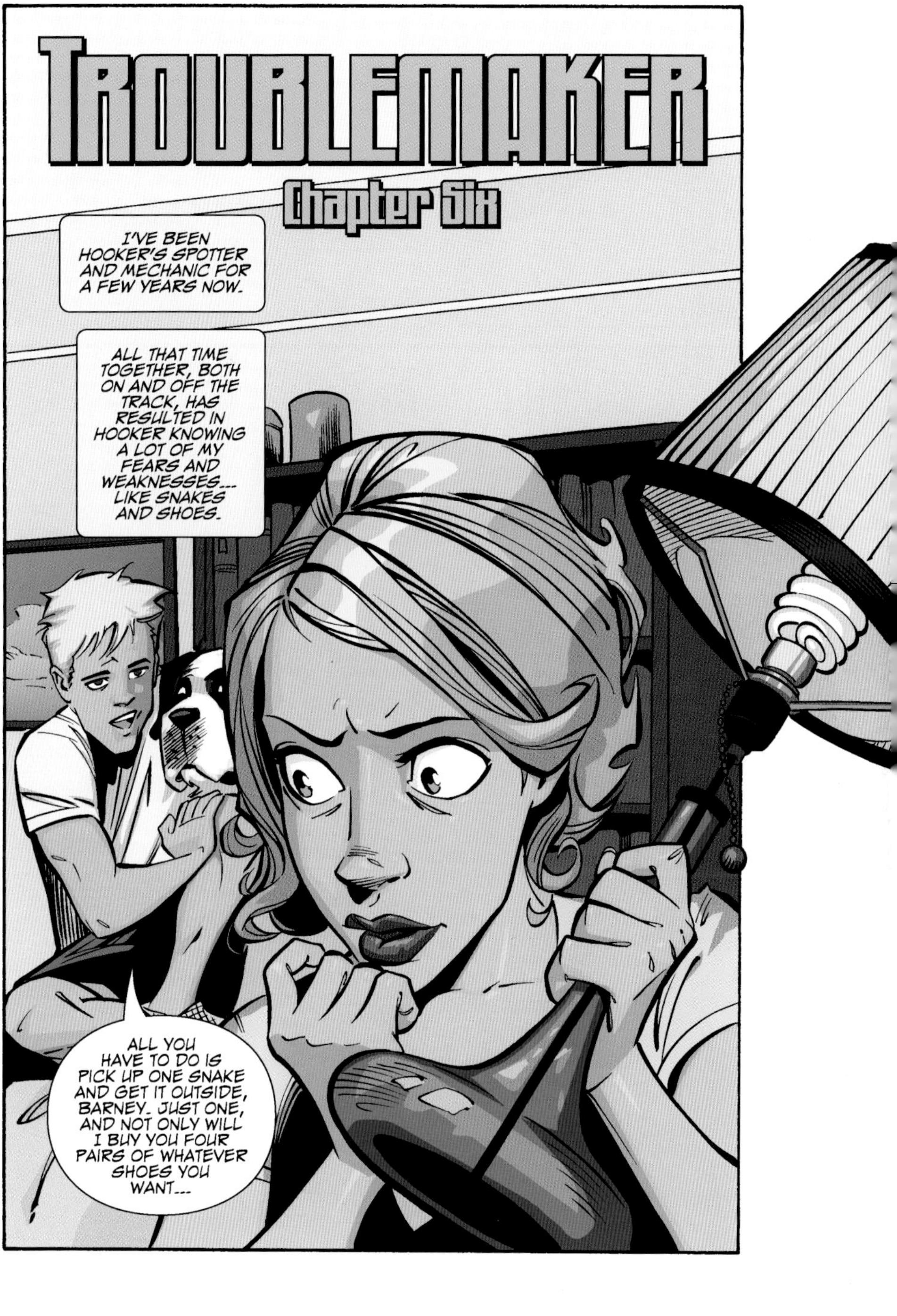
TROUBLEMAKER
Chapter Six
I'VE BEEN HOOKER'S SPOTTER AND MECHANIC FOR A FEW YEARS NOW.
ALL THAT TIME TOGETHER, BOTH ON AND OFF THE TRACK, HAS RESULTED IN HOOKER KNOWING A LOT OF MY FEARS AND WEAKNESSES... LIKE SNAKES AND SHOES.
ALL YOU HAVE TO DO IS PICK UP ONE SNAKE AND GET IT OUTSIDE, BARNEY. JUST ONE, AND NOT ONLY WILL I BUY YOU FOUR PAIRS OF WHATEVER SHOES YOU WANT...

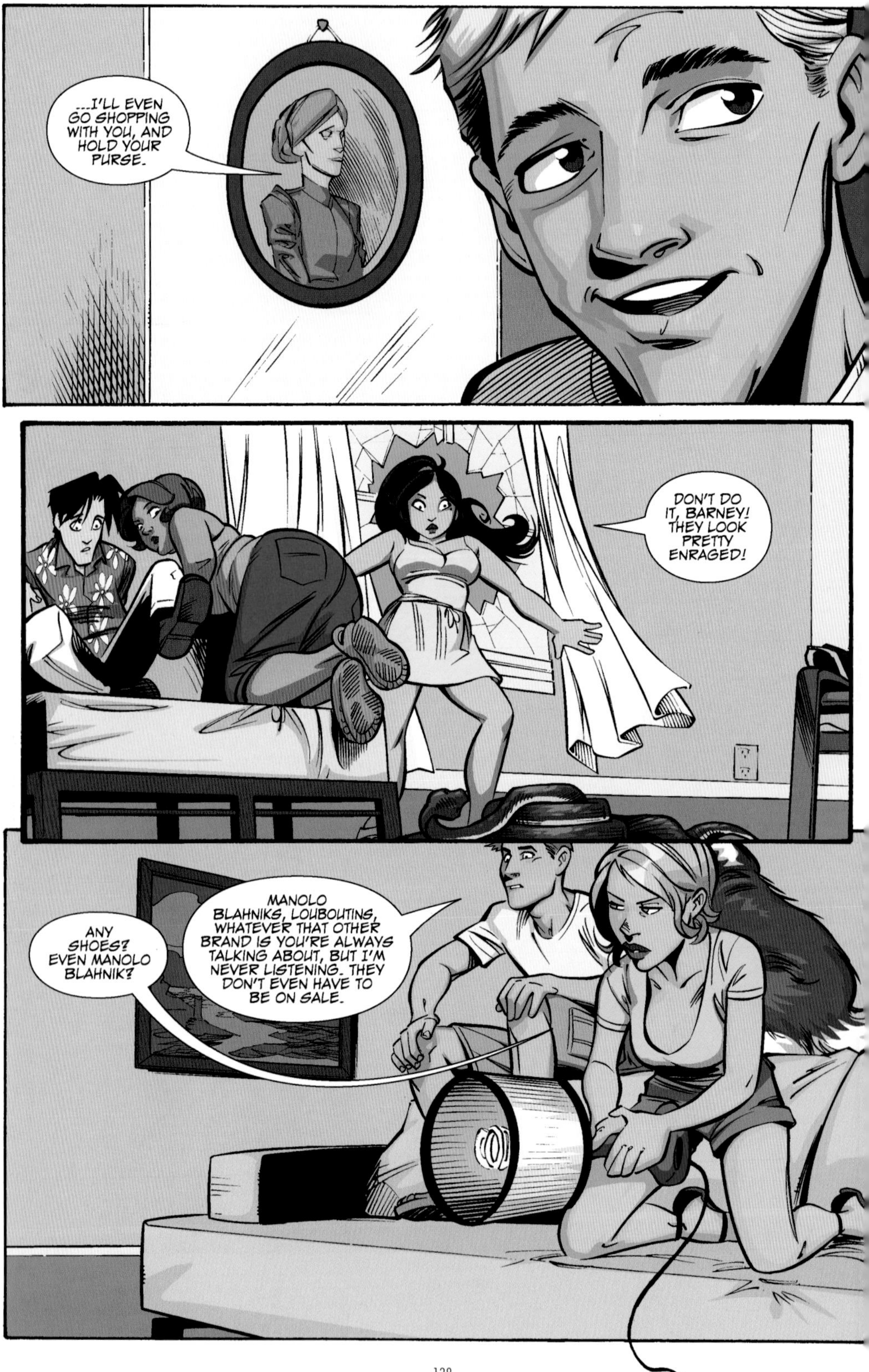
...I'LL EVEN GO SHOPPING WITH YOU, AND HOLD YOUR PURSE.
DON'T DO IT, BARNEY! THEY LOOK PRETTY ENRAGED!
ANY SHOES? EVEN MANOLO BLAHNIK?
MANOLO BLAHNIKS, LOUBOUTINS, WHATEVER THAT OTHER BRAND IS YOU'RE ALWAYS TALKING ABOUT, BUT I'M NEVER LISTENING. THEY DON'T EVEN HAVE TO BE ON SALE.

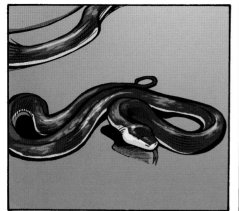

DEAL.

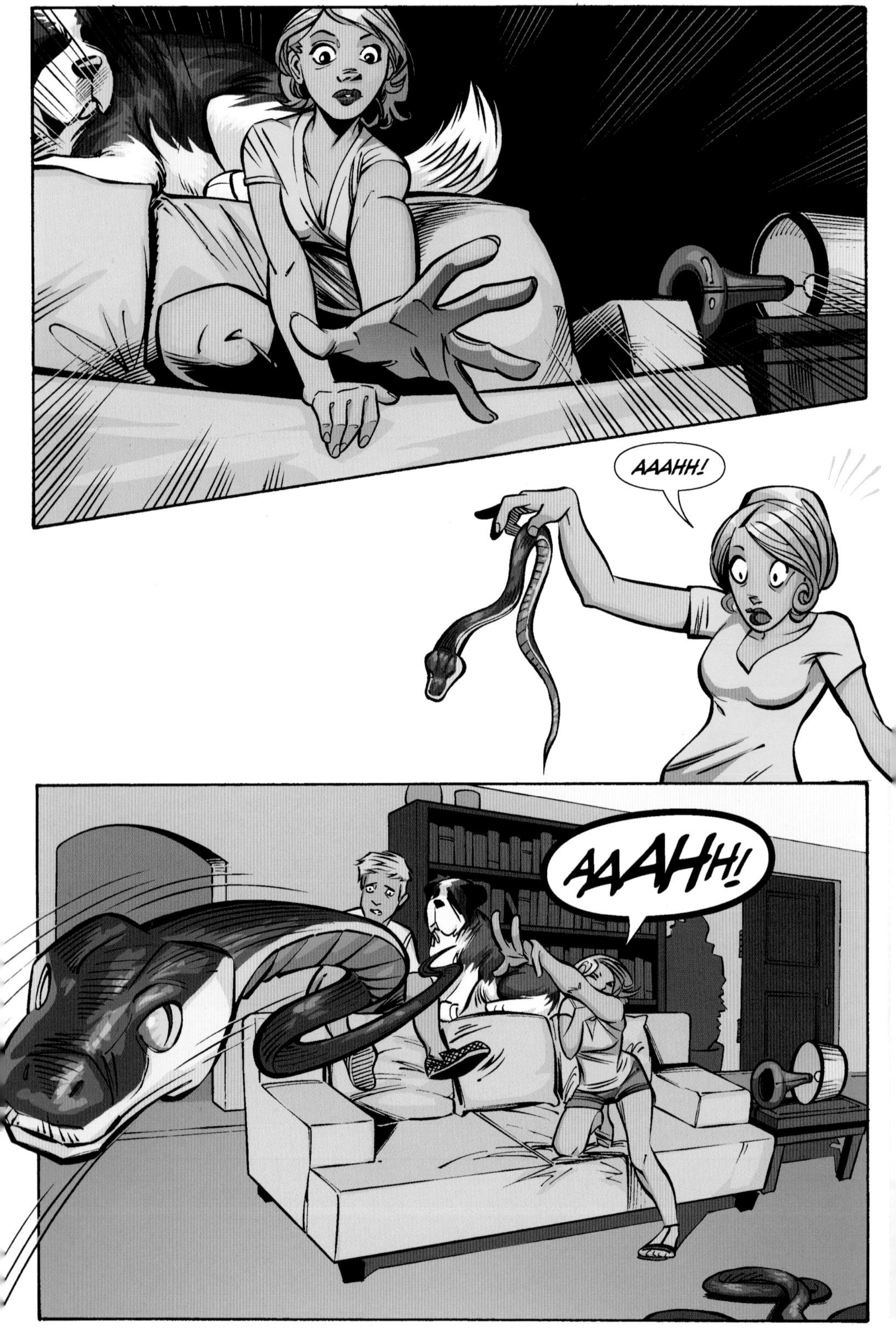
AAAHH!
AAAHH!

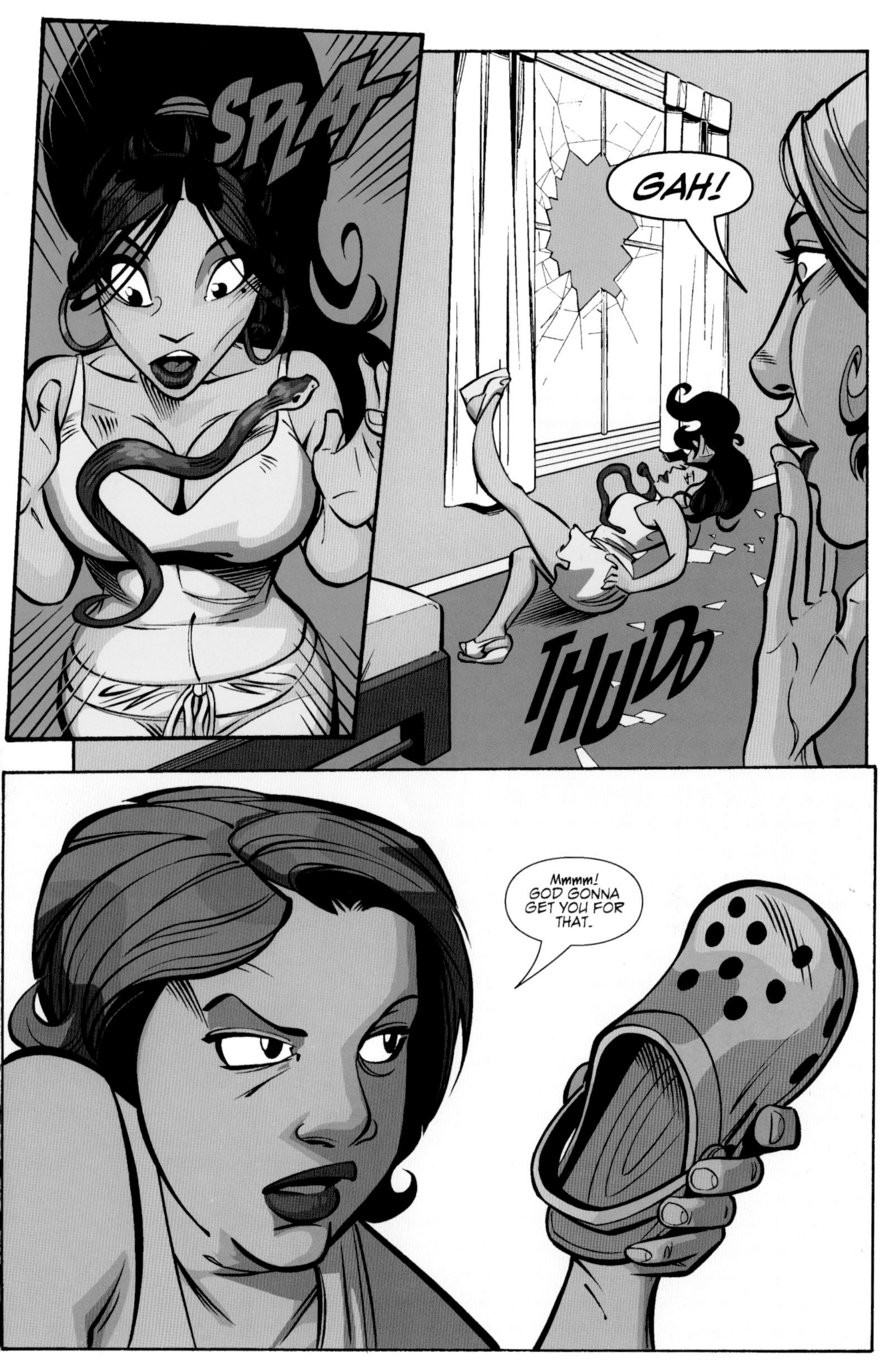
SPLAT
GAH!
THUDD
Mmmm!
GOD GONNA
GET YOU FOR
THAT.

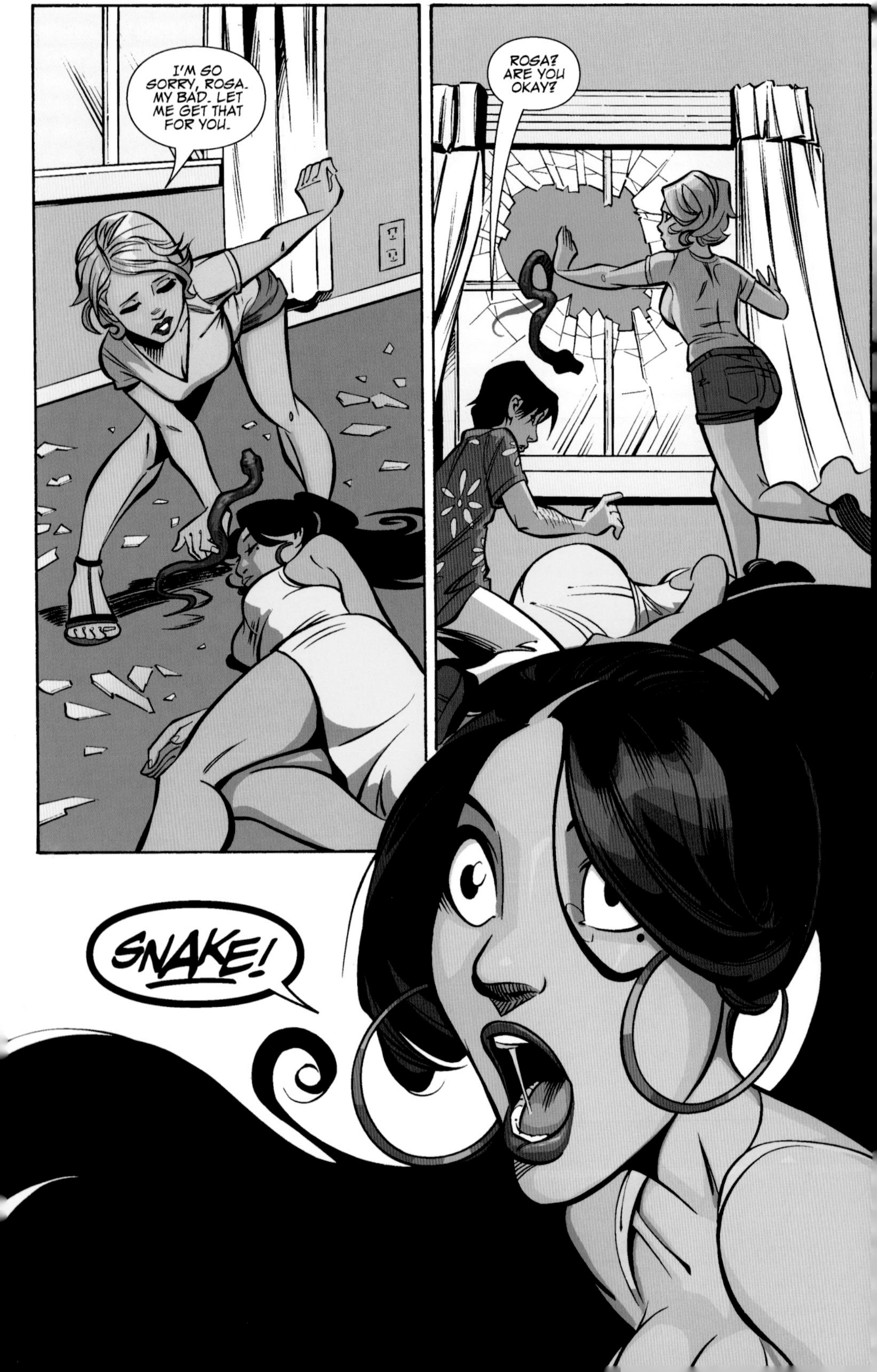
I'M SO SORRY, ROSA. MY BAD. LET ME GET THAT FOR YOU.
ROSA? ARE YOU OKAY?
SNAKE!

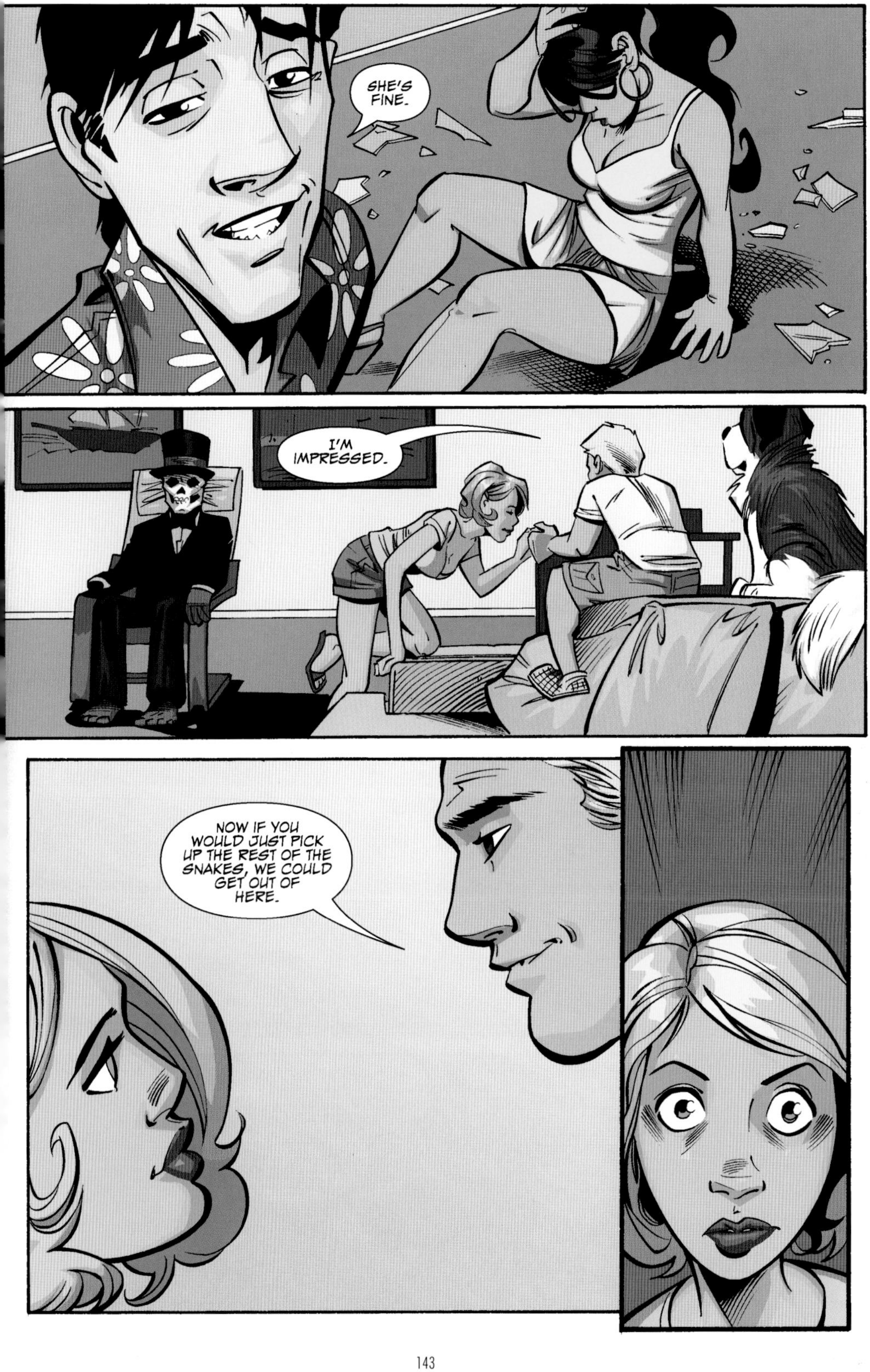
SHE'S FINE.
I'M IMPRESSED.
NOW IF YOU WOULD JUST PICK UP THE REST OF THE SNAKES, WE COULD GET OUT OF HERE.

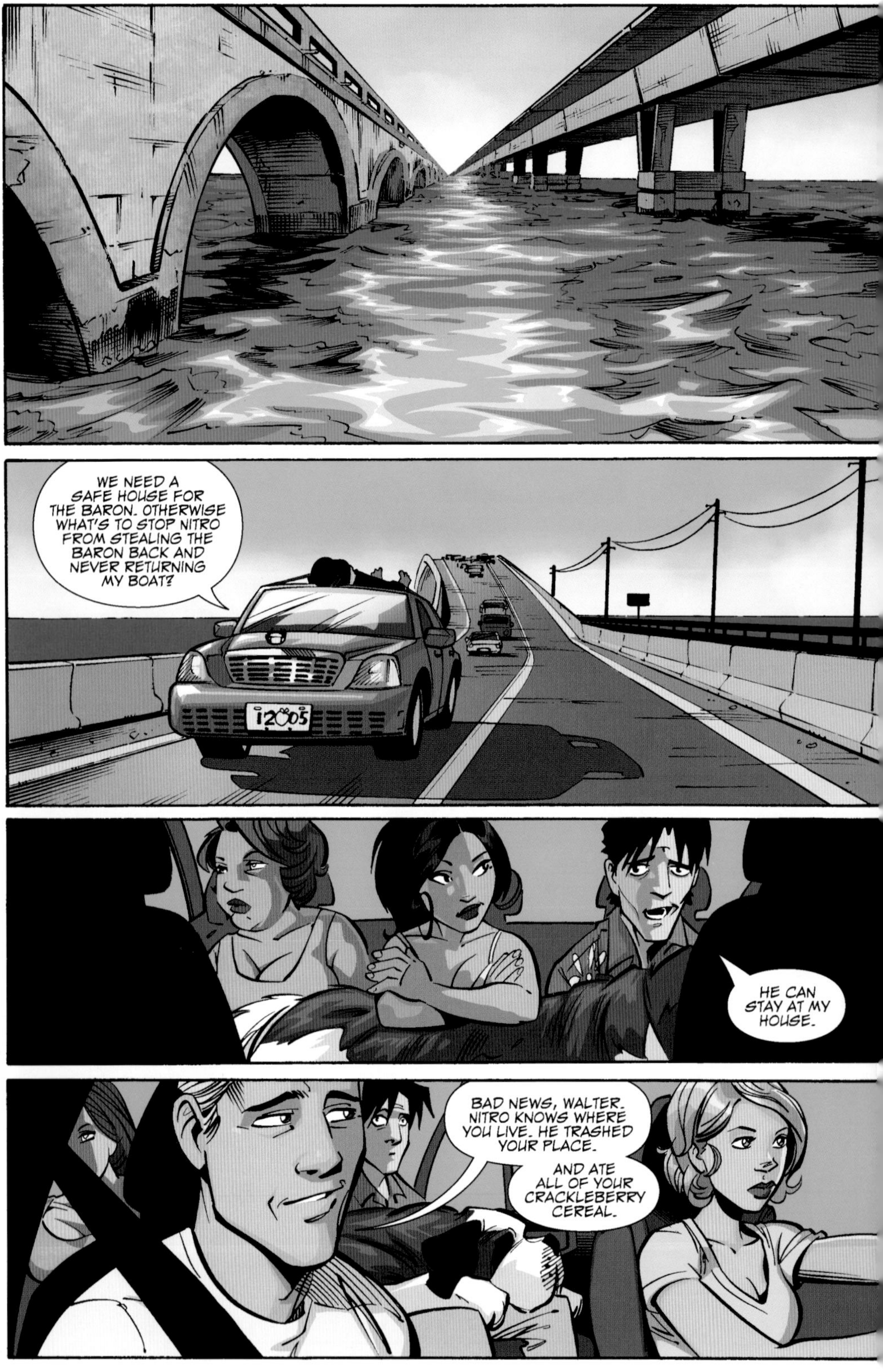
WE NEED A SAFE HOUSE FOR THE BARON. OTHERWISE WHAT'S TO STOP NITRO FROM STEALING THE BARON BACK AND NEVER RETURNING MY BOAT?
HE CAN STAY AT MY HOUSE.
BAD NEWS, WALTER. NITRO KNOWS WHERE YOU LIVE. HE TRASHED YOUR PLACE.
AND ATE ALL OF YOUR CRACKLEBERRY CEREAL.

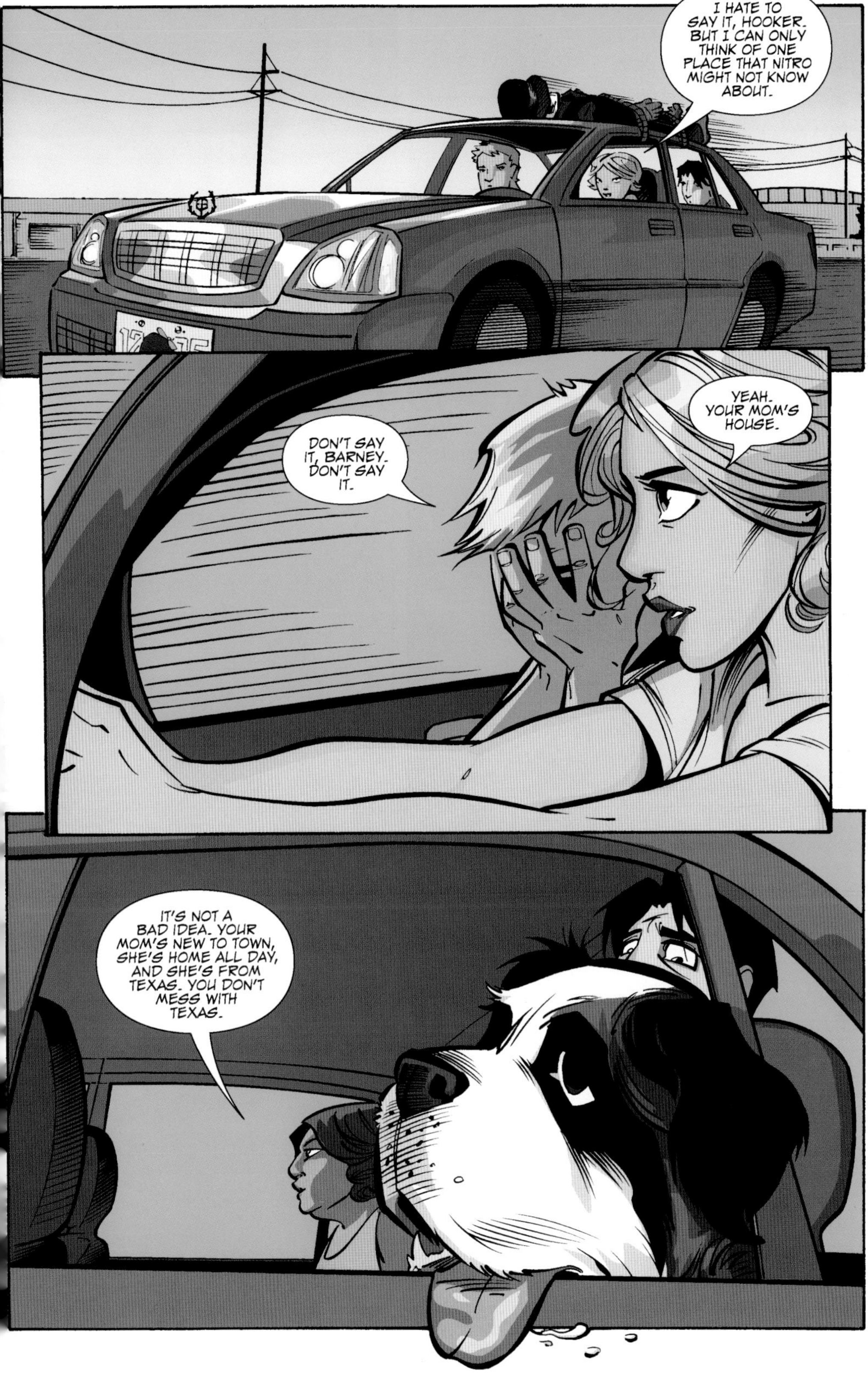
I HATE TO SAY IT, HOOKER. BUT I CAN ONLY THINK OF ONE PLACE THAT NITRO MIGHT NOT KNOW ABOUT.
DON'T SAY IT, BARNEY. DON'T SAY IT.
YEAH. YOUR MOM'S HOUSE.
IT'S NOT A BAD IDEA. YOUR MOM'S NEW TO TOWN, SHE'S HOME ALL DAY, AND SHE'S FROM TEXAS. YOU DON'T MESS WITH TEXAS.

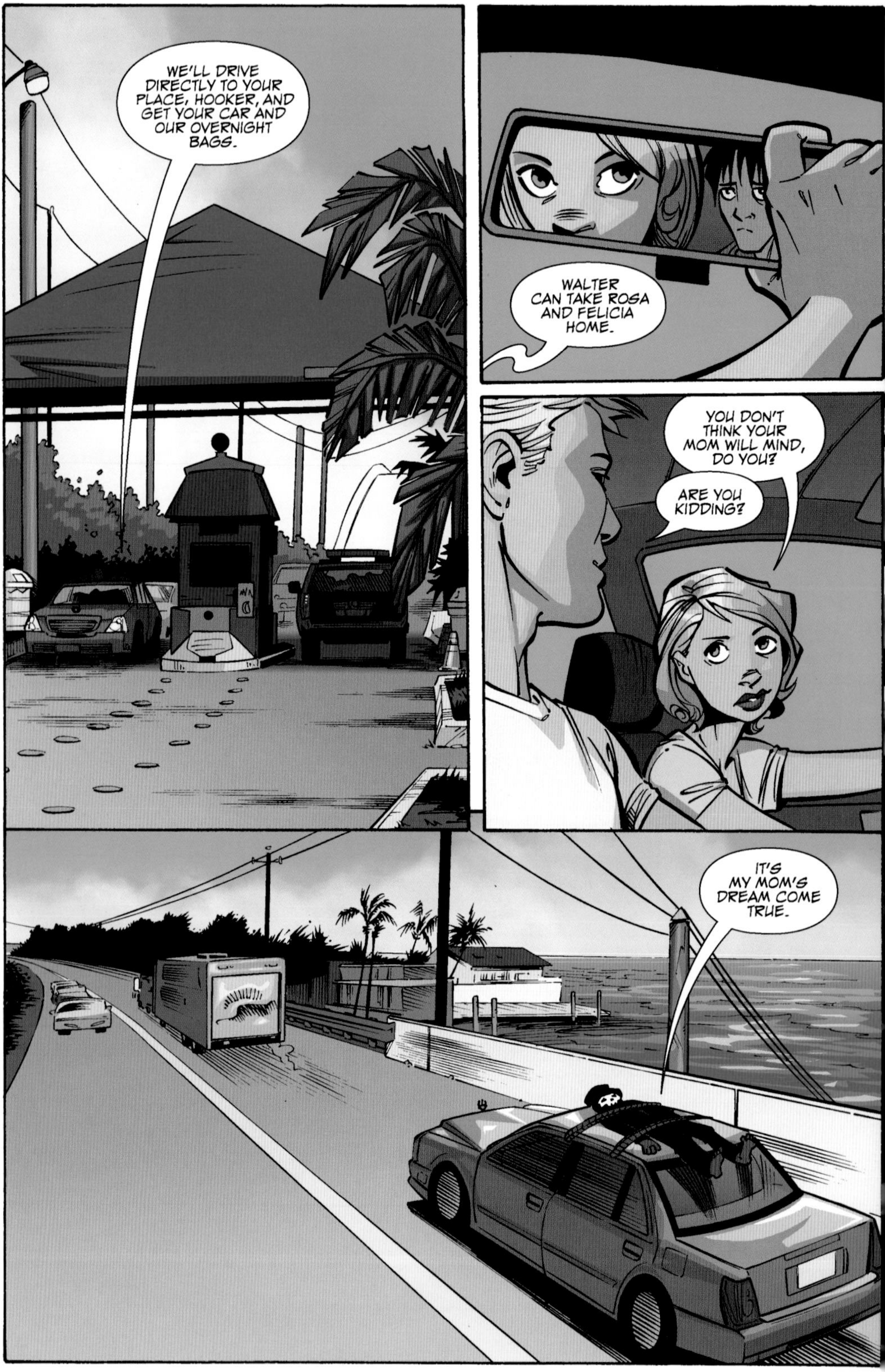
WE'LL DRIVE DIRECTLY TO YOUR PLACE, HOOKER, AND GET YOUR CAR AND OUR OVERNIGHT BAGS.
WALTER CAN TAKE ROSA AND FELICIA HOME.
YOU DON'T THINK YOUR MOM WILL MIND, DO YOU?
ARE YOU KIDDING?
IT'S MY MOM'S DREAM COME TRUE.

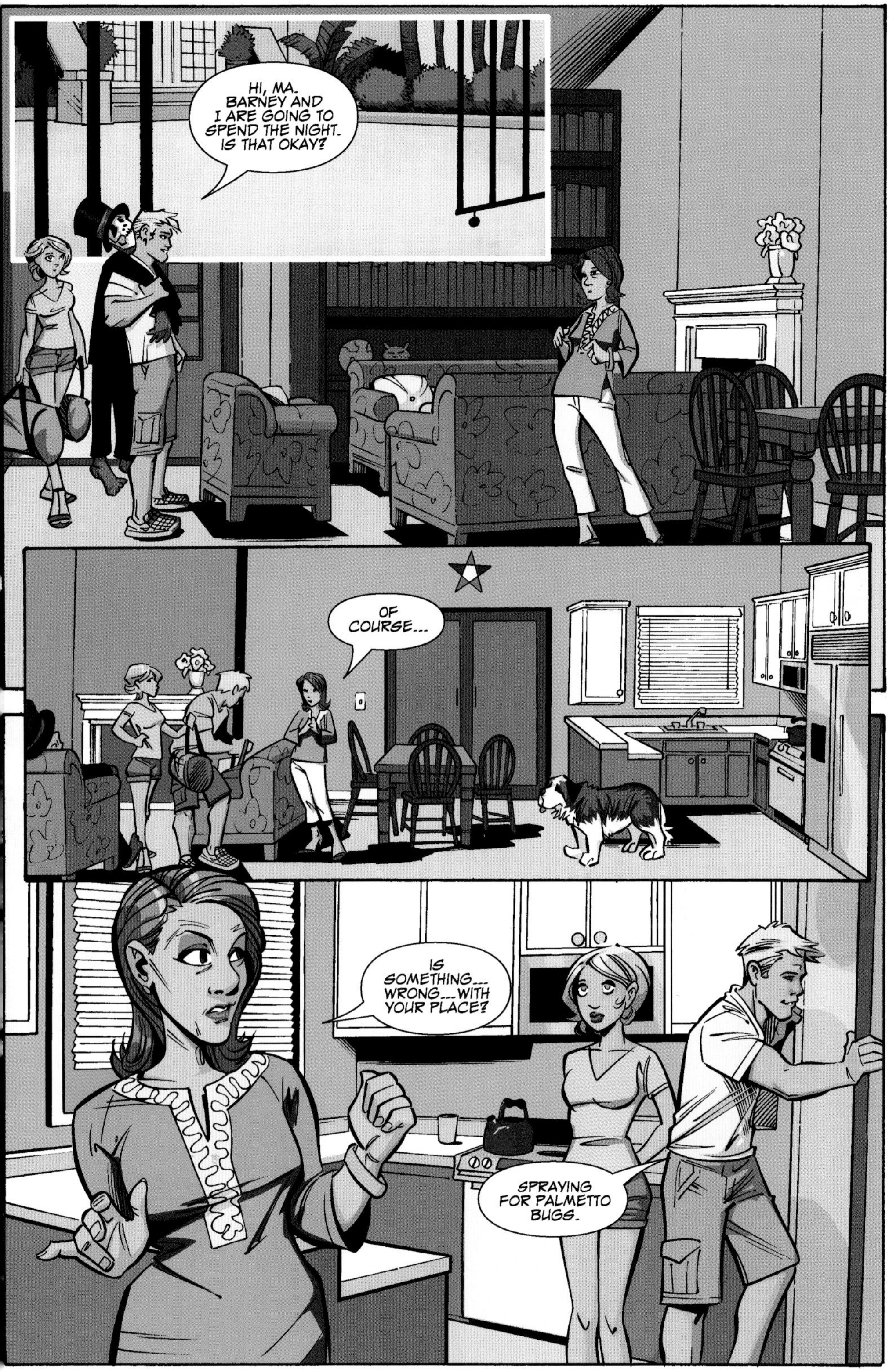
HI, MA. BARNEY AND I ARE GOING TO SPEND THE NIGHT. IS THAT OKAY?
OF COURSE...
IS SOMETHING... WRONG... WITH YOUR PLACE?
SPRAYING FOR PALMETTO BUGS.

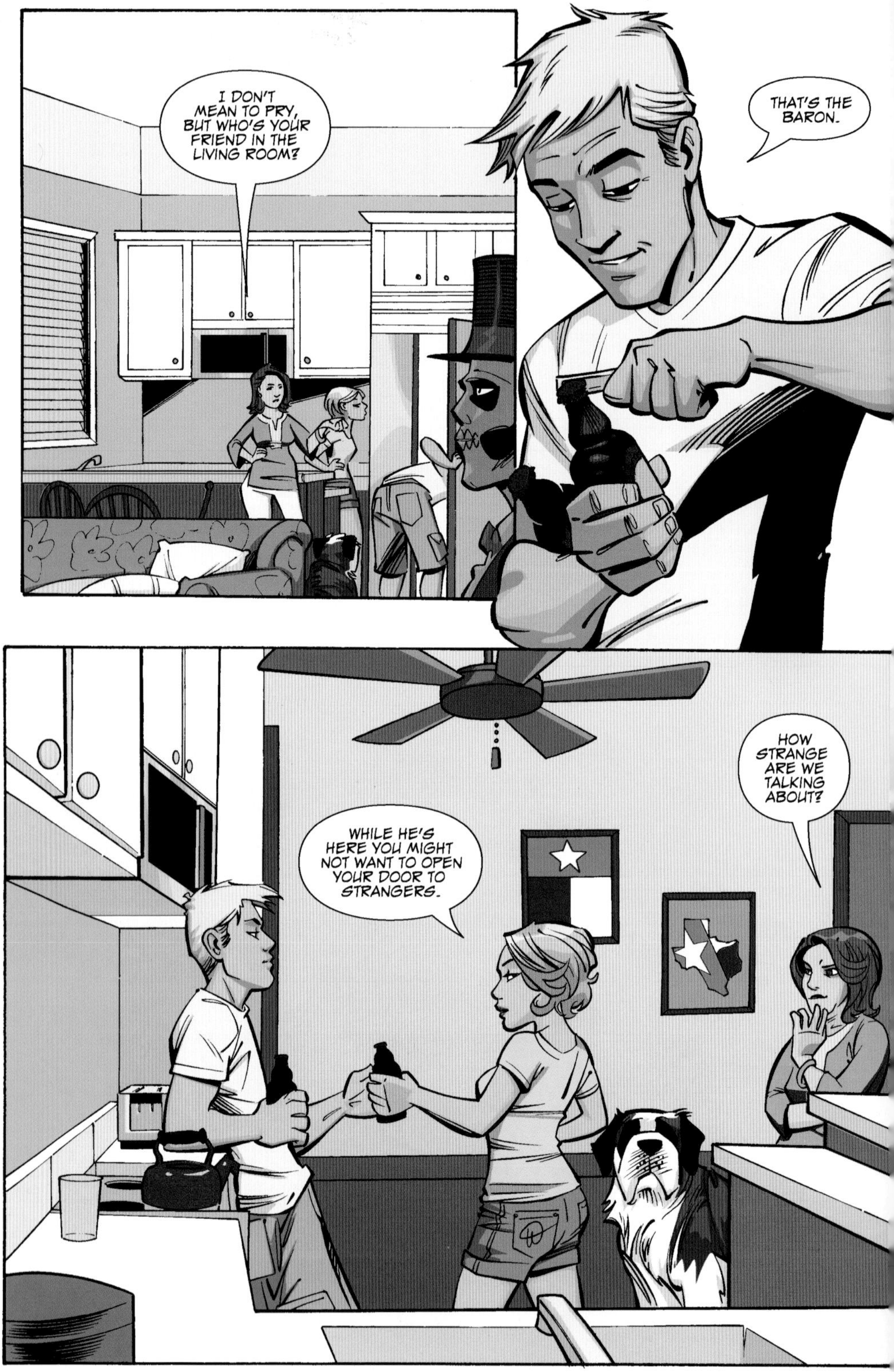
I DON'T MEAN TO PRY, BUT WHO'S YOUR FRIEND IN THE LIVING ROOM?
THAT'S THE BARON.
HOW STRANGE ARE WE TALKING ABOUT?
WHILE HE'S HERE YOU MIGHT NOT WANT TO OPEN YOUR DOOR TO STRANGERS.

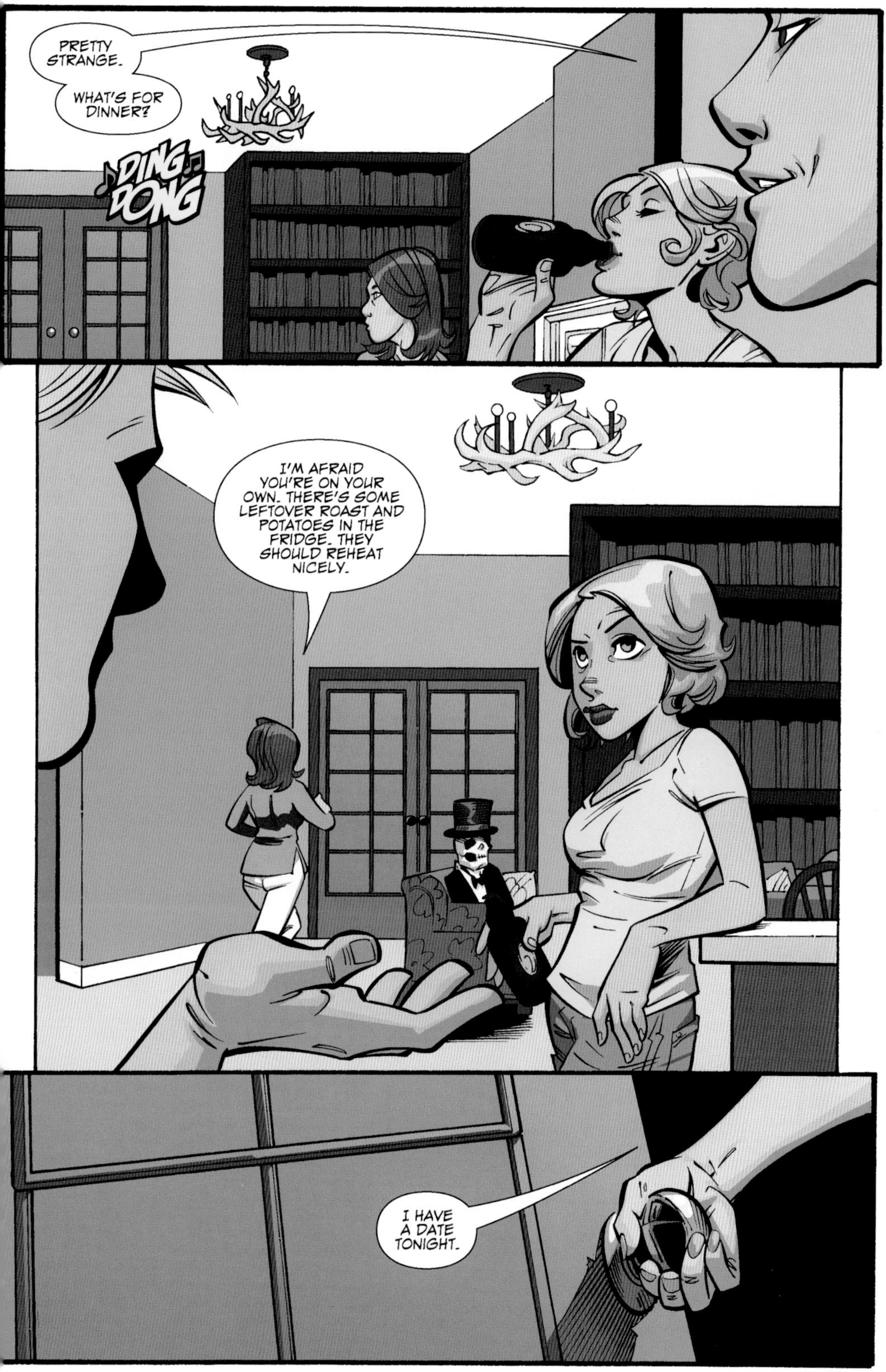
PRETTY STRANGE.
WHAT'S FOR DINNER?
DING DONG
I'M AFRAID YOU'RE ON YOUR OWN. THERE'S SOME LEFTOVER ROAST AND POTATOES IN THE FRIDGE. THEY SHOULD REHEAT NICELY.
I HAVE A DATE TONIGHT.

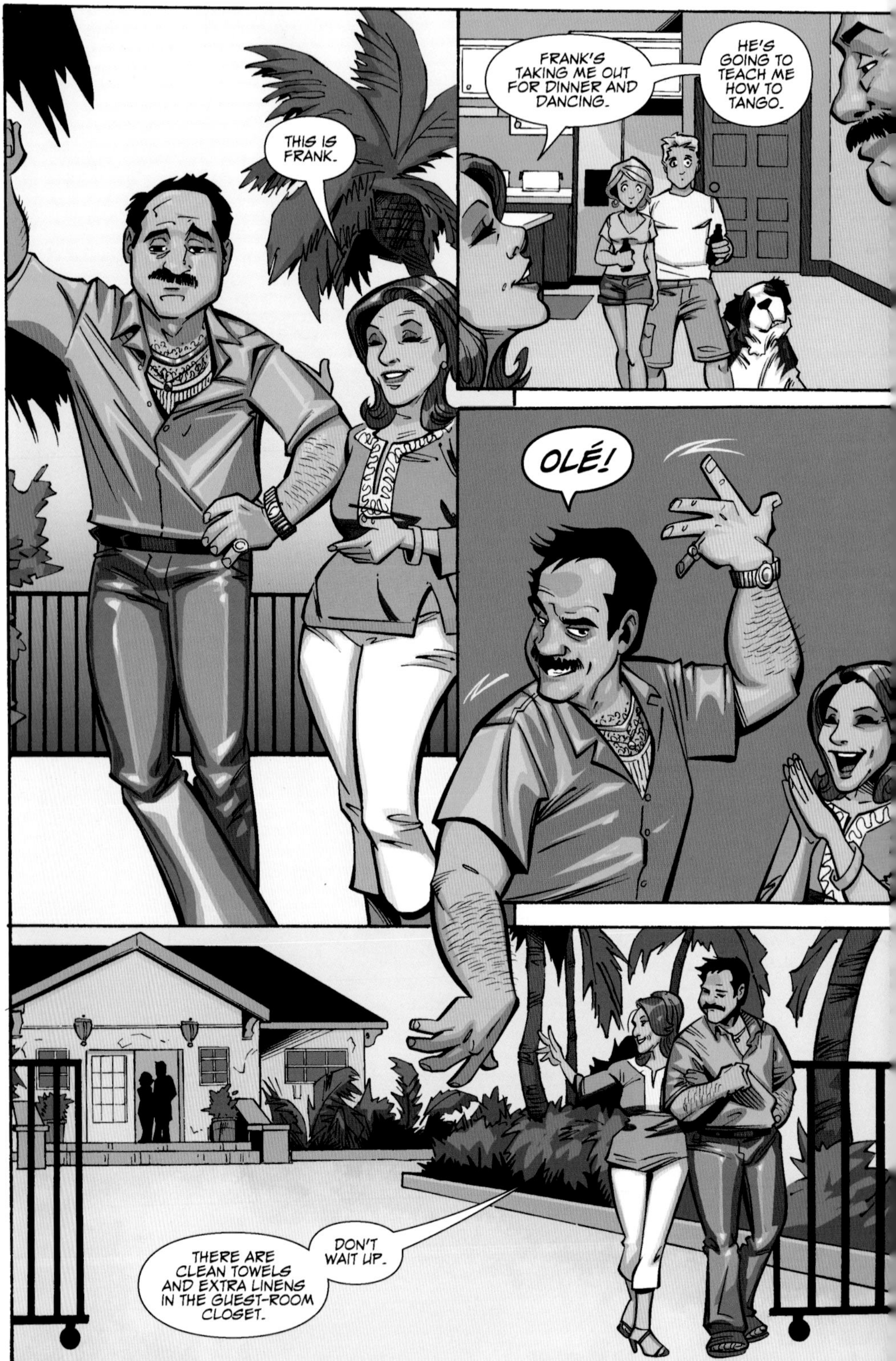

THIS IS FRANK.
FRANK'S TAKING ME OUT FOR DINNER AND DANCING.
HE'S GOING TO TEACH ME HOW TO TANGO.
OLÉ!
DON'T WAIT UP.
THERE ARE CLEAN TOWELS AND EXTRA LINENS IN THE GUEST-ROOM CLOSET.

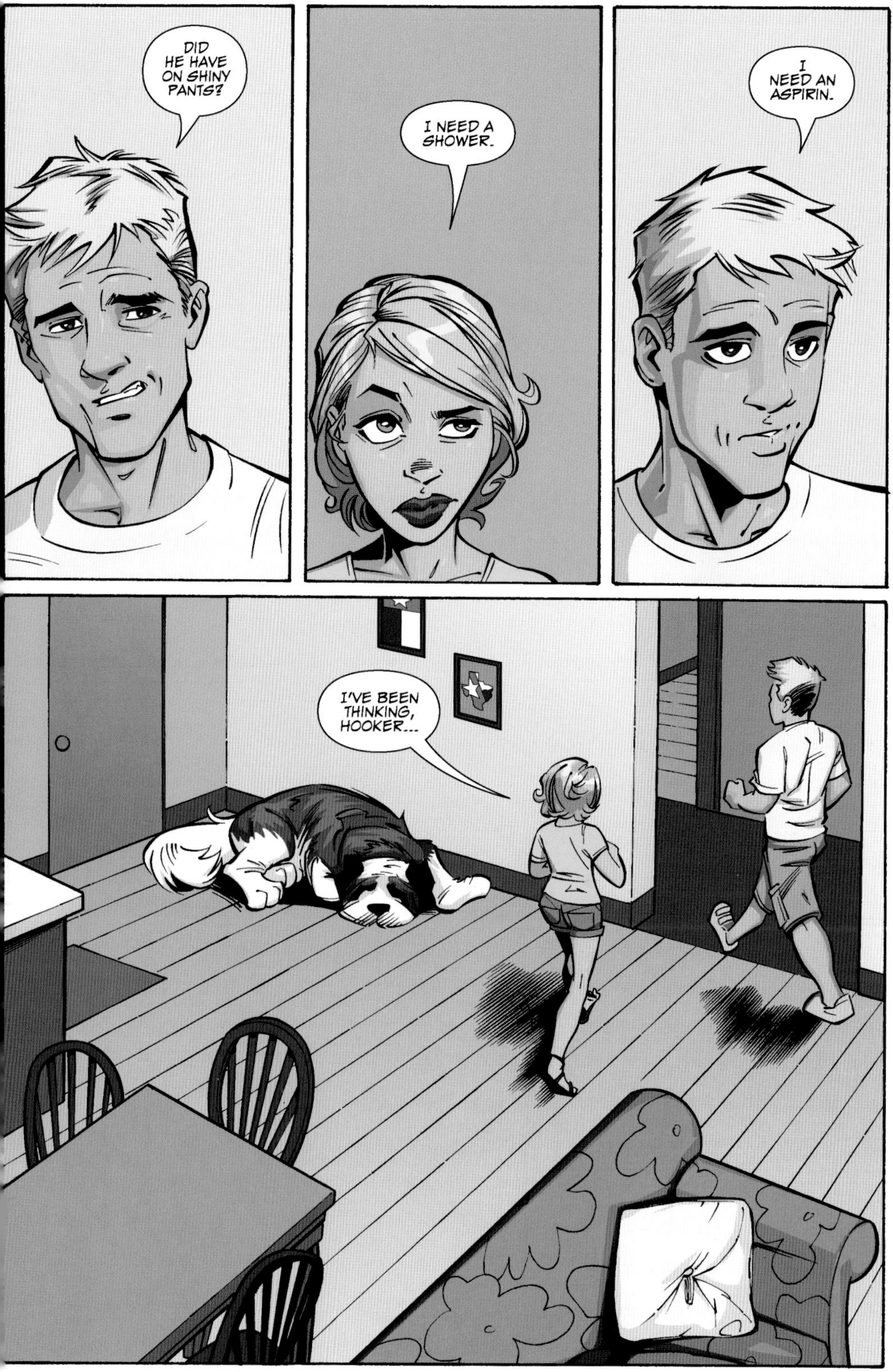
DID HE HAVE ON SHINY PANTS?
I NEED A SHOWER.
I NEED AN ASPIRIN.
I'VE BEEN THINKING, HOOKER...

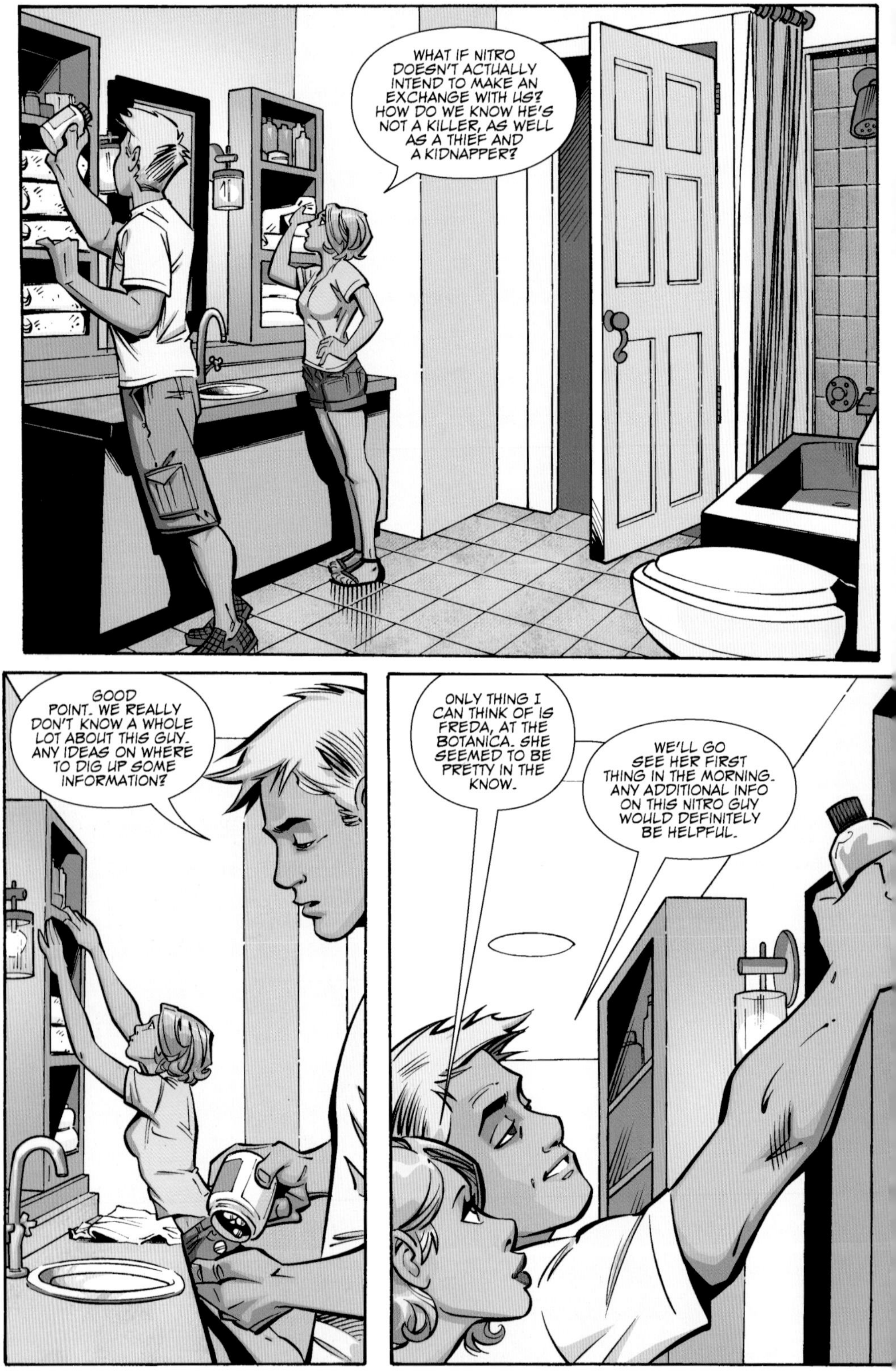
WHAT IF NITRO DOESN'T ACTUALLY INTEND TO MAKE AN EXCHANGE WITH US? HOW DO WE KNOW HE'S NOT A KILLER, AS WELL AS A THIEF AND A KIDNAPPER?
GOOD POINT. WE REALLY DON'T KNOW A WHOLE LOT ABOUT THIS GUY. ANY IDEAS ON WHERE TO DIG UP SOME INFORMATION?
ONLY THING I CAN THINK OF IS FREDA, AT THE BOTANICA. SHE SEEMED TO BE PRETTY IN THE KNOW.
WE'LL GO SEE HER FIRST THING IN THE MORNING. ANY ADDITIONAL INFO ON THIS NITRO GUY WOULD DEFINITELY BE HELPFUL.

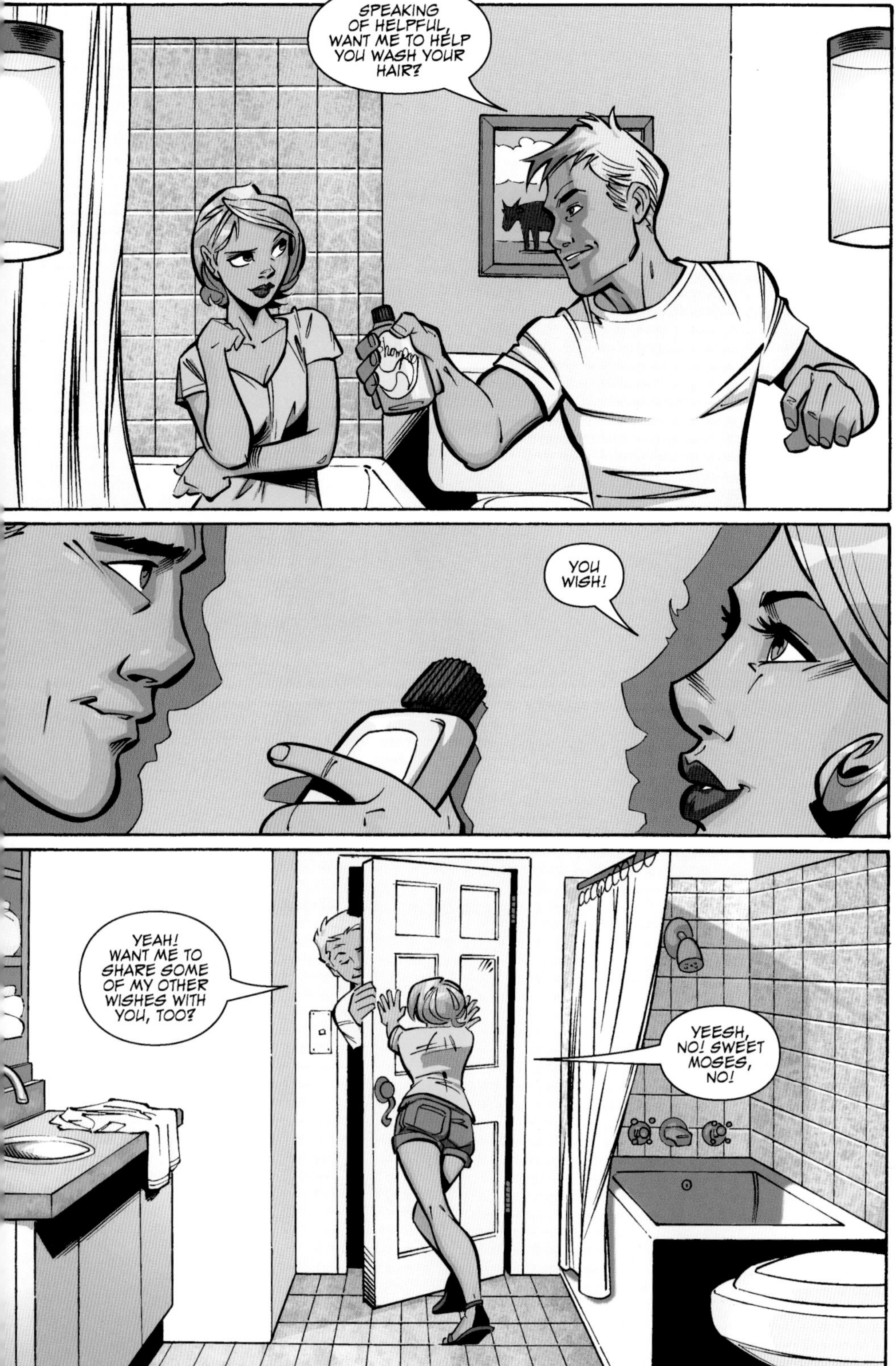
SPEAKING OF HELPFUL, WANT ME TO HELP YOU WASH YOUR HAIR?
YOU WISH!
YEAH! WANT ME TO SHARE SOME OF MY OTHER WISHES WITH YOU, TOO?
YEESH, NO! SWEET MOSES, NO!

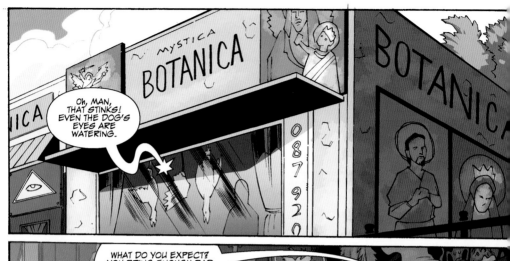

MYSTICA BOTANICA

BOTANICA

Oh, MAN, THAT STINKS! EVEN THE DOG'S EYES ARE WATERING.

WHAT DO YOU EXPECT? YOU BRING ENOUGH BAD JUJU INTO MY STORE TO TAKE OUT ALL OF RHODE ISLAND AND YOU THINK FIXING IT WILL SMELL LIKE ROSES?

NOW, WHAT CAN I DO FOR YOU?

REMEMBER THE HAND WE BROUGHT IN A FEW DAYS AGO? WE PUT IT BACK ON THE STATUE OF BARON SAMEDI AND WE'D LIKE TO GIVE THE STATUE BACK TO THE MUSEUM, BUT...

...COMPLICATIONS AROSE.

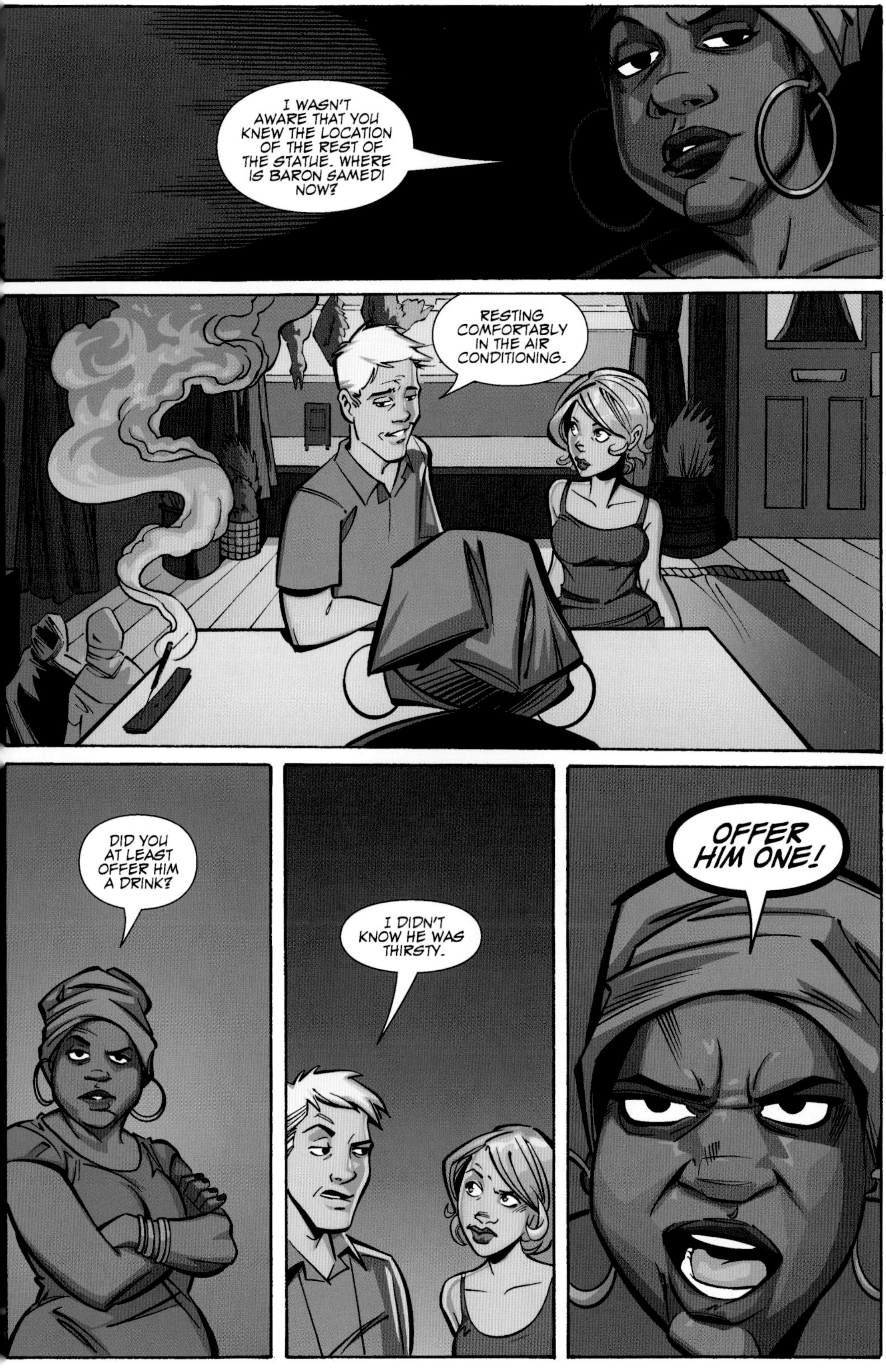
I WASN'T AWARE THAT YOU KNEW THE LOCATION OF THE REST OF THE STATUE. WHERE IS BARON SAMEDI NOW?
RESTING COMFORTABLY IN THE AIR CONDITIONING.
DID YOU AT LEAST OFFER HIM A DRINK?
I DIDN'T KNOW HE WAS THIRSTY.
OFFER HIM ONE!

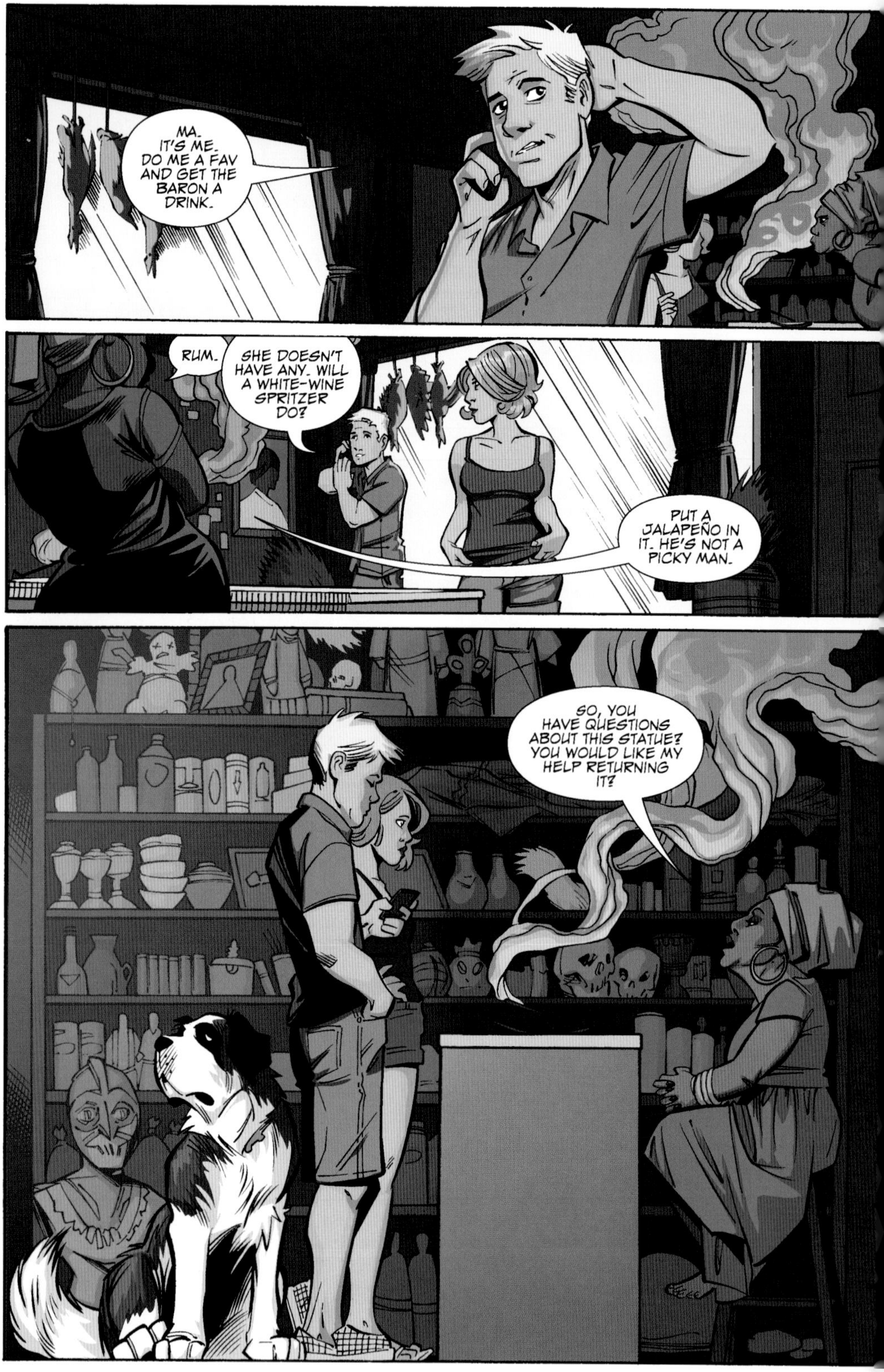
MA. IT'S ME. DO ME A FAV AND GET THE BARON A DRINK.
RUM.
SHE DOESN'T HAVE ANY. WILL A WHITE-WINE SPRITZER DO?
PUT A JALAPEÑO IN IT. HE'S NOT A PICKY MAN.
SO, YOU HAVE QUESTIONS ABOUT THIS STATUE? YOU WOULD LIKE MY HELP RETURNING IT?

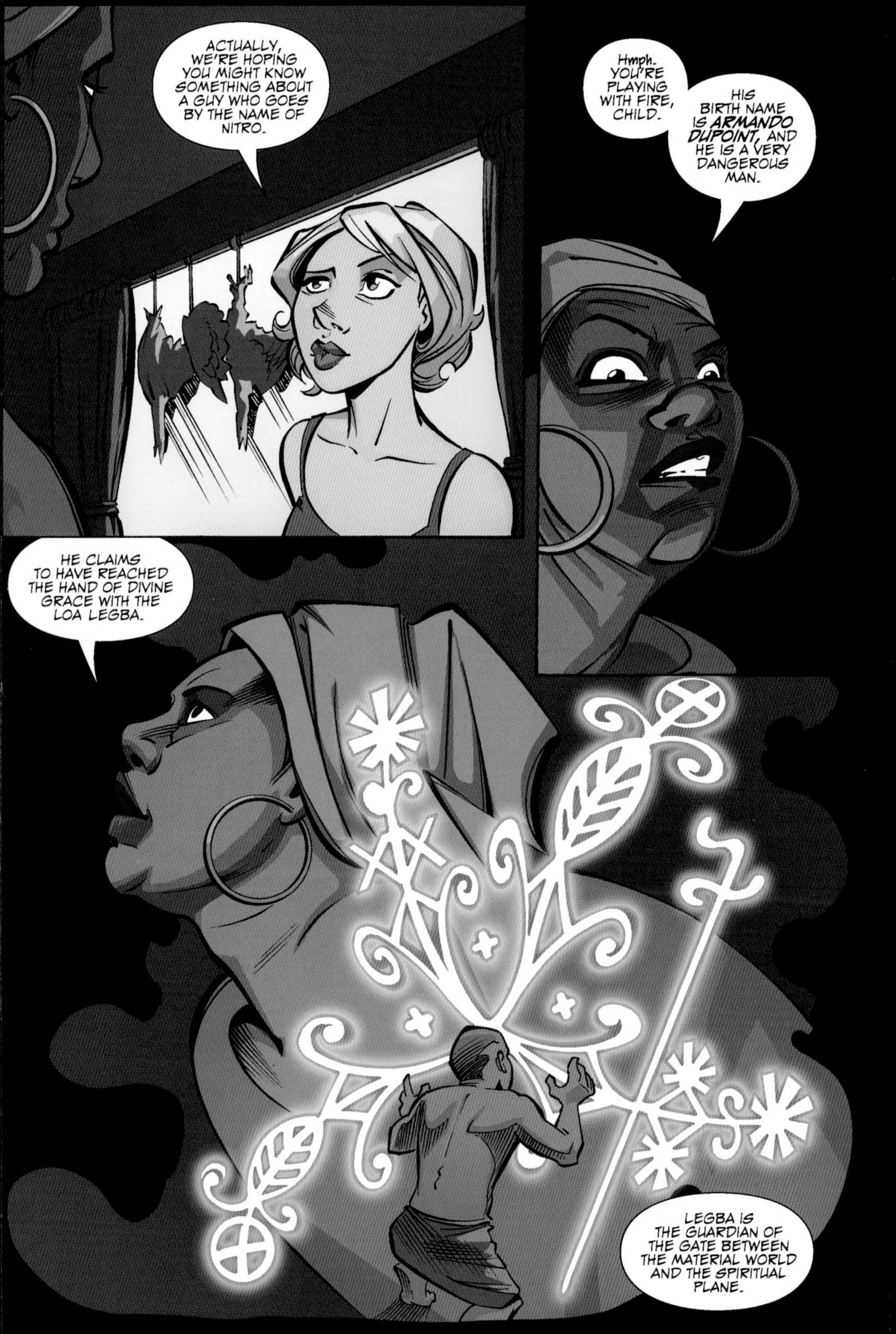
ACTUALLY, WE'RE HOPING YOU MIGHT KNOW SOMETHING ABOUT A GUY WHO GOES BY THE NAME OF NITRO.
Hmph. YOU'RE PLAYING WITH FIRE, CHILD.
HIS BIRTH NAME IS ARMANDO DUPOINT, AND HE IS A VERY DANGEROUS MAN.
HE CLAIMS TO HAVE REACHED THE HAND OF DIVINE GRACE WITH THE LOA LEGBA.
LEGBA IS THE GUARDIAN OF THE GATE BETWEEN THE MATERIAL WORLD AND THE SPIRITUAL PLANE.

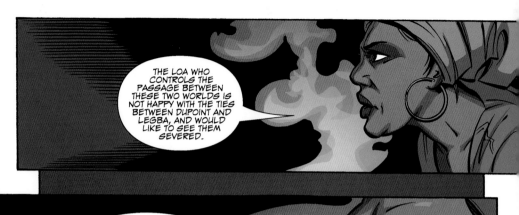

THE LOA WHO CONTROLS THE PASSAGE BETWEEN THESE TWO WORLDS IS NOT HAPPY WITH THE TIES BETWEEN DUPOINT AND LEGBA, AND WOULD LIKE TO SEE THEM SEVERED.

ARMANDO DUPOINT IS A *BOKOR.* A PRIEST OF BLACK MAGIC. HE IS DECEITFUL AND BLACK HEARTED. HE THINKS HE IS IN CONTROL OF THE LOA AND USES THEM FOR HIS OWN MISDEEDS, AN ACT I FIND DESPICABLE.

TAKE CARE IN YOUR DEALINGS WITH HIM. HE HAS A FOLLOWING OF DEVOTED SERVITORS, SOME OF WHOM WOULD DO *ANYTHING* FOR THEIR BOKOR.

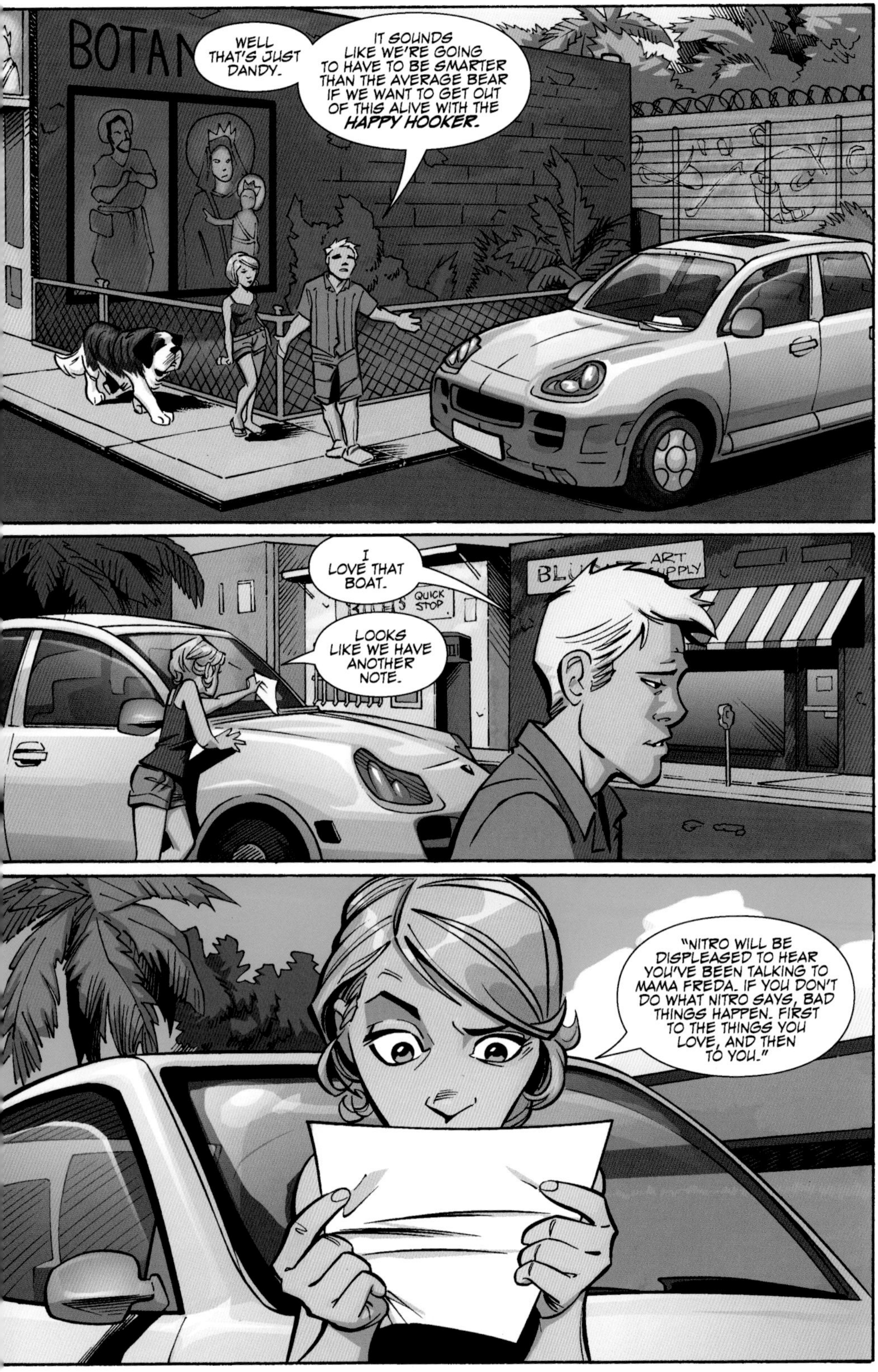
BOTAN
WELL THAT'S JUST DANDY.
IT SOUNDS LIKE WE'RE GOING TO HAVE TO BE SMARTER THAN THE AVERAGE BEAR IF WE WANT TO GET OUT OF THIS ALIVE WITH THE *HAPPY HOOKER.*
I LOVE THAT BOAT.
QUICK STOP
ART SUPPLY
LOOKS LIKE WE HAVE ANOTHER NOTE.
"NITRO WILL BE DISPLEASED TO HEAR YOU'VE BEEN TALKING TO MAMA FREDA. IF YOU DON'T DO WHAT NITRO SAYS, BAD THINGS HAPPEN. FIRST TO THE THINGS YOU LOVE, AND THEN TO YOU."

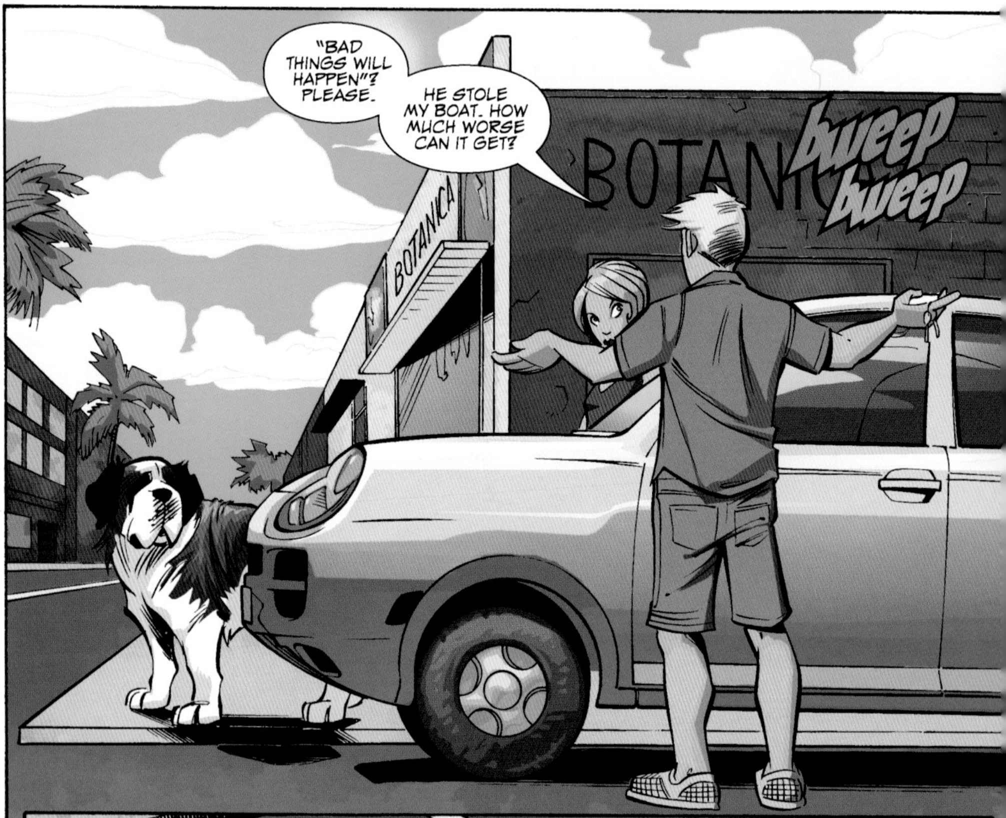
"BAD THINGS WILL HAPPEN"? PLEASE.
HE STOLE MY BOAT. HOW MUCH WORSE CAN IT GET?
BOTANICA
BOTANICA
BOTANICA
bweep bweep

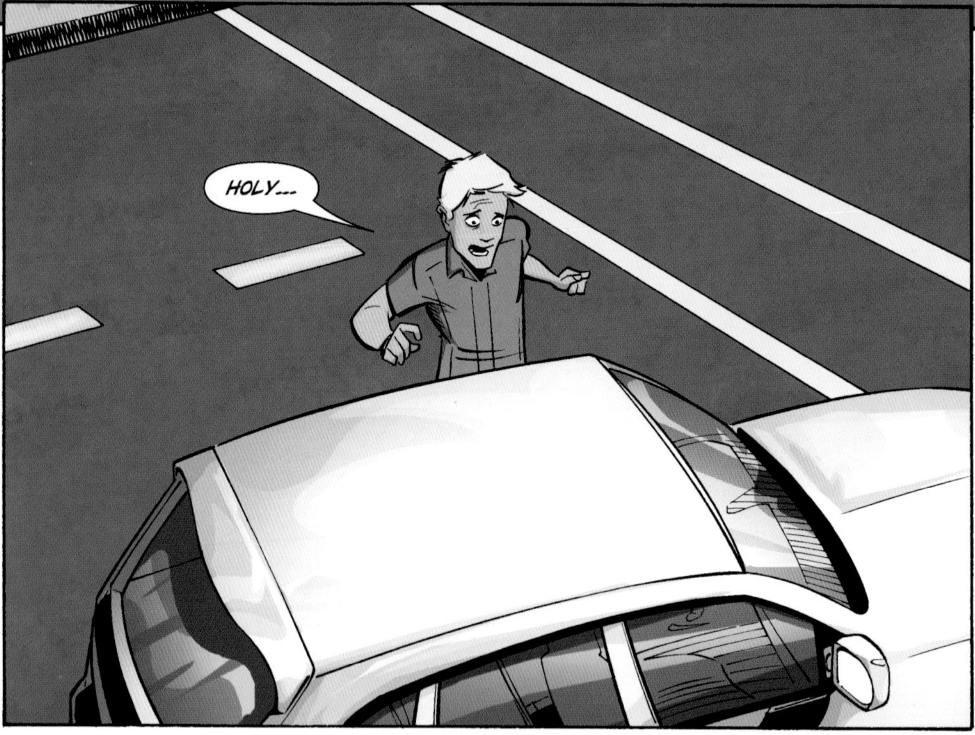
HOLY...

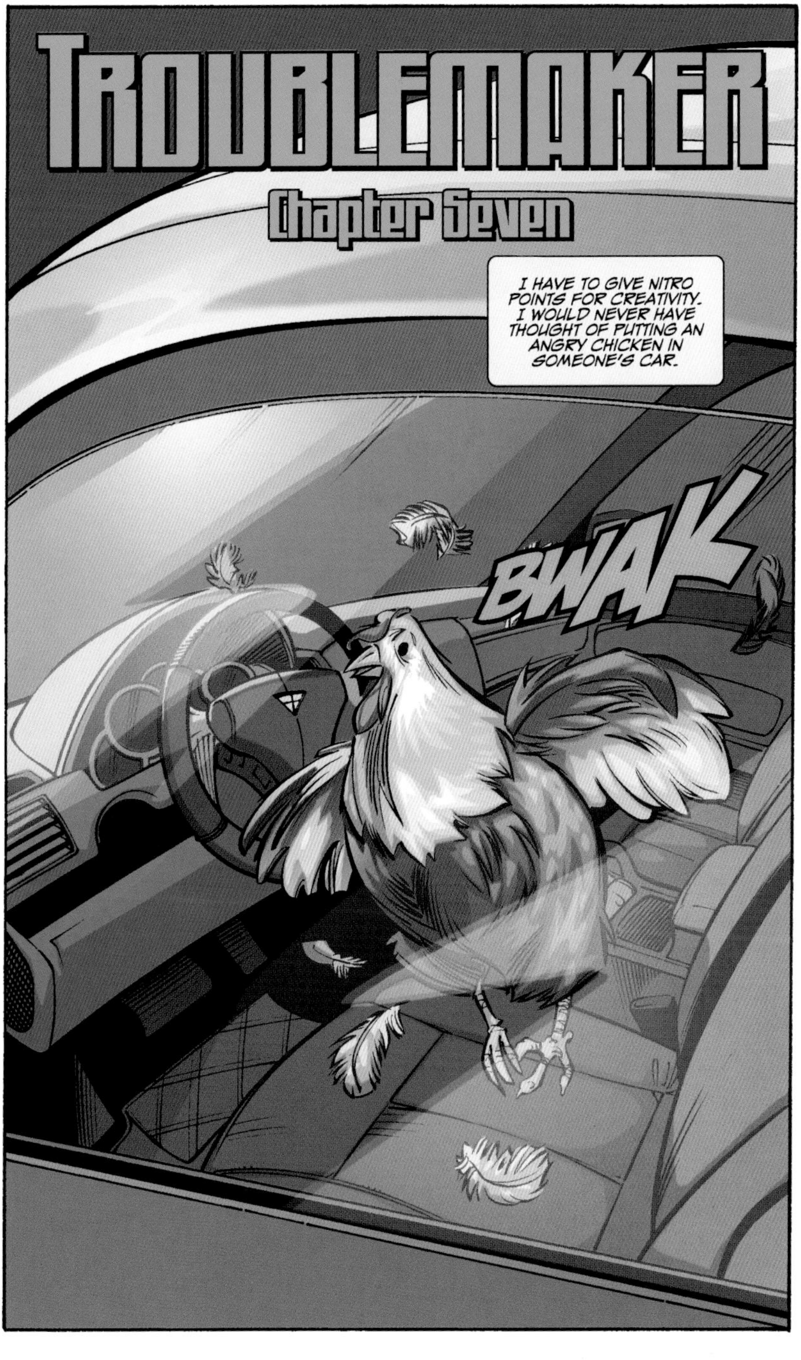
TROUBLEMAKER
Chapter Seven
I HAVE TO GIVE NITRO POINTS FOR CREATIVITY. I WOULD NEVER HAVE THOUGHT OF PUTTING AN ANGRY CHICKEN IN SOMEONE'S CAR.
BWAK

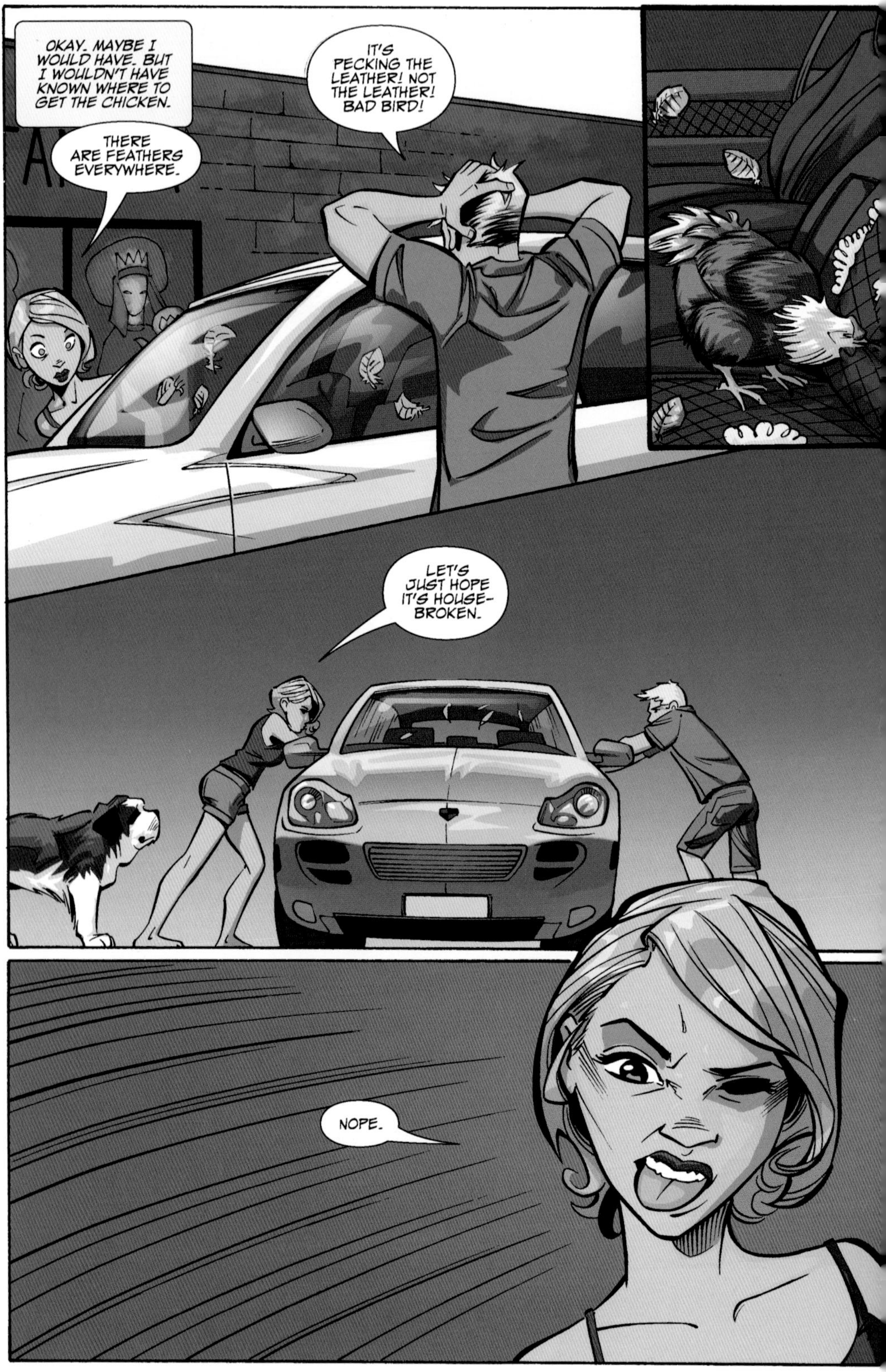
OKAY. MAYBE I WOULD HAVE. BUT I WOULDN'T HAVE KNOWN WHERE TO GET THE CHICKEN.
THERE ARE FEATHERS EVERYWHERE.
IT'S PECKING THE LEATHER! NOT THE LEATHER! BAD BIRD!
LET'S JUST HOPE IT'S HOUSE-BROKEN.
NOPE.

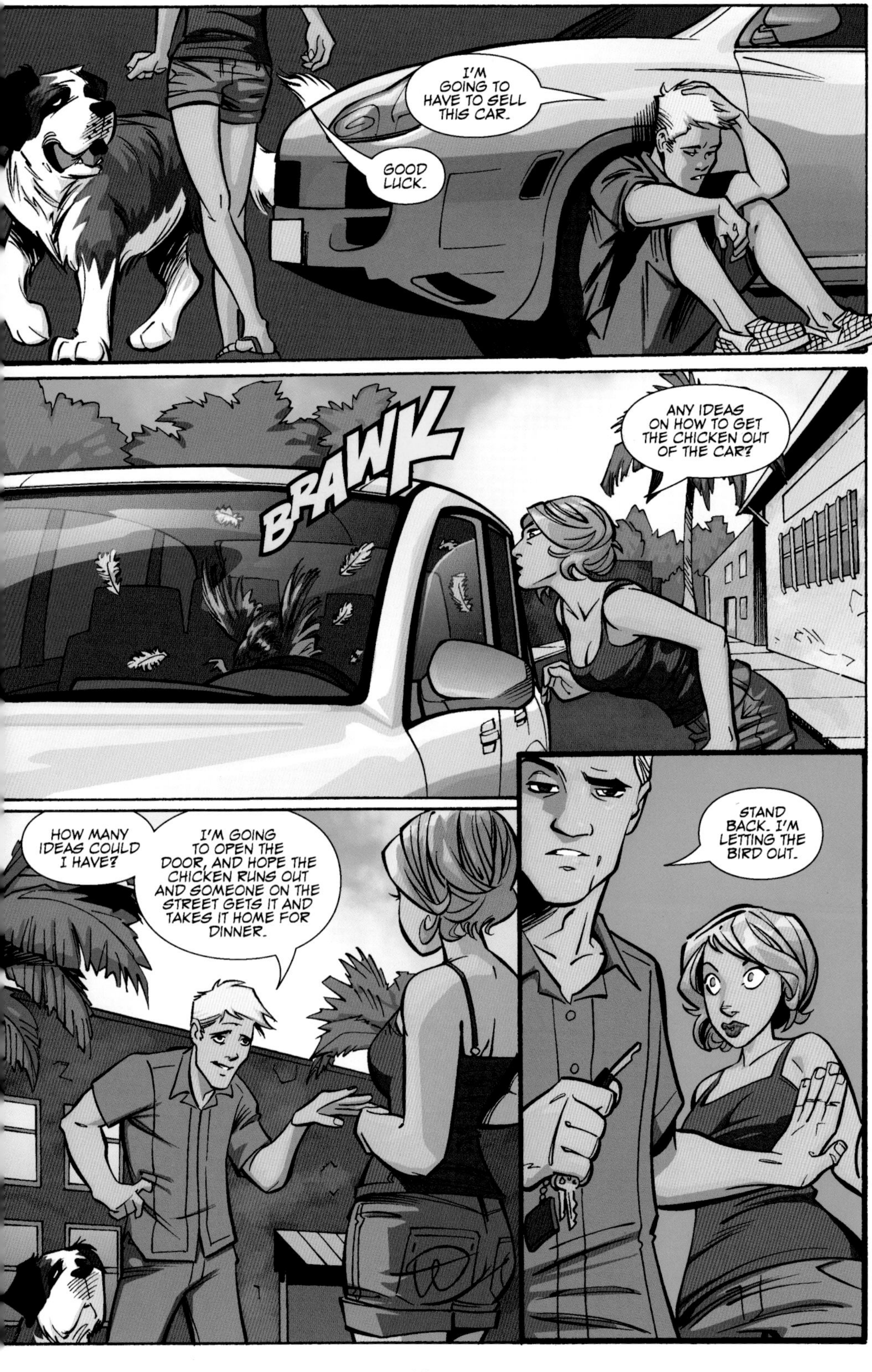
I'M GOING TO HAVE TO SELL THIS CAR.
GOOD LUCK.
BRAWK
ANY IDEAS ON HOW TO GET THE CHICKEN OUT OF THE CAR?
HOW MANY IDEAS COULD I HAVE?
I'M GOING TO OPEN THE DOOR, AND HOPE THE CHICKEN RUNS OUT AND SOMEONE ON THE STREET GETS IT AND TAKES IT HOME FOR DINNER.
STAND BACK. I'M LETTING THE BIRD OUT.

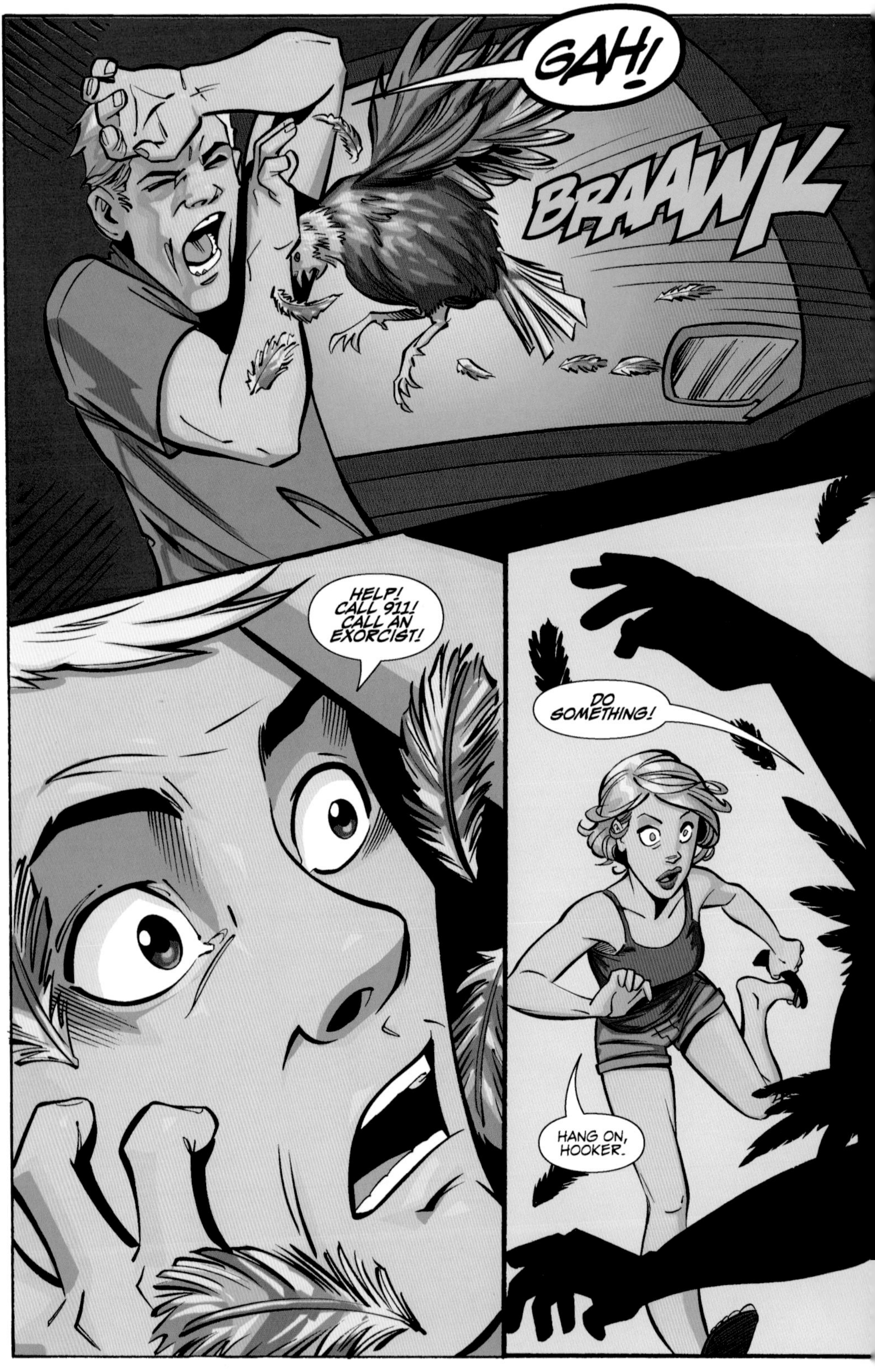
GAH!
BRAAWK
HELP! CALL 911! CALL AN EXORCIST!
DO SOMETHING!
HANG ON, HOOKER.

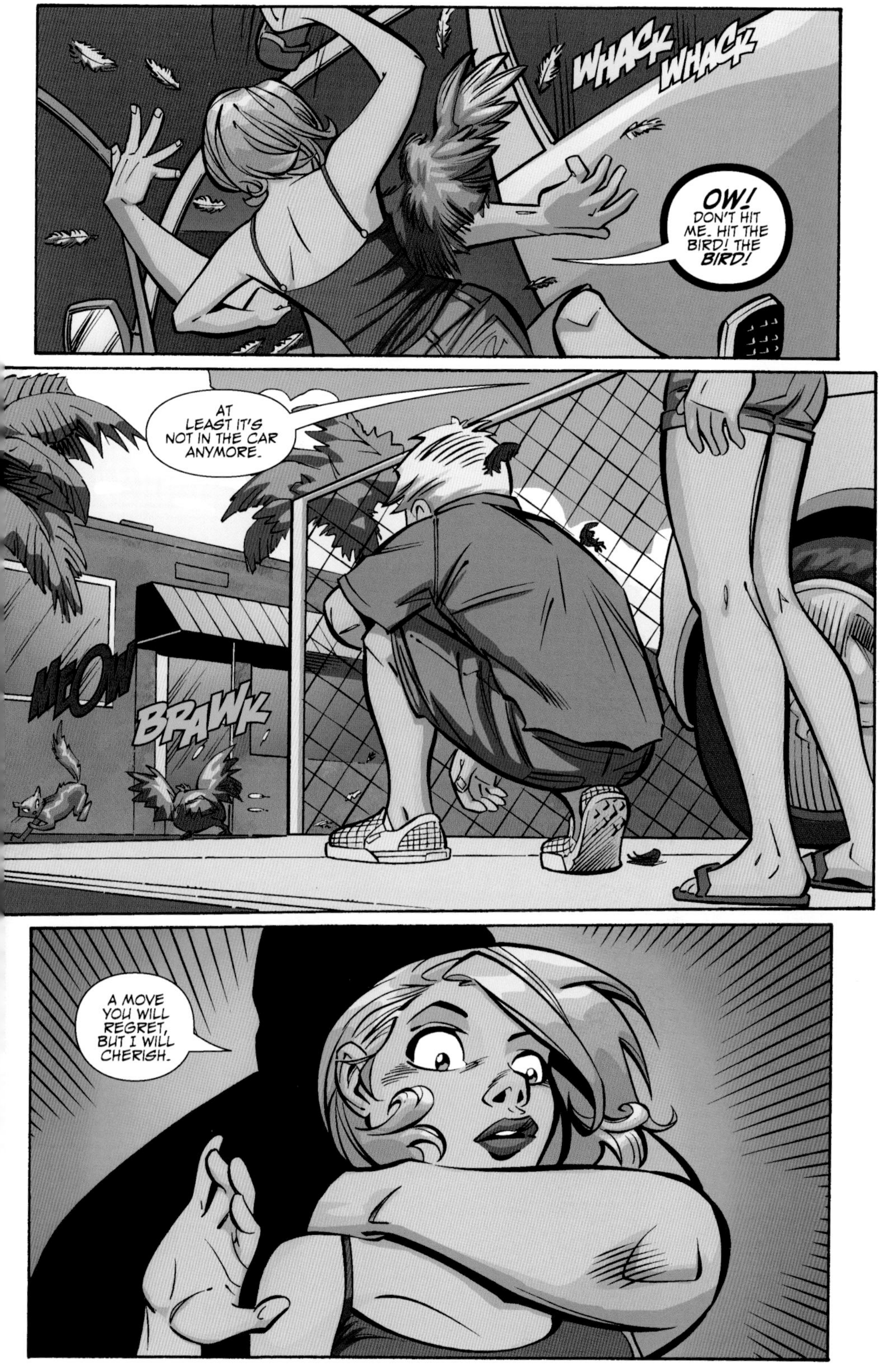
WHACK
WHACK
OW! DON'T HIT ME. HIT THE BIRD! THE BIRD!
AT LEAST IT'S NOT IN THE CAR ANYMORE.
MEOW
BRAWK
A MOVE YOU WILL REGRET, BUT I WILL CHERISH.

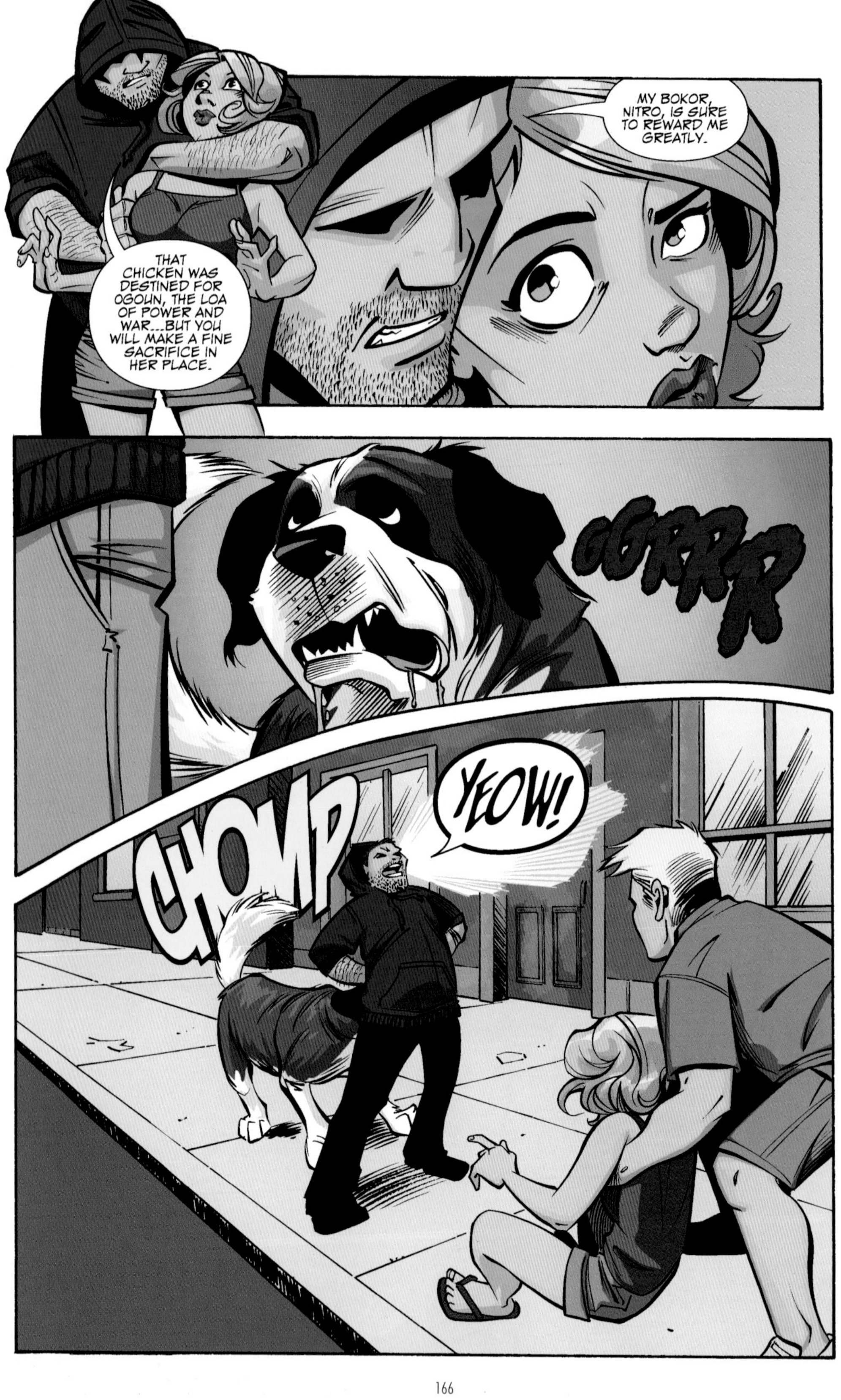
THAT CHICKEN WAS DESTINED FOR OGOUN, THE LOA OF POWER AND WAR...BUT YOU WILL MAKE A FINE SACRIFICE IN HER PLACE.
MY BOKOR, NITRO, IS SURE TO REWARD ME GREATLY.
GGRRRR
CHOMP
YEOW!

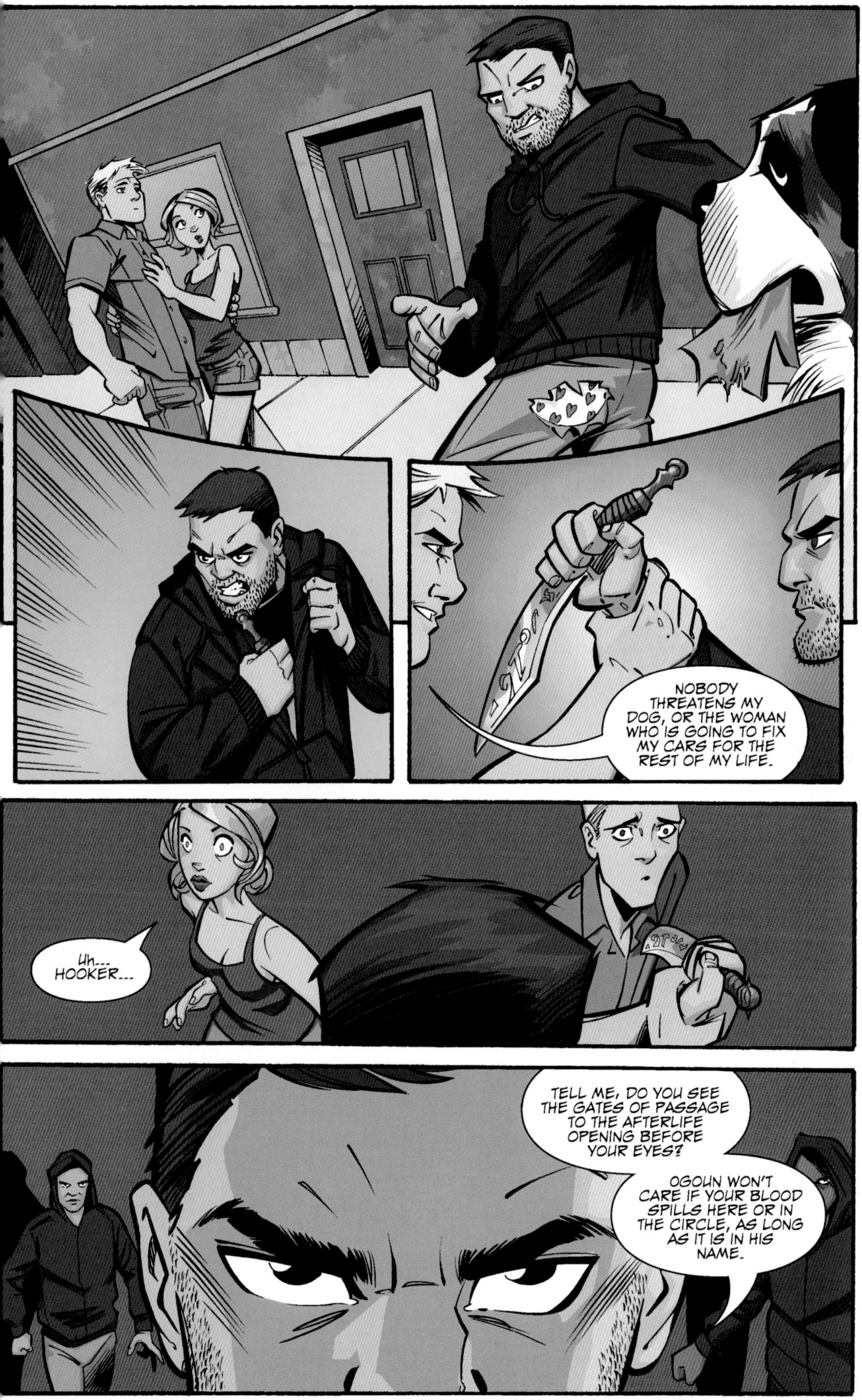
NOBODY THREATENS MY DOG, OR THE WOMAN WHO IS GOING TO FIX MY CARS FOR THE REST OF MY LIFE.
Uh... HOOKER...
TELL ME, DO YOU SEE THE GATES OF PASSAGE TO THE AFTERLIFE OPENING BEFORE YOUR EYES?
OGOUN WON'T CARE IF YOUR BLOOD SPILLS HERE OR IN THE CIRCLE, AS LONG AS IT IS IN HIS NAME.

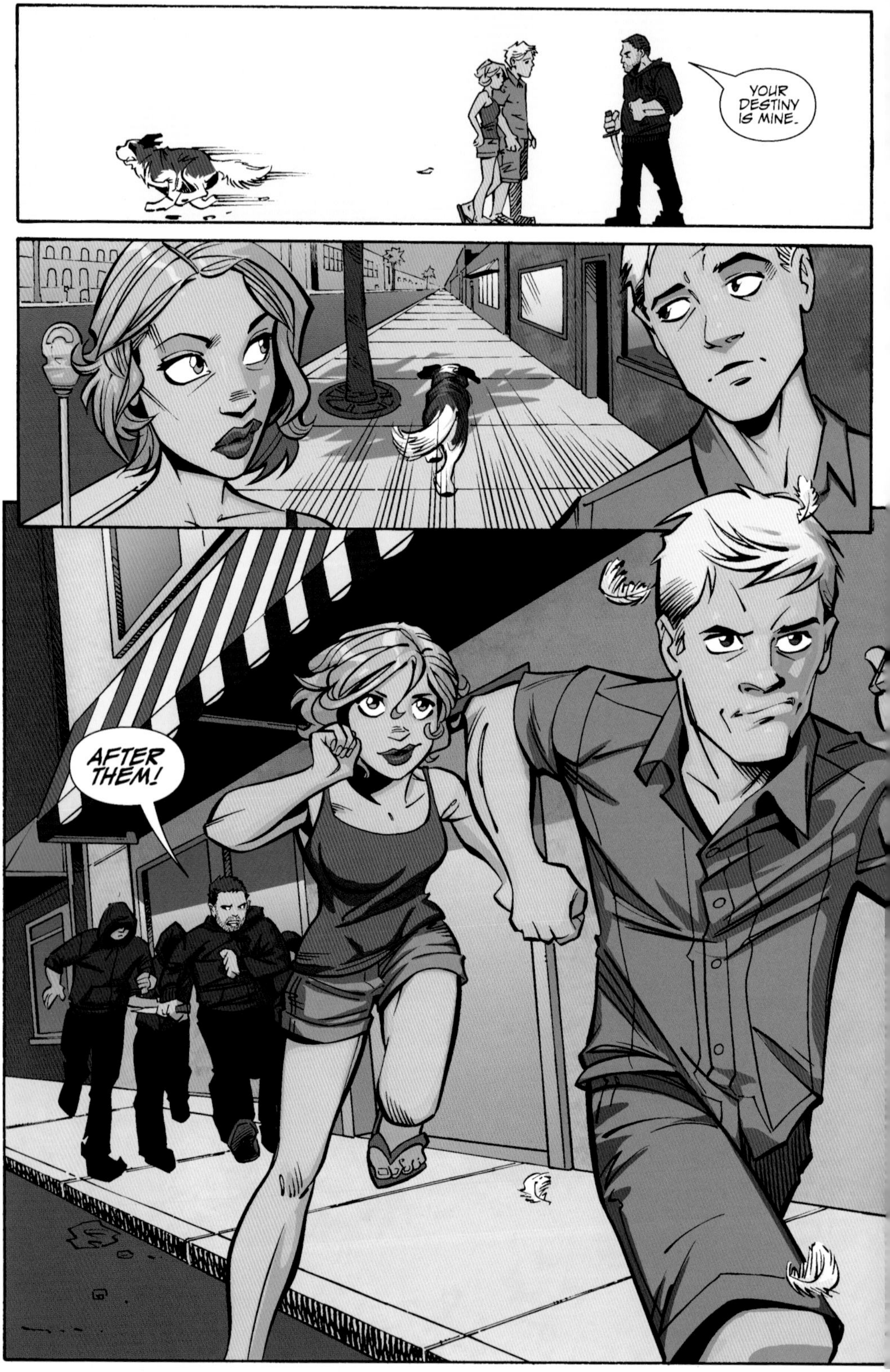
YOUR DESTINY IS MINE.
AFTER THEM!

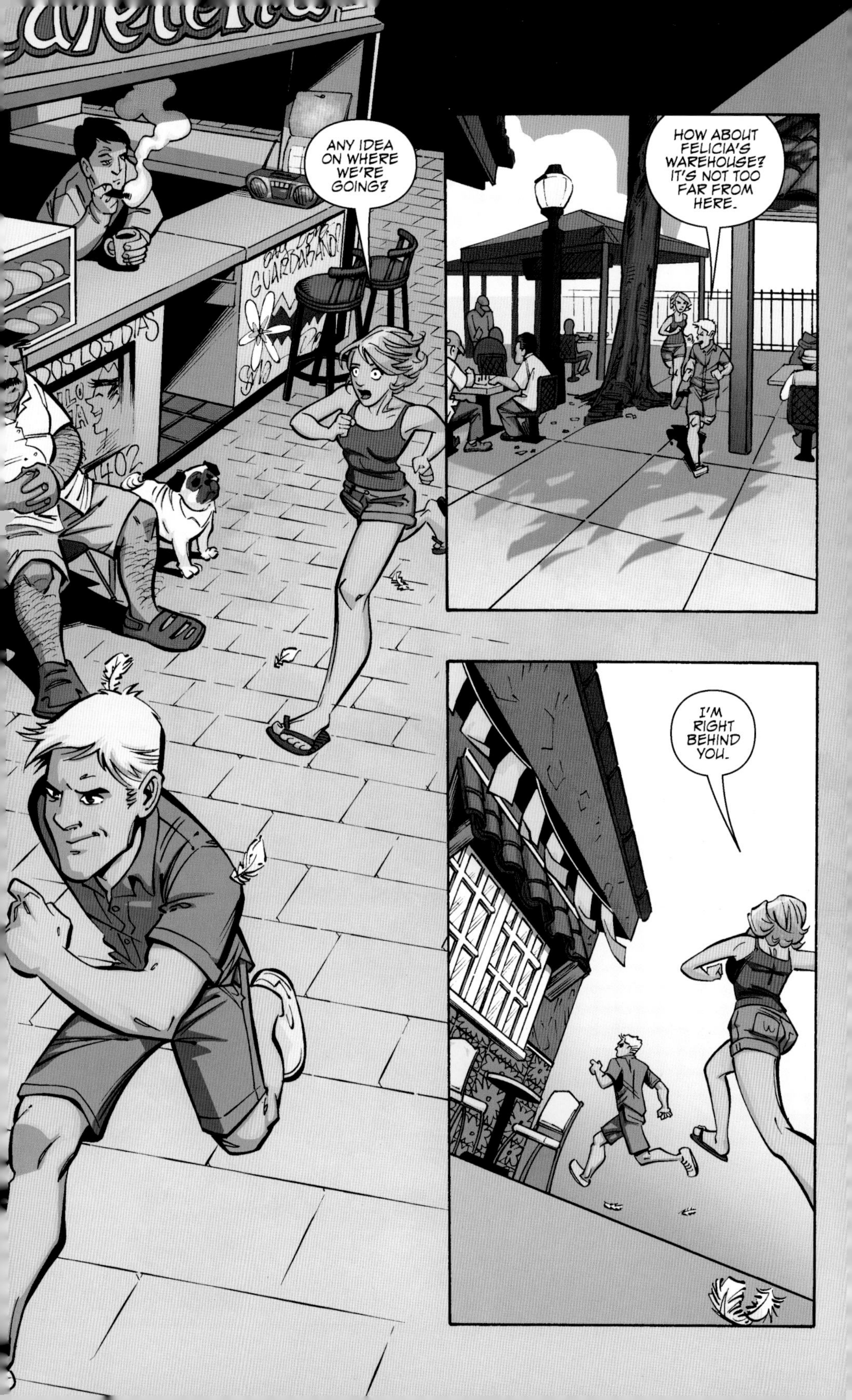
ANY IDEA ON WHERE WE'RE GOING?
HOW ABOUT FELICIA'S WAREHOUSE? IT'S NOT TOO FAR FROM HERE.
I'M RIGHT BEHIND YOU.

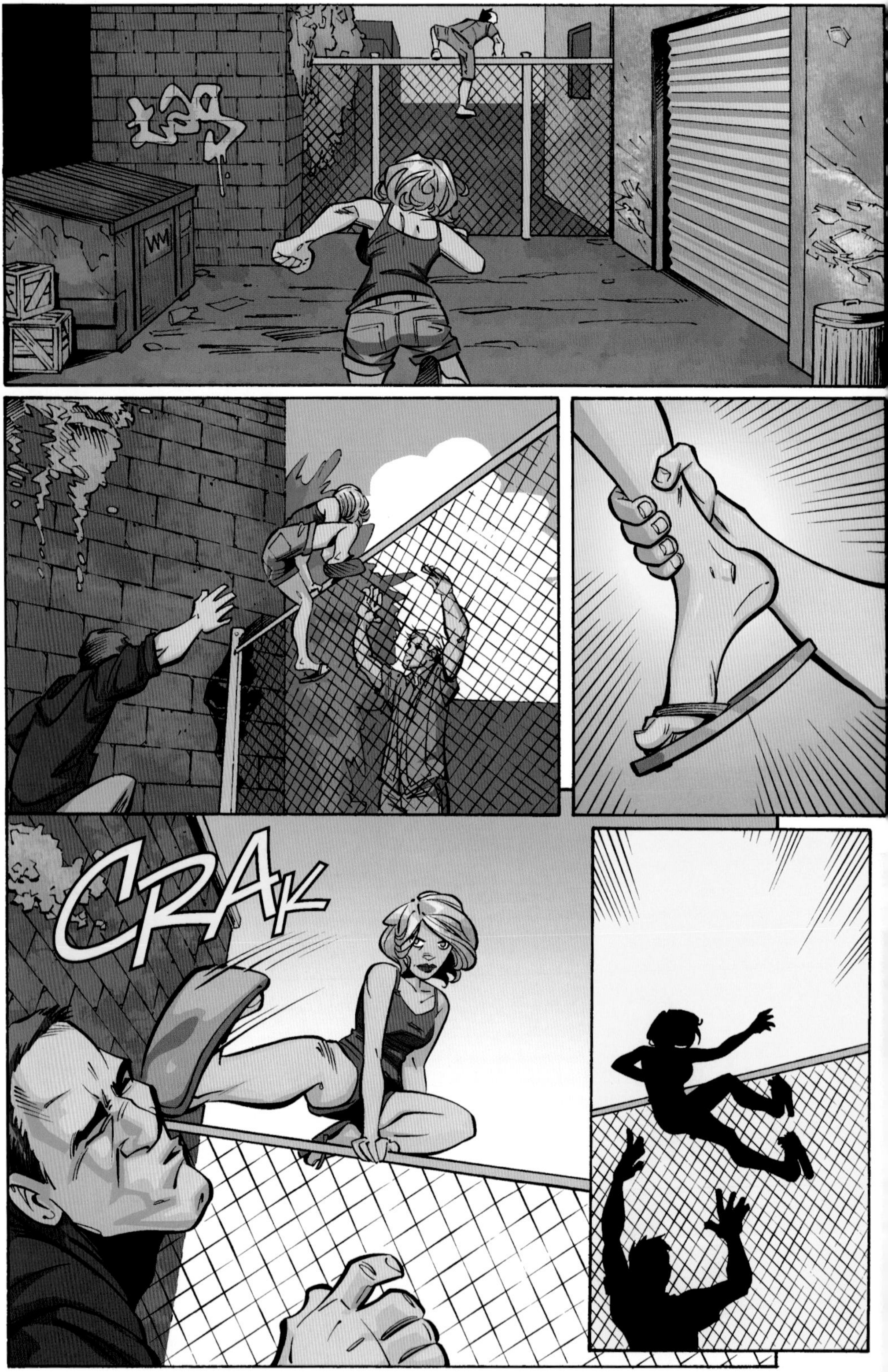
CRAK

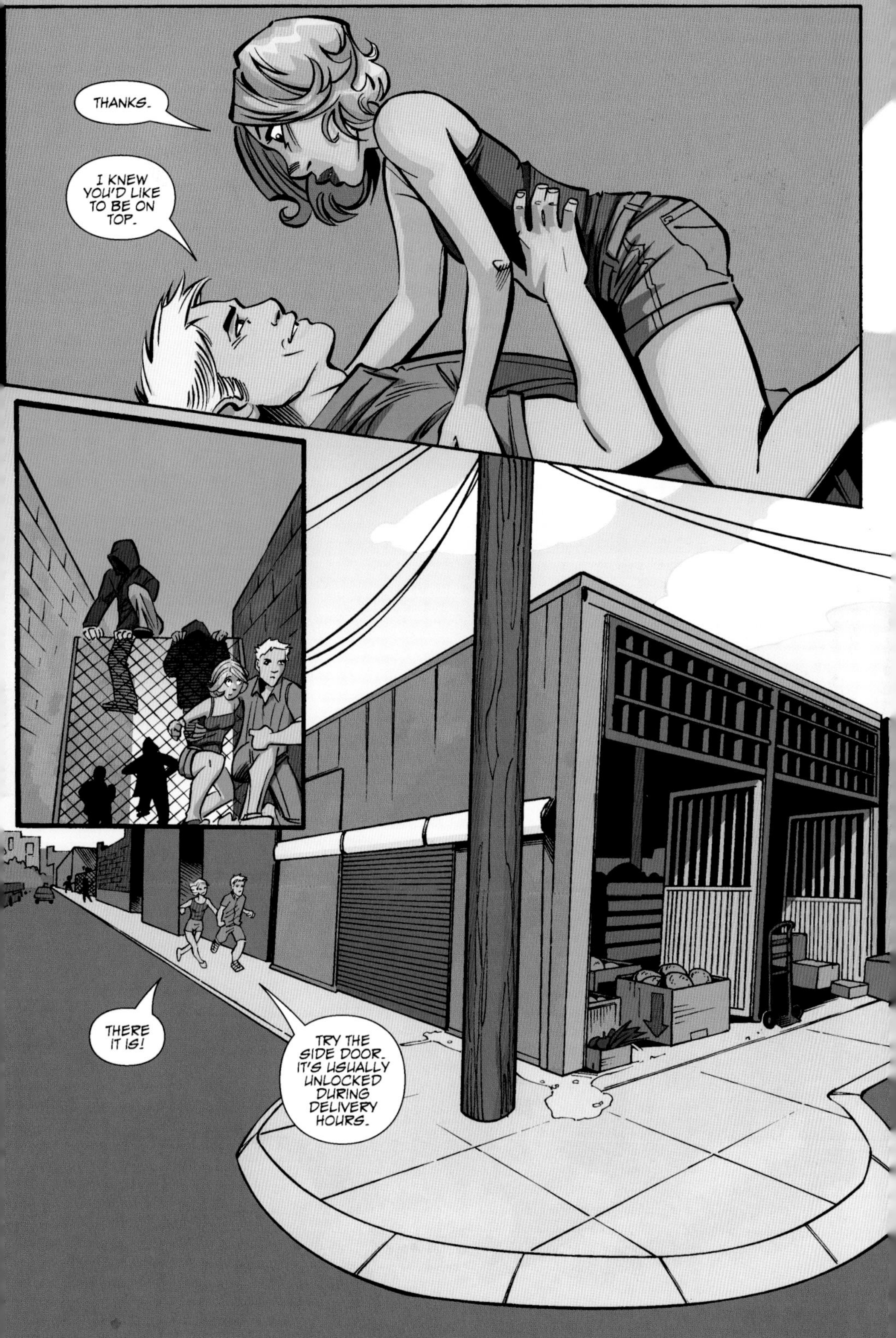
THANKS.
I KNEW YOU'D LIKE TO BE ON TOP.
THERE IT IS!
TRY THE SIDE DOOR. IT'S USUALLY UNLOCKED DURING DELIVERY HOURS.

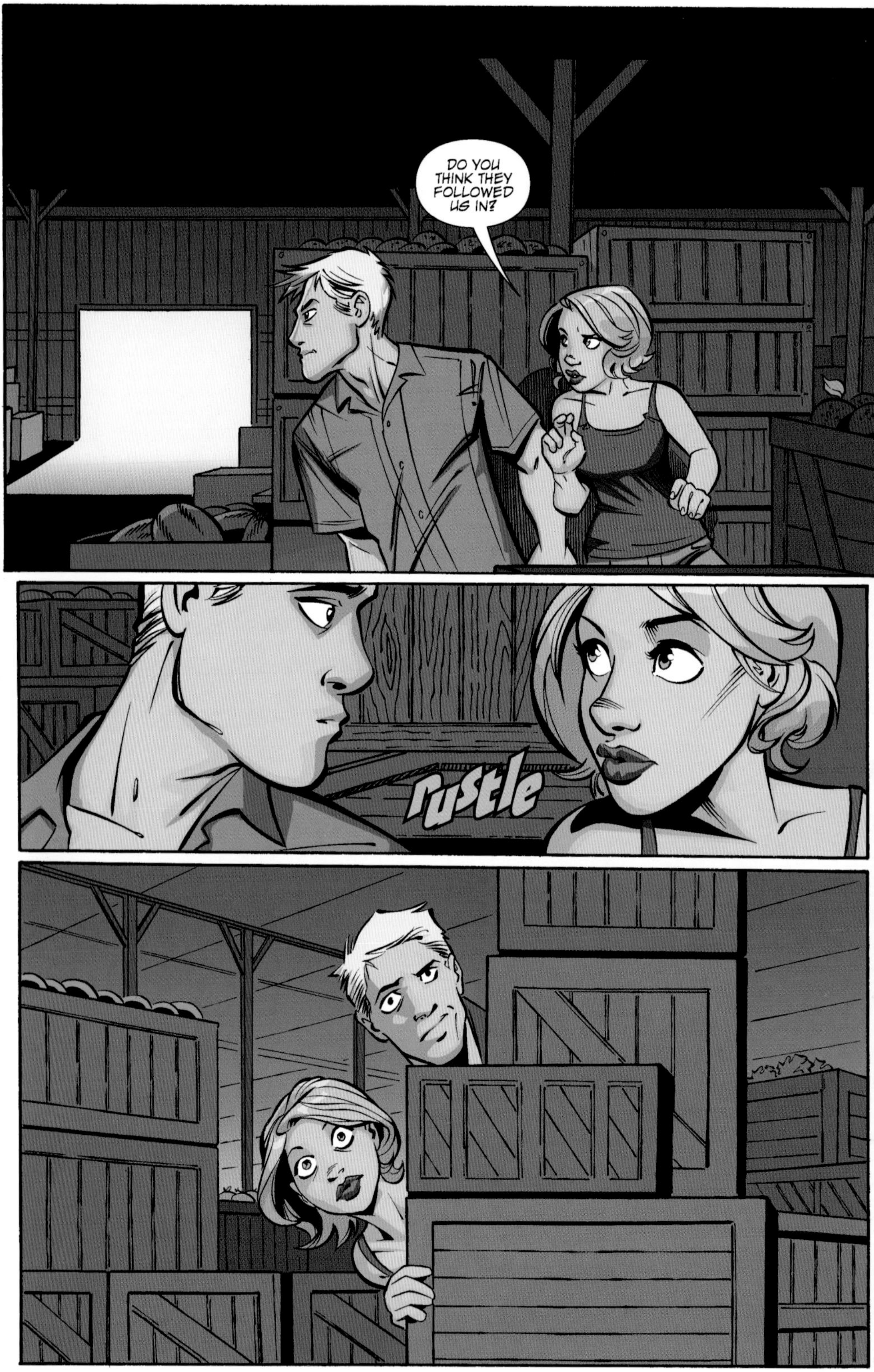
DO YOU THINK THEY FOLLOWED US IN?
rustle

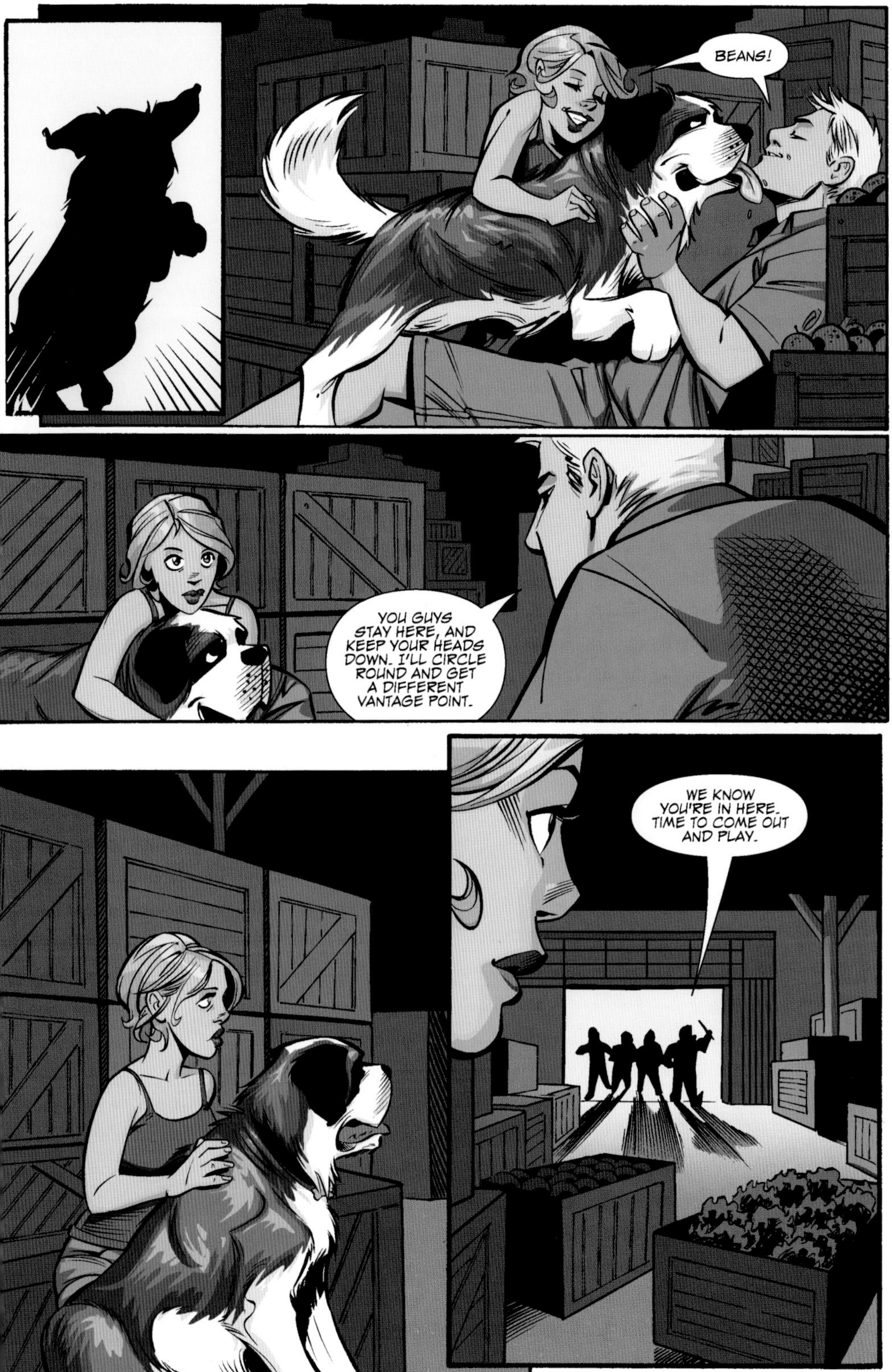
BEANS!
YOU GUYS STAY HERE, AND KEEP YOUR HEADS DOWN. I'LL CIRCLE ROUND AND GET A DIFFERENT VANTAGE POINT.
WE KNOW YOU'RE IN HERE. TIME TO COME OUT AND PLAY.

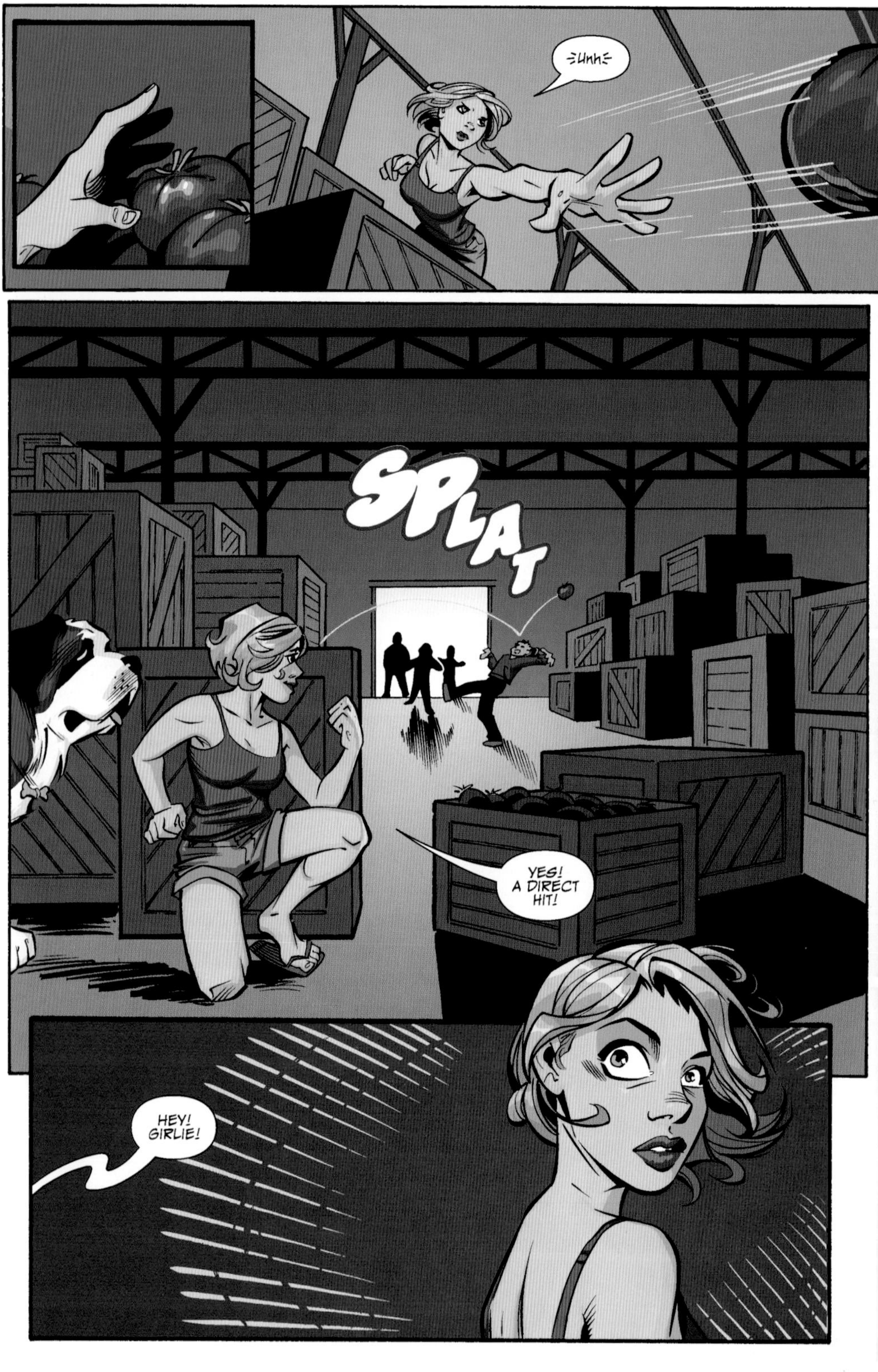

=Unnh=
SPLAT
YES! A DIRECT HIT!
HEY! GIRLIE!

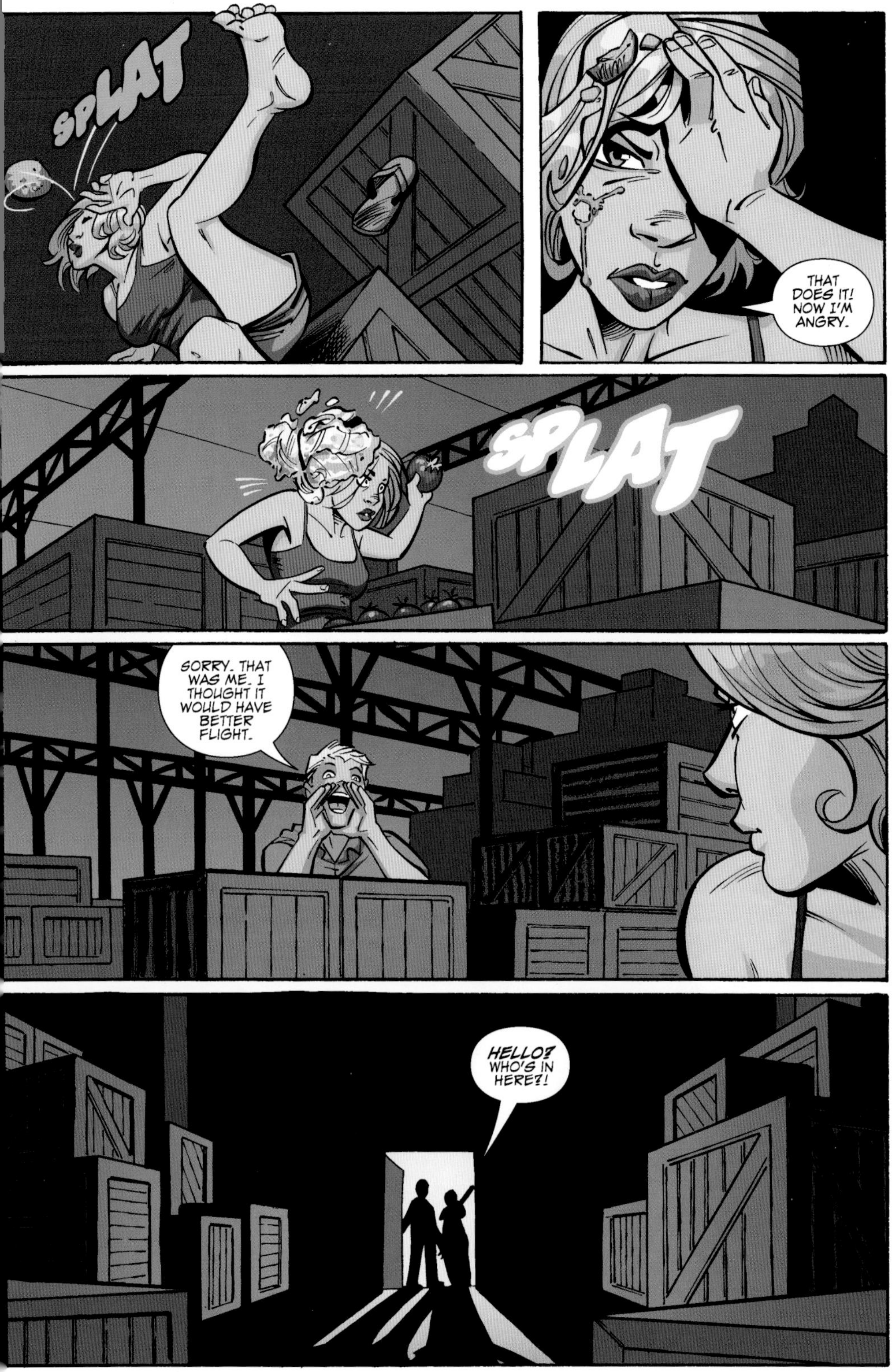
SPLAT
THAT DOES IT! NOW I'M ANGRY.
SPLAT
SORRY. THAT WAS ME. I THOUGHT IT WOULD HAVE BETTER FLIGHT.
HELLO? WHO'S IN HERE?!

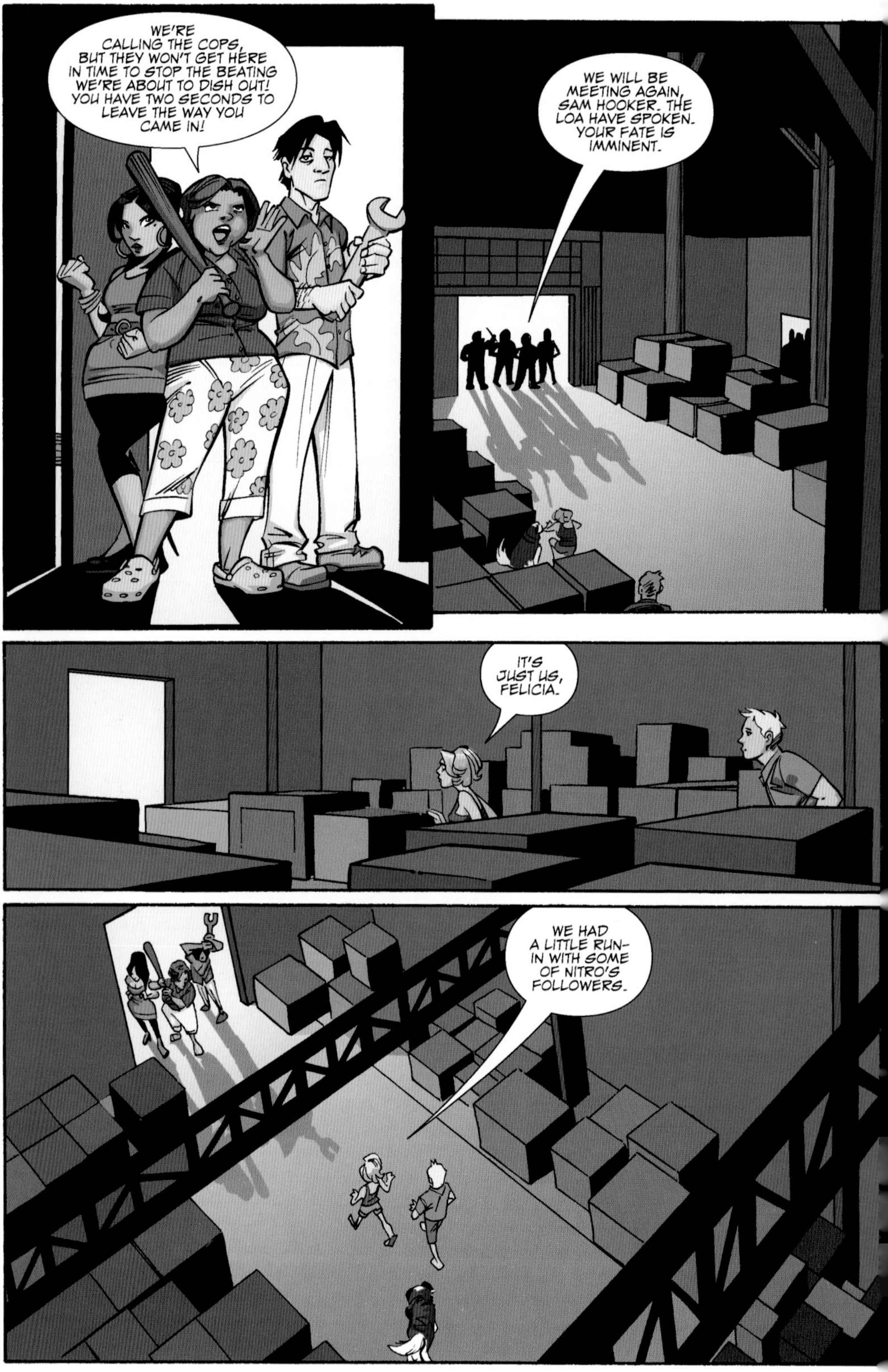
WE'RE CALLING THE COPS, BUT THEY WON'T GET HERE IN TIME TO STOP THE BEATING WE'RE ABOUT TO DISH OUT! YOU HAVE TWO SECONDS TO LEAVE THE WAY YOU CAME IN!
WE WILL BE MEETING AGAIN, SAM HOOKER. THE LOA HAVE SPOKEN. YOUR FATE IS IMMINENT.
IT'S JUST US, FELICIA.
WE HAD A LITTLE RUN-IN WITH SOME OF NITRO'S FOLLOWERS.

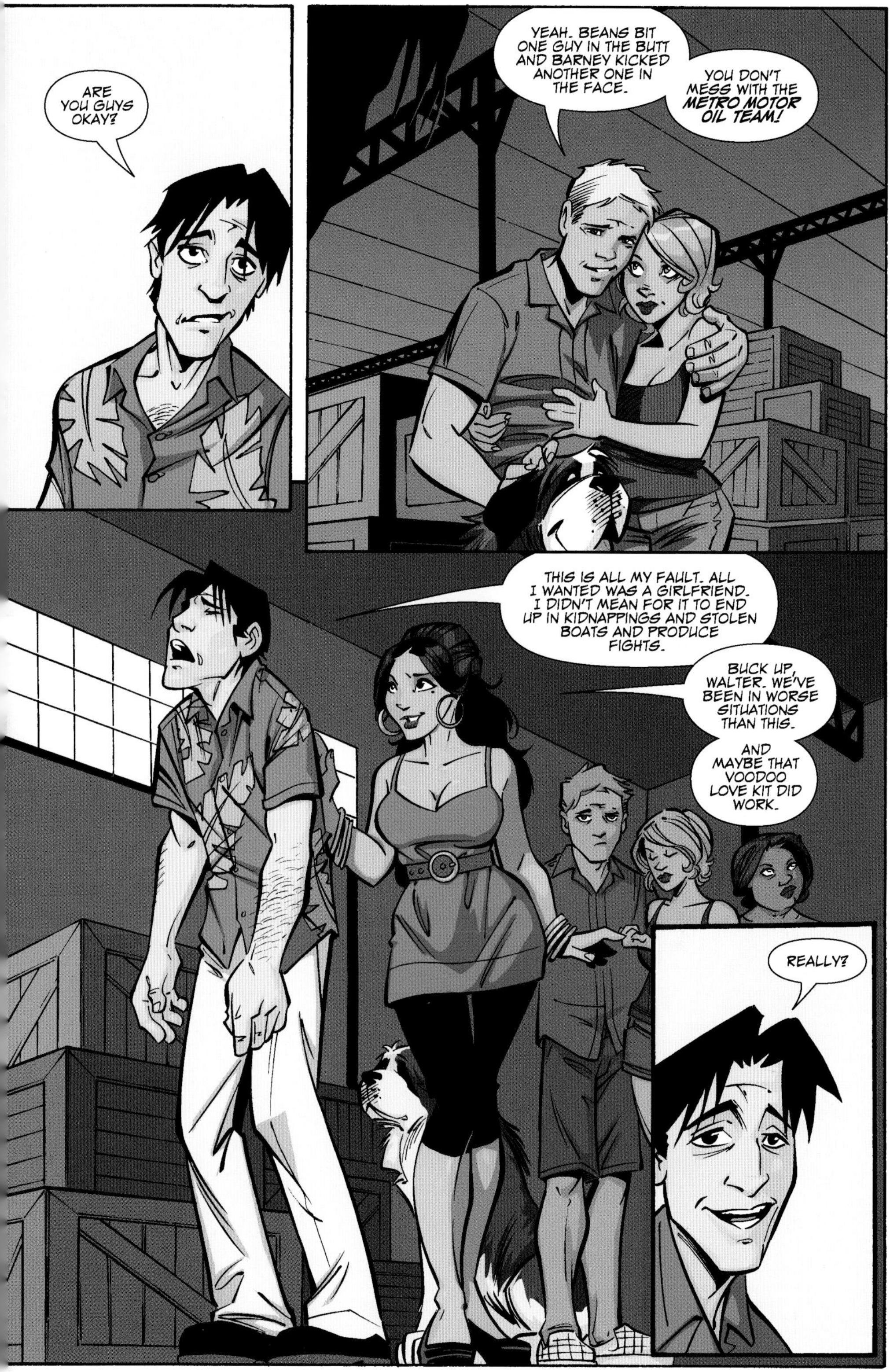
ARE YOU GUYS OKAY?
YEAH. BEANS BIT ONE GUY IN THE BUTT AND BARNEY KICKED ANOTHER ONE IN THE FACE.
YOU DON'T MESS WITH THE ***METRO MOTOR OIL TEAM!***
THIS IS ALL MY FAULT. ALL I WANTED WAS A GIRLFRIEND. I DIDN'T MEAN FOR IT TO END UP IN KIDNAPPINGS AND STOLEN BOATS AND PRODUCE FIGHTS.
BUCK UP, WALTER. WE'VE BEEN IN WORSE SITUATIONS THAN THIS.
AND MAYBE THAT VOODOO LOVE KIT DID WORK.
REALLY?

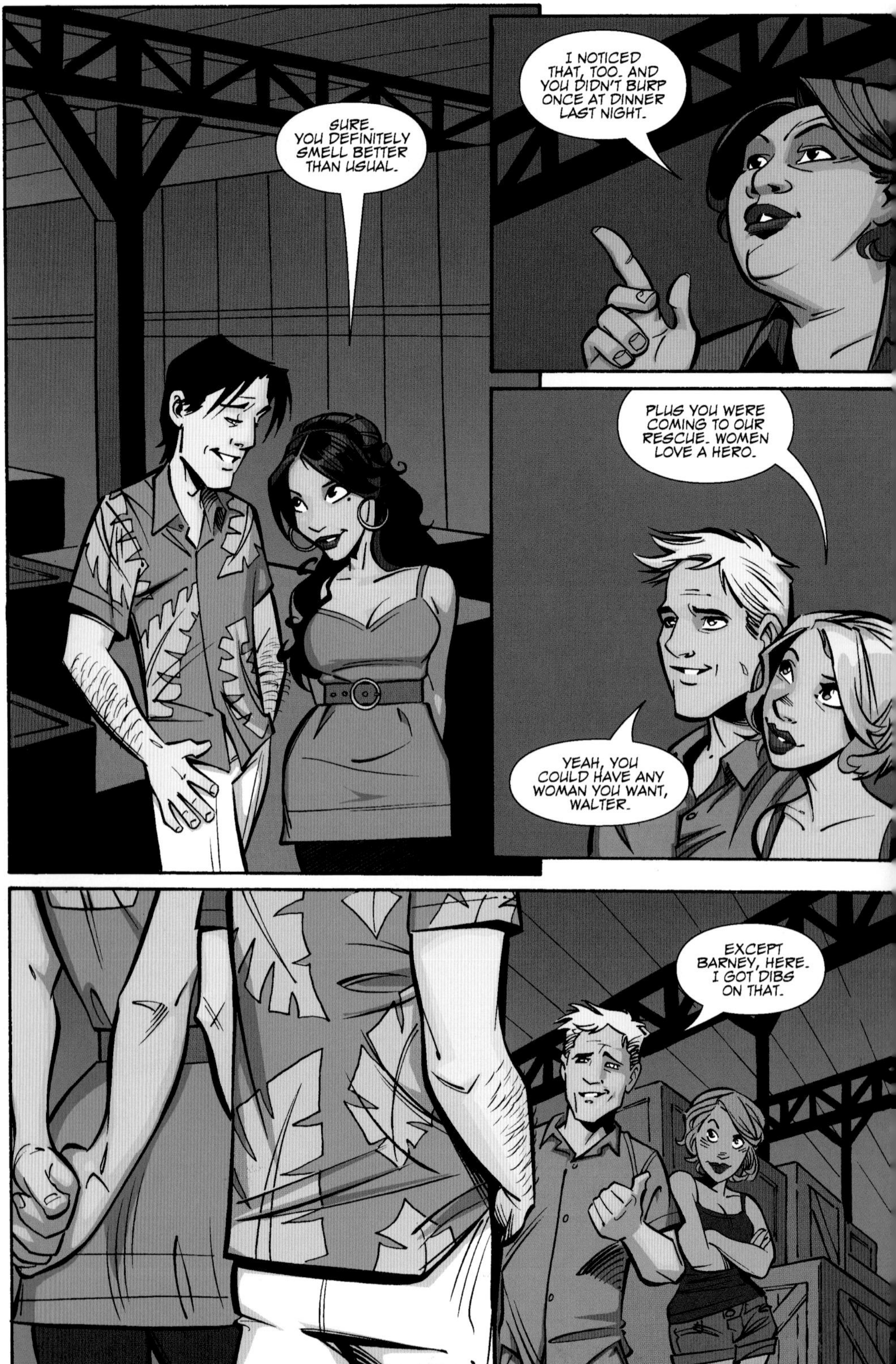
SURE. YOU DEFINITELY SMELL BETTER THAN USUAL.
I NOTICED THAT, TOO. AND YOU DIDN'T BURP ONCE AT DINNER LAST NIGHT.
PLUS YOU WERE COMING TO OUR RESCUE. WOMEN LOVE A HERO.
YEAH, YOU COULD HAVE ANY WOMAN YOU WANT, WALTER.
EXCEPT BARNEY, HERE. I GOT DIBS ON THAT.

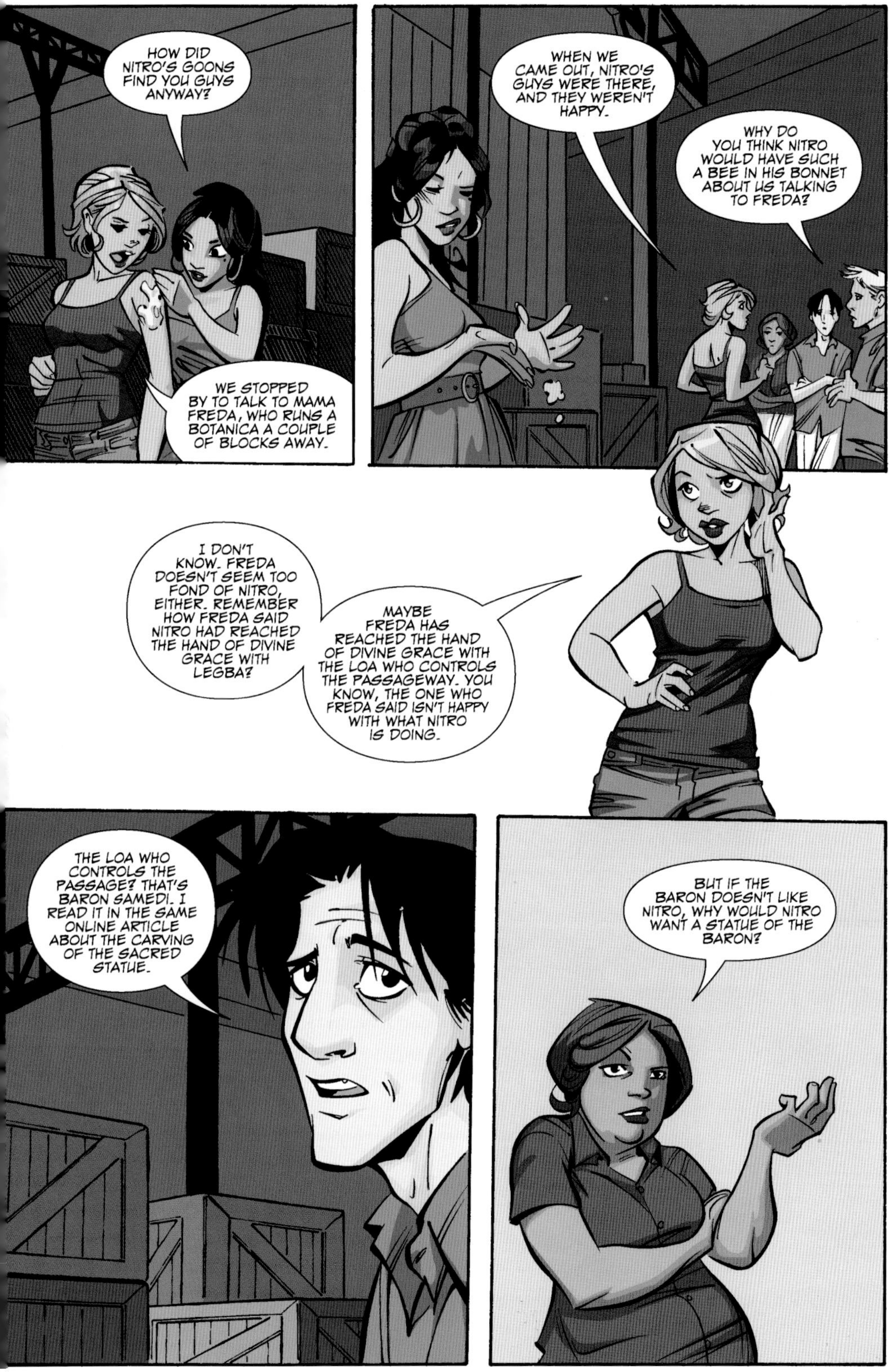
HOW DID NITRO'S GOONS FIND YOU GUYS ANYWAY?
WE STOPPED BY TO TALK TO MAMA FREDA, WHO RUNS A BOTANICA A COUPLE OF BLOCKS AWAY.
WHEN WE CAME OUT, NITRO'S GUYS WERE THERE, AND THEY WEREN'T HAPPY.
WHY DO YOU THINK NITRO WOULD HAVE SUCH A BEE IN HIS BONNET ABOUT US TALKING TO FREDA?
I DON'T KNOW. FREDA DOESN'T SEEM TOO FOND OF NITRO, EITHER. REMEMBER HOW FREDA SAID NITRO HAD REACHED THE HAND OF DIVINE GRACE WITH LEGBA?
MAYBE FREDA HAS REACHED THE HAND OF DIVINE GRACE WITH THE LOA WHO CONTROLS THE PASSAGEWAY. YOU KNOW, THE ONE WHO FREDA SAID ISN'T HAPPY WITH WHAT NITRO IS DOING.
THE LOA WHO CONTROLS THE PASSAGE? THAT'S BARON SAMEDI. I READ IT IN THE SAME ONLINE ARTICLE ABOUT THE CARVING OF THE SACRED STATUE.
BUT IF THE BARON DOESN'T LIKE NITRO, WHY WOULD NITRO WANT A STATUE OF THE BARON?

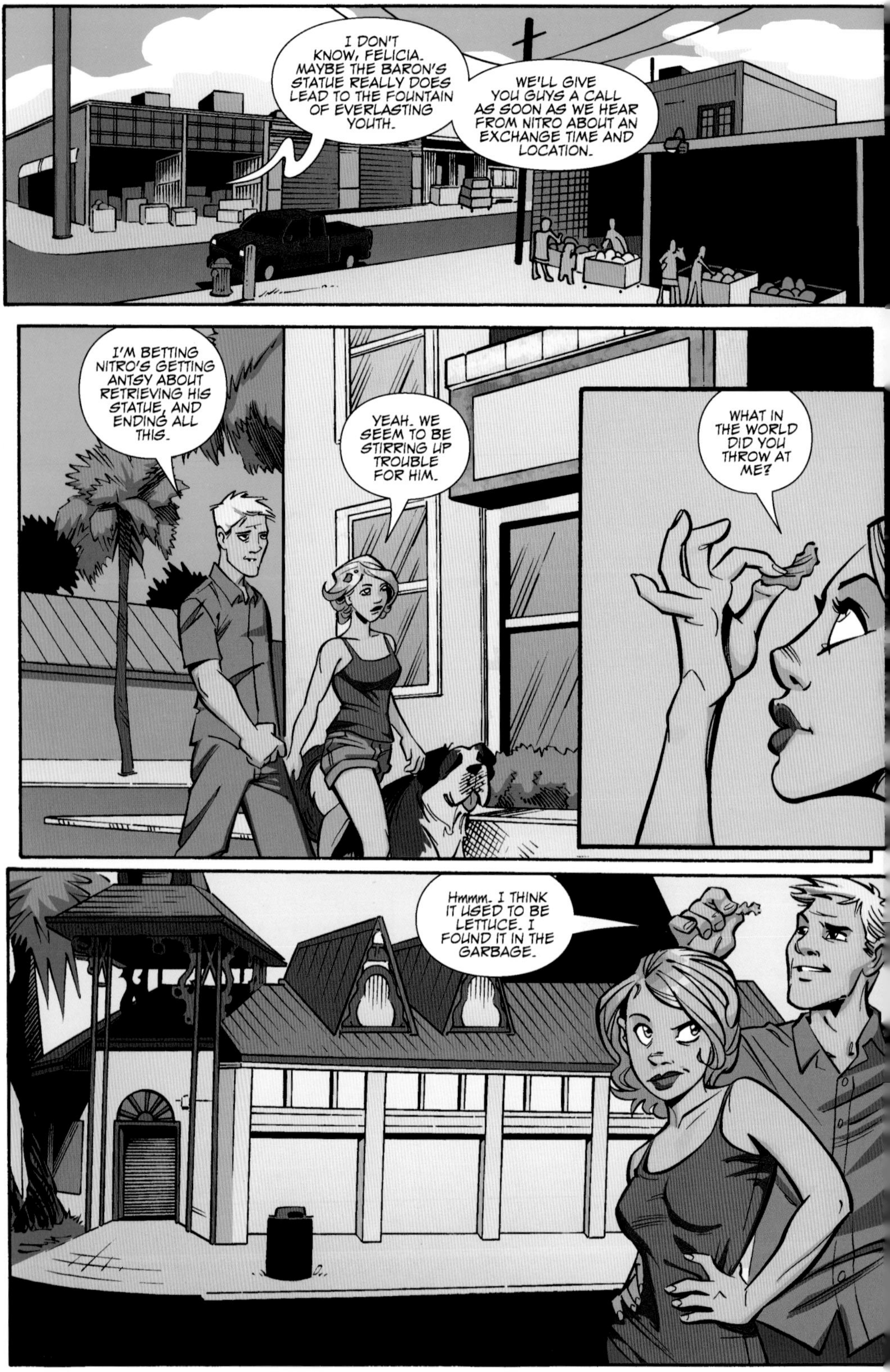
I DON'T KNOW, FELICIA. MAYBE THE BARON'S STATUE REALLY DOES LEAD TO THE FOUNTAIN OF EVERLASTING YOUTH.
WE'LL GIVE YOU GUYS A CALL AS SOON AS WE HEAR FROM NITRO ABOUT AN EXCHANGE TIME AND LOCATION.
I'M BETTING NITRO'S GETTING ANTSY ABOUT RETRIEVING HIS STATUE, AND ENDING ALL THIS.
YEAH. WE SEEM TO BE STIRRING UP TROUBLE FOR HIM.
WHAT IN THE WORLD DID YOU THROW AT ME?
Hmmm. I THINK IT USED TO BE LETTUCE. I FOUND IT IN THE GARBAGE.

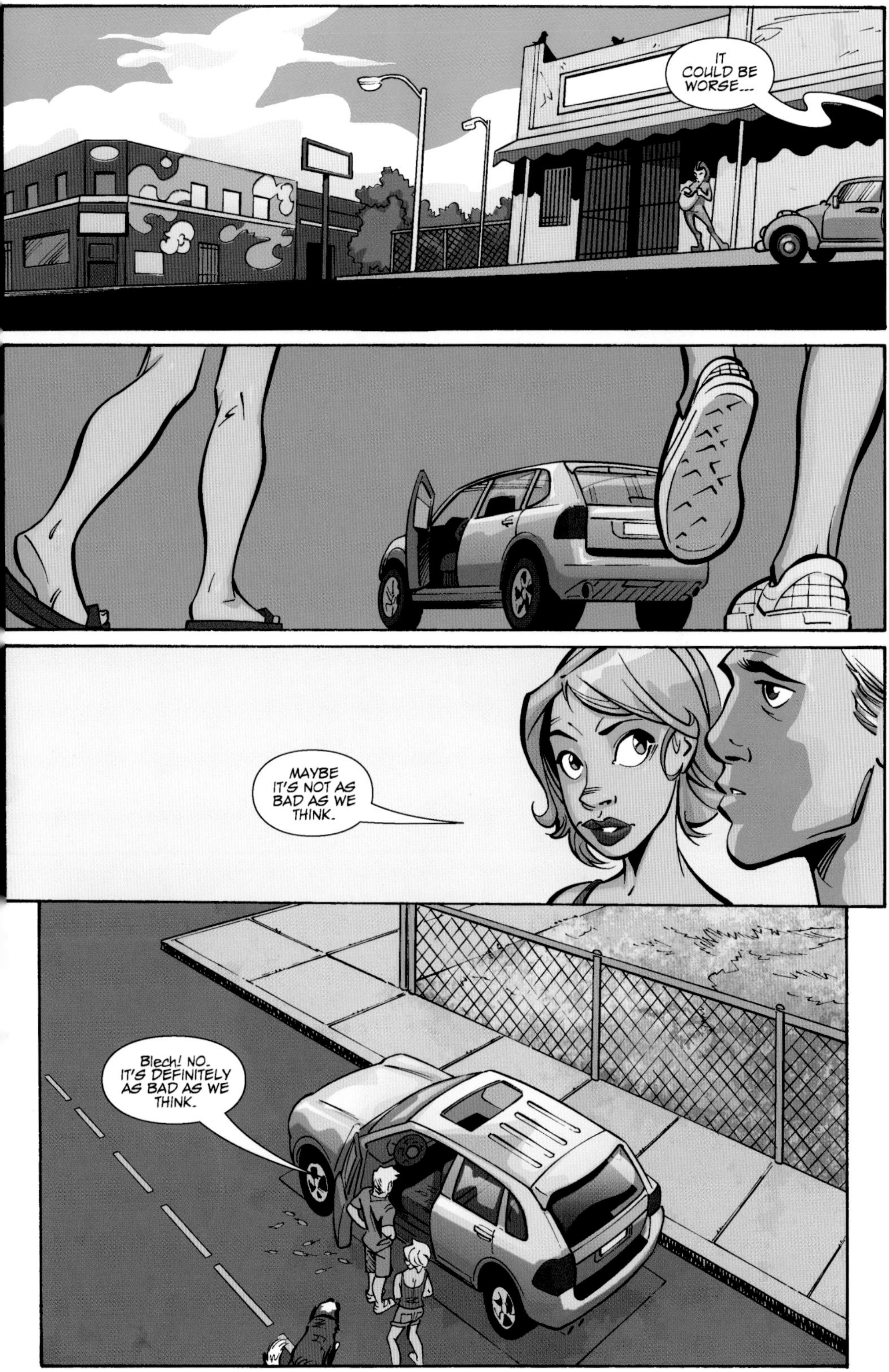

IT COULD BE WORSE...
MAYBE IT'S NOT AS BAD AS WE THINK.
Blech! NO. IT'S DEFINITELY AS BAD AS WE THINK.

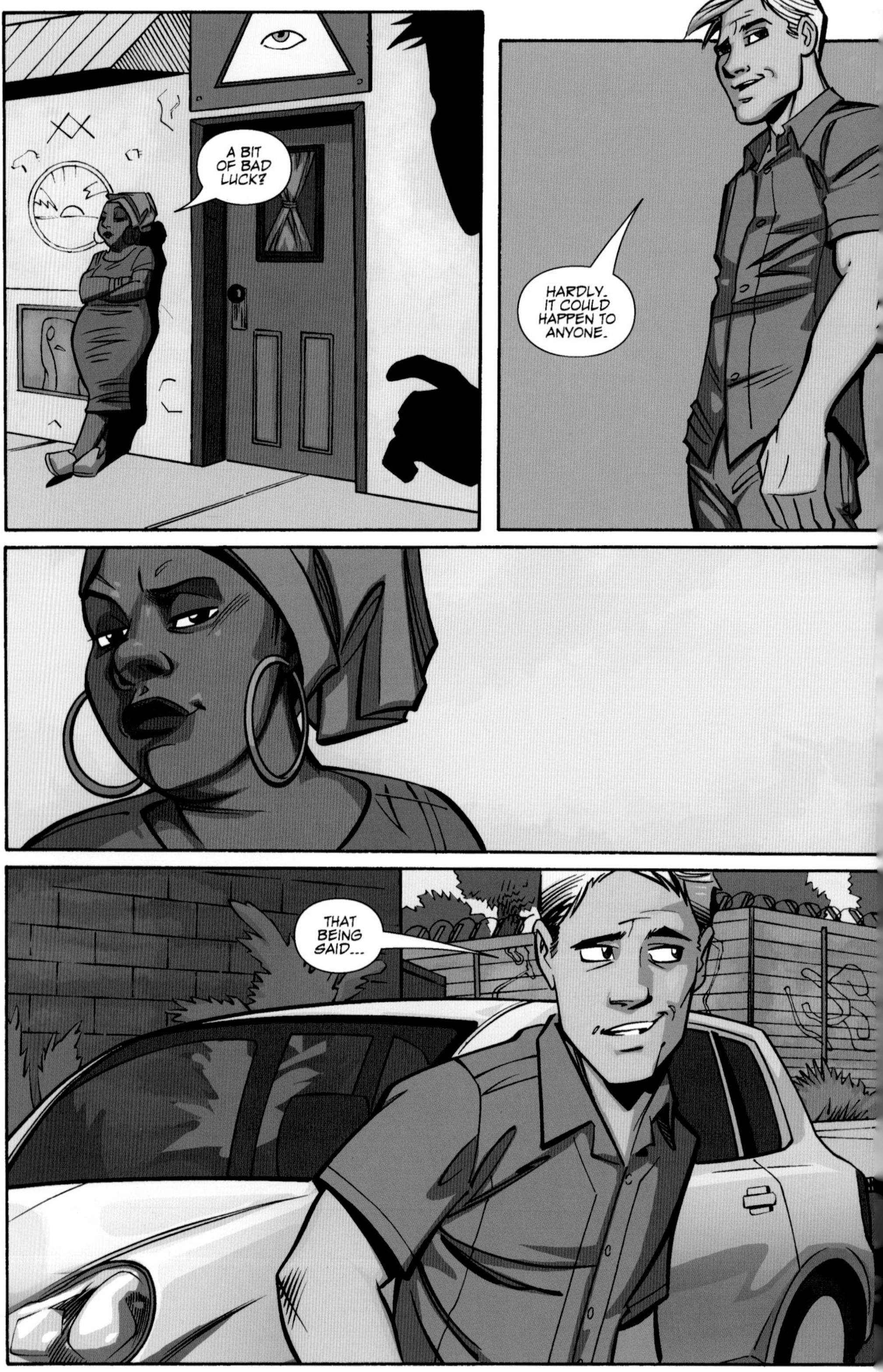
A BIT OF BAD LUCK?
HARDLY. IT COULD HAPPEN TO ANYONE.
THAT BEING SAID...

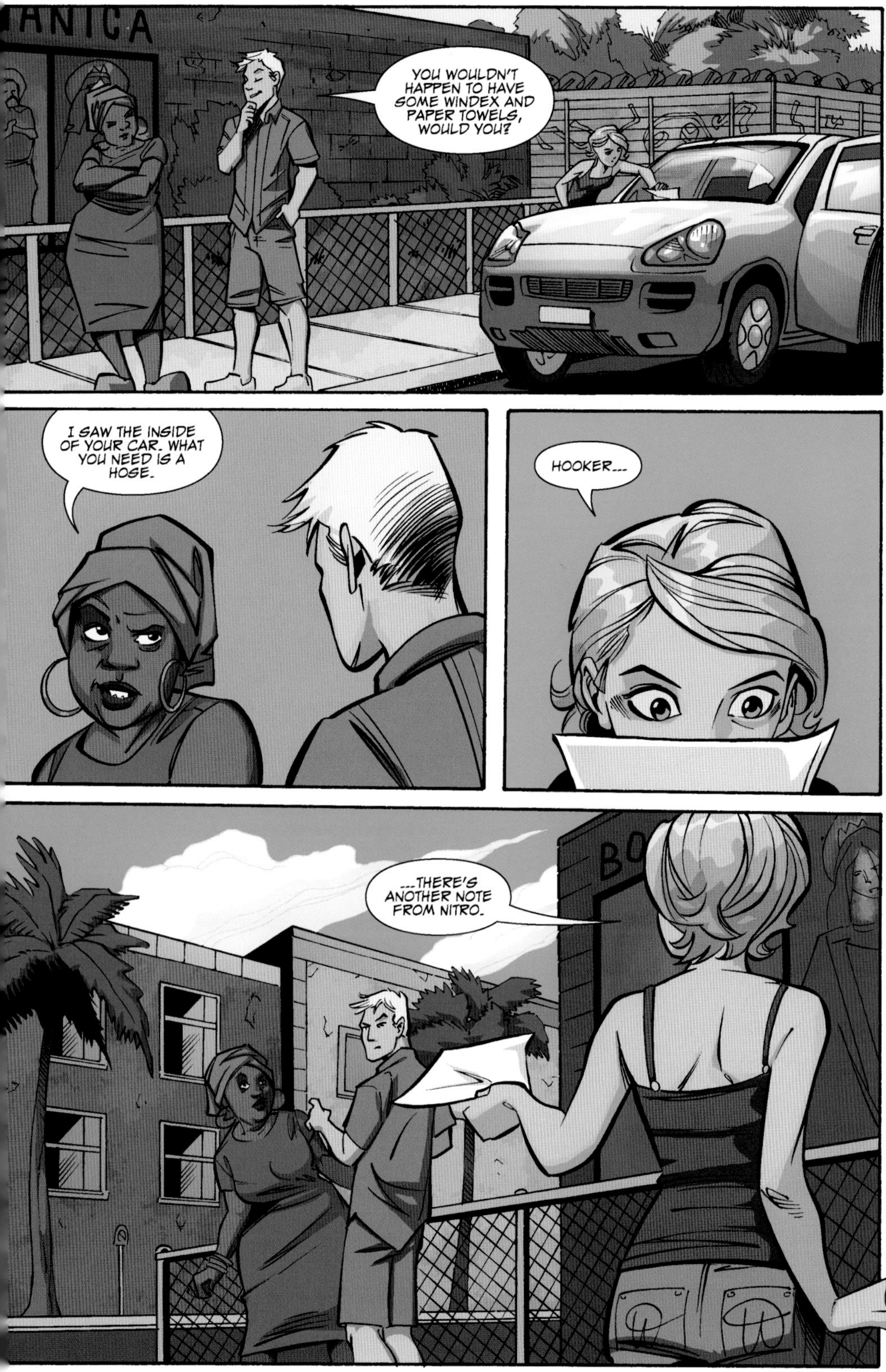
YOU WOULDN'T HAPPEN TO HAVE SOME WINDEX AND PAPER TOWELS, WOULD YOU?
I SAW THE INSIDE OF YOUR CAR. WHAT YOU NEED IS A HOSE.
HOOKER...
...THERE'S ANOTHER NOTE FROM NITRO.

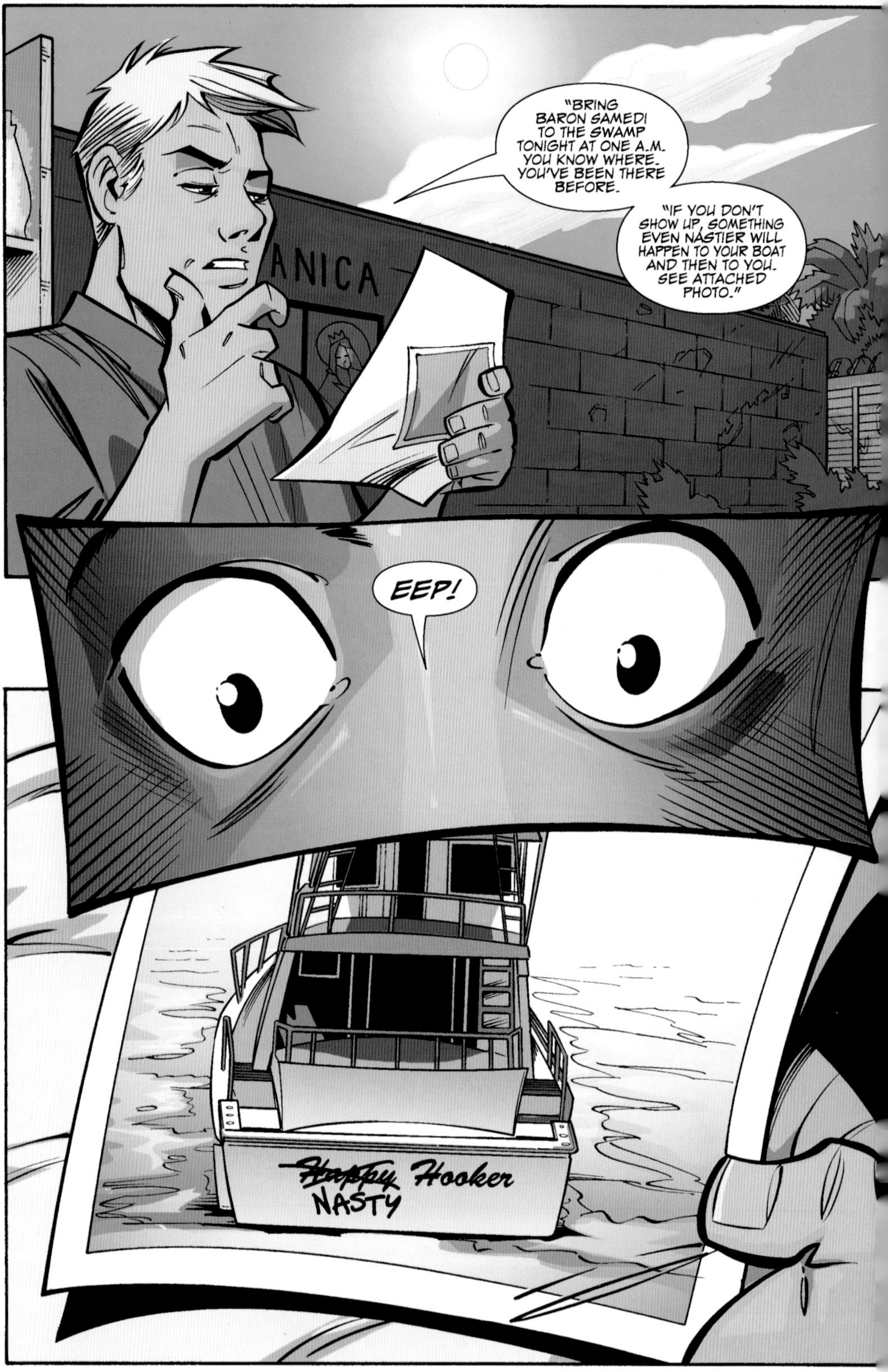
"BRING BARON SAMEDI TO THE SWAMP TONIGHT AT ONE A.M. YOU KNOW WHERE. YOU'VE BEEN THERE BEFORE.
"IF YOU DON'T SHOW UP, SOMETHING EVEN NASTIER WILL HAPPEN TO YOUR BOAT AND THEN TO YOU. SEE ATTACHED PHOTO."
ANICA
EEP!
~~Happy~~ Hooker
NASTY

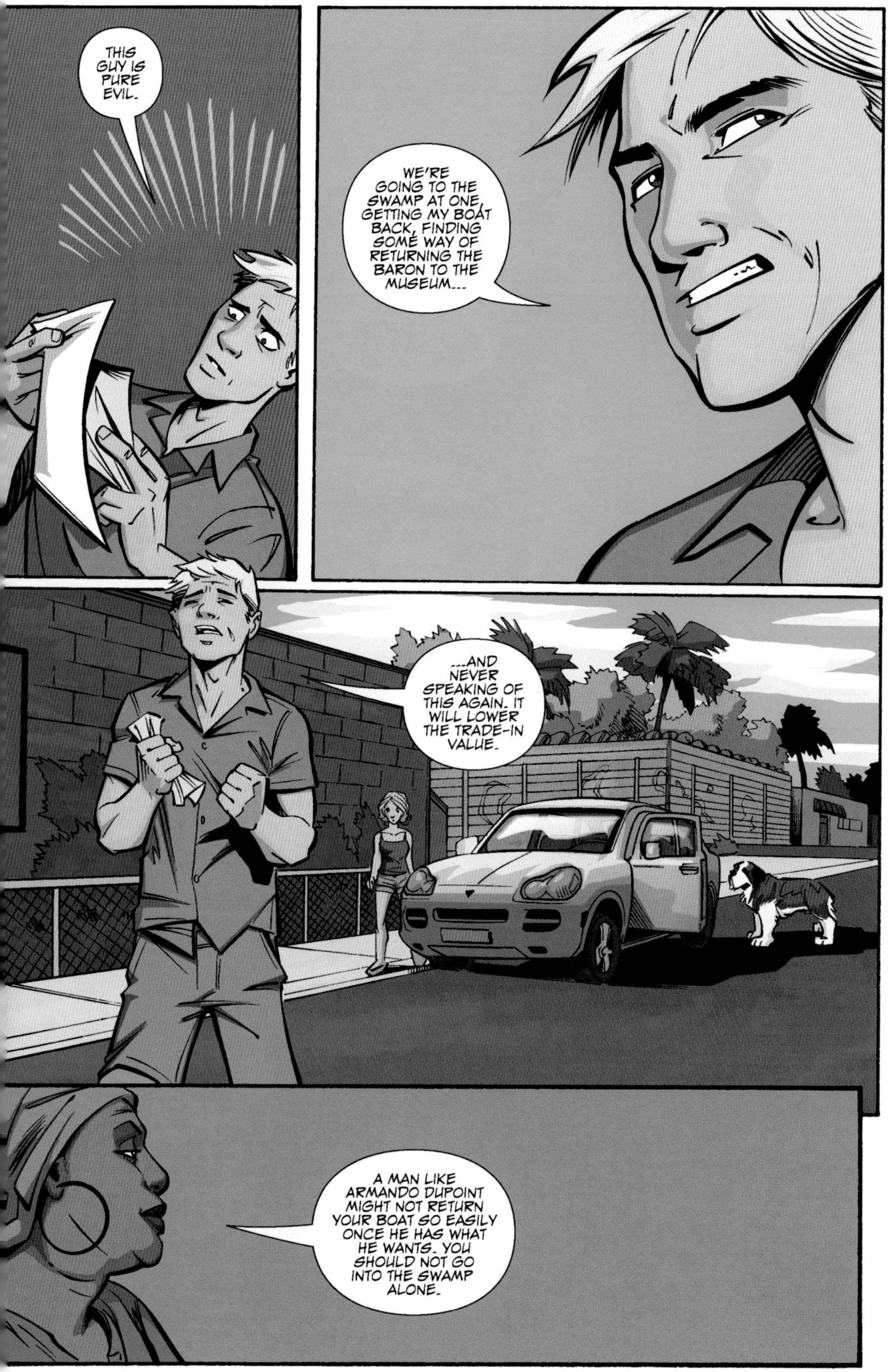
THIS GUY IS PURE EVIL.
WE'RE GOING TO THE SWAMP AT ONE, GETTING MY BOAT BACK, FINDING SOME WAY OF RETURNING THE BARON TO THE MUSEUM...
...AND NEVER SPEAKING OF THIS AGAIN. IT WILL LOWER THE TRADE-IN VALUE.
A MAN LIKE ARMANDO DUPOINT MIGHT NOT RETURN YOUR BOAT SO EASILY ONCE HE HAS WHAT HE WANTS. YOU SHOULD NOT GO INTO THE SWAMP ALONE.

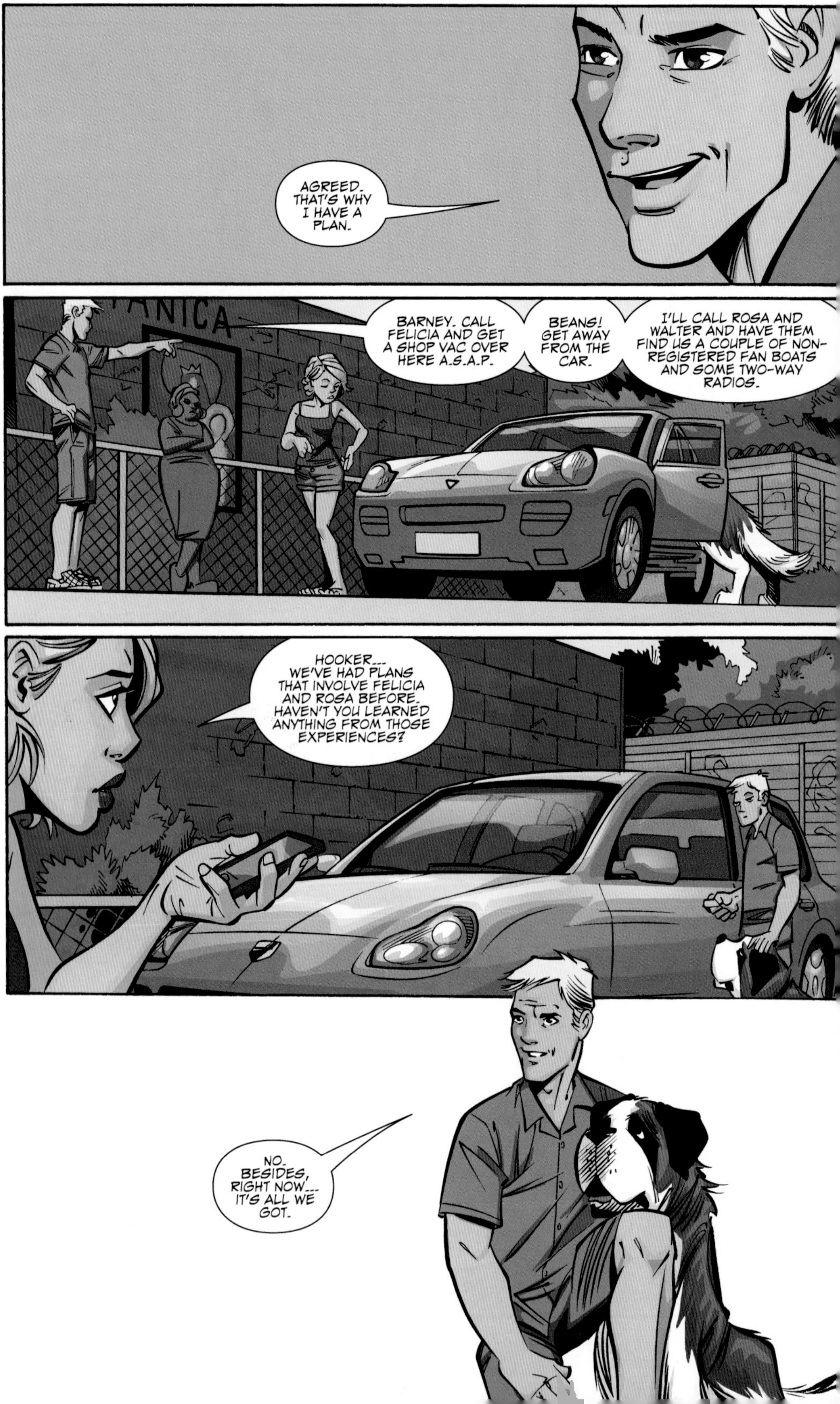
AGREED. THAT'S WHY I HAVE A PLAN.
BARNEY. CALL FELICIA AND GET A SHOP VAC OVER HERE A.S.A.P.
BEANS! GET AWAY FROM THE CAR.
I'LL CALL ROSA AND WALTER AND HAVE THEM FIND US A COUPLE OF NON-REGISTERED FAN BOATS AND SOME TWO-WAY RADIOS.
HOOKER... WE'VE HAD PLANS THAT INVOLVE FELICIA AND ROSA BEFORE. HAVEN'T YOU LEARNED ANYTHING FROM THOSE EXPERIENCES?
NO. BESIDES, RIGHT NOW... IT'S ALL WE GOT.

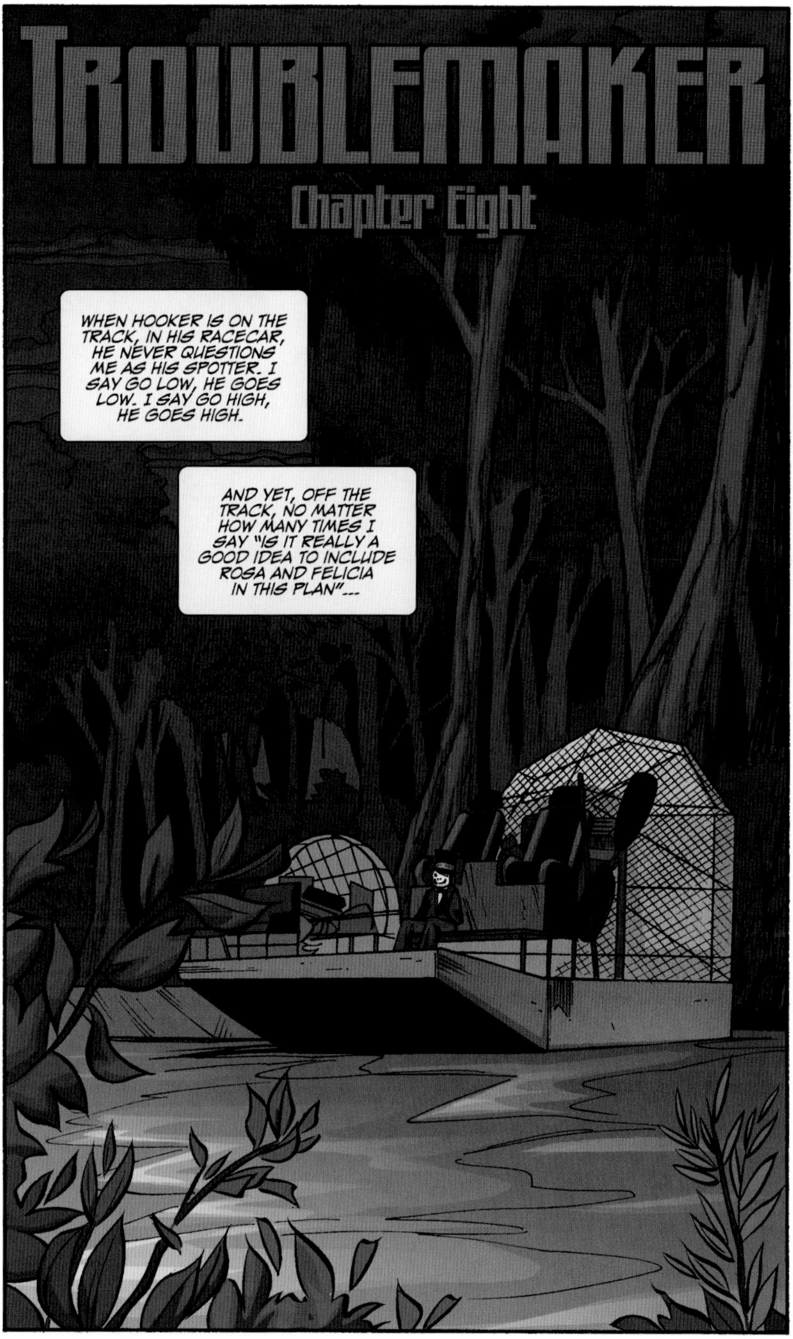
TROUBLEMAKER
Chapter Eight
WHEN HOOKER IS ON THE TRACK, IN HIS RACECAR, HE NEVER QUESTIONS ME AS HIS SPOTTER. I SAY GO LOW, HE GOES LOW. I SAY GO HIGH, HE GOES HIGH.
AND YET, OFF THE TRACK, NO MATTER HOW MANY TIMES I SAY "IS IT REALLY A GOOD IDEA TO INCLUDE ROSA AND FELICIA IN THIS PLAN"...

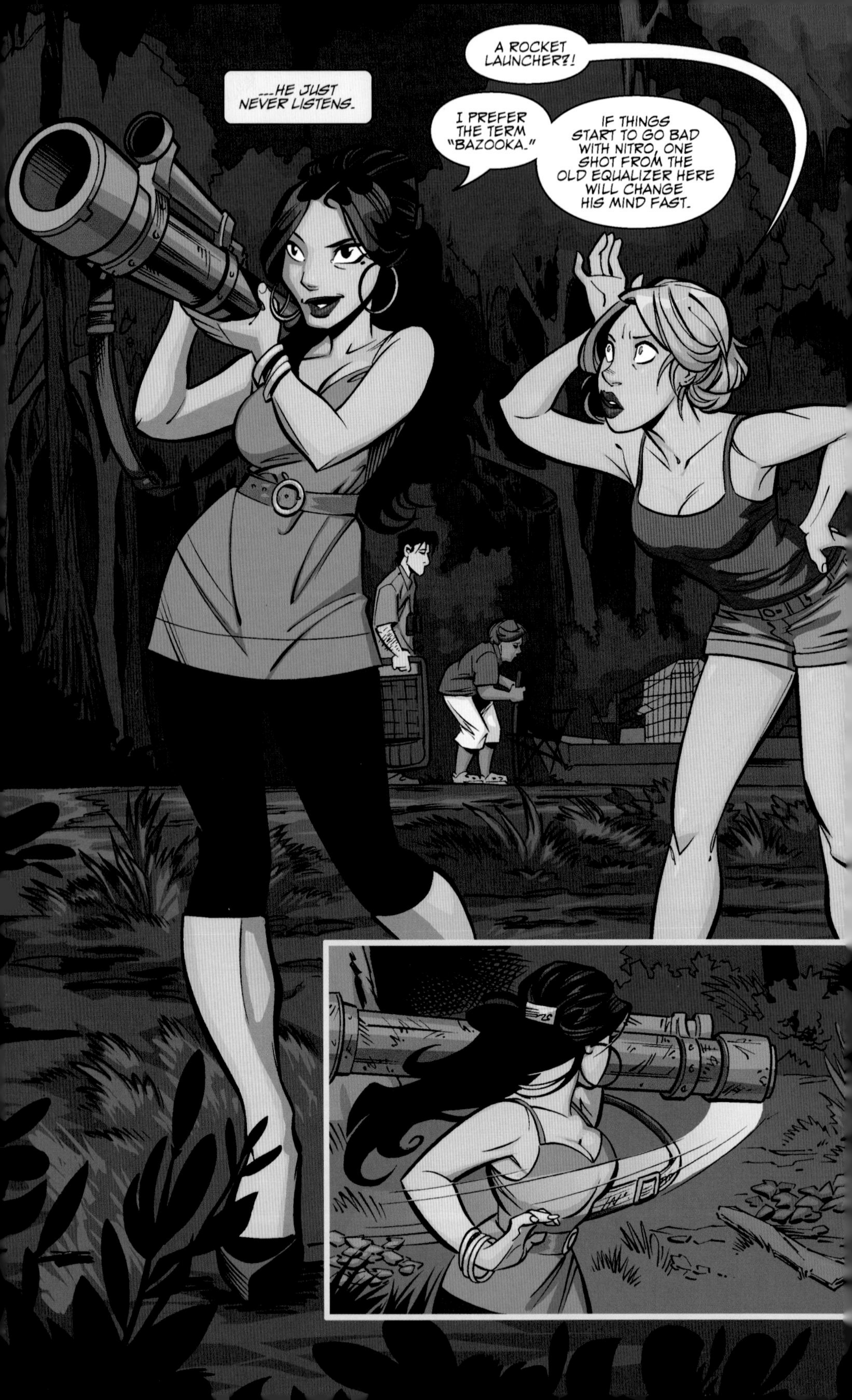
...HE JUST NEVER LISTENS.
A ROCKET LAUNCHER?!
I PREFER THE TERM "BAZOOKA."
IF THINGS START TO GO BAD WITH NITRO, ONE SHOT FROM THE OLD EQUALIZER HERE WILL CHANGE HIS MIND FAST.

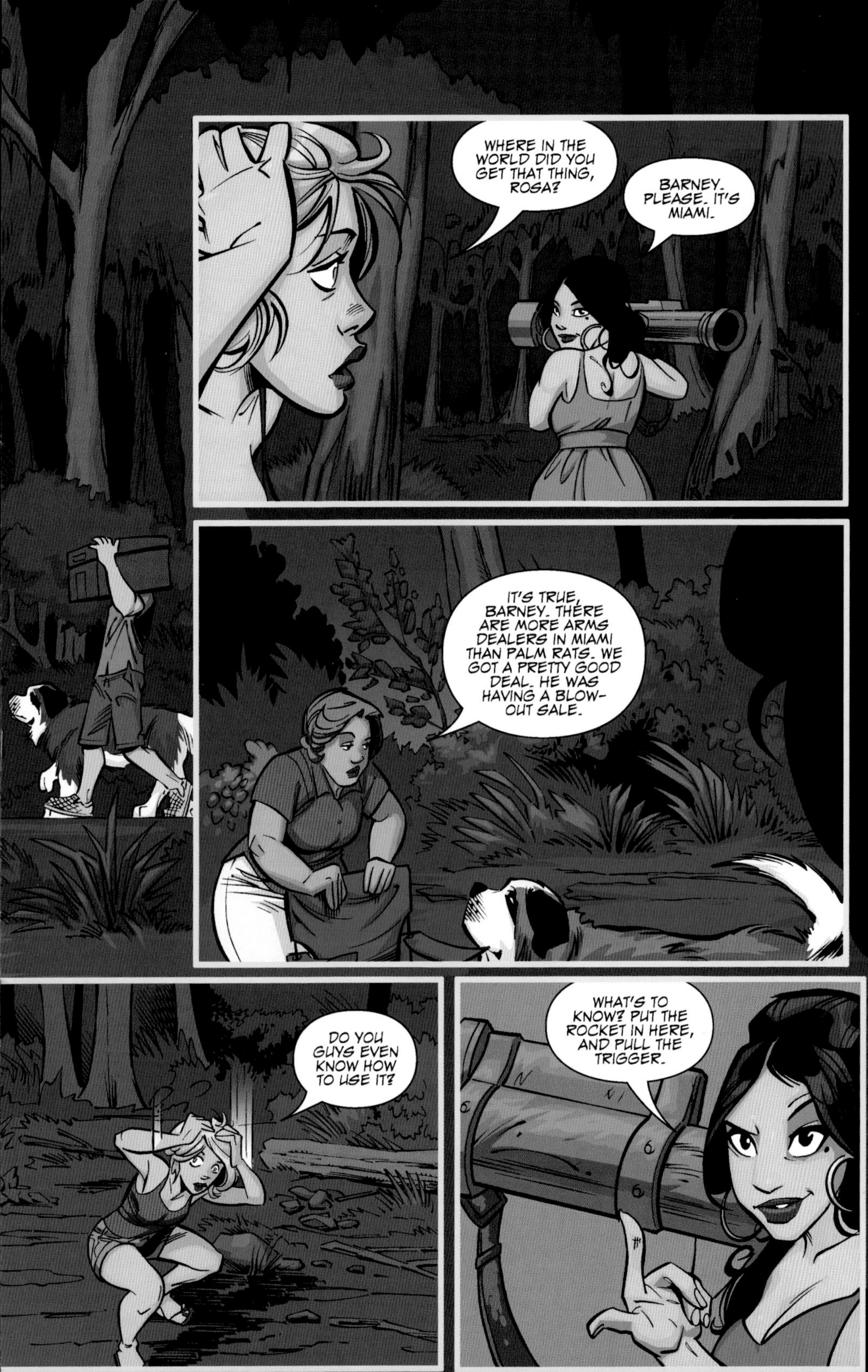
WHERE IN THE WORLD DID YOU GET THAT THING, ROSA?
BARNEY. PLEASE. IT'S MIAMI.
IT'S TRUE, BARNEY. THERE ARE MORE ARMS DEALERS IN MIAMI THAN PALM RATS. WE GOT A PRETTY GOOD DEAL. HE WAS HAVING A BLOW-OUT SALE.
DO YOU GUYS EVEN KNOW HOW TO USE IT?
WHAT'S TO KNOW? PUT THE ROCKET IN HERE, AND PULL THE TRIGGER.

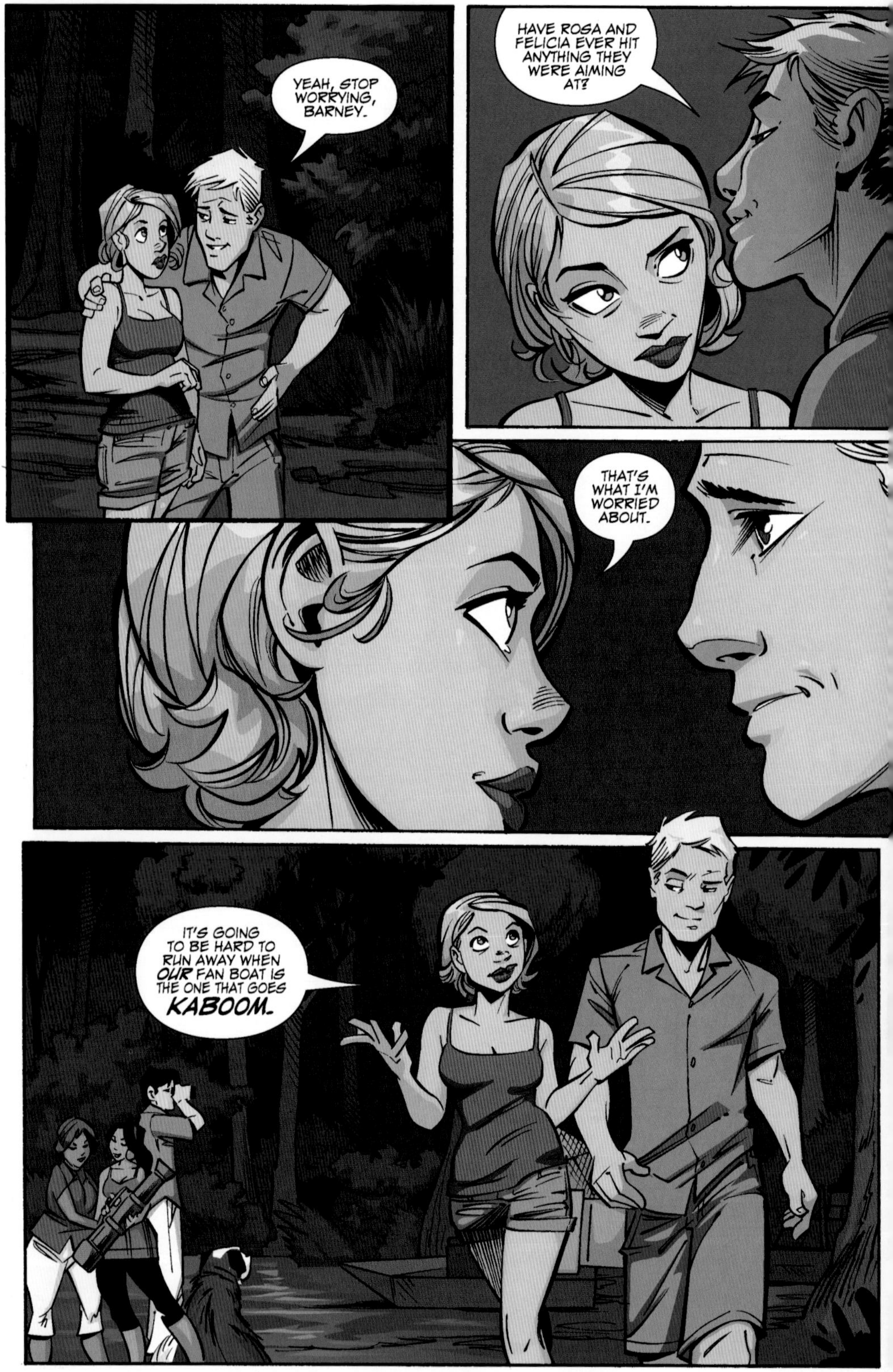
YEAH, STOP WORRYING, BARNEY.
HAVE ROSA AND FELICIA EVER HIT ANYTHING THEY WERE AIMING AT?
THAT'S WHAT I'M WORRIED ABOUT.
IT'S GOING TO BE HARD TO RUN AWAY WHEN OUR FAN BOAT IS THE ONE THAT GOES KABOOM.

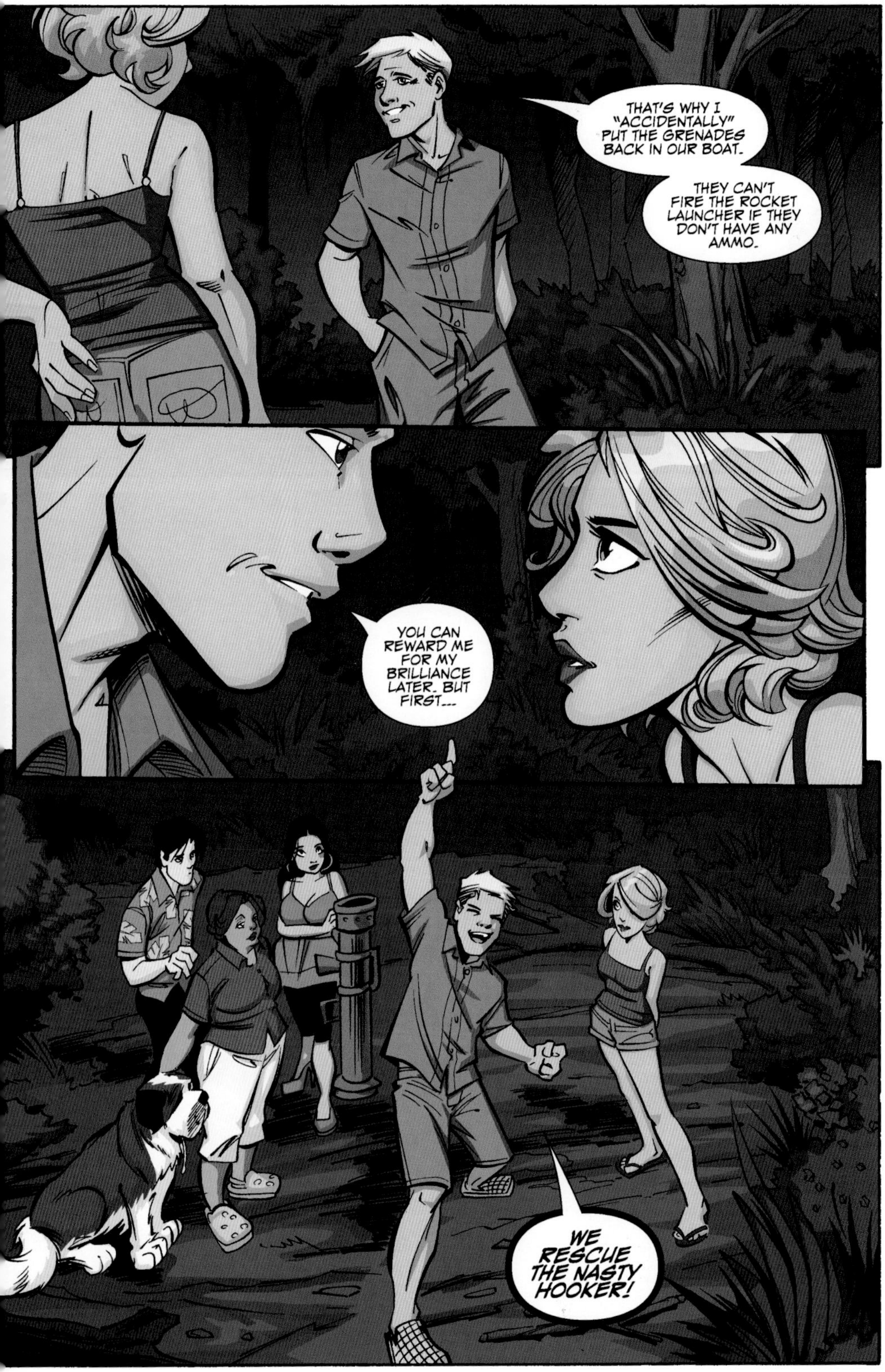
THAT'S WHY I "ACCIDENTALLY" PUT THE GRENADES BACK IN OUR BOAT.
THEY CAN'T FIRE THE ROCKET LAUNCHER IF THEY DON'T HAVE ANY AMMO.
YOU CAN REWARD ME FOR MY BRILLIANCE LATER. BUT FIRST...
WE RESCUE THE NASTY HOOKER!

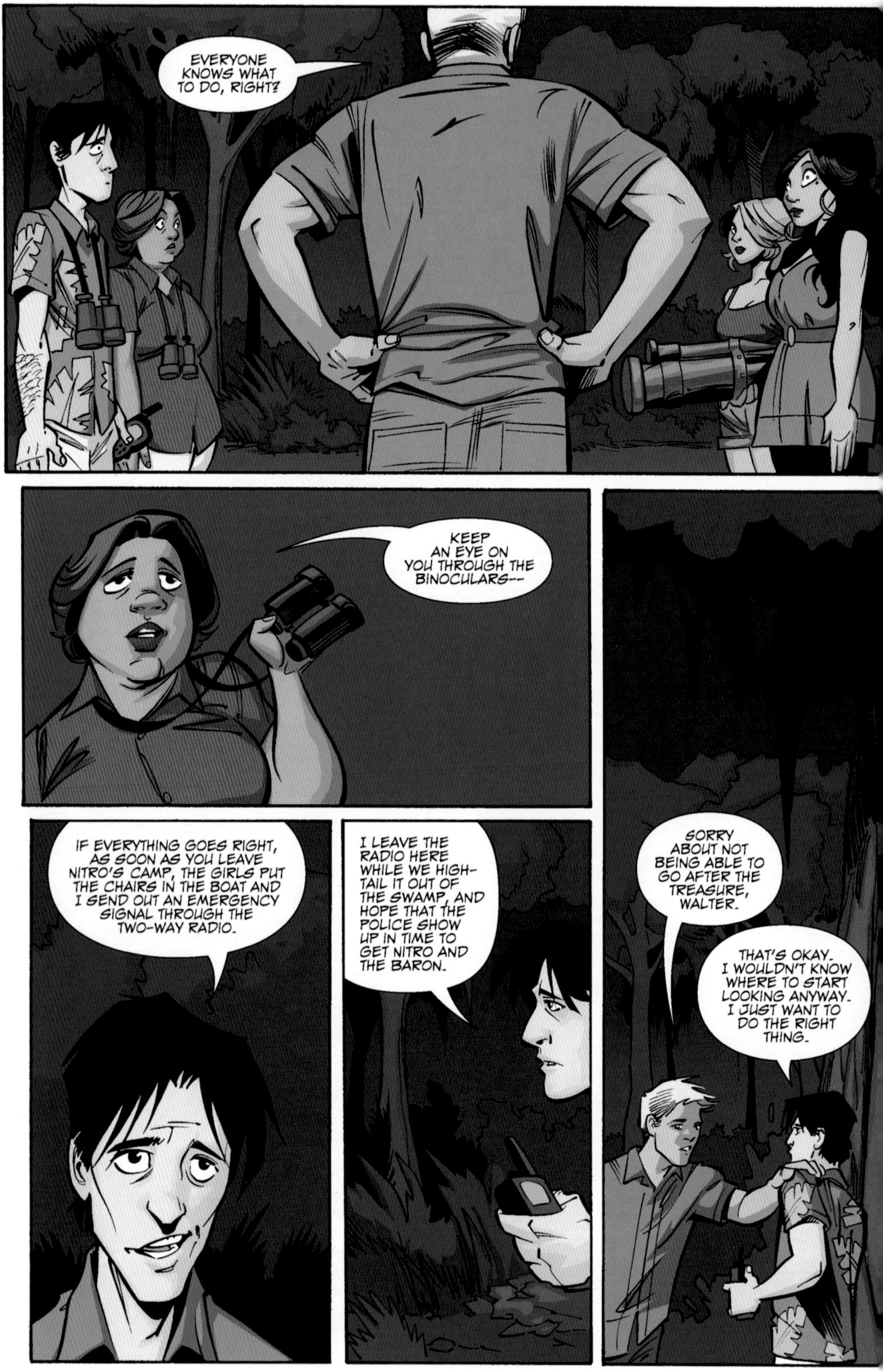

EVERYONE KNOWS WHAT TO DO, RIGHT?
KEEP AN EYE ON YOU THROUGH THE BINOCULARS--
IF EVERYTHING GOES RIGHT, AS SOON AS YOU LEAVE NITRO'S CAMP, THE GIRLS PUT THE CHAIRS IN THE BOAT AND I SEND OUT AN EMERGENCY SIGNAL THROUGH THE TWO-WAY RADIO.
I LEAVE THE RADIO HERE WHILE WE HIGH-TAIL IT OUT OF THE SWAMP, AND HOPE THAT THE POLICE SHOW UP IN TIME TO GET NITRO AND THE BARON.
SORRY ABOUT NOT BEING ABLE TO GO AFTER THE TREASURE, WALTER.
THAT'S OKAY. I WOULDN'T KNOW WHERE TO START LOOKING ANYWAY. I JUST WANT TO DO THE RIGHT THING.

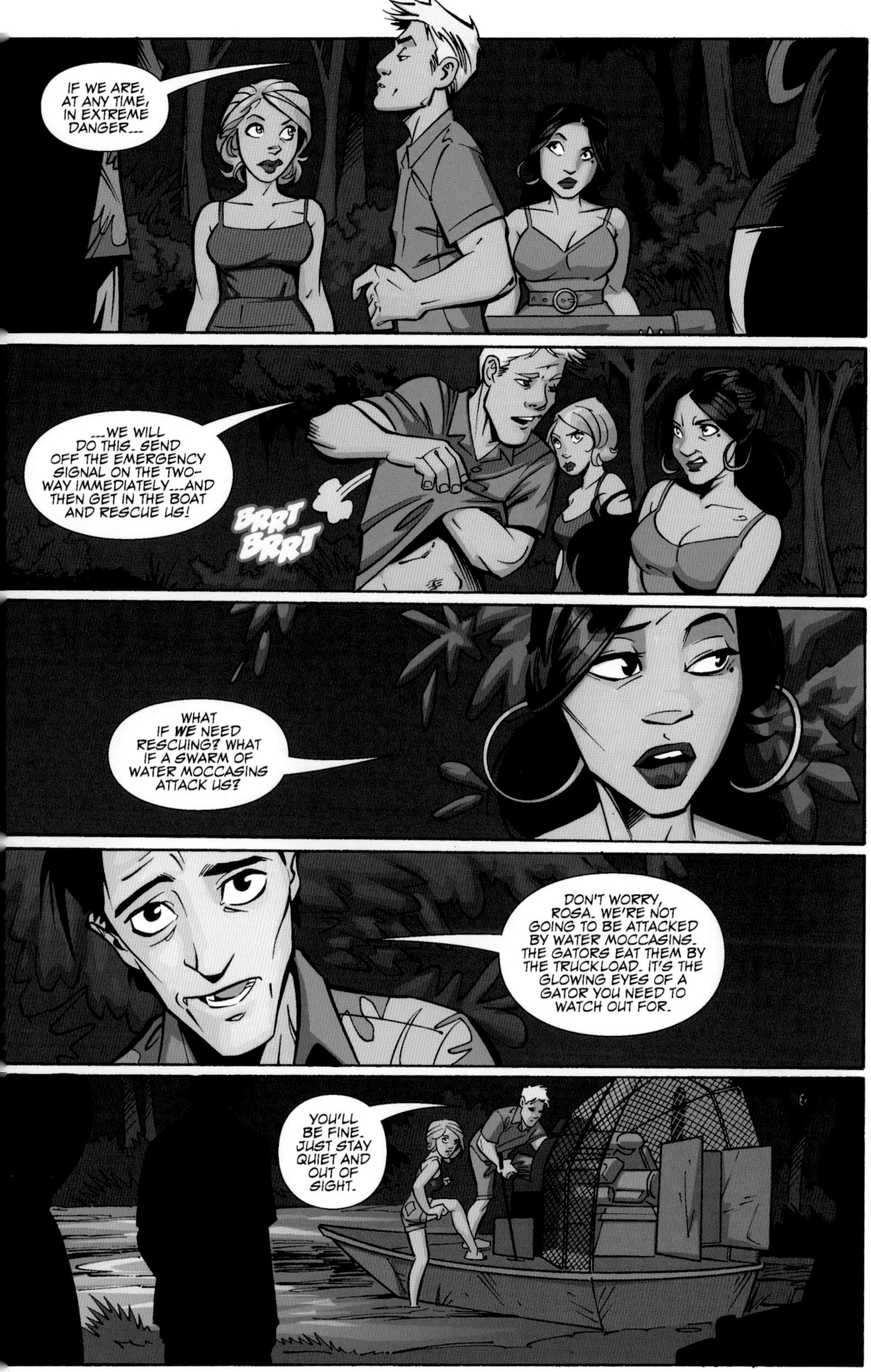

IF WE ARE, AT ANY TIME, IN EXTREME DANGER...
...WE WILL DO THIS. SEND OFF THE EMERGENCY SIGNAL ON THE TWO-WAY IMMEDIATELY...AND THEN GET IN THE BOAT AND RESCUE US!
BRRT BRRT
WHAT IF WE NEED RESCUING? WHAT IF A SWARM OF WATER MOCCASINS ATTACK US?
DON'T WORRY, ROSA. WE'RE NOT GOING TO BE ATTACKED BY WATER MOCCASINS. THE GATORS EAT THEM BY THE TRUCKLOAD. IT'S THE GLOWING EYES OF A GATOR YOU NEED TO WATCH OUT FOR.
YOU'LL BE FINE. JUST STAY QUIET AND OUT OF SIGHT.

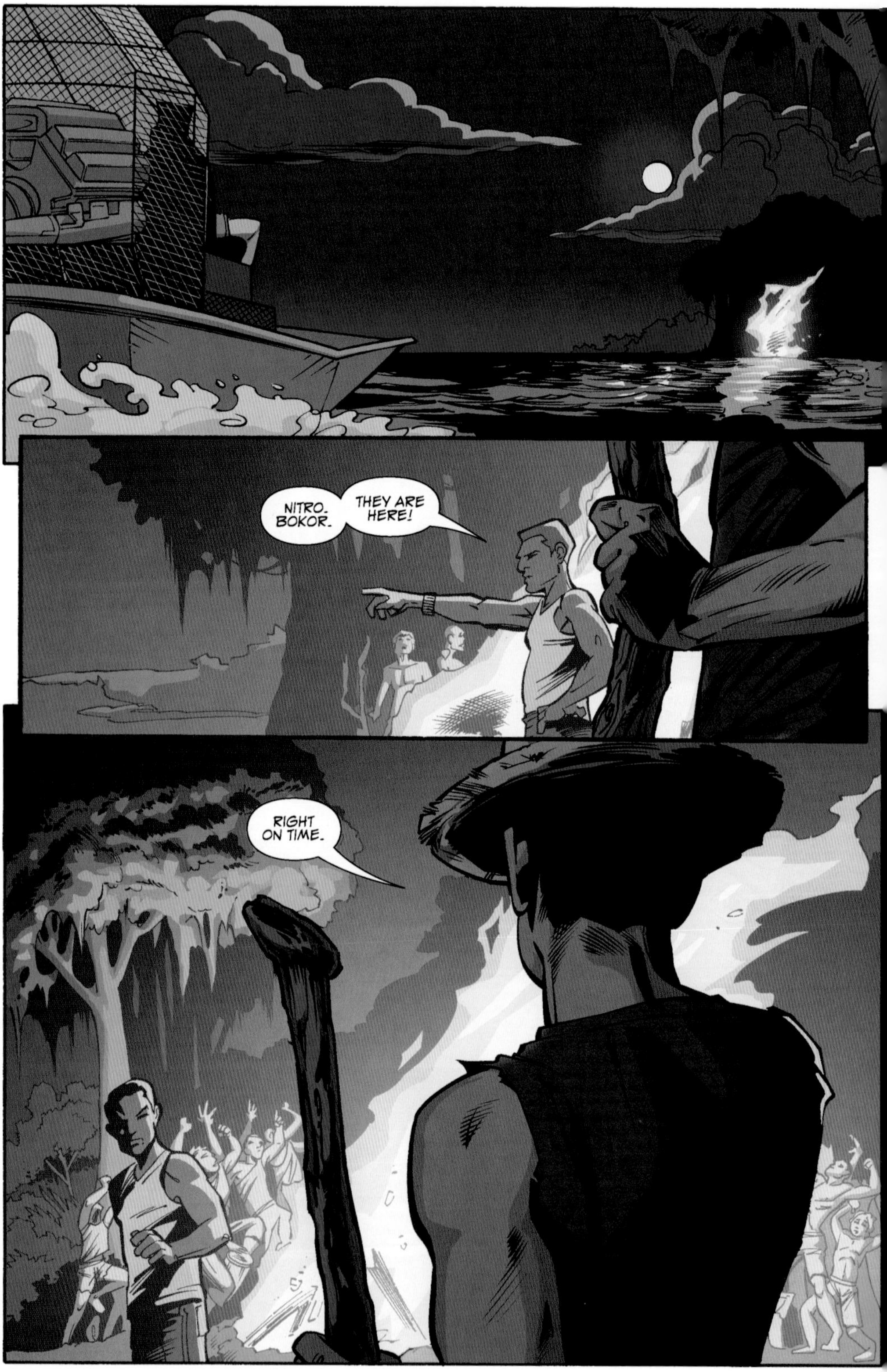
NITRO. BOKOR.
THEY ARE HERE!
RIGHT ON TIME.

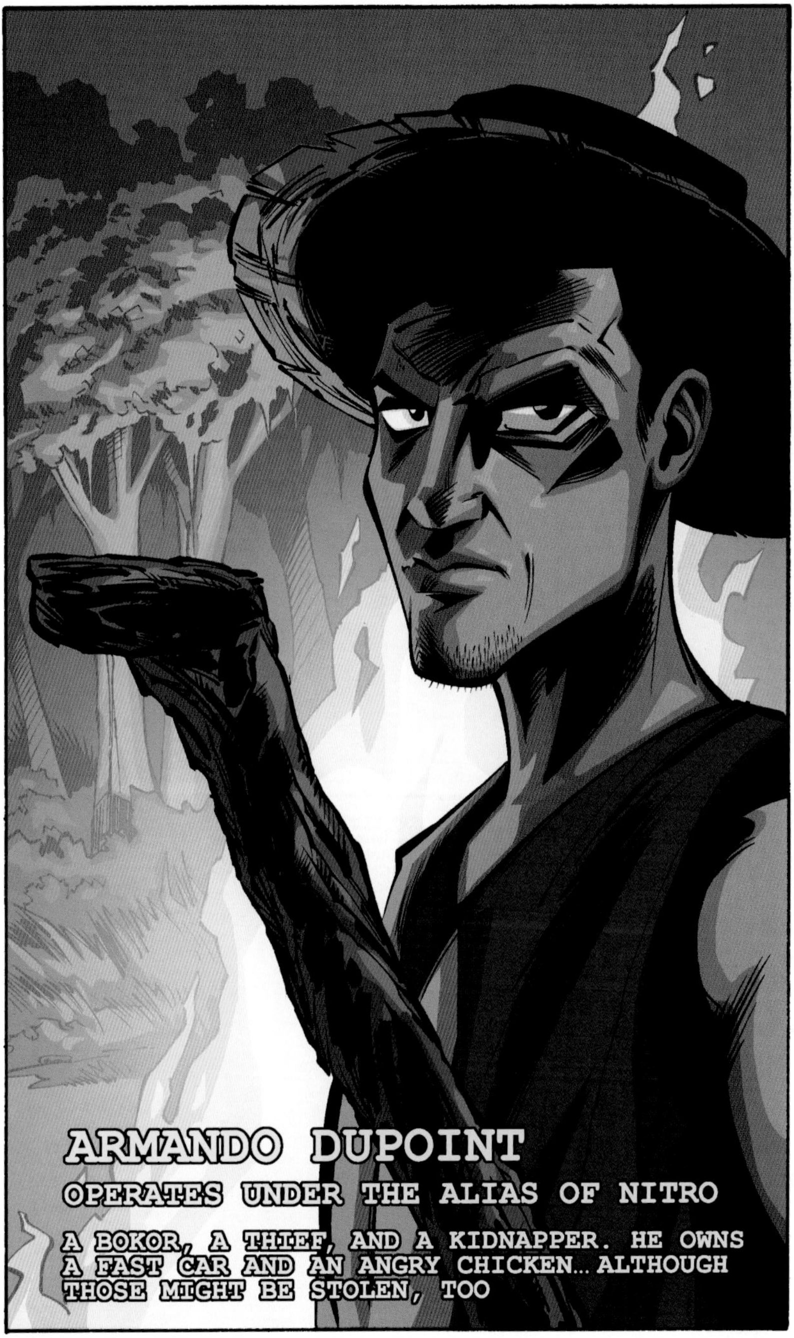
ARMANDO DUPOINT
OPERATES UNDER THE ALIAS OF NITRO
A BOKOR, A THIEF, AND A KIDNAPPER. HE OWNS A FAST CAR AND AN ANGRY CHICKEN... ALTHOUGH THOSE MIGHT BE STOLEN, TOO

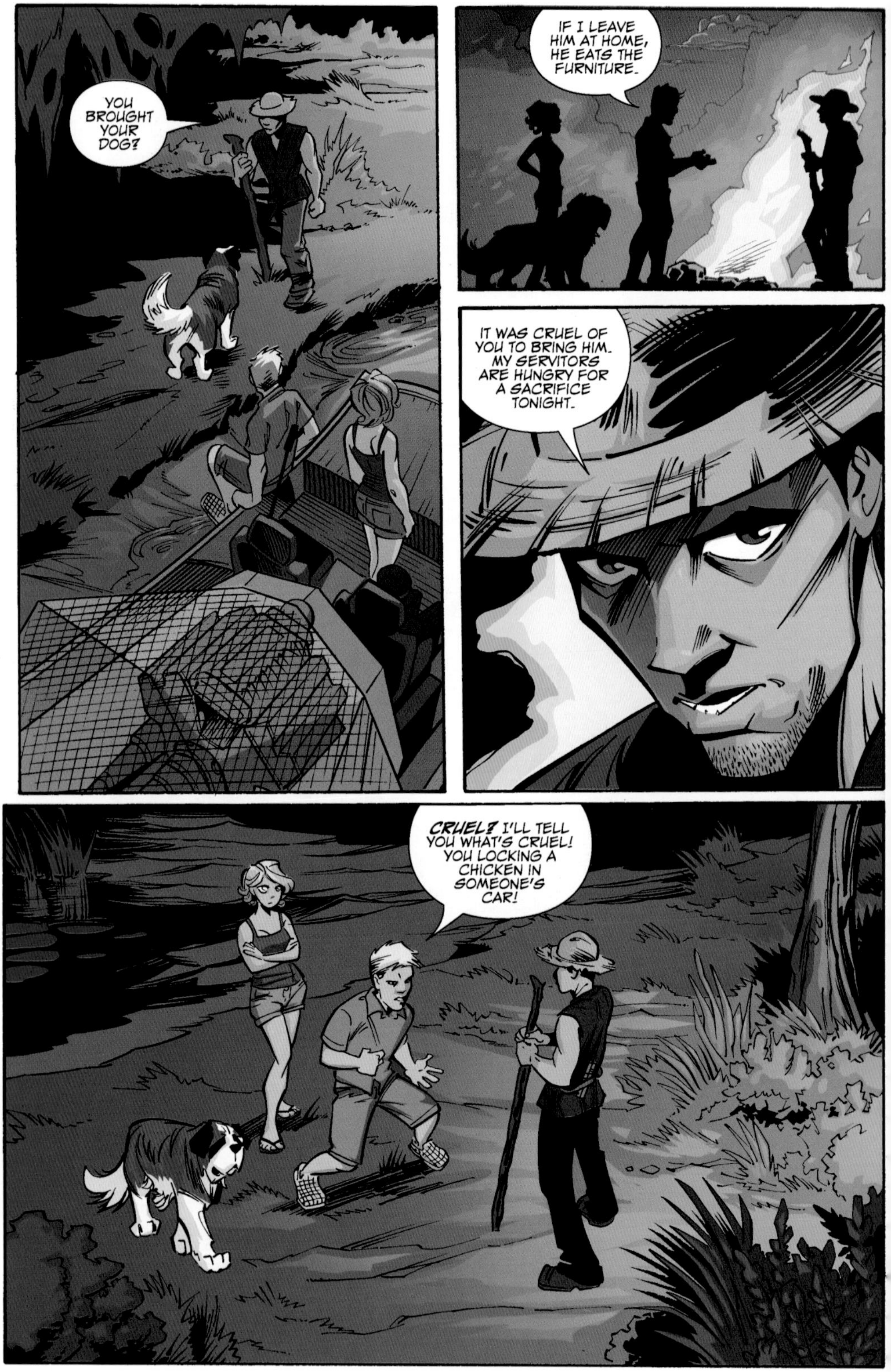
YOU BROUGHT YOUR DOG?
IF I LEAVE HIM AT HOME, HE EATS THE FURNITURE.
IT WAS CRUEL OF YOU TO BRING HIM. MY SERVITORS ARE HUNGRY FOR A SACRIFICE TONIGHT.
CRUEL? I'LL TELL YOU WHAT'S CRUEL! YOU LOCKING A CHICKEN IN SOMEONE'S CAR!

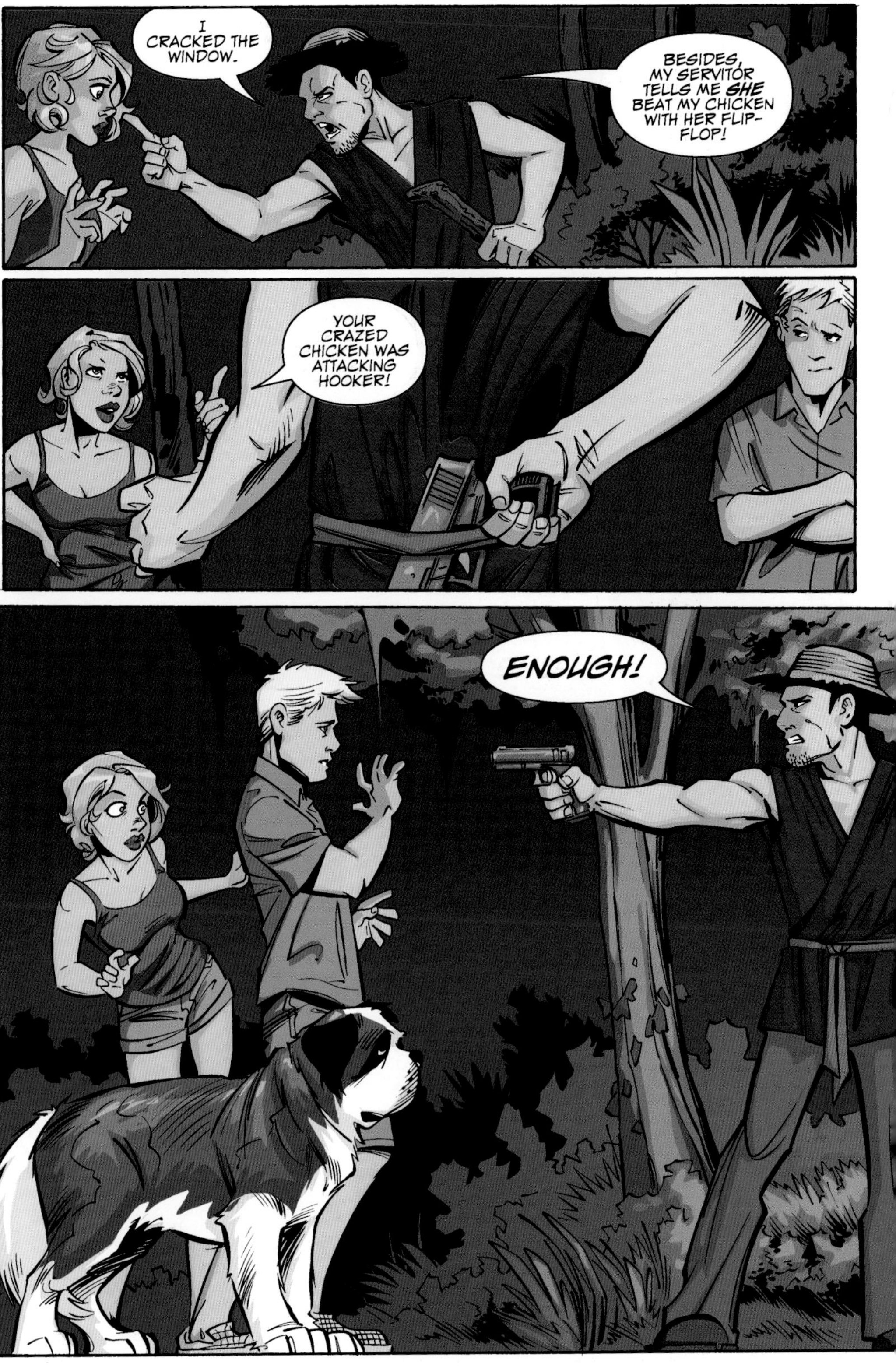
I CRACKED THE WINDOW.
BESIDES, MY SERVITOR TELLS ME SHE BEAT MY CHICKEN WITH HER FLIP-FLOP!
YOUR CRAZED CHICKEN WAS ATTACKING HOOKER!
ENOUGH!

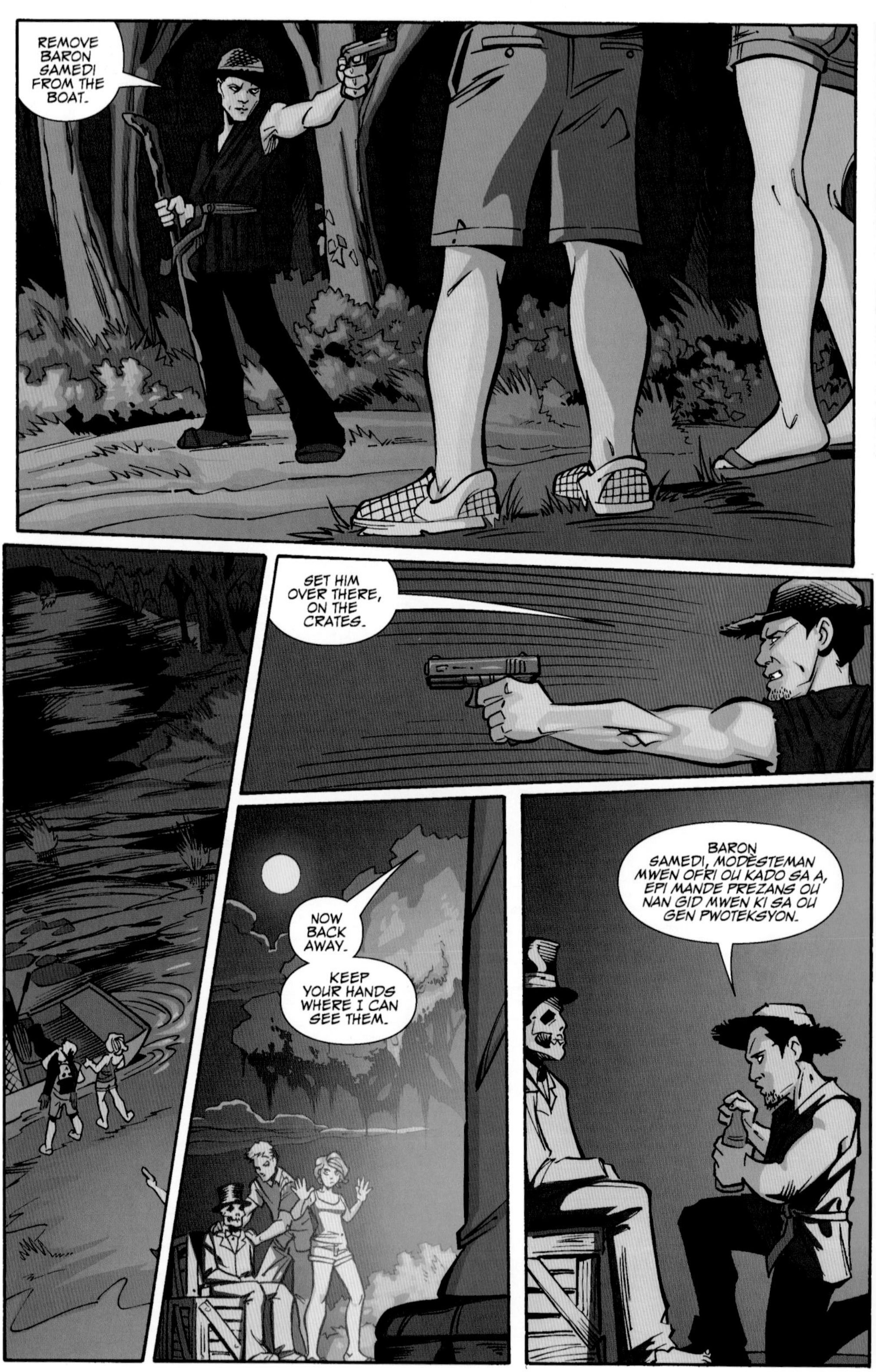
REMOVE BARON SAMEDI FROM THE BOAT.
SET HIM OVER THERE, ON THE CRATES.
NOW BACK AWAY.
KEEP YOUR HANDS WHERE I CAN SEE THEM.
BARON SAMEDI, MODÈSTEMAN MWEN OFRI OU KADO SA A, EPI MANDE PREZANS OU NAN GID MWEN KI SA OU GEN PWOTEKSYON.

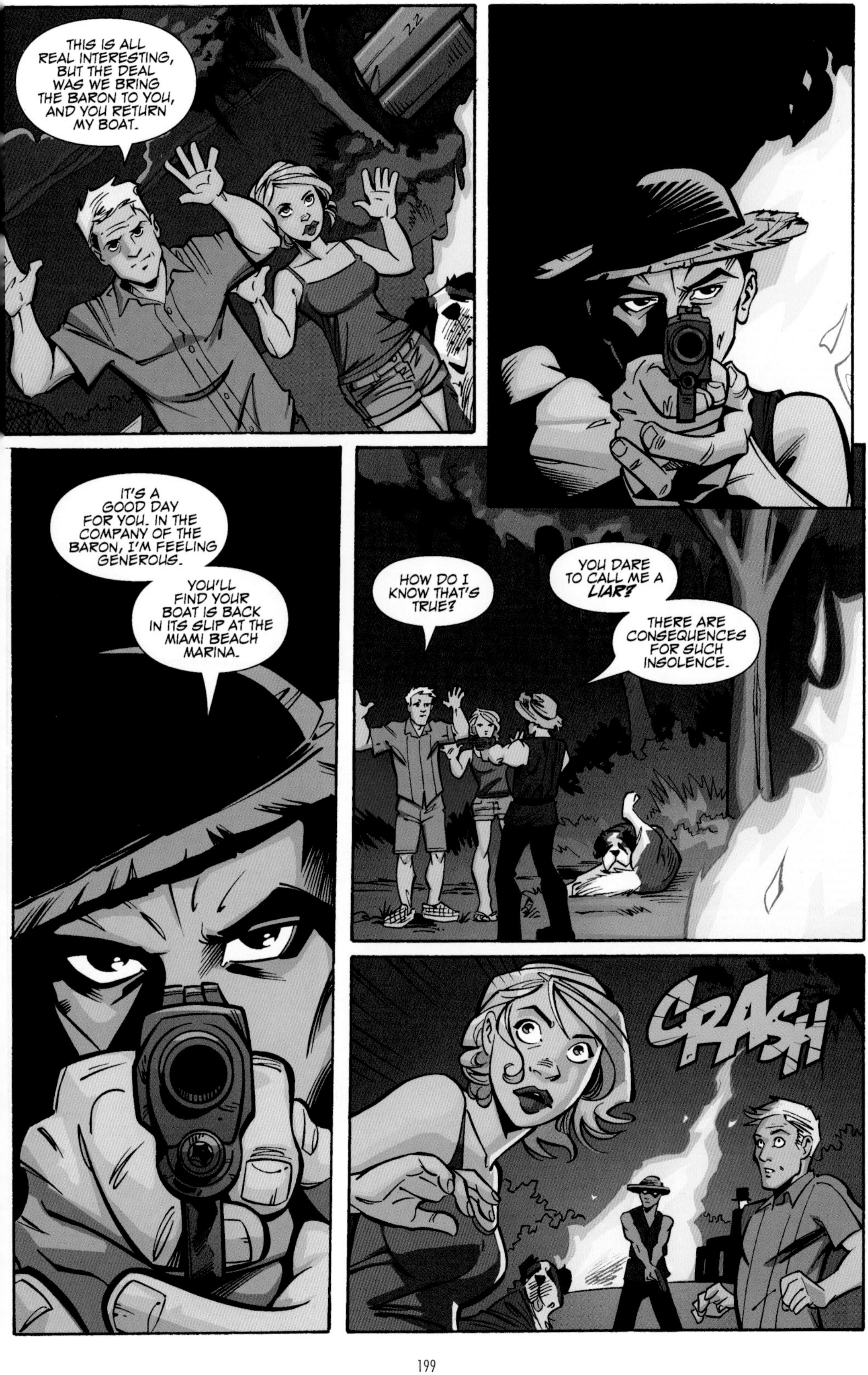

THIS IS ALL REAL INTERESTING, BUT THE DEAL WAS WE BRING THE BARON TO YOU, AND YOU RETURN MY BOAT.
IT'S A GOOD DAY FOR YOU. IN THE COMPANY OF THE BARON, I'M FEELING GENEROUS.
YOU'LL FIND YOUR BOAT IS BACK IN ITS SLIP AT THE MIAMI BEACH MARINA.
HOW DO I KNOW THAT'S TRUE?
YOU DARE TO CALL ME A *LIAR?*
THERE ARE CONSEQUENCES FOR SUCH INSOLENCE.
CRASH

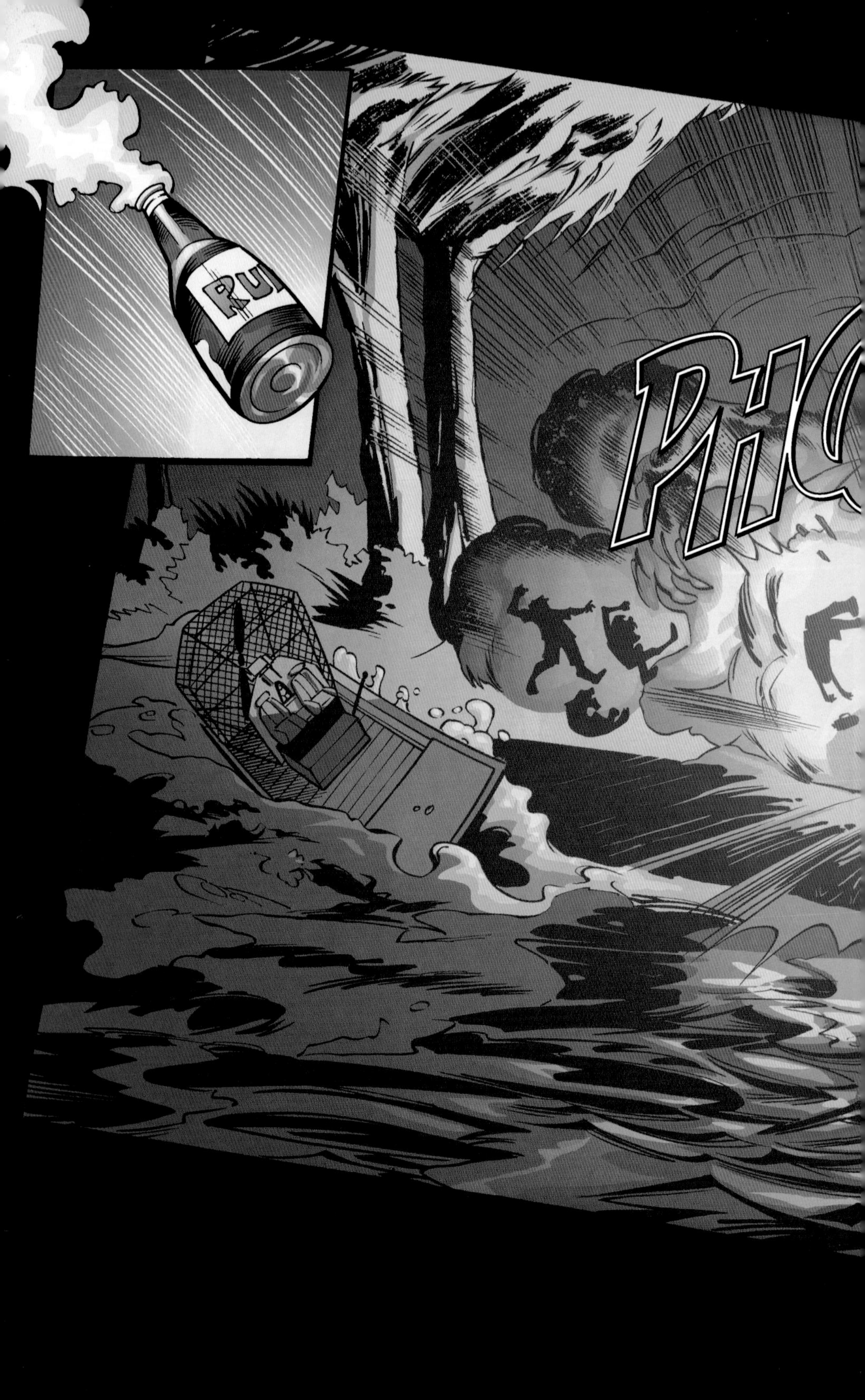
RU
PHO

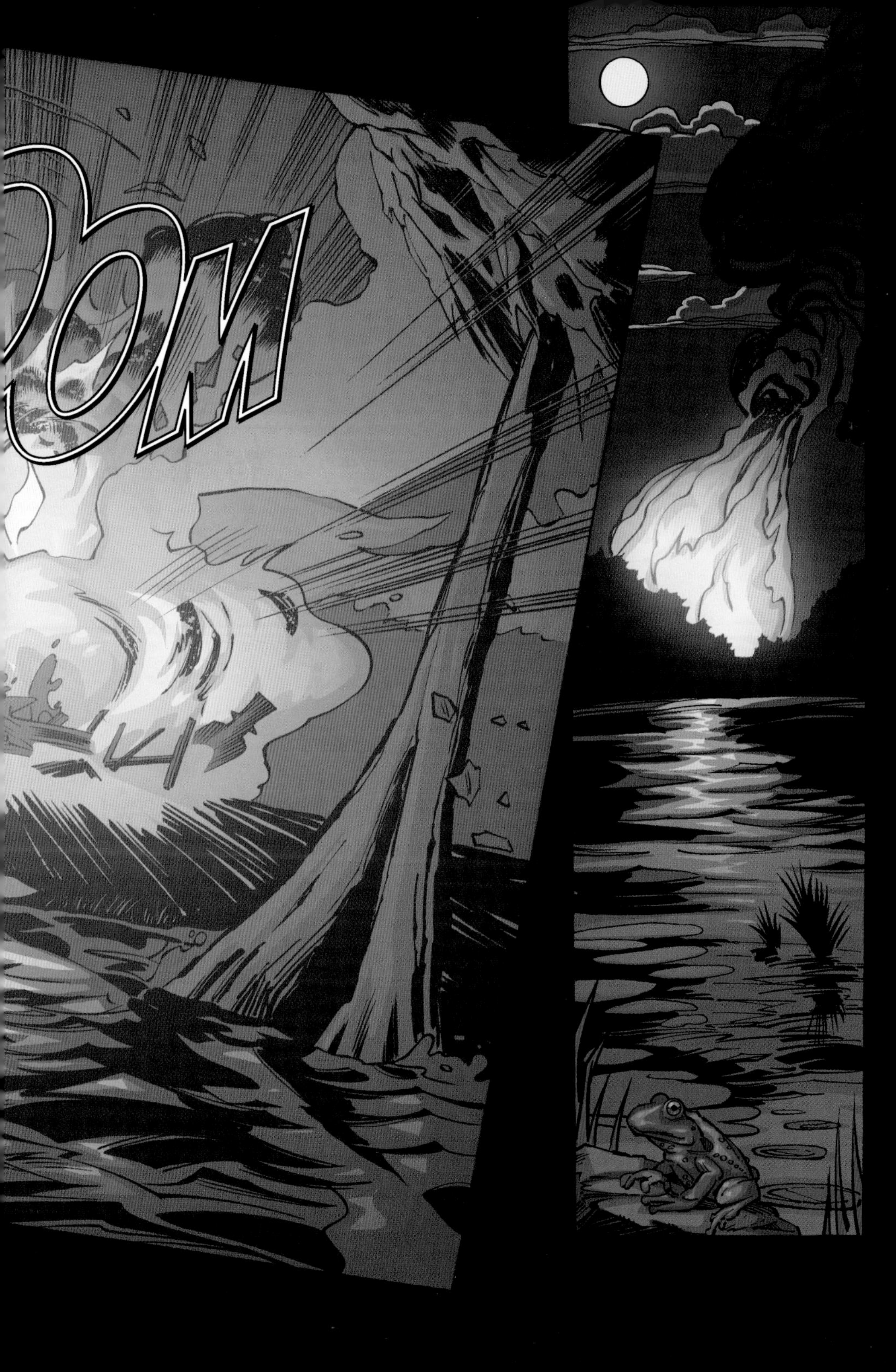
OOM

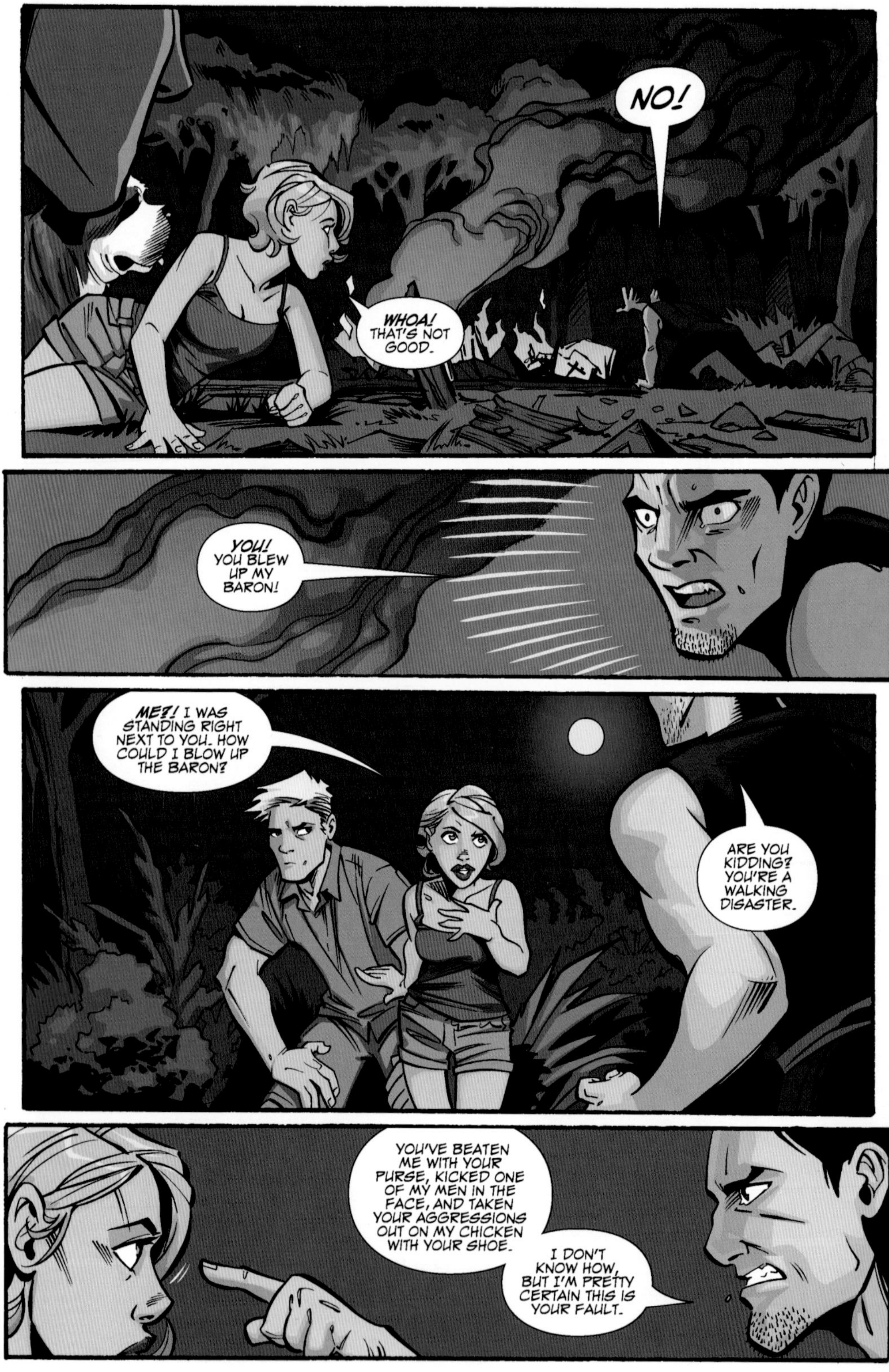
NO!
WHOA! THAT'S NOT GOOD.
YOU! YOU BLEW UP MY BARON!
ME?! I WAS STANDING RIGHT NEXT TO YOU. HOW COULD I BLOW UP THE BARON?
ARE YOU KIDDING? YOU'RE A WALKING DISASTER.
YOU'VE BEATEN ME WITH YOUR PURSE, KICKED ONE OF MY MEN IN THE FACE, AND TAKEN YOUR AGGRESSIONS OUT ON MY CHICKEN WITH YOUR SHOE.
I DON'T KNOW HOW, BUT I'M PRETTY CERTAIN THIS IS YOUR FAULT.

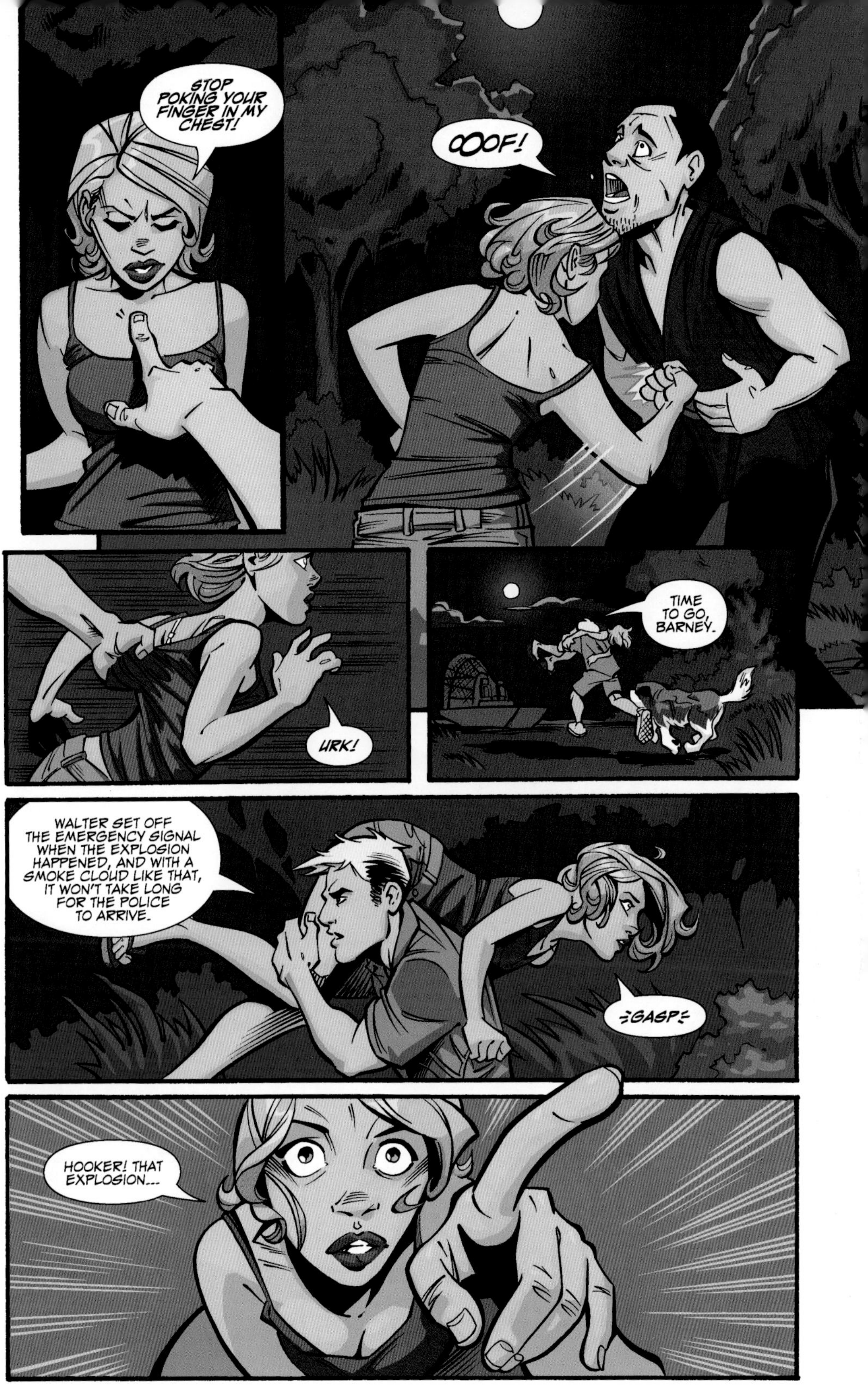
STOP POKING YOUR FINGER IN MY CHEST!
OOOF!
URK!
TIME TO GO, BARNEY.
WALTER SET OFF THE EMERGENCY SIGNAL WHEN THE EXPLOSION HAPPENED, AND WITH A SMOKE CLOUD LIKE THAT, IT WON'T TAKE LONG FOR THE POLICE TO ARRIVE.
GASP
HOOKER! THAT EXPLOSION...

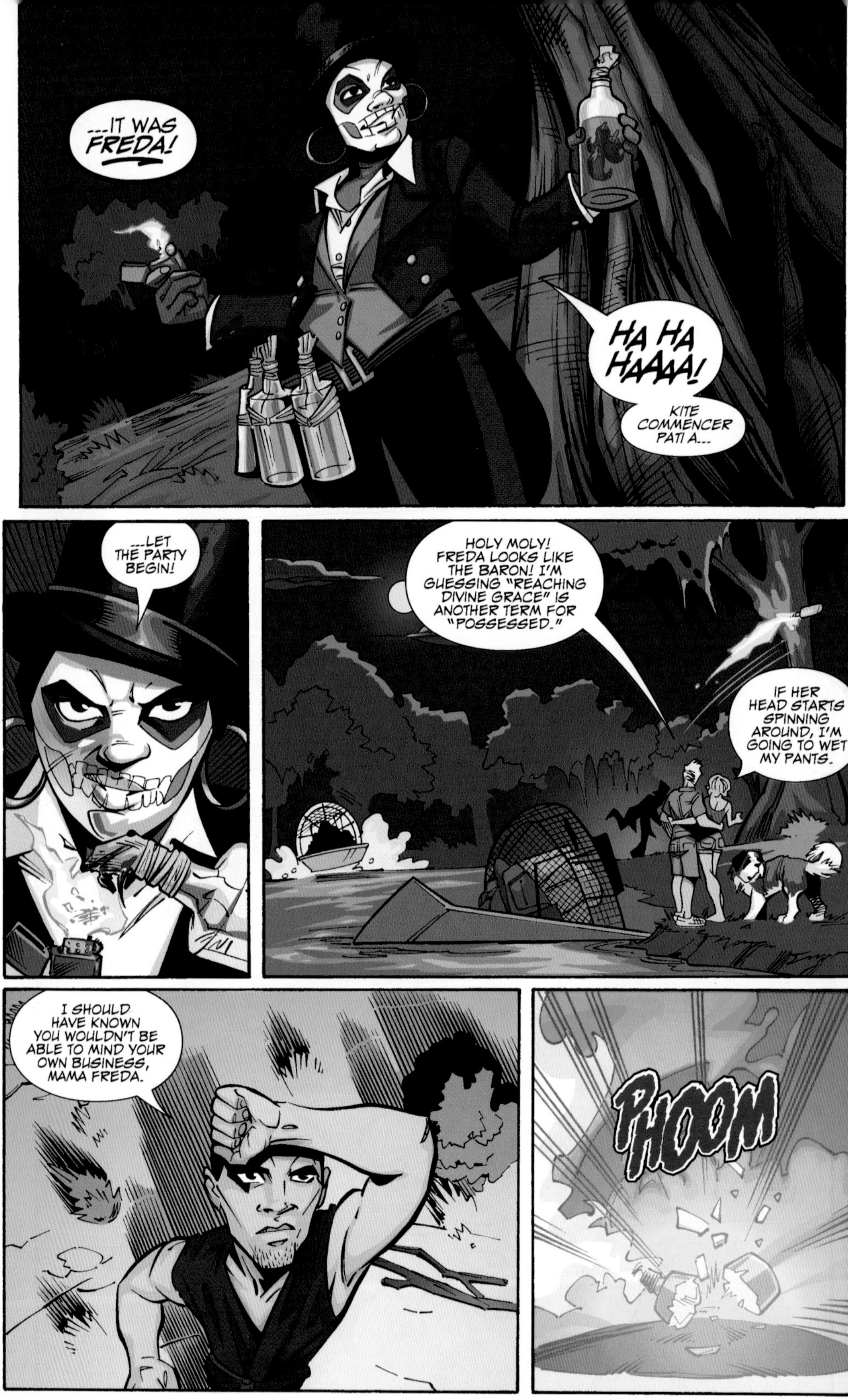
...IT WAS FREDA!
HA HA HAAAA!
KITE COMMENCER PATI A...
...LET THE PARTY BEGIN!
HOLY MOLY! FREDA LOOKS LIKE THE BARON! I'M GUESSING "REACHING DIVINE GRACE" IS ANOTHER TERM FOR "POSSESSED."
IF HER HEAD STARTS SPINNING AROUND, I'M GOING TO WET MY PANTS.
I SHOULD HAVE KNOWN YOU WOULDN'T BE ABLE TO MIND YOUR OWN BUSINESS, MAMA FREDA.
PHOOM

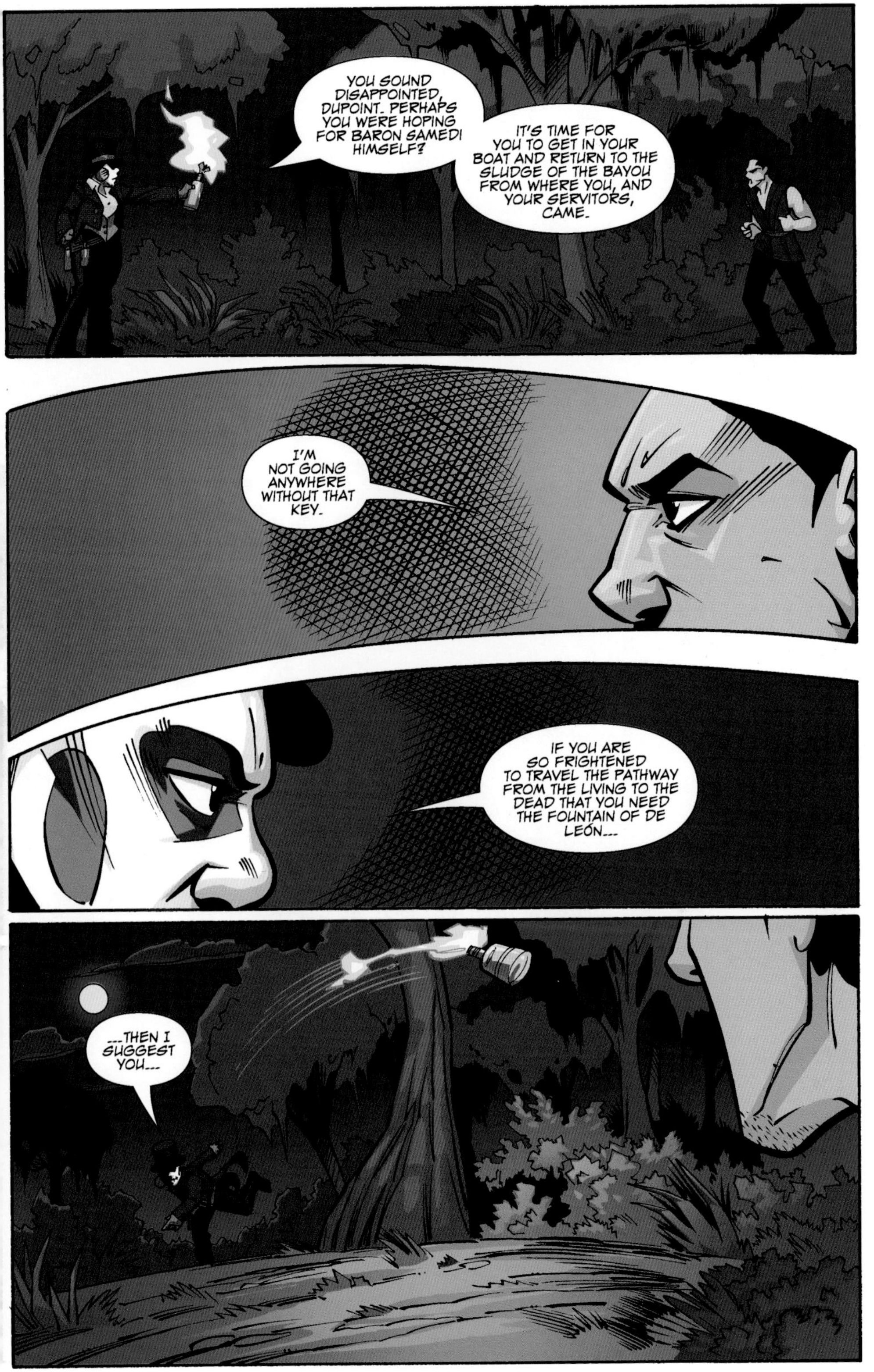
YOU SOUND DISAPPOINTED, DUPOINT. PERHAPS YOU WERE HOPING FOR BARON SAMEDI HIMSELF?
IT'S TIME FOR YOU TO GET IN YOUR BOAT AND RETURN TO THE SLUDGE OF THE BAYOU FROM WHERE YOU, AND YOUR SERVITORS, CAME.
I'M NOT GOING ANYWHERE WITHOUT THAT KEY.
IF YOU ARE SO FRIGHTENED TO TRAVEL THE PATHWAY FROM THE LIVING TO THE DEAD THAT YOU NEED THE FOUNTAIN OF DE LEÓN...
...THEN I SUGGEST YOU...

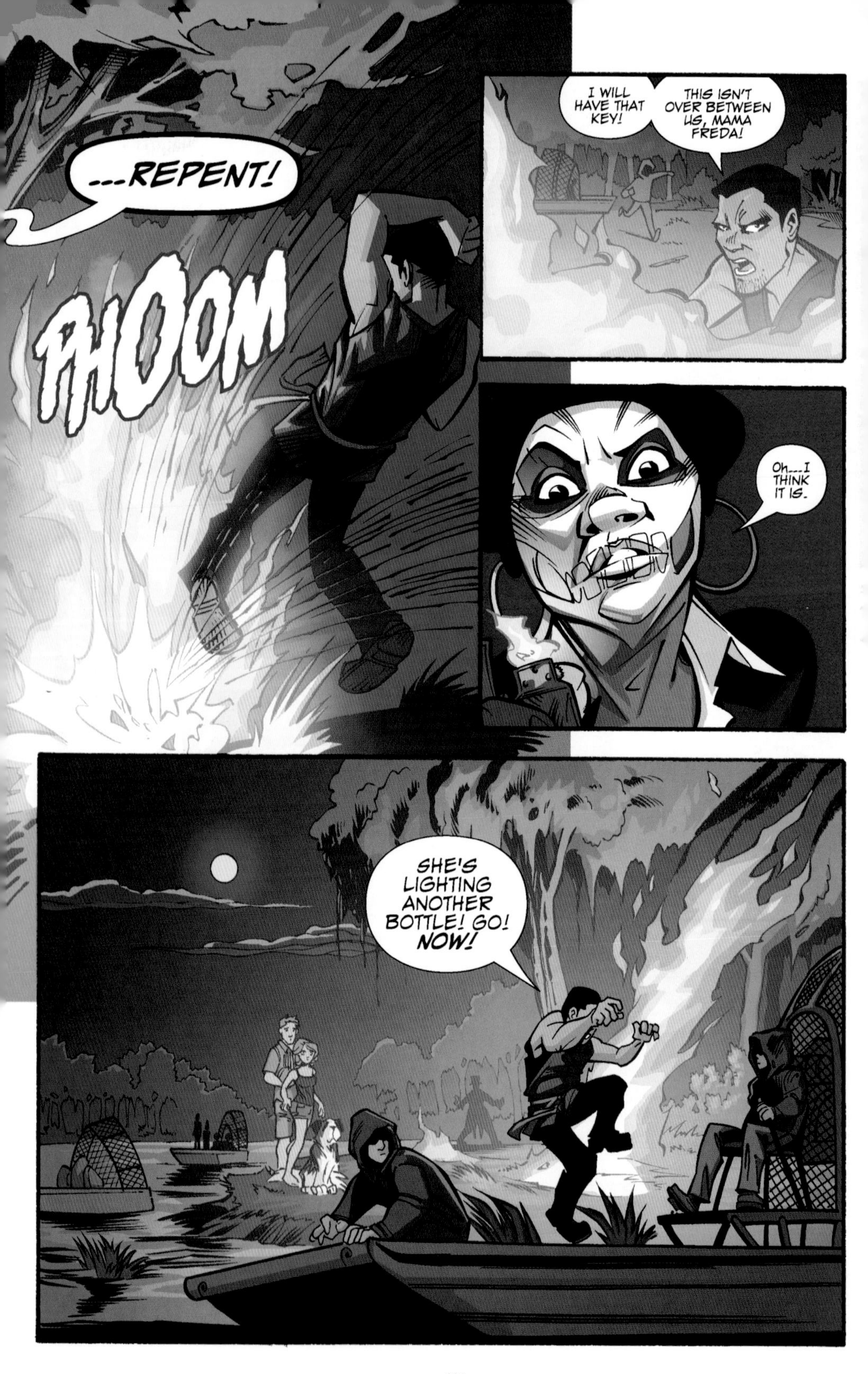

---REPENT!
PHOOM
I WILL HAVE THAT KEY!
THIS ISN'T OVER BETWEEN US, MAMA FREDA!
Oh---I THINK IT IS-
SHE'S LIGHTING ANOTHER BOTTLE! GO! NOW!

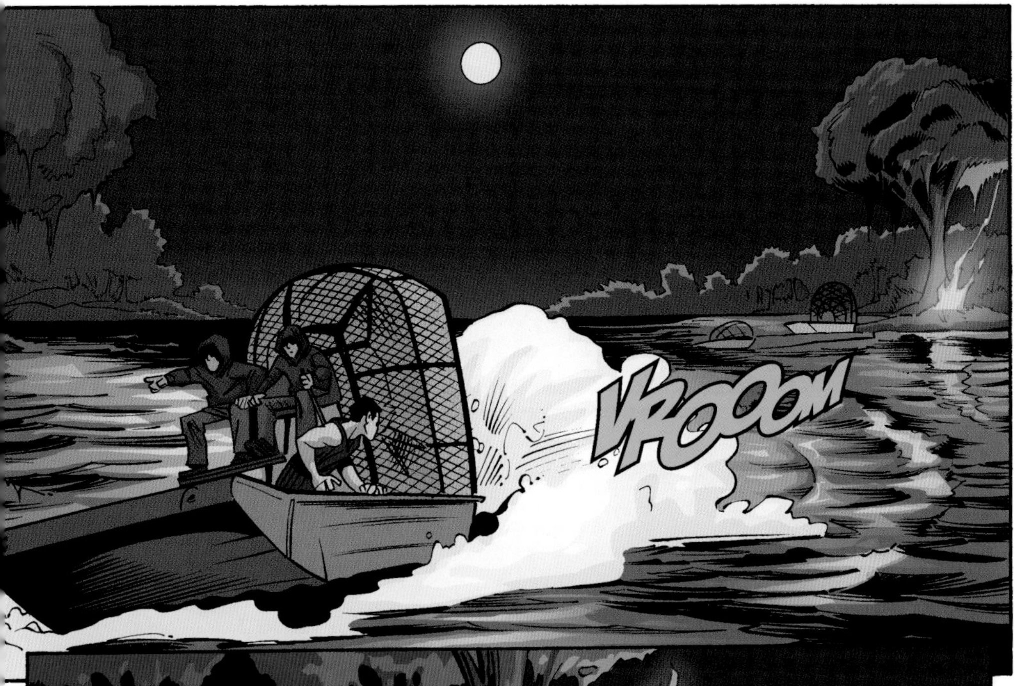
VROOOM

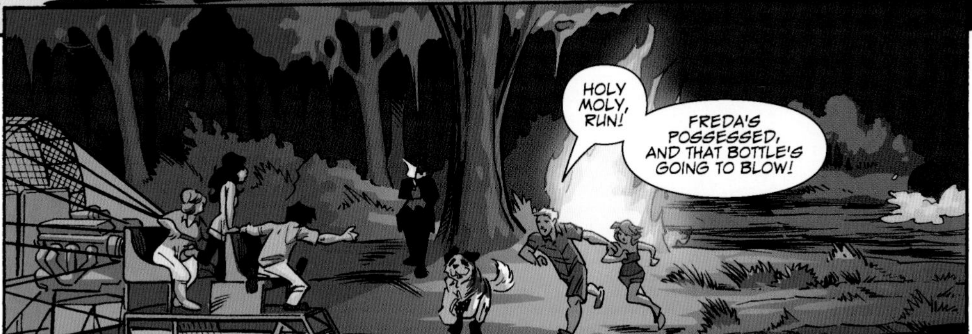
HOLY MOLY, RUN!
FREDA'S POSSESSED, AND THAT BOTTLE'S GOING TO BLOW!

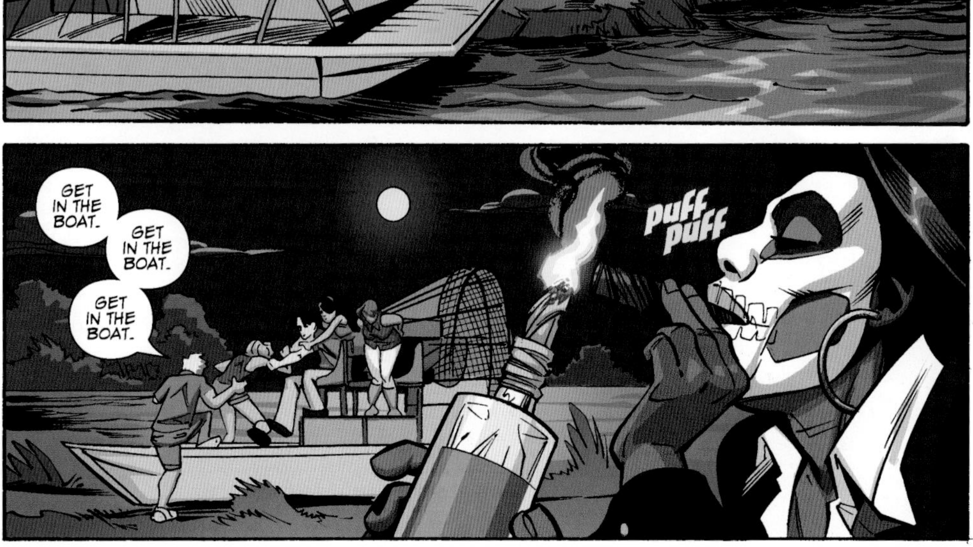
GET IN THE BOAT.
GET IN THE BOAT.
GET IN THE BOAT.
puff puff

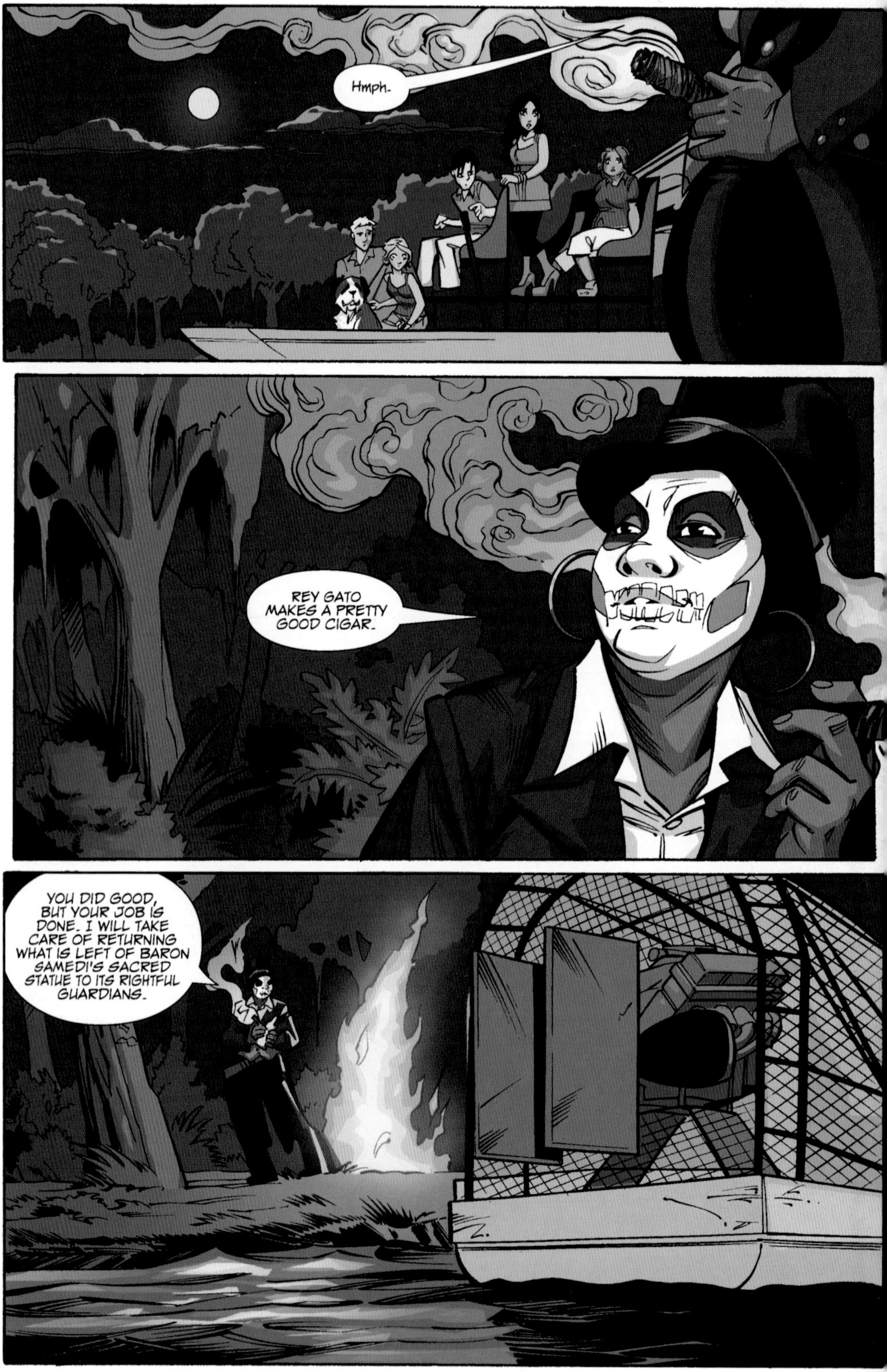
Hmph.
REY GATO MAKES A PRETTY GOOD CIGAR.
YOU DID GOOD, BUT YOUR JOB IS DONE. I WILL TAKE CARE OF RETURNING WHAT IS LEFT OF BARON SAMEDI'S SACRED STATUE TO ITS RIGHTFUL GUARDIANS.

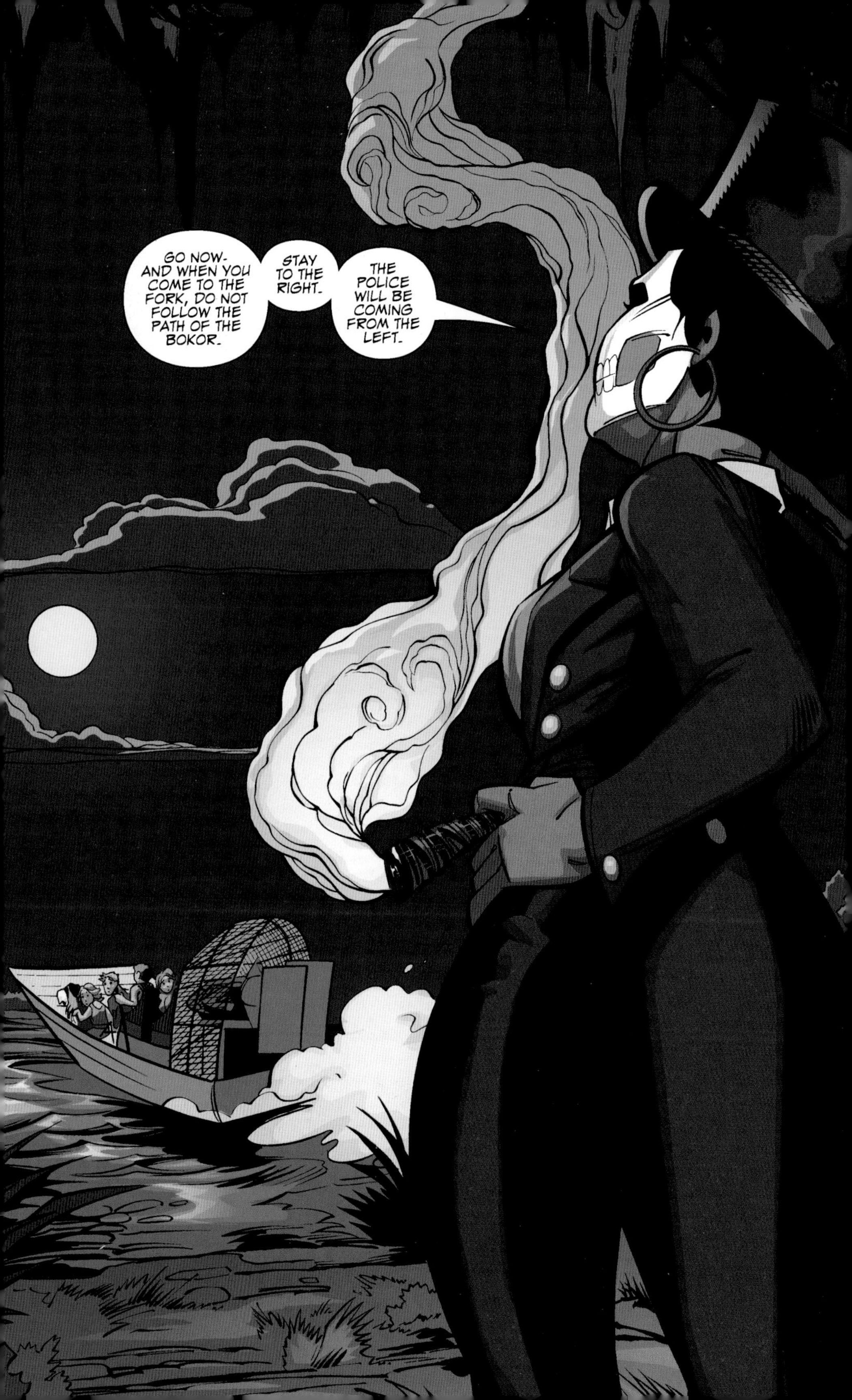
GO NOW- AND WHEN YOU COME TO THE FORK, DO NOT FOLLOW THE PATH OF THE BOKOR.
STAY TO THE RIGHT.
THE POLICE WILL BE COMING FROM THE LEFT.

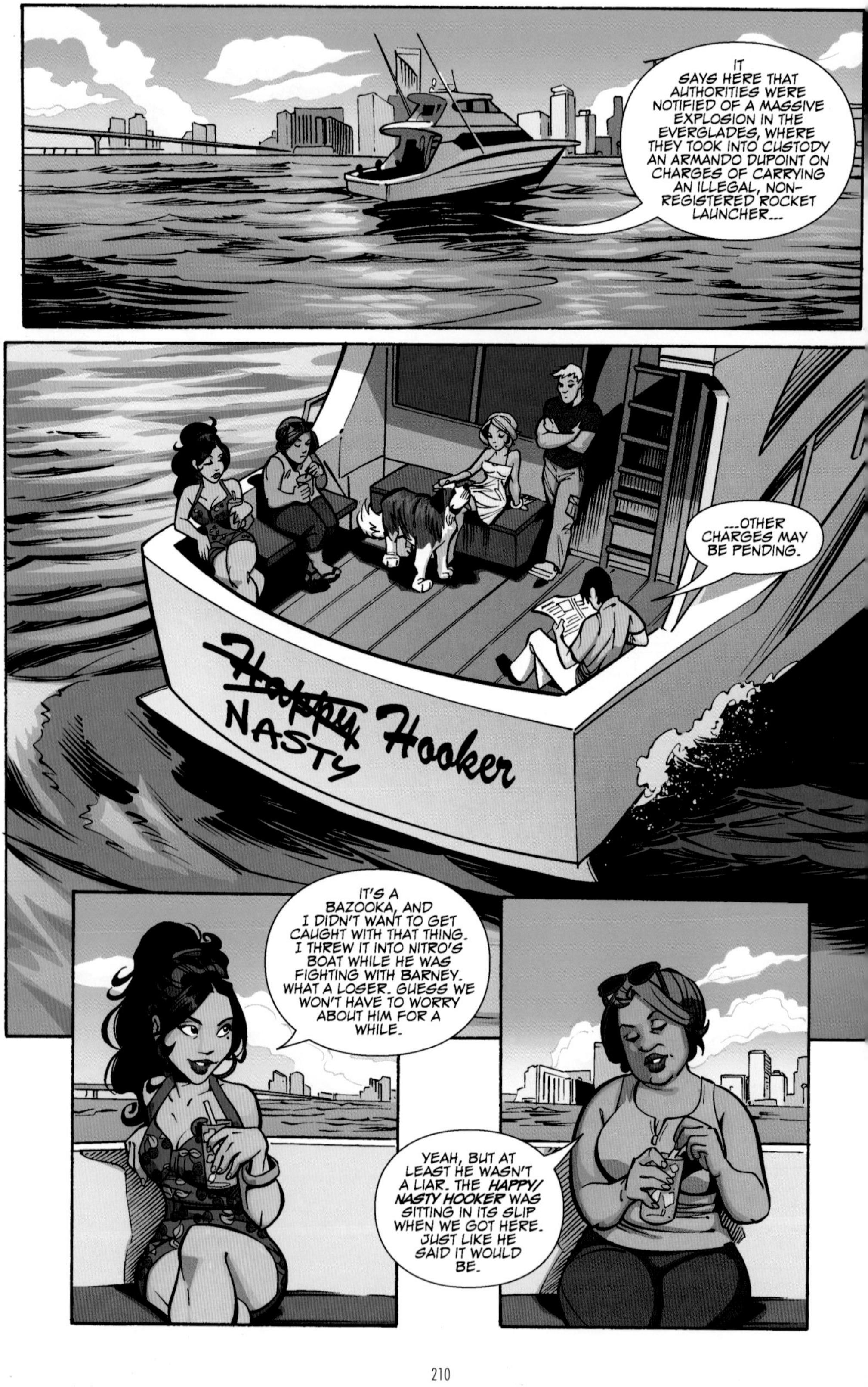
IT SAYS HERE THAT AUTHORITIES WERE NOTIFIED OF A MASSIVE EXPLOSION IN THE EVERGLADES, WHERE THEY TOOK INTO CUSTODY AN ARMANDO DUPOINT ON CHARGES OF CARRYING AN ILLEGAL, NON-REGISTERED ROCKET LAUNCHER...
...OTHER CHARGES MAY BE PENDING.
~~Happy~~ NASTY Hooker
IT'S A BAZOOKA, AND I DIDN'T WANT TO GET CAUGHT WITH THAT THING. I THREW IT INTO NITRO'S BOAT WHILE HE WAS FIGHTING WITH BARNEY. WHAT A LOSER. GUESS WE WON'T HAVE TO WORRY ABOUT HIM FOR A WHILE.
YEAH, BUT AT LEAST HE WASN'T A LIAR. THE *HAPPY/ NASTY HOOKER* WAS SITTING IN ITS SLIP WHEN WE GOT HERE. JUST LIKE HE SAID IT WOULD BE.

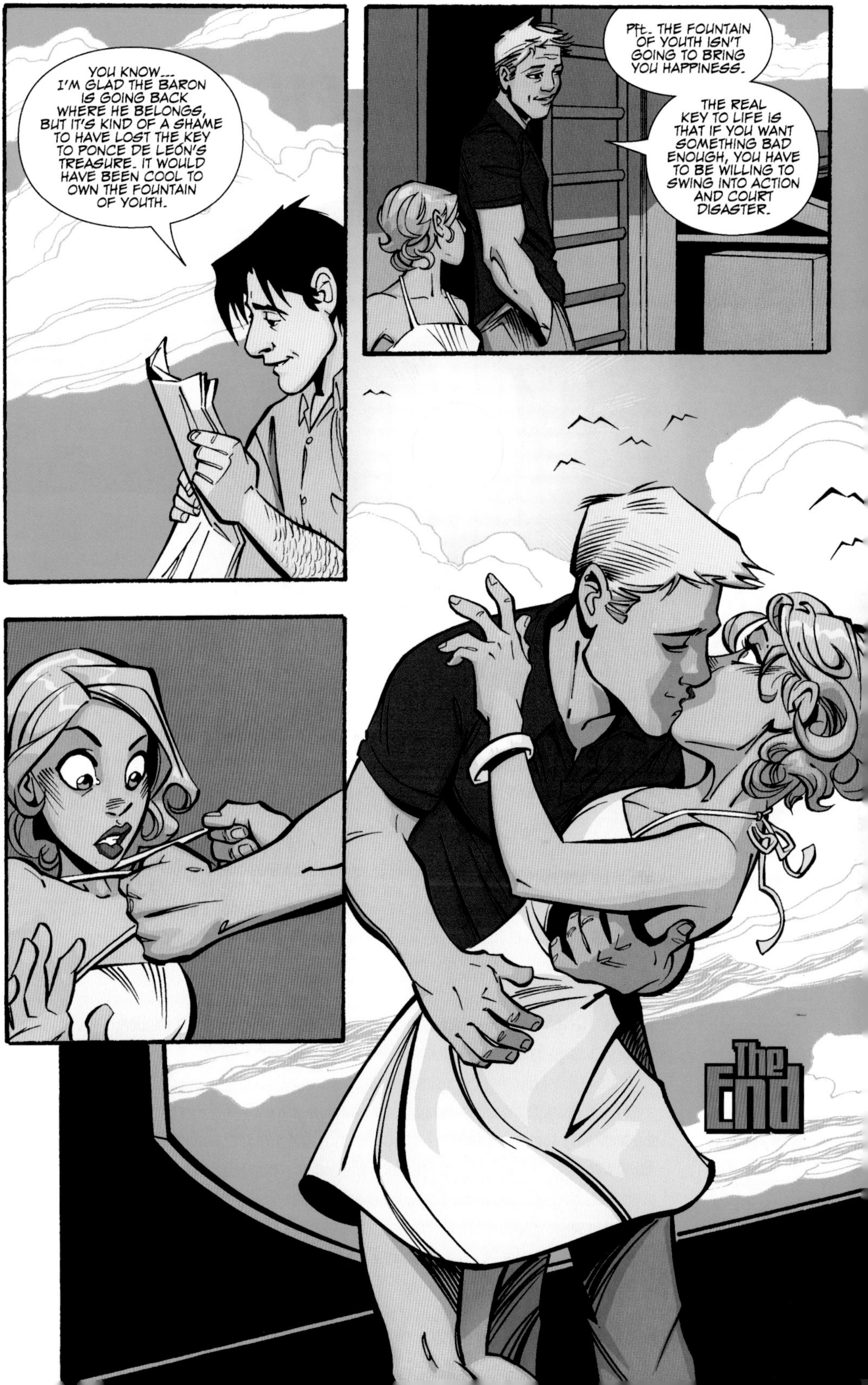
YOU KNOW... I'M GLAD THE BARON IS GOING BACK WHERE HE BELONGS, BUT IT'S KIND OF A SHAME TO HAVE LOST THE KEY TO PONCE DE LEÓN'S TREASURE. IT WOULD HAVE BEEN COOL TO OWN THE FOUNTAIN OF YOUTH.
PFT. THE FOUNTAIN OF YOUTH ISN'T GOING TO BRING YOU HAPPINESS.
THE REAL KEY TO LIFE IS THAT IF YOU WANT SOMETHING BAD ENOUGH, YOU HAVE TO BE WILLING TO SWING INTO ACTION AND COURT DISASTER.
The End

CREATOR BIOGRAPHIES

Photo © Roland Scarpa

Janet and her granddog, Barnaby.

JANET EVANOVICH is the number-one *New York Times* best-selling author of the Stephanie Plum series, as well as the Alex Barnaby and Sam Hooker series *Metro Girl* and *Motor Mouth*. Janet lives in Florida with her husband and her Havanese, Ollie. This is her first foray into writing comics.

ALEX EVANOVICH is the daughter of Janet Evanovich. She's been working with Janet for over fourteen years doing Internet work, newsletters, and editing, and is one of the coauthors of *How I Write*. She lives in Florida with her husband and her St. Bernard, Barnaby.

JOËLLE JONES debuted in comics in 2006, contributing a short story to the Dark Horse anthology *Sexy Chix*. She followed this a year later with the full graphic novel *12 Reasons Why I Love Her*, her first collaboration with author Jamie S. Rich. She then went on to illustrate the crime graphic novel *You Have Killed Me* and, most recently, the teen-witch comedy *Spell Checkers*. Joëlle has also drawn the youngadult book *Token* with Alisa Kwitney, worked with Zack Whedon on a comic-book spinoff of the popular *Dr. Horrible's Sing-Along Blog* web series, and drawn two issues of the Eisner-nominated series *Madame Xanadu*, written by Matt Wagner. She is currently working on a long-form comic for DC/Vertigo called *The Starving Artist*. You can visit her online at www.JoelleJones.com.

BARNABY AND HOOKER HAD A BEGINNING.
SOME WOULD CALL IT A PAST.

Janet Evanovich's
#1 *New York Times* Bestsellers
METRO GIRL and *MOTOR MOUTH*

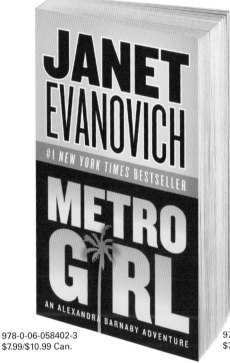

978-0-06-058402-3
$7.99/$10.99 Can.

978-0-06-058405-4
$7.99/$10.99 Can.

Read how Barnaby and Hooker blast through Florida to expose bad guys, right wrongs, and see that justice is done. And meet Rosa the cigar roller!

Now you are ready for **TROUBLEMAKER**, the first graphic novel in the series.

HARPER

AN IMPRINT OF HARPERCOLLINS*PUBLISHERS*

www.harpercollins.com

FROM DARK HORSE DELUXE . . .

TROUBLEMAKER PLAYING CARDS
$4.99
ISBN 978-1-61659-074-1

BEANS T-SHIRT
$24.99
ISBN 978-1-61659-089-5

LOGO AND PALM TREES T-SHIRT
$24.99
ISBN 978-1-61659-066-6

BARNABY AND HOOKER T-SHIRT
$24.99
ISBN 978-1-61659-069-7

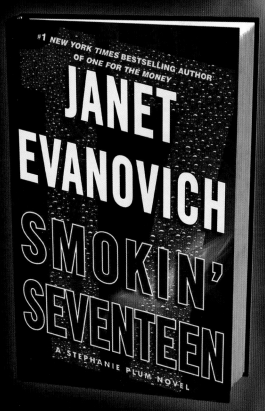

RECOMMENDED
DARK HORSE READING . . .

JOSS WHEDON GEORGES JEANTY
Buffy the vampire slayer
THE LONG WAY HOME

BUFFY THE VAMPIRE SLAYER SEASON EIGHT VOLUME 1: THE LONG WAY HOME

JOSS WHEDON, GEORGES JEANTY

Since the destruction of the Hellmouth, the Slayers—newly legion—have gotten organized and are kicking some serious undead butt. But not everything's fun and firearms, as an old enemy reappears and Dawn experiences some serious growing pains. Meanwhile, one of the "Buffy" decoy slayers is going through major pain of her own.

Buffy creator Joss Whedon brings Buffy back to Dark Horse in this direct follow-up to season seven of the smash-hit TV series.

$15.99
ISBN 978-1-59307-822-5

BEASTS of BURDEN
ANIMAL RITES
EVAN DORKIN JILL THOMPSON

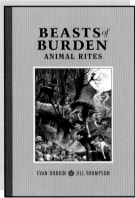

BEASTS OF BURDEN VOLUME 1: ANIMAL RITES

EVAN DORKIN, JILL THOMPSON

Welcome to Burden Hill—a picturesque little town adorned with white picket fences and green, green grass, home to a unique team of paranormal investigators. Beneath this shiny exterior, Burden Hill harbors dark and sinister secrets, and it's up to a heroic gang of dogs—and one cat—to protect the town from the evil forces at work. Can our heroes overcome these supernatural menaces? Can evil be bested by a paranormal team that doesn't have hands? And even more importantly, will Pugs ever shut the hell up?

$19.99
ISBN 978-1-59582-513-1

GIANT SIZE
Little Lulu
1

GIANT SIZE LITTLE LULU VOLUME 1

JOHN STANLEY, IRVING TRIPP

John Stanley and Irving Tripp's long run on *Little Lulu* is a milestone in American comics, as hilarious to grownups as it is to their children. With Stanley's popularity at an all-time high, Dark Horse is proud to take you back to the beginning of this legendary run. Collecting some of the earliest out-of-print volumes of Dark Horse's acclaimed reprint series, this massive 664-page omnibus contains the first fourteen issues where Little Lulu appeared.

$24.99
ISBN 978-1-59582-502-5

Oh My Goddess!
ああっ女神さまっ
1
藤島康介
KOSUKE FUJISHIMA

OH MY GODDESS! VOLUME 1

KOSUKE FUJISHIMA

Alone in his dorm, Nekomi Tech's Keiichi Morisato dials a wrong number that will change his life forever—reaching the Goddess Technical Help Line. Granted one wish by the charming young goddess Belldandy, Keiichi wishes she would stay with him always! Complications are bound to ensue from this; the immediate first being the new couple getting tossed out of the dorm—it's males only! How is his new "exchange student" companion going to be received on the NIT campus? A little too well for normal life to ever return . . .

$10.99
ISBN 978-1-59307-387-9

DARK HORSE BOOKS

AVAILABLE AT YOUR LOCAL COMICS SHOP OR BOOKSTORE
To find a comics shop in your area, call 1-888-266-4226.

For more information or to order direct visit darkhorse.com or call 1-800-862-0052 • Mon.–Fri. 9 AM to 5 PM Pacific Time.
*Prices and availability subject to change without notice.